PRAISE FOR JASON LEWIS AND
To The Brink

"We see a man who is – as Mowgli put it in *The Jungle Book* – prepared
to pull the whiskers of death."
—*London Times*

"Arguably, the most remarkable adventurer in the world today.
Many people would certainly go insane if they weren't killed first."
—*The Daily Mail*

"I believe it is important in our era of cars, trains and aeroplanes that
we are reminded what human beings can achieve using their own
strength and resources."
—*His Holiness the Dalai Lama*

"*Zen and the Art of Motorcycle Maintenance* meets Bill Bryson's
A Walk in the Woods. A thoroughly entertaining and insightful read."
—*Charlie Boorman*, Long Way Down

"An extraordinary adventure."
—*The Independent*

"An enthralling read."
—*Outdoor Photography*

D1447770

THE
EXPEDITION

TRUE STORY OF THE FIRST HUMAN-POWERED
CIRCUMNAVIGATION OF THE EARTH

 TO THE BRINK

JASON LEWIS

BILLYFISH
BOOKS

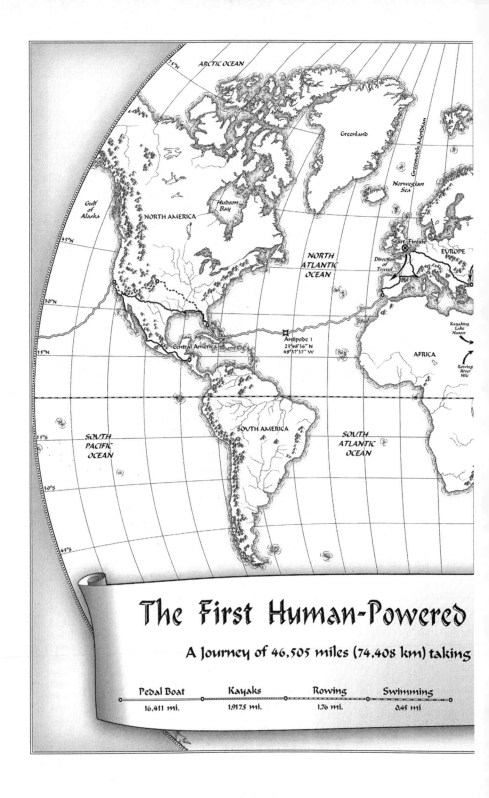

ARCTIC OCEAN

Greenland

Norwegian Sea

Gulf of Alaska

NORTH AMERICA

Hudson Bay

45°N

NORTH ATLANTIC OCEAN

Start-Finish

EUROPE

Direction of Travel

30°N

Kayaking Lake Nasser

15°N

Central America

Antipode 1
23°48'36" N
48°37'37" W

AFRICA

Rowing River Nile

SOUTH AMERICA

SOUTH PACIFIC OCEAN

15°S

SOUTH ATLANTIC OCEAN

30°S

45°S

The First Human-Powered

A Journey of 46,505 miles (74,408 km) taking

Pedal Boat	Kayaks	Rowing	Swimming
16,411 mi.	1,917.5 mi.	1.76 mi.	0.45 mi

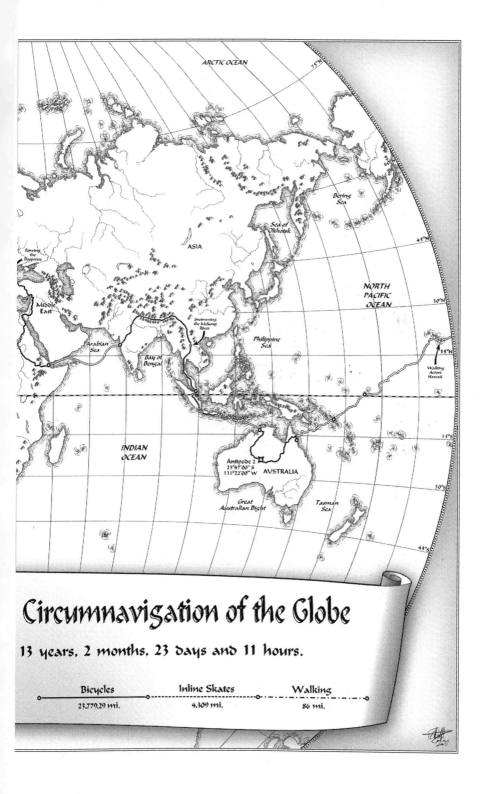

Circumnavigation of the Globe

13 years, 2 months, 23 days and 11 hours.

Bicycles	Inline Skates	Walking
23,779.29 mi.	4,309 mi.	86 mi.

First BillyFish Books edition 2016

For permission requests, write to the publisher: permissions@billyfishbooks.com
www.billyfishbooks.com

ISBN 978-0-9849155-2-1 (pbk.)

British Library Cataloguing in Publication Data. A catalogue record for this book is available
from the British Library.

Publisher's Cataloging-in-Publication data
Lewis, Jason, 1967 -.
To the brink : true story of the first human-powered circumnavigation of the earth / Jason
Lewis.
p. cm.
ISBN 978-0-9849155-2-1
Series : The Expedition.
1. Lewis, Jason, 1967 - --Travel. 2. Adventure travel. 3. Voyages and travels. 4. Voyages
around the world. 5. Human powered vehicles. 6. Spirituality. I. Title. II. Series.
G465 .L495 2016
910.4 --dc23   2012902556

All wood product components used in print versions of this book meet Sustainable Forestry
Initiative® (SFI®) Certified Sourcing (USA) and Forest Stewardship Council™ (FSC®)
Mixed Credit (UK) standards.

Cover photograph © Kenny Brown
Maps © Rob Antonishen/Cartocopia
Cover design by Kevin Jones

10 9 8 7 6 5 4 3 2 1

Excerpt from *The Road* by Cormac McCarthy reprinted by permission of Vintage, a division
of Random House, Inc. Excerpt from *Neither Here, Nor There: Travels in Europe* by Bill Bryson
reprinted by permission of William Morrow Paperbacks. Excerpt from *The Songlines* by Bruce
Chatwin reprinted by permission of Penguin Books. Excerpt from *House of the Tiger King: The
Quest for a Lost City* by Tahir Shah reprinted by permission of John Murray.

Every effort has been made to contact the copyright holders of third party content used in this
publication. Rights holders of any copyrighted works not credited should write to the publisher
at permissions@billyfishbooks.com in order for a correction to be made.

Synopsis

This is the third instalment of *The Expedition* trilogy.

In his first book, *Dark Waters,* window cleaner Jason Lewis teams up with former college friend, environmentalist Steve Smith, to attempt the first human-powered circumnavigation of the Earth. Aided by Steve's father, Stuart, a fun-loving insurance salesman with the gift of the gab, filmmaker Kenny Brown, Scotland's answer to MacGyver, and a loyal band of oddball volunteers, the unlikely duo struggle to attract sponsors. After two years, with little to show for themselves but bungled sea trials, run-ins with the police, and a humiliating inaugural press event, the aspiring adventurers set off anyway, biking from the Greenwich meridian. Low on funding but high on hope, world maps and oceanic charts in tow, they immediately become lost having forgotten to bring a London A to Z street atlas.

From Rye, they manage an illegal crossing of the Channel to Boulogne in their one-of-a-kind craft, *Moksha*, constructed by first-time boat builders Chris and Hugo. Next, they wheel south through Europe, visiting schools along the way, using the expedition to champion world citizenship and environmental responsibility.

Their determination and friendship are put to the test during a gruelling 111-day crossing of the Atlantic. Early on they are nearly crushed by a rogue trawler, and Jason suffers hypoxia when he almost drowns. They endure extreme fatigue, painful salt sores, bitter disagreements, and a monster wave that capsizes the boat, throwing Steve overboard.

But their ruthless initiation is also tempered by occasional forays into the sublime: resplendent sunsets, fathomless night skies, and a surprise Christmas dinner served by a passing ship. In the closing stages of the voyage, following months of meditative contemplation, Jason undergoes a life-changing transformation: a spiritual epiphany providing a comforting glimpse into the interconnectedness of all life.

The peace isn't to last, however.

After running aground on a reef in the Caribbean and a brush with Cuban pirates, our fledgling explorers stumble ashore in Miami. They face months of monotonous fundraising before resuming their journey separately across the US, giving each other much needed space before the longer Pacific voyage. Steve bikes through the Southern states while Jason learns to rollerblade on a more northerly route to San Francisco. He falls foul of ravenous fire ants, parsimonious Baptists, and gun-toting rednecks who take exception to his long hair and unorthodox choice of travel. Nevertheless, it is in the hospitality of strangers that he discovers another America, one where those less fortunate are often the first to offer food and shelter.

At the end of an exhausting 70-mile skate across the Eastern Plains of Colorado, complete with thunderstorms and sexual solicitations, Jason enters the town of Pueblo and becomes the victim of a brutal hit and run.

We pick up the story in *The Seed Buried Deep* with Jason lying by the side of the road, both his legs horribly broken. He spends the next five weeks in Parkview hospital, contemplating losing his left leg to bone infection and the likelihood of having to pull out of the expedition due to lack of funds. When the orthopaedic surgeon hears of this, he invites Jason to stay at his family's mountain cabin, cared for by Stuart who flies in to help. The pair tour local schools, where they meet a fifth grade teacher, April, who helps create a range of educational programmes and reveals her lifelong ambition to bike old Route 66. After nine months of recuperation, his legs now reinforced with titanium rods, Jason sets off with April from the spot he was hit, and together they scale the Rockies and complete the remaining 1,700 miles of the North American leg to California.

Reunited again, Steve and Jason expand their new vision of inclusiveness by encouraging others to ride along, south through Central and South America. After weathering the winter storms of the California coast and an infestation of poison ivy, the group cross the border into Mexico and are robbed on their first night. The learning curve steepens further kayaking the Sea of Cortez: the supply boat sinks, a gasoline stove explodes in Jason's face, and they run out of water. On top of all this, Jason loses the woman he loves when she chooses to return to her former life instead of the more uncertain future with the expedition.

Heartbroken, Jason withdraws to the mountains of Sinaloa to resolve whether he should continue the circumnavigation or go after Theresa. After four days without food or water, he makes his decision and pushes on through Guatemala, El Salvador, and Honduras, implementing cultural exchange activities with UNESCO affiliated schools along the way. In Tegucigalpa, however, he learns of the devastating effects of El Niño on the Southeast Pacific region, and the 7,000-mile leg through the Americas has to be aborted.

Back in San Francisco, Steve and Jason are forced to consider the less-favoured Plan B to Australia—island-hopping diagonally across the Pacific. It takes two attempts to reach the Big Island of Hawaii. The first voyage is curtailed by a storm, resulting in *Moksha* capsizing and

nearly sinking on a mooring buoy south of Big Sur. The second, following a year of boat restoration and fundraising, concludes successfully
after a 53-day pedal to Hilo. Despite getting along with Jason much
better than on the first voyage, Steve knows that after five long years
on the road he has reached his journey's end. Before leaving, he hikes
the 90 miles to Kailua-Kona and helps Jason prepare *Moksha* for the
upcoming voyage to the tiny atoll of Tarawa, 2,500 miles away.

Alone at sea for the first time, Jason finds himself lapsing into bouts
of lassitude, and his efforts to recreate the Samadhi he attained on the
Atlantic are thwarted by the constant distractions of technology that
didn't exist at the beginning of the expedition. After 43 days of pedalling he enters the doldrums, a 400-mile-wide countercurrent that nautical experts warned would be virtually impossible to cross in a human-
powered craft. Unable to make forward progress for weeks on end, his
resolve begins to waver, and he experiences hallucinations triggered by
an outbreak of septicaemia contracted through open sores while swimming. It is during these dark days at the end of his tether when Jason
starts talking to the resident pilot fishes underneath the boat, a desperate bid for companionship that expands to include an imaginary circle
of bickering friends.

One of the original boat builders, Chris, joins the next voyage, providing Jason with some much-needed camaraderie as far as the Solomon Islands. On arrival, the pair learns of a recent coup, which has
rekindled an age-old feud between the islands of Malaita and Guadalcanal. Chris nevertheless manages to trade places with April, who has
signed up to crew the remaining 1,400 miles to Australia. The voyage
is beset with difficulties from the beginning. A boatload of militia try to
steal April's prize cabbage on the first day, and once around the shel-

tered eastern edge of Guadalcanal, all hell breaks loose. The Southeast Trades are blowing full strength with sixty mile-an-hour gusts, keeping the inside of the cabin drenched and pushing the boat northwest towards Papua New Guinea. For April, who has never been to sea before, achieving even basic tasks like peeing over the side or washing her hair is further complicated by chronic nausea. After 32 days of seasickness and related malnutrition, the schoolteacher is in desperate need of medical attention.

We begin *To the Brink* with Jason and April battling to keep *Moksha* from being wrecked on the Great Barrier Reef.

CONTENTS

To my mother
For the extra grey hairs I put on your head

And to you, the Reader
For sticking with me until the end

There's magic in fighting battles beyond endurance ... It's the magic of risking everything for a dream that nobody sees but you.

—*Million Dollar Baby*

Once there were brook trout in the streams in the mountains. You could see them standing in the amber current where the white edges of their fins wimpled softly in the flow. They smelled of moss in your hand. Polished and muscular and torsional. On their backs were vermiculate patterns that were maps of the world in its becoming. Maps and mazes. Of a thing which could not be put back. Not be made right again. In the deep glens where they lived all things were older than man and they hummed of mystery.

—Cormac McCarthy, *The Road*

August 15
Wind: SE 20 knots. Heading: 320M. Position: 14°28'21"S 145°46'12"E

6:17PM. "KENNY. QUICK QUESTION. Have you got any credit cards on you?"

Even over the satellite phone, I can sense the tartan wallet pucker. "Why, you tois thinkin' ay goin' oan a cruise or somethin'?"

"Very funny, Kenny. Listen, I need to ask you a favour. A pretty big favour, actually."

Our Man Brown has been in Cairns less than a day. As usual, he's hit the ground running, drumming up local media interest and scouting around for a boat to come out and film our arrival. This time he has the added task of organizing a relief effort.

Drifting on the sea anchor, we've been taken five miles north and six miles west since our last fix. The problem is our northing, rendering Cormorant Pass no longer an option. We've had to shift our sights instead to Half Mile Opening, ten miles to the northwest. The forecast doesn't look good, though. South-southeasterlies are predicted for the next week, which will blow us parallel to the Ribbon Reefs and make them even harder to cross. As with Cormorant, we have a half-hour window to catch the tide going in the right direction through the narrow opening. If we miss it and get swept into the barren wasteland above Cape Melville, any prospect of getting April to a doctor will be lost.

Evacuating the schoolteacher has to be the first priority, saving *Moksha* second. Earlier, I got Kenny to phone the five-star resort on Lizard Island and request assistance with an emergency crew transfer outside the reef. The answer was a categorical no. Their entire resort fleet, including a blue water dive boat more than capable of operating in big seas, needed to remain on site in case any of their $4,000-a-night guests wanted to go snorkelling.

Dumfounded by the response, Kenny tried the research station. The warm, affable Tanya Lamb, one of two caretaker managers, informed him that although the research station didn't have any craft seaworthy enough to venture beyond the reef, she and her husband, Bob, would be on standby to help in any other way they could.

Kenny broadened his search. None of the commercial vessels operating out of Cooktown showed interest in coming out. Not for any price. In the two and a half centuries since Captain James Cook ploughed *HMS Endeavour* into a coral bommie, the seas north of Cape Flattery have earned themselves a fearsome reputation. Even today large portions of the chart are marked as unsurveyed, with no indication of the hazards lying beneath the surface.

After hours of phone bashing, Kenny finally tracked down one outfit prepared to do the job, a charter boat based in Port Douglas, one hundred and twenty nautical miles south of Lizard. When I called to firm up the booking, a figure of $2,000 a day plus fuel was quoted to me by "John-o," the skipper. The round trip from Port Douglas to Half Mile Opening will take no less than three days, apparently, costing in excess of $8,000.

Kenny coughs. "Sae what's thes big favour, then?"

"Well, how should I put this, Ken …" I pause. "The expedition is bankrupt. I don't suppose you'd be in a position to—"

"Nae problem," he cuts in. "I think I've got some space oan ma Mastercard."

A brown-and-white-chested booby joins us before dark, making several laps of the boat before touching down. The first thing the little shitehawk does is squeeze out a celebratory turd on the Perspex hatch, before settling down to an animated bout of cleaning, wiggling its beak through its plumage and using an enormous pink foot to scratch the back of its head. As the evening wears on, the wind increases to storm force. *Moksha* lunges and yaws on the sea anchor like an enraged bull, and by midnight waves are crashing over the deck. One submerges the boat completely. There's a muffled squawk. When I peer out of the hatch, our feathered comedian is gone.

August 16

Wind: SSE 35 knots. Heading: 320M. Position: 14°16'15"S 145°33'49"E

6:30 AM. HAND OVER fist, April and I pull in the sea anchor together, the rope cinched around the port side oar to stop each hard-won inch from being dragged back out. The conditions are atrocious, the wind gusting forty knots and waves towering all around.

"Kinda reminds me of workin' cattle," April remarks as she heaves on the saturated line, her expression wracked in concentration. "With a cow on the end of a rope and trying not to let her get away."

Each time the boat rocks to port, we pull in a little more slack.

"Then again," she adds, "the rope isn't usually this wet."

The yellow canvas chute comes alongside. I haul it onto the sliding hatch and lash it down with bungee cords to keep the wind from catching hold. Now we have to start pedalling south as hard as we can.

We've been blown too far north in the night even to make Half Mile Opening. All remaining hope lies with Kenny and the aptly named *Wee Jock*. Having motored overnight from Port Douglas to Lizard, they plan to follow latitude 14°12'S from the east. We'll follow the same line of latitude from the west and hope our paths cross. But if either vessel strays off course by half a mile, we'll miss each other.

This we cannot let happen. As John-o pointed out before leaving Bob and Tanya's house in the early hours, we only have one chance to get it right. "Once you guys disappear around the corner into Bathurst Bay," he warned, "we can't help you."

9:40 AM. HALF MILE Opening is now well to the southeast. In less than three hours, we'll be in Bathurst Bay. I try to remain calm, but inside I'm screaming: *Where the hell is Wee Jock?*

For the umpteenth time, I hail them on the VHF.

"*Wee Jock, Wee Jock*, this is pedal boat *Moksha*, over."

Silence.

While April pedals, I call Bob Lamb on the satellite phone. With a phone line and the research station's high-powered radio at his disposal, he's acting as the communications go-between.

"Bob, anything from *Wee Jock?*"

"Nah, mate. They're out of range now. But they've got that gantry for sighting marlin, so they've got a better chance of spotting you than you have them."

"Okay. If we don't make contact by ten thirty, I'll start sending up a flare every fifteen minutes."

"Sounds good, mate."

I offer to take over pedalling from April, but she's quick to remind me that she hasn't yet missed a shift, and she's not about to start. Today is her thirtieth consecutive day of seasickness. I try to picture how she looked leaving Tulagi but fail. In just one month, she's been reduced to a bony chassis stretched with human skin: tanned, leathery, streaked with salt, eyes buried in their sockets, the right one partially closed. Her hair, or what's left of it from the ongoing starvation, is gathered in a loose bun on her head. It hasn't been washed in a fortnight.

Her body is close to breaking, but her spirit remains strong. I smile fondly at her. "April, do you remember saying at the start of the voyage how you wanted to be like the Energizer Bunny?"

She nods, a flicker of recognition behind the mask.

"Well, regardless of what happens today, we can be sure of one thing. The Energizer Bunny would have conked out a long time ago."

Her eyes soften, and two glittering beads slice the parched landscape of her face like the first runnels of desert rain.

10:20 AM. AT FIRST, I dismiss it as a new sound coming from the ailing pedal unit. *Thing's about to crap itself again and at the worst possible time.* Then the noise gets louder and clearer, the unmistakable throb of a diesel engine. I jump up and scan the horizon.

"There they are."

A white motor cruiser surges over a rolling crest, outriggers and fishing poles bristling from the stern. Revving noisily and belching out black plumes of soot, *Wee Jock* announces its arrival by pulling the marine equivalent of a doughnut.

"The Coral Sea Cavalry has arrived!" laughs April.

Bloody show-offs, I mutter under my breath.

The deckhand is barely contained in a pair of terrifyingly tight swimming trunks. This must be "Dave-o," John-o's partner. He throws a line.

"Thanks for coming out," I holler, scooting forward on my knees to tie the line through the eyebolt on *Moksha's* bow.

"No worries, mate," he grunts.

The tow to Lizard Island is brutal. Punching headlong into the breakers, *Moksha* spends whole seconds underwater before launching missile-like from the back of each wave and slamming with bone-jarring force into the next. April and I hang on for dear life. That the boat doesn't disintegrate with the merciless pounding is yet another testament to her builders, Hugo and Chris.

Two hours of this and the Barrier Reef looms, a jumbled altar of stony corals exposed by the hissing tide. Beyond it, Lizard rises from the sea like the lost kingdom of Atlantis. A small yellow boat appears with Lizard Island Research Station printed along the side. The driver, an athletic man with dark wiry hair, introduces himself as Bob Lamb—a rarity amongst his kind, it seems. He is the first Australian we've met without an "o" attached to the end of his name.

Bob escorts us to the west side of the island where, in the shelter of the lee, the water is calm. For the first time since Coral Sea Corner a month ago, the ocean isn't trying to kill us. We secure Moksha alongside *Wee Jock* and transfer to the research vessel. Bob throws the helm hard over and aims for a beach of impossibly white sand. As we slip effortlessly across the translucent bay, coral shimmering a few feet beneath us, I listen in to April and Kenny's conversation.

"Yeah, it's been pretty levelling." April is sitting on one of the cross planks, wrapped in a green fleece jacket. "The ocean has taken me to the basement emotionally. But it's been good to see how far down I could get. Now I know there's nothing in life that can intimidate me."

She shifts position to take the weight off her sitting bones and smiles. "But boy, that sure was one helluva ride."

Kenny has his video camera resting on his knees. "I'd ask for my money back if I were you."

April laughs.

"Looking forward to getting back to Colorado?" Kenny asks.

April nods. "Looking forward to holding my daughter and my dog."

"Probably got a billion things to do, eh?"

"It'll be fall. I'll need to cut firewood for the winter. And get to know a hundred kids. I have three fourth and fifth grade classes to teach this year."

The island expands to our full field of vision as we near the beach. I marvel at the subtle gradations of textures and colours connecting the smooth coral shore with the ragged green peak on which Captain Cook once stood, repairs to the *Endeavour* complete, scouring for an escape route through the reef. It is one of the most beautiful islands I have seen on the expedition so far.

I turn to Bob. "What a dump. How can you stand living here?"

He breaks into a grin. "I know, it's tough, but someone's gotta do it."

"Wow," April breathes, soaking it all in. "The first colours I've seen in a month that aren't blue or steel grey. I can't believe how green it is."

Kenny lifts the camera to his shoulder and starts filming. "First thing you'll do on land, April?"

She thinks for a moment. "Find out what it's like to hold vegetation in my hand again. And sand, what it feels like between my toes."

We come to a bumping rest in the lapping shallows. A handful of inquisitive people from the research station have gathered to behold this human flotsam washed in from the sea. One, a suntanned woman in dark glasses, reaches forward to take the painter. "Hi," she smiles. "I'm Tanya."

I debark first. April follows. She makes a graceful pirouette and lands plumb on her arse.

"I can't believe this!" April giggles in embarrassment. The High Seas Hair has slipped forward at a rakish angle, completing the picture of a pirate princess.

Bob helps her to her feet. I steady her left elbow. "You alright?" I ask.

Bracing her bruised, emaciated legs at ten to two, April teeters like a newborn foal.

"Yeah, it's just that ..." She pauses and laughs again.

"It's not moving, is it?" says Bob.

"No, it's not moving. It's not moving anymore."

Cairns, Australia
ROUGHING IT IN THE RATHOLE

We used to build civilizations. Now we build shopping malls.
—Bill Bryson, *Neither Here, Nor There: Travels in Europe*

"LOOK, GINI. SAYS 'ERE this bloke's pedallin' round the wode. Says 'e started in Landon 'n awl."

Landon. Was that Cockney I was hearing?

"I could do that. Nah problem."

"Do wot, Tony, pedoo' round the wode? You couldn't pedoo' round the block!"

Pedoo'. Wode. Definitely East End.

"Course I could, Gini. Get me fit for a bit of 'ows ya father n' awl."

In that semi-conscious dream state before waking fully, I heard fumbling, a woman giggling. "Oooh, stop it, Tony. People're watchin'!"

Then I remembered where I was.

Ah yes. The Rathole, The Pier Shopping Centre, Cairns, Australia.

If Steve had told me in Paris that the circumnavigation would require us to live in a shopping mall for an extended period, I would have laughed in his face. Part of the expedition's appeal had been to put as much distance between these black holes of the human soul and me as possible. Yet, in a warped twist of fate, my worst nightmare had come true. I was now a full-time mall rat, whoring out my stories in air-conditioned consumer hell, competing for the attention of the glassy-eyed shoppers as they passed.

At the end of each workday, flogging tee shirts and names on the boat for $20, I hid in the Rathole while the security guards did a final sweep. In the morning, once the place was unlocked, I snuck out and pretended I'd just arrived. Today, I'd obviously overslept.

I levered myself out and wrestled into a shirt and a pair of shorts. Fluorescent lights blazed overhead, and invisible gambling machines known as "pokies" whirred and chimed in the background. Against the shopping centre drone, I could hear Tony and Gini following the route on the map provided. "Cross the Atlan'ic, America on rowllerblades." There were other display items drawing passers-by to the exhibit: photographs, laminated press clippings, info cards on how the boat worked, a three-minute video of journey highlights looping on a television, and so on. If people had questions, I was on hand to answer them—and to clobber them for $20, of course.

I had the kettle on, boiling water for tea, when I heard footsteps mount the viewing podium.

"Bloke must be off 'is rocker crossin' the Pacific in this fing," Gini was saying. "'Ere, Tony, you can see where 'e sleeps."

Two pink faces appeared over the side.

"Oops, pardon us!" Tony looked as if he'd just barged into a stranger's house—which, in a way, he had. Since making landfall, *Moksha* had become my home and base of operations. Laughing self-consciously, he added, "Didn't fink anyone was innit."

"No problem." I waved a hand. "Take a look around. This is the stove for cooking. This is where you pedal …"

For my first three weeks in Australia, I'd based myself in Port Douglas, one hundred kilometres north of Cairns. Early fundraising efforts had been a disaster. With twenty of the twenty-nine dollars I'd stepped off the boat with, I bought some paint, brushes, and a sheet of plywood, and made up a sign that read, "You Too Can Pedal the World Famous *Moksha*. $10 for 15 minutes." I'd then tied her up to the boat ramp, sat back, and waited for the moolah to roll in. A recent article in the *Cairns Post* would bring the punters flocking, I was sure of it.

In two days, I had just two takers: a purple-faced man, who snarled "this better be good," and his fleshy, eight-year-old son, who was bored out of his mind the moment he stepped aboard. "Daaad," the ozling whinged as he pedalled, "it smells in he-ya." When we arrived back at the ramp, the father, now an even deeper shade of purple, demanded his money back.

Exhausted, broke, and alone, living in a car park next to a mosquito-infested swamp with crocs eyeing me from the darkness, my introduction to Terra Australis Incognita, the unknown land of the south, was different to what I imagined. Okay, so life on the expedition was never going to be glamorous, but the destination I had in my mind's eye crossing the Pacific was a little more exotic than this. In the coming weeks, I was to be reminded that circumnavigating the planet on a shoestring was as much about forgoing expectations and being adaptable as it was dogged determination. Any dum-dum with enough money could human power their way across an ocean or a continent. Far more challenging was arriving skint in an unfamiliar part of the world and immediately switching from a linear, miles-under-the-belt mindset to that of an all-singing, all-dancing networking machine to start bringing in the dough. This typically took the form of holing up in the nearest phone box for several days armed with a bag of coins and a copy of the Yellow Pages.

Through Ray and Dorelle of the Port Douglas Yacht Club, I secured permission to display *Moksha* on the Marina Mirage boardwalk used by tourists to reach charter boats heading to the Great Barrier Reef. Mornings and evenings were best, when passengers were embarking and disembarking. Slowly, the funds trickled in. The priority was to repay Steve and my sister, Julia, who had loaned the money to pay off Kenny's credit card.

Tony blinked at me. "You're not … you're not actually the bloke doin' this fing are you?"

I nodded. "U-huh."

"Cor! Bit cramped in 'ere innit? 'Ow jew get any exercise?"

I stared at him. "Umm, I pedal?"

The Londoners laughed good-naturedly. They lived in Kent. It had taken a little over 24 hours to reach Cairns from Heathrow via Singapore. "Bit quicker than you!" They'd just spent two weeks scuba diving on the reef. Next they were going on a rainforest trek to the Daintree River.

"We'll be back in England this time next week," said Tony.

"Another four or five years for me," I said.

"Did you see any sharks?"

Fuck me, here we go.

A few months earlier, a simple mouse click on E*trade and thousands of dollars would magically appear. Now it was back to the blather, the same old hackneyed yarns wheeled out repeatedly. Lying in the Rathole at night, I took to brooding, slipping into a slough of depression, hating the expedition and myself more and more. Thankfully, however, despair is only a state of mind, an arbitrary perspective with no basis in reality. Just when you think you can't take it anymore, someone who has it much worse rolls up and makes you feel like a complete wimp.

"That's an interesting-looking boat," a man said to me one day. He was in his seventies, wearing a straw hat and khaki trousers. *Military man,* I thought to myself, *or a priest.* He'd wandered up to the stand just as I was closing down for the day.

"Yes," I replied half-heartedly. "It's …" Then I fell silent. I was tired. I was hungry. I was storied out. I had a streaming head cold and a splitting headache from the fluorescent lights.

He looked impatiently at me. "Well, aren't you going to tell me about it?"

Reluctantly, I started to, and egged on by his encouraging commentary—"Oh, really?" and "How extraordinary!"—I felt my enthusiasm return.

George Abbott was his name. "May I take a look inside?" He nimbly scaled the podium and poked his head through the hatch. "Goodness, quite narrow, isn't she?"

But life aboard *Moksha* was nothing compared to what he'd endured. The conversation wound its way round to his own experiences as a prisoner of war in Crete in 1941.

"Escaped six times." George frowned at the memory. "Each time I was recaptured, they put me in solitary confinement for two and a half months." It was at this point I noticed his withered left hand. "I couldn't move my arm after that, what with the arthritis."

He belonged to a dying breed of Australians, tough, no-nonsense pioneers who'd built a nation, many fighting for a country they'd never seen.

"Thousands of us allies sought refuge with the Russians." George was describing his seventh, successful escape attempt now, after which he'd headed east. "We ended up on the frontline as cannon fodder ahead of the tanks."

Later, I saw him on the esplanade hurrying for a bus, dodging the dawdling tourists and dog walkers. *After all he's been through,* I said to myself, *still running like a teenager. What the hell have you got to complain about?*

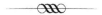

In order to maintain the integrity of the circumnavigation, I needed to backtrack the thirty-five miles *Moksha* was towed through the Great Barrier Reef and complete them by human power.

It took two attempts, both nearly ending in disaster. Pete and Russ, two brothers I'd met in Port Douglas, owned a fishing boat docked in Cooktown. Taking a week away from fundraising, I hitched a ride on *Sirius II* back to the latitude and longitude position where *Wee Jock* had intercepted *Moksha* five months before. This time I was in a canvas kayak.

After five hours of paddling, I'd made it through Half Mile Opening and was part way to Lizard Island when the boat started to feel sluggish. The port side rudder cable suddenly snapped. The kayak had sprung a leak and was sinking.

Lucky for me, a documentary cameraman was shadowing in another kayak. Rafting up alongside, Todd Paulsen steadied my waterlogged craft, while I fumbled under the spray skirt for a bailing cup. It didn't

take long to establish that in the confusion of launching from *Sirius II,*
neither kayak had been provisioned with one. Cursing my stupidity, I
yanked off the outer of two plastic bags waterproofing the handheld
VHF and began ladling the water rising in my lap. Todd, meanwhile,
managed to reach the brothers on Channel 16 before *Sirius II* disappeared over the horizon.

For the second attempt, this time from Lizard Island, Bob Lamb
found some industrial silicon to seal the leaking rudder pintle and a
wire coat hanger to fix the steering cable. Pete, Russ, and Todd had
already returned to Cooktown, so I struck out for the mainland on
my own. Twenty-two miles later, having recrossed my earlier wake, I
rounded Lookout Point and felt the hairs on the back of my neck stand
up.

That was when I glanced behind me and saw two lidless eyes and
a snub nose closing in, my reptilian welcoming committee to Australia
proper.

By March 2001, I was staying with family friends north of Cairns.
Abutting native rainforest echoing to the cackling calls of kookaburras,
the Edwards' pleasant two-storey home offered a very different base of
operations to the mayhem of the shopping mall. The *Wee Jock* debt was
now paid off, so I turned my attention to securing funding for the overland leg to Darwin. With the circumnavigation two-thirds complete and
four one-hour shows recently sold to Discovery Channel, hooking a title
sponsor would be easy, I told myself. Yet, of the one hundred and sixty
proposals I sent to companies in the UK and Australia, only twenty-
seven even elicited a response. They were all refusals.

"After careful consideration, we regret to inform ..."

As Tony Whale, marketing manager for Silva UK, explained to me

over the phone, these days it was all about fitting the corporate marketing prescription of round shapes for round holes and square shapes
for square holes. "If you don't fit the right hole," he said, "you're buggered."

Expedition 360, a veritable bricolage of misfit jigsaw pieces, was
clearly beyond buggered.

But just as I was beginning to lose heart, an offer came through from
a publisher catering to the secondary schools market in the UK. Reddo
Publishing proposed developing a CD-ROM pack and textbook series
for Key Stage 2 and 3—nine through thirteen year olds. In return, they
agreed to underwrite Overland Australia.

I was ecstatic. After all the mishaps and disappointments, the expedition was about to take off as the ultimate experiential learning tool
and get paid to boot. A custom website, created and managed by a
dedicated online team, would host a unique multimedia experience for
classes to follow live. Reddo planned to invest £100,000 over twelve
months, establishing an expedition brand with a view to continuing the
partnership to Greenwich and beyond.

April and May vanished in a blur of activity. I needed to recruit two
teachers and ten teenagers from different countries around the world,
forming a multicultural classroom without walls to explore the outback
with me. Two of the young explorers would be Australians acting as
local ambassadors.

As well as mountain biking an average of sixty kilometres a day,
the team would target Discovery Zones en route, generating content
centred around geography, history, language, ecology, and science.
The World Wildlife Fund commissioned lesson activities relevant to
Education for Sustainable Development (ESD), written in the field
and beamed back via satellite. The Photo Exchange and Video Exchange Programs were also included, tying as they did into social studies. Picking up from where Annie left off on Tarawa, a photographer

from Minneapolis, Rebecca Lawson, would work with four groups of teenagers from both European settler and aboriginal backgrounds in Cairns and Alice Springs. With our cutting-edge website, films and photo albums would be viewable online for the first time.*

This took hundreds of hours to organize, in addition to working out a route. Using topographic maps provided by the Australian Surveying Land and Information Group (AUSLIG), I planned a 4,800-kilometre off-road journey from the shores of the Pacific to the Top End. The route took in lush rainforest, scorching desert, and every ecosystem in between, exposing classrooms to a wide variety of plant and animal species, including twenty of the world's most venomous snakes. Plus, there was Australia's rich cultural heritage. Tracing a finger over the maps, the names of the aboriginal settlements felt awkward in my mouth:

Urandangi. Kaltukatjara. Kalkarinji. Yuendumu.

The departure date was set for July 1, midwinter in the Southern Hemisphere. This ensured the Red Centre would be at its coolest, a modest ninety-seven degrees Fahrenheit for a daily mean, and the eighty-six-day trek would overlap the UK winter term for schools to participate in the live event.

As May rolled into June, the sponsorship momentum became infectious. Cannondale agreed to loan a selection of full-suspension mountain bikes capable of handling the rugged terrain. Mitsubishi Australia came on board with a 4WD Canter, the ideal support vehicle. With hundreds of kilometres between waterholes in the Simpson and Tanami Deserts, it was unrealistic to expect the young explorers to carry their own water or the plethora of electronic gadgetry we would need to share our daily adventures with schools.

By mid-June, everything was in place—except one crucial thing. The promised advance against royalties still hadn't arrived from Reddo,

---

*   In a pre-YouTube world, having the ability to stream video was both expensive and technologically complex.

making me extremely anxious. The head of content wasn't returning emails. Silence, too, from the commissioning editor. Finally, I managed to reach the project manager as she was driving home from work one day.

"Is the website up and running yet?" I asked.

"Another week," came the reply. "Don't worry, everything's on track to go live the first of July. And a cheque is definitely on its way."

THREE DAYS LATER, an email from the CEO of Reddo Publishing appeared in my inbox. *We rather underestimated the amount of lead-in time required*—blah, blah, blah—*we've had problems with our server*—blah, blah, blah. In other words, work hadn't even begun on the website. *Can you delay a year?*

I had eight people, plane tickets in hand, arriving in less than a week. Buying time to scrape some cash together, I postponed the departure for a fortnight. My sister, Julia, re-loaned the expedition $2,000. ROHO Cushions, who were designing custom padding for *Moksha's* pedal seat, donated another $2,500.

It would be bare bones. Three young explorers relying on a bursary had to drop out, and each member of the team would now have to pay their own costs. Then there was the small matter of the website. Jake and Skip from Video Free America in San Francisco stepped up to the plate, knocking together a basic site capable of streaming video and hosting live webcasts. Students from James Cook University in Cairns improvised an instant messaging service for classrooms to communicate with the team in the field. Sheryll Oliver, a teacher at the Cairns School of Distance Education, put us in touch with host families along the route.

As usual, it was the folks the expedition came into contact with who made it all happen.

THE OUTBACK
YOU'LL NEVER MAKE IT TO DARWIN

The migration itself, like the pilgrimage, is the hard journey: a "leveller" on which the 'fit' survive and the stragglers fall by the wayside. The journey thus pre-empts the need for hierarchies and shows of dominance. The 'dictators' of the animal kingdom are those who live in an ambience of plenty. The anarchists, as always, are the 'gentlemen of the road'.

—BRUCE CHATWIN, *The Songlines*

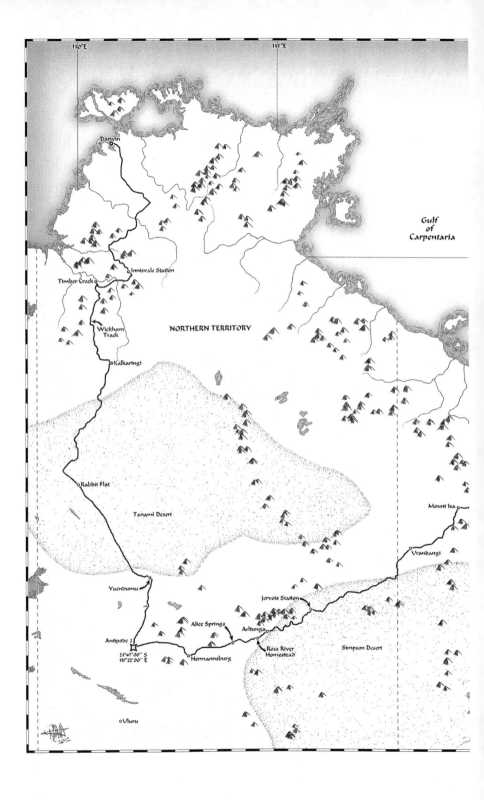

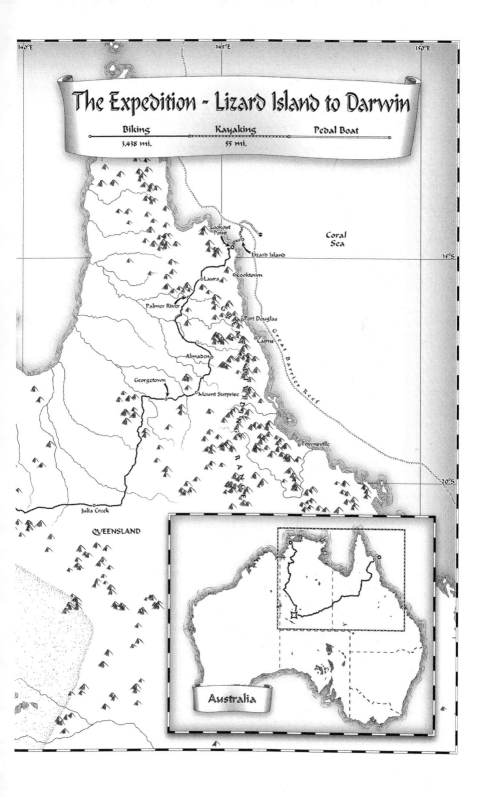

"SCUSE ME MATE. Is this the Starcke River?"

"Course it's the fuck'n Starcke River."

Fiftyish, Joe Sicorra was the quintessential outback ocker in his flip-flops, scant shorts, and tee shirt advertising drill bits. His beard, more salt than pepper, framed a battered hooknose put even more out of joint by our sudden appearance. A tattered, sweat-encrusted hat completed the picture of feral decay.

"Fuck me. Look at all you cunts."

Fastened to the end of his right arm was a stubbie can of Castlemaine XXXX, his only apparent means of survival in the outback. He shook it at us. "You're fuck'n mad, comin' up 'ere to ride them mongrel push bikes. You can do that wherever you fuck'n loike. Why here?"

We were lost, as we'd been for most of the day, blundering around north of Cooktown on washed out tracks. Many of those marked on our thirty-year-old maps had grown over from lack of use, and more recently bulldozed trails sprang out of nowhere, taking us kilometres in the wrong direction.

It didn't matter. After being bogged down in Cairns for ten months, getting lost in the outback felt bloody marvellous. Dry eucalypt forest covered the ferrous-red terrain, over which fleeting wallabies bounced. Camouflaged goannas froze against the flaking trunks of ironwood trees as we passed. Magnetic termite hills littered the surrounds, their east-west-facing elliptic shape drawing maximum benefit from the sun. These brick-red mounds were home to three species of parrot, according to one of the young explorers, nineteen-year-old Bell Chamberlain, a moon-faced bird lover from Victoria with wild hair.

Joe leaned against his Holden Ute and nodded at our Cannondales. "Bet they're not yours."

"On loan," I confirmed.

He took a swig of his beer, revealing a weathered hand, fingers claw-like and cracked with abrasions.

"Where d'you think you're takin' them cunts anyway?"

"Darwin."

He didn't even blink. "Any more of yooz cunts comin'?"

"Yeah, a few more," replied John-o. John-o was a drinking chum of our support-driver-cum-outback-survival-expert John Andrews, nick-named Blue Dog. The New Zealander had taken a few days off work to help out. "But they haven't turned up yet, which means—"

"Which means yer fuck'n lost!" Joe crowed triumphantly. "Listen, leave your shit here and go an tie a bag or some fuck'n thing on the fuck'n track up there, something they can recognize so they don't miss the fuck'n turn-off."

Blocking the way ahead was a body of opaque water, green and stagnant, its muddy banks bristling with mangroves that resonated to the whoops and whistles of invisible birds.

"But you've gotta cross the Starcke, haven't ya?" said John-o, squint-ing at the map in his hands.

Joe sucked on his teeth. "No, yer don't. There's another road. You'll end up in Lakefield if you take that one."

"So where's the mouth, then?"

"One kilometre in front o' you."

"But why does the map say—"

"Fuck the map yer fuck'n lost yer cunt. Yer didn't read the fuck'n map properly."

"It crosses the river, though."

"It does not."

"Does."

Joe rolled his eyes. "Does not! Listen, oi don't give a fuck. Oi'll give you a hundred fuck'n dollars yer dumb Kiwi cunt. How can you cross to the other side when there's no fuck'n bridge to cross the fuck'n thing?" He waved his stubbie at the river behind him. "Fuck me dead. Com-mon fuck'n sense." He shook his head and grinned. "Japanese fuck'n maps. Fuck the fuck'n maps!"

"Maybe the map's wrong?" John-o offered timidly.

"Nah, you just read the cunt wrong."

The rest of the team finally caught up, and we slumped exhausted into our tents. Tomorrow was a big day. We had to get fully organized before leaving from the beach at first light.

Joe was up first. "C'mon, yer fuck'n poofters. Roise and fuck'n shoine!"

I looked at my watch. It was 5:00 am—still dark.

Two hours later, properly rested, I unzipped the tent flap and stuck my head outside. Joe and Bell were standing at the entrance to Blue Dog's tent, a mud crab the size of a steering wheel in Bell's hands. It flourished its pincers at her in defiance.

"Go on! Go on!" Joe was yelling excitedly. "Just open his tent and stick it in there!"

"Isn't he still sleeping?" whispered Bell.

"Shit, yeah. Go and wake 'im up. Don't let it go on 'im, though. It'll take his fingers off if it gets a hold. Just stick it right in his face so when he opens his eyes he sees it."

Bell gingerly opened the flap.

"Throw it in there! Throw it in! C'mon, loosen yer bra strap. Don't be a girl."

Outback Education 101 in full swing, I thought despairingly, and reached for my sandals.

The team spent the morning sorting out gear for the trailers we'd be towing behind the bikes. Kenny, who'd come to film for the first week before handing over to Todd, gave the youngsters a map-reading lesson using topos and GPS. He and Todd also demonstrated how to use the video cameras—everyone had agreed to record a daily video diary for the Discovery series. There was a crash course in bike maintenance offered by sixteen-year-old Crister Brady, a pleasant, eager-to-please schoolboy from California. His father, Jim, a teacher at Santa Barbara

Middle School, was one of the team's two professional educators—
April being the other.

Joe was enjoying himself far too much to do any more fishing. He
laid into poor Todd, who was working on a camera outside his tent.
"You're a dumb fuck'n cunt," Joe told him. "Work on a tarp, not the
fuck'n sand. That way you can see where the fuck'n screws fall."

"So is this your new purpose in life, Joe?" April asked. "To harass
us?"

He leered and tipped his hat. "Nah, darl. I already got one o' those.
A woman's purpose in life is to empty the stubbie bin. A man's is to fill
it."

Little surprise then to hear his take on aborigines: "Know why they
invented the boomerang? 'Cos the cunts are too fuck'n lazy to go 'n
pick it up!"

But during lulls between theatrics, Joe was capable of astute observations. He was just lonely and liable to show off when he had an audience—like now. Beneath his hard outer shell, he was as soft as the mud
crabs he'd come all this way to find. And he wasn't the hard-drinking
beer monster he made himself out to be, either.

"I drink Castlemaine **XXXX** *Light* so I can drink sixteen of the
cunts to eight of the normal strength," he boasted to me that afternoon.

"So why not just drink eight of the regular strength and save your
money?" I said.

"'Cos that way I can still get up in the morning."

His logic was illustrated twelve hours later. The sun was already well
above the horizon by the time we wheeled our bikes down to the beach
and positioned our back wheels in the water for a "before" shot. We
were nine. The young explorers looked fresh faced and their gear—
bikes, yellow **BOB** trailers, CamelBaks, and **ICOM** radios—all brand
spanking new.

I tapped a lukewarm can of Victoria Bitter on my handlebars, and
flipped the ring pull, unleashing a fountain of white foam. "Here's to

Darwin!" I toasted to a chorus of whoops. Taking a swig, I passed it down the line.

"You took a lot there, Josh," said Jim when the can finally reached him.

A bushy-haired teenager from Cairns, Josh Grey had signed up after a last-minute appeal on the local ABC radio station for riders.

"Waddya mean?" he protested. "Hardly got a mouthful."

Kenny finished his roll of film. "Okay, last one to Darwin's a big grrrl's blouse."

Just then, there was a crash of foliage at the top of the beach. Camera in one hand and stubbie in the other, Joe emerged from the bushes in a clean blue shirt, hair neatly combed. He began marching down the beach, bawling at us.

"Useless bunch o' fuck'n cunts! Call yourself a fuck'n boike team? Oi fuck'n came down 'ere at twenty to fuck'n seven to see you cunts off." He stabbed at his watch. "Now it's fuck'n nine o'clock, and yooz is still fuck'n 'ere!"

One of the team was a mid-thirties truck salesman from Salt Lake City, along to make up numbers. "It's not even your birthday," said Mike Roney coolly. "And we gave you such a wonderful gift to bitch about this morning."

Joe chuckled. "Fuck me. You'll get along."

I said, "So, why don't you grab a bike and come along with us, Joe?"

He looked at me, appalled. "Look. Mate. By the time I got a fuck'n hundred metres down the fuck'n road I'd be puffin' and blowin' and fuck'n walkin' back to get a fuck'n beer."

There was part of him itching to come along, you could tell. For all the cursing and haranguing, Joe was already living vicariously through our adventure.

Then we were off, tyres crunching over the gravelly sand exposed by low tide. The air was cool, and sunshine glittered off a light chop in the bay. Overland Australia had begun. After three hundred metres, there was a shout behind us. Joe was standing ankle deep in the surf, his stubbie raised in an Aussie salute. And were those tears running down the old curmudgeon's cheeks?

"Oi'm fuck'n tellin' yer cunts!" he hollered. "You'll never fuck'n make it to Darwin."

To cross the Great Dividing Range, the mountains separating the Queensland coast from the rest of Australia, our route took us up the legendary Maytown Track, a rugged, at times impossibly steep trail blazed in the late 1800s by Chinese labourers wielding picks and shovels. It was the lifeline for 50,000 people eking out an existence on the Palmer River Goldfields two hundred and twenty-five kilometres inland. Bullock trains hauled supplies up the rutted path from the nearest port at Cooktown. Prospectors themselves had to walk, pushing wheelbarrows loaded with equipment and provisions.

Four days after leaving the coast, the team arrived at the Maytown turn-off near Jowalbinna. The plan was to rendezvous with the support vehicle at 12:30 pm, but by 2:00 pm there was no sign of it.

I made the decision to keep going. Already two weeks behind schedule, every additional delay increased the risk of being caught by the wet season in the Top End, cut off by swollen rivers and bogged in the mud. Progress, however, was slow. For the first three kilometres, we were pushing our bikes through deep sand. This was the Quinkan Reserve, home to both good and evil spirits, according to local aborigines. If a child went missing, a bad Quinkan was to blame. But Quinkans could also be playful and mischievous, as we were about to find out.

It was the hottest time of day, ninety-seven degrees, and Mike was reaching the end of his tether. He was a big guy with a wrestler's build, and his wrap-around shades gave him the compound, bug-eyed look of a Mafioso. He'd fallen four times in the first hour out of Laura.

Then his bottom bracket came loose. Without the requisite tool, he'd resorted to sand trudging.

Now we were all sand trudging, sweating and cursing like the early pioneers, staggering through washed-out gullies and shoving our heavily laden trailers up the sheer slope, laughed at by the kookaburras and ambushed by biting green ants that leapt from the bushes. After three hours and a 1,300-foot climb in elevation, the track levelled out at Hell's Gate, a narrow pass between towering rocks where cannibalistic aborigines once picked off the stragglers. Legend had it Chinese diggers got it in the neck first, singled out for their sweeter flesh.

But where was the support vehicle? Running low on water and ravenously hungry (all we had with us was "scroggin," Aussie for trail mix), the team collapsed under a mulga bush and waited.

After twenty minutes, Josh jumped to his feet "Here's Kenny! Good on yer, matie."

The last time we'd seen him, Our Man Brown was in the support truck with Blue Dog. He was now riding one of the Cannondales, a pan, gallon container of water, and several bags of noodles bungeed behind his seat.

It was then we learned of the five and a half hours that Blue Dog had spent loading the truck that morning and his dismay at our continuing up the track without him.

"*Someone* must have realized I wouldn't be able to follow you."

We were back in Jowalbinna, sitting around a campfire, listening to Blue Dog's version of what had gone wrong. Raised on a station near Broken Hill in New South Wales, Blue Dog had the knowledge to keep the young explorers alive in the Australian bush for the first critical weeks.

Oblivious to the wood smoke billowing in his face, Blue Dog continued. "I mean, there's absolutely no way I could have made it up there in the truck."

The root of the problem lay in the dynamic between the nimble bike team and a support vehicle loaded with three hundred litres of drinking water, one-and-a-half tonnes of food, two generators for powering electronics, and a small library of reference books for supplementing the educational updates. We were tied to it like tots to a teet, yet the truck was what allowed us to take a more interesting off-road route in the first place.

Jim spoke up. A veteran of cycling expeditions with Educational Safaris, a non-profit organization that took children on awareness-learning adventures in different parts of the world, he'd seen this a hundred times, apparently.

"It's going to take a while to iron out the glitches." Lean and bookish in his John Lennon glasses, he spoke with measured precision, choosing his words carefully. "We need to establish a fluid system of loading the truck in the mornings, so we all set off together, the bikers and the truck within the same radio net. Give it ten days, and *maybe* we'll have a system worked out."

In the meantime, we needed to get over these mountains. A group decision was made to tackle the fifty-kilometre track without the support truck, which would take the long way round and meet us on the other side. The next day was spent repacking the trailers, exchanging tents and sleeping bags for food and water, and catering to the worst-case scenario—someone breaking their femur, for example, and having to be carried out on a makeshift stretcher, a two- to three-day ordeal.

Or getting bitten. The world's deadliest snake, the inland taipan, was native to the region, its venom three hundred times more potent than that of a rattlesnake. A single drop was enough to kill our entire team of twelve.*

---

* We carried pressure bandages for immobilizing venom and a shock device that broke down key enzymes with electricity, buying time to get someone to hospital for anti-venom.

At sunrise the following morning, we were back at Hell's Gate, having tackled the worst of the climb in the predawn cool. The next thirty kilometres were tremendous riding. In the words of Crister: "Gnarly, gnarly, technical, loose, down hills, drops, really steep up hills. *Awesome.*"

When he was fourteen, Crister had ridden the length of the Continental Divide from Canada to Mexico. He was an experienced rider and a tremendous asset in camp, constantly volunteering for chores—washing dishes, gathering firewood, helping prepare the evening meal—without ever needing to be asked.

At a ten-minute scroggin stop, Mike announced, "I'm doing things I never would have done even a day ago. Well, apart from one time when I slid down the hillside like a baby."

By early afternoon, we were well over halfway. The mood of the group was one of cautious optimism that we'd make it to the Palmer River before dark.

But the Maytown Track wasn't finished with us yet. First came the punctures—I had three in less than one hour. Then, after being treated to stunning views of north Queensland, we dropped off the escarpment, slicing through the twisting shadows of eucalyptus trees, and started up a nine-kilometre grade taking us up and over the final ridge. Mike, who hadn't had time to get properly fit before coming out, started to flag. Fifty metres short of the summit, he collapsed with heat exhaustion.

I found him sitting in the middle of the track, his eyes closed, hair sticking up on end, head resting in his hands.

"How you doing, Mike?"

"Freezing … freezing cold. I just need some food."

Mike was the odd one out in the group. He wasn't a student or a teacher. He wasn't on the end of a camera like Todd and Kenny or behind the wheel of the support truck like Blue Dog. When Kenny interviewed him at the Starcke and asked why he'd joined up, Mike replied that he needed to "break out of a routine situation of selling trucks."

Using his fingers as a shovel, Mike began excavating scroggin from a plastic bag and spooning it into his mouth. I slipped off my CamelBak, pointed the nozzle at his head, and squeezed. Nothing came out, just air and bubbles.

"Just teasing you, Mike."

He forced a dry laugh.

Finally, a trickle ran down his upturned face.

With daylight fading, the prudent thing to do was to camp and allow Mike to fully recover. But it would be a cold night without our sleeping bags, and in the end, Mike insisted we carry on. I agreed on one condition, that we take some weight out of his trailer.

And so, we pushed on into the dusk, passing a sign that warned: "Beware of Open Mine Shafts." In its heyday of 1870, Maytown would have been crawling with prospectors hoping to strike it rich. Now it was a ghost town, not a soul in evidence. It was strange to imagine the mass of eager faces hurrying here to live like rats, underground, stabbing at the quartz reefs with hand tools. Ninety-nine per cent walked out with nothing. The rest either made a fortune or, too weak to leave, starved to death.

Abandoned machinery littered the surrounds: rusting boilers, winches, mills, crushers, ore stamps, and grinder pans. A five-tonne flywheel lay cracked in half, the inscription revealing it had been cast in Manchester, England. Transported halfway around the world by sailing ship, it was then hauled up the Maytown Track by bullock cart and winched over the steeper inclines by block and tackle.

It was too dark to ride anymore, so we walked the last three kilometres by moonlight. By the time we made it to the truck, we'd been out for nearly sixteen hours. Everyone was shattered.

"Home safe," I muttered to Kenny's waiting camera, heading for the campfire that Blue Dog had started.

Mike was behind me, walking zombie-like with fatigue.

"Hoos it goin?" asked Kenny.

"Done," Mike replied wearily. "Absolutely done. That's how it's go-ing."

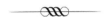

MOUNTAINS BEHIND US, we descended into the flattish scrubland of the Great Artesian Basin, serenaded by the melancholic strains of creaking windmills as we skimmed over the dark, hard-packed loam. A rusting hubcap nailed to a tree on a property line warned: "Private Property. Keep Out. No Camping. NO ANYTHING!" The sky stretched in a sheet of untrammelled azure ever westwards, the monotony broken only by solitary cotton ball clouds. Beneath us, underground aquifers drip-fed with rainfall seeping west from the Great Dividing Range pro-vided the only source of the water for the region's vast cattle stations.

The biggest of these was Wrotham Park, weighing in at an impres-sive 10,200 square kilometres, the size of Belgium. We stopped in to say "G'day." Blue Dog traded four expedition tee shirts for some fresh fruit and cuts of meat for the flesh eaters. The station was so vast they used helicopters for the annual muster of 32,000 head of tick-resistant Brah-ma cattle destined for the halal markets of the Middle East. Fired up by the sight of our bicycles, the cream-coloured leviathans thundered ahead of us in a great snorting mob as we left, throwing up billowing clouds of bull dust into our faces.

"Later, bovines!" Crister hollered once they'd peeled off into the eucalyptus trees. "Catch ya' down the road in my burger, dude."

This was hard country, home to hard people. We called in at the Kruckow's, a pioneer family who'd bought enough land to set up a station at Pinnacle Springs, sixty kilometres south of the railhead at Almaden. Sheryll Oliver had arranged for us to film a Discovery Zone segment on how the children, Emma and Laura, received their education through the School of the Air.

The girls met us at the gate with their newly weaned black-and-tan kelpie puppies peering over the lip of a wheelbarrow. Blue Dog bent down to scratch one of them under the chin. "This one's a big fatty, isn't he?"

"We call him Rolly," said Emma, the older of the two. Like her sister, she was barefoot and wore khaki shorts, a long-sleeved shirt for the sun, and a domed hat with a wide brim made out of felt. The girls were waiting for their parents and Uncle Frog to return from branding and castrating weanlings in a nearby corral.

Verna was petite with fair skin and wore the same distinctive hat as her daughters. "The first year we were here was the worst. Terrible!" We were standing next to the original homestead, a dilapidated tin shed. "Of the two hundred cattle we started out with, we lost about a hundred to drought the first season."

As she talked, a tall, broad-shouldered man with dark untidy hair ambled up. This was her husband, Peter.

"It was an absolutely shocking way to start a cattle station," Verna continued, smiling wryly.

The land was marginal, valued at four dollars an acre in 1991. They'd managed to scrape together sixty-four-and-a-half square kilometres, enough to sustain a family at a ratio of one animal to forty acres—or so they reckoned. But starting from scratch, life had been immeasurably hard.

"This is where I had Laura." Verna adjusted her steel-rimmed specs and squinted up at the cobwebs sagging under the roof. "There was no running water, just a tank on stilts, and a donkey."

This was not the family pet, but a DIY hot water heater made from a forty-four-gallon drum.

Verna laughed, but she obviously wasn't laughing back then.

Judging by the teasing glances she kept throwing at her husband, I suspected that it was all Peter's idea, and his long-suffering wife had sucked it up so he could live his dream.

"Ever since I was fourteen," Peter confirmed in a low Aussie lilt, "I wanted to run cattle. But you don't notice the hardship when you're doing what you love."

"That's easy for you to say!" Verna poked her husband's ribs playfully. "No phone. No electricity. Everything washed by hand. Dust and filth everywhere. And with a new baby!"

On top of the drought, the crude living conditions, and the stunning indifference of the outback, Emma had been diagnosed with leukaemia three years earlier. Twice a week for six months, the family had driven the twelve-hour, nine-hundred-kilometre round trip to Townsville for treatment. For now, at least, her cancer was in remission, and she was able to lead a normal, healthy life.

Next morning, April and Jim helped the girls with their schoolwork, which we filmed in a little schoolroom set apart from the new house—a wooden bungalow with a wide veranda that Peter and Frog had recently completed. Over the crackle and whine of the high-frequency radio set, I could make out the familiar voice of Sheryll Oliver in Cairns. She was going through the roll call of her pupils, who were spread over an area the size of Wales. As each name was called, a shrill reply came warbling over the airwaves. When it came Emma's turn, the ten year old pressed the toggle on her handset and replied, "Good morning, Miss Oliver!"

Verna peered over her daughter's shoulder, and said, "Not being able to see their teacher or the other kids, they've learned to become good listeners." Emma looked up at her mother, who jokingly added, "But strangely that seems to disappear once they get in the house and I need some cleaning done, eh?"

Pressing on to Springfield, we passed a road-kill wallaby lying beside the track. A twitch between the animal's hindquarters caught my eye. Telling the others to go on ahead, I dismounted and turned the carcass over. It was a mother with a pair of bloodied feet protruding from the white fur of her pouch. The joey was still alive, scratching feebly at the dirt. Gently, I freed the tiny form, a furless puppy with elongated hind legs, a rat-like tail, and bulbous eyes struggling to focus in the midday sun.

Poor little guy must be burning up in this heat, I thought grimly.

Circling above, nature's waste disposal team was standing by: a dozen vultures ready to swoop. I knew I couldn't take the joey with me.

As I rode away, gloves splattered with blood, I thought of the Kruckows and their struggle in the heart of Australian darkness. Sure, the country was unforgiving, but they were still "Having a go!" as Joe Sicorra would have said. They weren't trying to get rich. They were just following a dream, doing it the hard way, without safety nets, delighting in teetering along the outermost edge of life, thumbing their noses at the culture of entitlement elsewhere, at those content to sleepwalk along the well-trodden path. They'd taken everything the bush had thrown at them so far, and they were still standing, still working, and, with the dry humour I'd come to associate with True Blue Aussies, still laughing. As Jim acknowledged in his blog description of them for that evening: "Strength is adaptability. It isn't a matter of what happens to you, but how you react to what happens."

"IT'S ANOTHER TEN k's to the road, and it's all this shit." Blue Dog nodded at the tall grass lining the track. "So we'll just camp here for the night by this dam."

Bell stared impassively at him. "It's the perfect place for disease," she whispered. Like the birds she so loved, her voice rarely rose above a cheep. "Flies. Cow shit. And we'll be in the way of the cows getting to water. They're having a hard enough time out here as it is."

We'd come to an earthen tank holding surface run-off for livestock. Black crested cockatoos mobbed the branches of nearby ghost gums, chattering and shrieking at each other, before swooping down to drink at the water's edge.

Blue Dog glared at Bell. "Well, where the fuck do you want to camp, then? You choose a better place."

Less than a week into the trip, and Blue Dog and Bell already shared an intense dislike for each another. Seeing where this latest exchange was heading, I quickly stepped in. "So, what's the problem with camping a little farther down the road?"

Blue Dog leaned out of his cab window. "Because if we have a campfire here, we won't set the whole place alight."

He had a point. The grass in the surrounding bush was tinder dry.

"Bell's right, though," Mike chipped in, "This place is really dirty."

Blue Dog made a face. "Bit of cow shit ain't gonna hurt anybody. And the cattle will still make it to the water."

We took a vote whether to stay put or carry on. Despite the filth, the consensus was to stay where we were, so we could light a fire and cook a meal.

Tensions had been building between other group members for several days. Besides Bell and Blue Dog, Mike was becoming increasingly frustrated with my minimalist mode of leadership. For him, getting to Darwin posed a near-impossible challenge, requiring military-style discipline if we hoped to make it there intact. One of his biggest fears was the wildlife. He was convinced that every snake, spider, and wild pig was out to get us.

"Bell," I said. "Camp wherever you like, just as long as you tell us where you go, okay?"

This became the norm. The team would make camp. Bell would

stick around long enough for a wash-up meeting, in which the following day's plan would be laid out, and to write one or more of the educational updates. She'd then take off and find her own campsite.

It was partly to do with her allergy to dust. That and Bell loved to roam freely in the moonlight, listening and smelling, fine-tuning her faculties to nature's mainframe. At the Starcke River, she'd informed me that back in Victoria she often rode her bike "at night, in the snow, and always alone."

No one ever saw her eat a meal. I once caught her sucking a tomato half-heartedly, another time nibbling on a eucalyptus leaf. Otherwise, nothing. Apart from a small cotton bag of wild rice stashed in the support vehicle, she lived off the land, foraging bush tucker.

I'd known from the start that taking such an eclectic band of individuals into the outback wasn't going to be easy. Allowing personal freedoms while at the same time keeping everyone safe required a delicate balancing act. A degree of structure is inevitable within any group, and the larger the group, the more structure typically needed. But structure for its own sake was something I'd always found irksome. The fine line between the two became blurred when different perceptions of risk and corresponding tolerances for fear entered the mix. I never had any doubt we'd make it to Darwin. Neither did Bell. "Difficulties?" she'd replied in her Starcke interview, when asked what she thought the main difficulties were facing the team. "Whatever people want to make difficult." Mike, on the other hand, saw things differently. If he were in charge, as he said he was used to, he'd lead from the front and "get the whole team ticking like a well-oiled machine."

That was the last thing I wanted. A machine. I wanted the young explorers to pursue individual interests and passions, to spread their wings, and espouse a sense of ownership in our collective endeavour. With this in mind, I planned for them to take a leadership day once a week, giving the youngsters experience in making key decisions, reading maps, chairing meetings, interfacing with the support vehicle, and so on. As Steve had once pointed out, people didn't belong to the expedition, they *were* the expedition.

In any case, lack of structure wasn't at the root of Mike's grievances, as it turned out. He was wrestling with a much more sinister issue. "I'm a ticking time bomb," he confided to his video diary one evening, going on to explain that as well as needing to take a break from selling trucks, the reason he'd joined the expedition was to confront and destroy his innermost demons, before they destroyed him.

AFTER A THOUSAND kilometres of dirt tracks, we hit our first stretch of asphalt, the Gulf Development Road, notable for the festering abundance of corpses littering its length.

Indeed, it could be said that road kill is the one defining feature of roads in Australia. In the first kilometre alone heading towards Mount Surprise, we encountered five carcasses belonging to three different animal species: an eastern grey kangaroo, a red fox, and a wallaby. The stench was incredible, and worse was to come. We passed mutilated possums, mangled dogs, and toads squashed into coasters. Then more grey kangaroos and wallabies at various stages of dismemberment, with many of the scavengers themselves becoming a menu item. The tally of death was so impressive we used the numbers for a statistics lesson for schools following online.

The primary engines of this demise were the road trains. Obstinate and unwieldy, these three-tailed monsters pounded the Never-Never 24/7, annihilating everything in their paths. They did so because they could. Distributing everything from beer to bullied beef to all four corners of the red continent, they were the undisputed kings of the highway. This and at fifty metres in length, slamming on the brakes could result in the most appalling jackknife. In open range country where the cost of fencing was prohibitive, the drivers relied instead on the truck's bull bars to clear the road of hopping roos and cringing possums.

BOOOMMM!!!

"Someone's been hit!" A second later, a flash of white blew past: a road train thundering into the haze, its trailers fishtailing wildly.

We were twenty kilometres west of Georgetown, riding single file. The drill was for the tail-end Charlie to yell "Road train UP!" when he or she heard one coming from behind. The call would be passed up the line, and the entire team would pull off the road, dismount, and wait for the colossus to pass. The person riding point would do the same for vehicles coming in the opposite direction.

On this occasion, it appeared that Josh, riding tail, had been caught unawares. Looking over my shoulder, I saw a twisted knot of limbs and bicycle sprawled in the gravel.

By the time I leapt off my bike and ran back to the crash site, Jim was already at the scene, holding Josh's head and administering Rescue Remedy under his tongue. A wave of relief swept through me. His elbow and left hand were severely grazed, he was badly shaken, but the youngster was alive. The last trailer had missed him by a whisker, the back draft bowling him over his handlebars.

Something changed after that. Josh's near miss served as a reality check, putting a temporary stop to the endemic bickering. The group closed ranks and began pulling as one. Loading the truck in the mornings was honed down from two hours to thirty minutes. People volunteered for camp chores without having to be told. A system was finally emerging, as Jim said it would. We took turns rising at 3:30 am to start a fire and get breakfast going. The rest of the team would be up by 4:30—packing tents, scoffing porridge, and swilling black tea—ready to load the truck and be on the bikes by sunrise.

Much of this streamlining was thanks to Blue Dog. "Survival is not always about whether you're going to die or not," he told me one evening, imparting what I took to be his guiding philosophy in the outback, "but the difference between enjoying yourself and having a terrible time."

He showed us some of his tricks, including letting the water in the billycan get "lumpy" before throwing in a handful of loose tea for smoko, mid-morning break, so the leaves didn't float. And which wood made the best coals to bake damper, the simple but delicious bread made from flour and water and cooked in a camp oven buried underground. On the Mitchell River, he'd taught Crister how to pan for gold and fish for the freshwater shrimp Australians called "yabbies."

With their adolescent appetites, keeping Crister and Josh properly fed was crucial. One reliable hunger indicator was Josh's deteriorating table manners.

"What *are* you doing?" I asked him during a smoko break. He was standing at the back of the truck, spooning breakfast leftovers onto a slice of damper.

"Porridge sandwich," he replied, continuing to lather the bread.

Josh was the spitting image of Sideshow Bob, one of *The Simpsons* animated cartoon characters, his ginger mattress of hair sprouting in all directions.

I said, "Do you realize how utterly depraved that is?"

Josh threw his head back, rocked on his heels, and unleashed his trademark hyena laugh. "He-he-he!" Then he took a bite of his sandwich. A gob of porridge oozed out and landed on his right foot.

"You—are—re—volting!" I said.

"It's not the end of the world," Josh replied, his cheeks bulging.

Another clot welled, detached itself, and landed on his left foot. Mike was also watching. "I saw a kink in that plan right off," he laughed.

Despite his atrocious eating habits, Josh had a big heart. He was a happy-go-lucky kid with a seemingly inexhaustible capacity for telling jokes.

"Did I ever tell you my six-legged-chicken joke?" he asked me as we rode together one day.

"You did," I replied. "Except last time it had three legs."

"Well then!" the teenager cried triumphantly. "You haven't heard my six-legged-chicken joke, have you?"

It wasn't all fun and games. Unaccustomed to rising much before 10:00 at home, Josh was finding the 4:00 am starts a struggle. And in the third week, when he forgot to charge the radios for the fifth night in a row, I let them remain flat so he would face the consequences in the morning. Without a radio net, the safety of the group was compromised, prompting angry demands for Josh to "get his shit together."

Feeling the heat, Josh vented his frustrations during one of his evening "video diarrhoeas."

"Sick of Jason at the moment," he fumed, running his fingers through his hair and popping his eyes at the camera, which was set up on the outskirts of camp for privacy. The teenager had red blotches on his face, and he was sweating. "Pissing me off … I'm sick of this shit." He stuck his face in the lens. "Sick of *your* shit, Jason!"

Being homesick didn't help. Josh missed his family and friends terribly. "I've been thrown together with these people," he went on. "They're my mates whether I like it or not."

Behind him, the light was fading and the cockatoos were screeching. He looked miserably at his feet. "My only outlet is this camera. Today has been so difficult. No one's talking. I've been thinking about what I'm doing here and why I'm doing this. If I had the choice, I'd go home right now. It's too much. This expedition seemed like a really good idea at the time. But now I'm having second thoughts."

WE ENTERED JULIA Creek, "Home of the Fat-tailed Dunnart," according to the sign, a claim borne out by the abundance of furry placemats on the road leading into town.

This was where we were to lose Jim. With school starting soon, he had to return to his teaching job in Santa Barbara. April, who'd been given a two-month sabbatical, would take over his duties as education coordinator.

Crister would remain with us, making it his first time away from both parents. He put on a brave face as April squeezed his arm and smiled encouragingly. "Don't worry," she said gently. "We'll take good care of you." April and I had agreed to act as Crister's surrogate parents for the remainder of the trip to Darwin.

"Aw, c'moan, momma." Grinning sadistically, I pinched the youngster's left cheek. "You gonna spoil Junior. 'Sides, his ass is mine now his daddy's gawn!"

Jim laughed nervously. "This won't be like the Marine Corps, will it?"

"Boot camp starts today. Now drop and give me twen'y, boy!"

A BRUISER WEARING an orange boiler suit, a miner's headlamp, and a pair of black rubber gumboots grinned inanely from the roadside and hollered, "Welcome to The Isa. Now you're a real Aussie!"

The tourist billboard was strategically positioned to steer the visitor's eye away from the phalanx of belching chimneys in the background, the damask red slag heaps, and the sallow pall of smoke hanging over the town. We'd been told that when the wind blew from the southeast in Mount Isa, the town's copper smelter was turned off to keep the 18,000 inhabitants from being asphyxiated.

After three weeks in the bush, we were looking forward to stocking up on provisions and running some errands. Since the Starcke, Bell had managed to lose her ATM card, driver's license, all her cash, address book, notebook, dictionary, three pairs of sunglasses, a towel, eleven pens, three hairclips, two pairs of chopsticks for tying up her hair, and an entire set of clothes.

"All of it gone," she beamed, throwing up her hands in delight. "Just gone!"

On the way into town we called in at the Healy State School to meet two aboriginal teenagers who were joining the expedition. Part of the young explorer format was for native ambassadors to introduce themselves and their homeland to classrooms around the world. However, when we tracked down our contact, Joan Marshall, we were told the boys had changed their minds.

"You got here just a little too late," she said. "It's now the season for initiation. The kids are afraid the Kalkadoon elders will drag them into the bush if they travel with you."

"Why, what happens?" I asked.

"They, umm … get scarred."

The Aussie accent threw me. "Did you say scared or scarred?"

"Scarred. With stones."

To mark their transition to manhood, the boys apparently faced being circumcised with sharp rocks. No joke for a sixteen year old—or any year old, for that matter. "But a couple of the girls are interested in coming along," Joan added.

Kate and her cousin, Josie, were in their mid-teens. Despite not being fit and lacking experience on mountain bikes, the girls would help break the stereotype of indigenous males doing all the travelling while the women stayed at home barefoot and pregnant.

April interviewed them in the principal's office. "So, what interests you about coming along?" she enquired.

Kate looked at her cousin. "It'd be good to get away from Mount Isa, wouldn't it, Jo?"

Josie shrugged. "Yeah, get us off the ciggies and the grog for a bit."

I looked for the irony in their faces, but no, they were being deadly serious. This was not exactly the motivation we were looking for.

I'd been driving the team hard since the Starcke, and a couple of rest days were badly needed. A chance encounter with Greg, an Eco-Challenge veteran and fellow cyclist we'd met on the road from Cloncurry, landed us a quiet backyard on the outskirts of town with three of Greg's expedition camels for company.

After setting up his tent, Josh pulled me aside out of earshot of the others.

"I think I'm gonna head back to Cairns," he mumbled, kicking at a clod of dirt. "I need to concentrate more on my running."

I was flummoxed. Not privy to his video diaries to date, this was news to me. If anyone was about to throw in the towel, I'd expected it to be Mike. Josh explained that it was his dream to run in the Commonwealth Games one day, and he needed to start training. But this didn't seem to me the real reason. The way he kept avoiding my gaze suggested there was something else at play.

"Look," I said, "we're all tired. Why don't you just sleep on it? Make a decision in the morning when your head's a bit clearer."

Josh nodded reluctantly and wandered off to join the others, leaving me to ponder the root cause of his complaint. I remembered something Jim had told me at the Starcke: "The group's got to fall apart first before it can come back together."

But what if the group fell apart and didn't come back together?

MIKE LAY IN the middle of the track, his black cycling jersey coated with red dust, blood welling liberally from a deep gouge in his right elbow.

"Head," he grunted, nursing his right shoulder with his left hand. "Shoulder. Elbow."

A few seconds before, Mike and I had been tearing along the unpaved surface of the Plenty Highway, the country's main east-west artery, fooling around playing tag. Our handlebars locked horns for an instant, pitching Mike head first onto the hard-packed dirt.

"The only thing I'm worried about is my clavicle." Mike winced as Crister rinsed the elbow wound with Betadine. "Ouch! Don't rub it." Mike chuckled. "Hurts like a bastard when you do that."

Helping him to a sitting position, we took off his shirt and helmet, which had a two-inch-long crack along the right side.

"Bonged my head pretty good," said Mike. "Helmet saved my ass."

"Looks like your fruit took a hit, too," I said, extracting the remains of an apple and an orange from his hip pocket.

Earlier that morning, we'd emptied the Mount Isa Woolworths of porridge, potatoes, self-raising flour, peanut butter, and jam before cycling west out of town, past a creaking yellow sign gnawed by rust and riddled with bullet holes reminding visitors to "Keep Mount Isa Beautiful." The next supply point was Alice Springs, nine hundred kilometres away. Josh was still with us having had second thoughts after being interviewed by the local radio station. "The presenter was like, 'What you're doing is pretty amazing, a once in a lifetime experience'. And afterwards, I thought, yeah, she's right. The running can wait. I need to finish this first. I've never actually finished anything in my life before."

While Crister bandaged Mike's elbow, I fashioned a makeshift sling from an old bicycle inner tube. Mike sat staring at the undulating sand stretching south towards the Simpson Desert. "I'm starting to get superstitious," he said bitterly. "Like something's out to get me, and that something just won't let me finish this trip. I'm always the one to fall, always the one to get hurt." He shook his head. "Did I spit on a village witch or something?"

As well as countless falls, Mike had strained his hamstring racing Josh to one of the rest stops before Mount Isa. Later that same day, he'd aired his exasperation in a video diary entry: "It just pisses me off when I fail. I've had three years of nothing but shitty, shitty-assed luck."

We got him to his feet and picked up his bike.

"I'll try riding," he said, "Until my pain threshold tells me to stop."

"Carry on like this, Mike," I said, "and you'll arrive in Darwin looking like a mummy."

He laughed. "Yeah, you guys will be popping champagne, and there'll be this ball of gauze off to one side, holding up a bandaged finger, going, 'I was there, too!'"

He managed to tough it out the rest of the day riding with his good hand, but after a sleepless night he'd had enough—the pain was too great. He agreed to be taken back to Mount Isa in the truck for an x-ray.

"If it's just a bruise, I'll fly to Alice Springs and wait for you there. But if it's broken, I'll go home."

The sun was peering over the horizon as he stood there in his wide-brimmed hat and bug-eyed glasses, arm hanging feebly. "There's no point in me dragging myself around just to watch you guys work. I'd be even more grouchy than I am already."

A sober silence descended on the group as we contemplated the prospect of Mike not coming back. For me, this would help to avoid an unpleasant task. The truck salesman and I butted heads constantly. In Mount Isa, a furious argument had erupted over how much structure to incorporate into eating: whether to formalize meals at meeting times to prevent what Mike called "bored eating" or leave it up to the individual. After that encounter, I reminded myself that this was an educational endeavour, not a twelve-step programme for adults with anger-management issues. Both Crister and Josh had expressed unease at his outbursts, so I'd made up my mind to give Mike his marching orders once we reached Alice Springs.

But nothing is ever as it seems. With the video diary tapes kept confidential until Darwin, there was no way of knowing that Mike had run out of chewing tobacco a few days into the trip and was suffering from nicotine withdrawal. After splitting with his long-time girlfriend, he'd lived a solitary life, with only his beloved dog to keep him company. And when it died suddenly, anger and despair at himself and the world had sent him over the edge.

"I ended up in a hospital at my family's request," he confided to the camera. "Spent two or three days there, locked up to consider the fact that my family would like me to promise to find a point to my life. If my father hadn't been in Salt Lake City, I wouldn't be alive now."

If I'd known this at the time, I could have taken circumstances into account and been more sympathetic towards Mike. As it was, I breathed a sigh of relief as the truck set off for Mount Isa. Chances were he wouldn't be coming back.

The rest of us pushed west into landscape the colour of barley straw. The mornings were getting colder and the air drier the nearer we got to the Red Centre. Our lips chapped, our heels cracked, and we were still wearing fleece jackets and long johns at 11:00 in the morning during our yoga-cum-stretch break.

In the town of Urandangi, little more than a pub and a handful of flaking bungalows home to fourteen residents, we turned off the highway at the state school sign, an old car bonnet hand-painted with crude letters and propped against a tree. At the end of the dusty track, a dozen aboriginal children were waiting for us—the entire school, as it turned out.

Ranging in age from six to eighteen, the pupils were a sulky lot, scowling at us in their sweatpants and tee shirts. A few wore training shoes, but most went barefoot. Huddling together, they began to mutter to one another. *Look at these tourists with their fancy push bikes!*

In the schoolhouse, I gave a presentation about the expedition, but with their grasp of geography limited to local tribal areas, the notion of circumnavigating the planet meant little to them. The only thing we had in common was the amount of dirt we were wearing.

Trying a different tack, I asked the eldest, a sullen-looking youth in a blue football jersey, if he could tell us about bush tucker. According to Blue Dog, bush tucker tasted like shit, but you could live on it.

The adolescent stood staring at the ground, hands jammed under his armpits.

I tried again. "Goannas. What about goannas?"

We were back outside, the wind whipping the dry grass around our ankles. Scratching his elbow self-consciously, the teenager blew out his cheeks, sniffed, and bit his lower lip. He said nothing. The younger ones meanwhile spun on their heels and kicked the grass out of boredom. Some of them began to wrestle in it.

Crister came to the rescue. "Hey, why don't we do a trade? We show you some bike tricks, and you show us some bush tucker. Waddya say?"

He and Josh took the lead, pulling wheelies and bouncing on their back wheels. The kids laughed and squealed with delight. For the finale, Crister mounted the stairs to their classroom, jumping from step to step without putting his foot down.

Then it was the children's turn. A six-year-old urchin in a yellow shirt led us to a rather ordinary-looking bush next to the water tower. This was Marie, the expert. She was also the filthiest, her hair fortified with bull dust and sticking out at impressive angles, with a single lock curling down past her backside like a prehensile tail.

"They yellow," she whispered, describing the witchetty grubs that lived in the root systems.

"How big do they get?" I asked encouragingly. Even for an aborigine, she was painfully shy.

"Leedle," said the boy standing next to her. He held up two fingers four inches apart.

A jolly-faced woman in her mid-thirties was watching. This was the teacher, Fay. "And then you cook them in the fire, right? The same way as bush bananas? Just throw 'em in? Or in a saucepan? How?"

"Howl," corrected Marie.

"In a hole?"

"Yiss. And then"—Marie had her little hands cupped in front of her eyes—"pudda a fire inut."

Smiling proudly, Fay said, "Marie's our bush tucker queen. If you're lost, this is the one to be with." Turning back to the girl, she said, "So you put a fire in it and just cook them in the coals?"

"Yiss."

We'd already been introduced to witchetty grubs on a bush tucker tour in Mount Isa, so we declined Fay's offer to have the shrub demolished for us.

"So, how many do you need to eat before you're full?" I asked Marie.

She looked at me blankly.

Fay translated: "How mini wud yer noyd fer a gud foyd, Marie?"

"Foyve," the girl whispered shyly. "Maybe seex."

"And echidna. How do you eat an echidna?"

"Pull its guts out."

"Then?"

"Pull all the spines out."

"How, with pliers?"

"Yiss."

That evening, the team was camped off the road in a dry gully when the truck pulled up. Mike climbed gingerly out of the cab, and everyone crowded around to hear the prognosis.

"The doctors thought they found a hairline crack in the clavicle, but they couldn't be sure." He rubbed his close-shaven head with his good hand, a proper medical sling now supporting his right shoulder. "If it's still bad in Alice, I'll get another x-ray."

"So can you stay?" I asked in surprise.

"I'll be useless for a few more days, but if the group sees fit to have me ba—"

"Waahoodle!" cried Josh, throwing his arms around him. "I don't believe it!"

Crister stepped up. "Give me five, Pops! Good to have you back."

"Well, if you guys don't mind waiting on me hand and foot."

I smiled and reached out to shake his hand. "Small price for having you back, Mike." And I meant it. One thing had become clear to me during the course of the day. Although he chewed my brains and sent my blood pressure through the roof, Mike was one of us, an irreplaceable member of our little expedition family. So what if he put Crister and Josh on edge at times? They were growing up fast in the outback. They could handle it. And their genuine delight at his return illustrated the gaping hole that would have been torn in the fabric of the group had he left for good.

Mike looked relieved, like he'd passed a test. "The only problem is that my arm is pretty incapacitated."

"How far can you lift it?" I asked.

"To my waist."

"Well, that's far enough."

"For what?"

"For you not to be begging like a sorry bastard every time you need to get your Johnson out to take a whiz."

Mike chuckled.

"Hey, Mike!" Josh smirked. "I was afraid I was going to have to take over your role as Chief Bitcher."

"No, Josh. You're the one who needs bitching *at.*"

And we all had a good laugh at that.

"SO, YOU'RE SURE you want to join this smelly bunch of bikers," I said, trying not to sound too surprised.

She was blonde, pretty, wearing a white top, blue neckerchief, and khaki slacks. "Yeah, I'd like to be one of you if possible." The wind whipped her shoulder-length hair as she laughed. "It's all up to you, of course, if I meet your smelliness standards."

Five minutes before, a tour bus had pulled up, halogen lights blazing. The side door opened with a hydraulic hiss, unleashing a gust of air conditioning and fifty whey-faced tourists into the white heat of the outback. One of them, Git (pronounced Geet), a twenty-seven-year-old medical student from Cleveland, Ohio, had responded to an appeal for a new team member to fill the gap left by Jim. The group was now interviewing her by the side of the road.

"Can you ride a bike?" I asked.

"Not that it's a prerequisite," Mike cut in. "As I certainly can't."

A dead kangaroo thick with flies lay in the drainage ditch beside us. The stench was enough to gag a maggot.

Git replied that she could, having lived until she was eight years old in Holland. Holland was pretty much synonymous with bike riding, apparently.

Next, I asked, "So why do you want to come along?"

She crossed her arms and contemplated the bull dust at her feet. "I'm looking for space and time to figure some things out, and this bus tour is not giving me what I want."

Leaving her in the company of the maggoty roo, the team convened out of earshot.

"Works for me," said Mike. Then, in a comic voice, he added, *"I need a doctor … at all times!"*

The rest of the team also gave the thumbs up.

"Okay, Git," I said, walking back to where she stood. "Got your sunscreen?"

"Oh! Sweet!"

"But you should know that we're a disgusting bunch. We have horrible habits. We eat like pigs. Fart indiscriminately. We hardly ever wash."

"We get up way too early," chimed in Josh.

Git planted her hands on her hips and grinned. "And this is different from my daily life … how?" Then her expression turned serious. "But you should know something about me, too. I'm supposed to be back at med school in four days. I'll need to tell my parents."

I let her use the satellite phone in the truck. The rest of the group hovered within earshot.

"Hi, mom, dad? Yes … Hello? Good." Git was sitting in the passenger seat, clutching the receiver with both hands. "Listen. I met a group of people currently biking through Australia, and they said I could join them, and so I've joined them now, and it's going to take a month to get up to Darwin, and so I'm going to get permission from the dean to take the year off, which she said I could do anyway, and I'll be home the middle of October …"

She paused for a second. There was silence from the receiver. "Mom? Dad? Are you still there? Hello? Are you okay?"

A wave of sniggering rippled through the group.

"Mom, it's a completely legitimate, safe, and, um … above the board, financed operation."

More sniggering. None of the qualities she had used to describe the expedition sounded even remotely familiar.

Putting the phone back, Git put her hand to her forehead and closed her eyes. "Oh god, I need a little down time."

"That was the coolest call I've ever heard to someone's parents," said Mike, chuckling. "If I was your parent, I would have said, 'Are they holding a gun to your head? If so, just say *rosebud*.'"

THE LANDSCAPE UNDERWENT a noticeable transformation as we entered Northern Territory. Termite mounds as big as houses towered over the track, and clumps of spinifex grass with blades of porcupine quills studded the surrounds. On one spiny tussock, we spied a stick insect in the shape of a four-legged blade of hay.

"Let's see if he has any sight," said Crister, waving his radio antenna at one end.

"I think that's its bum," I said.

"How do you know?"

Mike was looking over my shoulder. "Maybe it's a pushmi-pullyu?"

The insect swayed back and forth, a clever evolutionary trick to mimic a grass stalk trembling in the breeze.

We turned off the Plenty Highway west of Jervois Station, heading south towards Arltunga, central Australia's first town, since faded to a nook of dust and flyblown anonymity. The sign on the gate read, "1080 Dingo Poison laid on this property," with another below it warning, "Disease Control Area. Tuberculosis and Brucellosis. This gate must remain closed!"

The track curved, rose, and fell, horizontal desert lines giving way to rolling hills and craggy summits. Carpets of wildflowers brought the dull scrub alive: blues, whites, yellows, purples, and mauves. We reached the crest of a rise and there, stretching before us like Earth before the fall, a remarkable crater-ringed valley protected by brooding sierra on all sides, the peaks broken and splintered.

We dismounted and climbed a hillock. In the mustard light, the vibrancy of the landscape thinned to a ragged pelt of tow-coloured scrub, patchy like the mangy rump of an old camel. Meandering veins of animal paths criss-crossed to the skyline.

"Diversity. It's all here!" trilled Bell, flicking at the flies with her tartan scarf.

But for all its beauty, the land wasn't worth squat, according to Blue Dog. "At four dollars an acre, you could buy this hill we're sitting on for a crate of piss," he said.

We carried on, hoping to notch a few more miles before nightfall. Mike, Git, and I rode together. I asked them how they were both doing.

"Shoulder feels good," said Mike. "Mind and soul feel good. Comfortable with the group. My expectations are now low. That way I can never, ever, be disappointed."

"Ah, Grasshopper. You learn much!"

"Acceptance. Acceptance. It's becoming my middle name," said Mike. "I'm learning to let go."

Git was riding a yellow Jekyll 600. "Legs doing fine," she said. She was sweating and panting, but otherwise holding her own in the heat. "Other parts of my body are beginning to make themselves known, though."

We hit a series of bumps, which almost had her over, but a few well-chosen expletives had her back on track. "In the first hour, I think I went through the whole litany of reactions from nervousness, anticipation, fear, exhilaration, doubt, confusion, boredom, exhaustion, happiness, to reproach of myself for getting into this!"

She laughed, but her video diarrhoea that evening was less cheerful.

"The thing that scares me most is the thought that I might not finish this. It may sound silly for me to think that way, but there are other things in my life, major things, that I haven't finished. And so this trip is very much about starting something, and no matter what the cost to yourself, having the—what my father would call the zitz fleisch—the endurance, to finish it. So it's a proving ground for myself."

The next day, we reached the last difficult stage before Alice Springs, a forty-six-kilometre bushwhack through virgin wilderness to the Ross River homestead.

Blue Dog voiced his doubts. "Well, say if you took off this afternoon and it started raining, and it rained for a week"—he was kneeling in the sand, running a finger over the 1:100 000 topographic map for the region that depicted an obstacle course of steep ravines and impossible escarpments—"then you'd be in real trouble. 'Cos nobody could get to you. I certainly couldn't in the truck. You'd have to try to walk out. It'd be very, very difficult in this terrain, crossing creeks and all that sort of thing."

He was right, of course. The relatively short but assertive colonization of Australia by Europeans since the arrival of the First Fleet in 1788 could almost be catalogued by instances of explorers, prospectors, and even modern day thrill-seekers taking off into the Never-Never, and never coming back.

"We have GPS," said Bell softly.

Blue Dog shook his head. "It doesn't matter if you have GPS or not. If you get lost, you could be out there for days."

I sensed a growing impasse. As our guide, Blue Dog felt it was his duty to get us to Darwin safely, and his goodwill as a volunteer was something we relied heavily upon. But the security of the alternative— albeit longer—route to Alice Springs on tarmac wasn't the reason we were here. As Todd pointed out, "So many places on this planet have been completely over-run, or are over-populated, or just heavily trampled on. And here's this spot on the map that hasn't been touched."

My thoughts wandered while the group argued the pros and cons. In twenty-first-century society, you get in your car, or push off on your bike, and know exactly where you're going. You know what the destination looks like before you even get there. Everything is guaranteed, foreseeable. Yet, as Git had illustrated, deep within the human psyche lies the primal need for intervals of *not* knowing how things are going to turn out. That's when you get a glimpse of who you are and what you're really made of, responding to the unseen challenges fate throws across your path.

This was the understanding lost to western living I'd originally joined the expedition to rediscover: to *un*know all that I thought I knew about the world and myself, and to relearn ways of thinking that offered insight into behaviour compatible with a sustainable future. The asphalt, like the modern consumer lifestyle, symbolized efficiency, predictability, mediocrity, boredom, and a slow acquiescence to mindlessness and a living death. I wanted the young explorers to experience the opposite—for a short while, at least. No asphalt. No support vehicle. No safety net to catch us if we fell.

I called everyone together. "Okay, option one is we backtrack to Arltunga, back along this tourist road—"

"It is actually quite pretty, that road," interrupted Blue Dog.

"To Trephina Gorge Park," I continued. "Or we see if we can find a way through to Ross River. Those up for the Ross River option, raise your hands, please."

A quorum of arms went up.

"But what if you can't get through?" protested Blue Dog.

"We think it's worth a try," said Bell, her hand raised.

Blue Dog glowered at her. After a month and a half in the outback, the two loathed each other more than ever.

"Then we'll just have to backtrack," I said.

Blue Dog sighed and looked off into the distance. "Well, whatever. But I strongly recommend that you don't even consider it."

"But why?" I asked in frustration.

"Well ... you could just be going down there for nothing."

Bell whispered, "Or we could miss something we'd never have the chance again to do in our lives."

The group voted six to two to take the off-road route. Starting at first light, we manhandled our bikes and trailers into a narrow, slab-sided canyon, gazing all the while at the blast-furnace-red walls polished by centuries of floodwater. Spindly trees jutted from the crevices high above us. Ghost gums flourished along the sandy bottom. After an hour of sand slogging, we came to a billabong blocking our path, the first water since the Einsleigh River, nineteen days earlier. The water came up to our necks as we waded across, sputtering at the freezing water, ferrying our bikes and trailers on our heads.

As the morning wore on, the canyon opened out to a swathe of grassland contained by a rim of low hills. There were hardy ironwood trees, wattles, and more ghost gums. Every few kilometres, Mike, riding point, stopped and checked our latitude and longitude position against the map. Today was his leadership day. Since Mount Isa, we'd rotated the day-to-day decision-making. Only in the event of a crisis, or a decision that conflicted with the long-term interests of the circumnavigation, would I intervene.

At one such break, which allowed the team a chance to grab some food, Mike froze. "April!" he whispered. "Quick, look!"

Ahead of us, through the trees, a herd of wild horses—brumbies, as Josh called them—were grazing. There were all sorts, bays and sorrels and grullas and blacks, and all of them fat and sleek. Trying not to make a sound, the team crept forward to get a closer look. Suddenly, we were spotted. Up went twenty-five pairs of ears, cocked in our direction. Then they were off, bucking and snorting with their manes and tails flying high, followed by two spooked kangaroos going flat out to keep up.

We entered another canyon—more sand trudging, more ferrous-red cliffs, more hauling our trailers over rocks and boulders—and joined a dry streambed lined with yellow Senna bushes. Wicked three-cornered jack thorns took a toll through the afternoon, but by this point in the trip, we were all puncture experts, completing repairs in less than three minutes. As the light began to fade, we stumbled across a graded track. "No Vehicles or Bikes Beyond this Point," the sign warned, indicating the direction we'd just come.

And that was when we knew our little foray into the abyss of not knowing was over. Our leap of faith had paid off.

ON ITS OWN merit, the Stuart Caravan and Tourist Park in Alice Springs was never going to be memorable. It was ideal for doing laundry, taking showers, mending gear, charging electronics, applying for permits to enter aboriginal lands, or just relaxing. But the location wasn't breathtaking. Our fellow residents weren't any more weird or obnoxious than what you might expect in such a place. There was nothing to elevate it above the massed repertoire of travel experience for its jarring qualities, its defiance of the norm. It was dull and easily forgettable, a grey interval in the otherwise rich tapestry of our journey, fated to slip from our minds as soon as we left it.

It is for this reason that I am struck by the clarity with which I remember the events of September 11, 2001, starting with being woken at four in the morning by Blue Dog.

"Hey, Jason."

"Is there a problem?" I murmured groggily.

"There's something you need to see."

Reluctantly, I unzipped my sleeping bag and wrestled on some warm clothes. Blue Dog was meanwhile yammering about airplanes.

"So there's this one that just tore through the side of the building …"

I followed him to a trailer belonging to George, one of the long-stay residents. Columns of black smoke were pouring from a pair of skyscrapers on the TV set. The strained voice of a male news presenter was describing the scene: *"Nine-fifty-nine am, the until now unthinkable, the south tower of the World Trade Center collapses, an unknown number of people still trapped inside."*

When they awoke, the rest of the team struggled to comprehend the scale of the destruction. They sat glued to George's TV like deer caught in the headlights, utterly transfixed. For the Americans, it was the worst attack on their country since Pearl Harbor. Mike, Todd, and Git circled the wagons back at our campsite to discuss what they'd seen.

"To know you're being flown directly into the World Trade Center, an entire airliner full of ..." Placing her hands over her black fleece hat, Git closed her moistening eyes and shook her head. "I mean ... it's seven twenty-five here, and it's almost six in Cleveland, and, um ... they're still lying on the ground being triaged, I'm sure."

Overwhelmed, she turned and walked out of the fold.

Mike was next. "New hate's been born right now." There was no anger in his voice, just sadness and a note of heavy resignation. He stared at the ground with his arms crossed. "The first thing that went into my mind was Bin Laden. But it could just as easily be one of our jackass fuckers who can't seem to get things right in their lives and decided to"—he used his fingers as quotation marks—"'die for their country'."

"Yeah, but it sounds too organized for it to be some militia group," said Todd, his tone characteristically measured and ambassadorial. "It's just crazy people!"

Git was back. She was also examining her feet, avoiding eye contact with the others. "But you can't call an entire nation of people crazy. They're not all clinically insane."

"That's what I'm saying," said Todd. "They're extremist groups who have taken an extreme interpretation of their doctrine."

Off to one side, April was kneeling on a silver tarpaulin, her head bowed in prayer. Crister was also off on his own, quietly processing it all.

"This could easily mean world war," Mike was saying. "And if *we* go to war, everybody goes to war. The world is changed as of right now."

Todd laughed again. "But who do you go to war against? How do you fight an enemy that doesn't have borders?"

The rest of us, the Aussies and the Brits, were loading up the truck, preparing to head out. Not that we didn't care. Citizens of ninety countries were lying buried under concrete and steel, after all. But every day in Alice was another day we could be stranded by the wet season in the Top End.

"I don't understand," sobbed Git. Her hand was pressed against her mouth, and tears were rolling down her cheeks. "Why are we packing up this truck? Why are we going? Why are we cycling? Why are we going through a fucking desert?"

I gathered everyone together.

"Okay, all the Americans here, I'd like to know your thoughts. Whether to continue, or stay here to call home and find out more information."

Crister was the first to speak. "I think I'd rather be out in the desert. Be able to think better."

April agreed. She said she'd managed to call her daughter, Lacy, and found it easier to deal with tragedy if she had something to do. Mike was the same: "Be out on the road, breathe, be in motion and dissect my feelings in a more positive way."

Git, on the other hand, was torn. She clearly didn't want to go anywhere, but as the newest member of the group, she was loath to hold up the expedition.

I said, "You need to be selfish here, Git."

She sniffed and cleared her throat. "Selfishly speaking, what I'd be doing if I was home right now would be sitting in front of the TV, watching the news broadcasts, and hearing more of what's going on. Heading off into the desert seems … irresponsible and preposterous."

I suggested we listen to reports on the truck radio and the next CNN bulletin at 8:00 am. "We'll just play the rest of the day by ear," I added.

Git wiped her eyes with the back of a gloved hand. "But if you all wanted to go now, I'd just suck it up, and I'd be fine." She stood to attention and stiffened her expression. "See? I can be completely fine. I just won't think about it."

"Okay," I said. "But bear in mind we have an opportunity to find out more information while we're here in Alice, not out in the desert."

"But there's the next town we stop in. What is it? A town with a k?"

"Hermannsburg?"

"Oh, yeah, Hermannsburg. There'll be a television there, too, right?"

I shook my head. "Unlikely."

Git looked at me in disbelief.

Blue Dog chuckled. "After Alice, there'll be nothing till Darwin."

That was 2,500 kilometres away.

The route north would take us along an old cattle-droving track bisecting one of the most isolated and arid places on Earth, the Tanami Desert. First we needed to hit a GPS coordinate two hundred and thirty kilometres west of Alice Springs, the matching antipode to one that Steve and I had crossed on the Atlantic, thereby ensuring a true circumnavigation as delineated by Guinness World Records and another adjudicating body, ExplorersWeb.*

By late morning, Git had had her fill of annihilation. "I just want to be home," she said miserably. "To be around the people this is happening to, and feel some sense of going through crisis with them."

The instinct to hunker down and share the burden was natural, but with the US in lock-down and all flights barred from leaving or entering the country, no one was going home anytime soon. With little other choice, we made for the desert.

The team was quiet and pensive as we rode single file through the suburbs of Larapinta Drive. To our left ran the jagged spine of the MacDonnell Ranges, calling to mind the precipitous buttes of the Arizona canyon lands. Then the tarmac gave out, and the reassuring sound of gravel was crunching under our tyres once more.

"So nowhere," murmured Josh, gazing around at the spartan landscape.

The emptiness that spun our tyres spun the wheels in my head, too.

---

* Expedition 360 antipodes: 23.48.36N, 48.37.37W (Atlantic); 23.47.00S, 131.22.00E (Australia)

The 9/11 attackers had succeeded not because they'd flown airplanes into buildings or murdered nearly 3,000 people, but because they'd accurately counted on Americans reacting like Americans, the same as they could Brits reacting like Brits if they'd targeted London, or Aussies reacting like Aussies if they'd bombed Sydney. At the end of the day, it all boiled down to tribalism, the oldest story in the relatively short book of human history. For the first time in their lives perhaps, the Americans in the team felt vulnerable, caught out in the open, away from their cave. And they were taking it personally, exactly as the terrorists had hoped.

THE TRACK TO Glen Helen petered first to grit, then to granular sand the colour of tomato soup. Trudging ankle-deep through the stuff and pushing our loads, twenty-five kilometres was a high estimate for the day.

Even when we got to ride on a hundred feet of packed surface here and there, it was barely worth the effort. The region was infested with thorns, three-cornered jacks up to a centimetre across, mean, slashing, skewering things shaped like ninja throwing stars. *Why does everything in Australia have to be so damn mean?* I thought. *Biting, spitting, stinging …*

There's good reason for it, of course. Isolated from the rest of the world for millions of years, Australia's plants and animals evolved unusually potent defence mechanisms to cope with the harsh conditions, and *Emex australis* was no exception. Our tyres were double-lined with Mr Tuffies and packed with puncture-prevention Slime, but the dagger-like spines still made it through. And it took only one person with a flat for the rest of the team to be stranded in the heat without shade.

On we slogged, following a series of bores marked on the topo with names like Bullocky Bore, Speares Bore, and Oondoomoola Waterhole.

They were all dry. In spite of this, the desert still found ways to support life. Mottled lizards froze under clumps of spinifex as we passed, tracking us with their beady black eyes, and stands of Xanthorrhoea, a tussocky desert grass with an average lifespan of six hundred years, brandished their single black flower spikes at us like giant toilet brushes. Tiny fat-tailed skinks and geckos blended seamlessly with the orange sand, yet another ingenious adaptation to life in the Red Centre.

Nearing Derwent Station, seven pillars of smoke hung over the windswept plain like a washing line of oily rags. There was nothing especially alarming in this. Bushfires raged constantly in the outback, sparked by lightning, or by aborigines practicing the same method of hunting they'd used for tens of thousands of years, one that attracted game by encouraging new growth. But the smell of burning spinifex intensified, catching the backs of our throats like cordite, forcing us to stop and tie wetted bandanas around our faces.

"You know the first thing you do when you meet a bushfire?" said Blue Dog at our mid-morning break. He was standing beside a circle of grey dusty coals, using a plastic washtub to mix flour and water together.

"No idea," I replied.

"Light another fire."

Seeing my confusion, he added, "To boil a billy of course!"

Was this some strange Aussie-ism? The equivalent of the English *"let's 'ave a cuppa tea and fink about it"* when faced with imminent doom?

He laughed. "If you light the fire downwind o' ya, it'll create a safe zone. Fire can't go where it's already burned."

I motioned to the tub. "What have we here?"

"Johnny Cakes."

"Like damper?"

"Sorta."

"Is there some magic ingredient?"

"Time," he said, smiling. Like many outback types we'd met—station owners, miners, bore runners—Blue Dog had perfected the art of carrying on a conversation with his teeth clamped together to stop the flies from buzzing in and out of his mouth. He tore off a fistful of wet dough and lobbed it into the coals. "Time to make 'em before *they* all get here." He nodded at Josh, Crister, and Todd, who were already circling. "Otherwise they eat all the dough on me. They won't wait till they're cooked!"

"They're swarming," I confirmed, watching the three of them edge closer, "getting ready for the feeding frenzy."

Blue Dog shook his tongs at them. "Now back! Back!"

Marauders temporarily deterred, he used his boot to nudge a Johnny Cake out of the coals. It was blackened on the underside, raw on top. "Hmm," he murmured, "might be a bit of a problem with temperature control."

My mouth filled with saliva. None of us were fussy about food anymore. We were all constantly hungry.

Blue Dog kicked another cake. It was similarly charred on one side. "Well, we're not expecting the Queen to come now are we?" he said cheerfully. "They're rising up pretty well. A nice cup of tea and a bit of jam and a scone—should be pretty good, eh?"

The water in the billy had come to a rolling boil, "nice and lumpy," as Blue Dog would say. He threw in some loose tea, then booted the rest of the cakes into the sand. The way the team fell on them, you'd think we hadn't eaten in a week.

After smoko, we discussed how to circumvent the bushfire raging in our path.

"We don't want to be separated," said Blue Dog. "That's the key. If you can judge where the fire is, which is really hard from ground level, you go upwind of it as best you can. Speed determines a lot. If the wind is in a constant direction, it's easier to predict. It's when it's calm that a fire will create its own wind, then you can't tell what it's gonna do next."

Making a sweeping loop, we reached the fire line after an hour of sand bashing. Clumps of resin-laden spinifex were exploding up ahead and whole trees bursting into flames like Roman candles. Fuelled by the wind, long licking tongues of yellow flame were leaping from canopy to canopy, faster than a human could run. There was no immediate danger to us, thankfully. With the wind at our backs, the bushfire was moving away from us.

Following cautiously in its wake, we entered an apocalyptic landscape dotted with the blackened remains of slow-moving skinks and lizards, and smouldering cinders rolling out for kilometre upon ashen kilometre. Three-cornered jacks were no longer a problem; they'd been incinerated along with the thorn bushes. That night we camped on burnt ground next to a stand of twisted skeletons that were once wattle trees. The scene was one of sobering destruction, but there was comfort in it, too. If the wind changed direction suddenly in the night, at least we wouldn't be running for our lives.

"Bloody kids," I growled. "Rug rats. The lot o' ya."

"Thirty-year-old mongrel," Josh muttered under his breath.

"What was that?"

"I said, thirty-year-old mongrel!"

"Ha! You'll regret this."

I'd just discovered a boulder in my trailer. It was the same one that did the rounds of all the trailers, sneaked in when the owner wasn't looking. Unbeknownst to me, I'd dragged it all the way from Alice Springs.

"You think life is just one long party, don't you?" I said. "Well, one day you teenagers will know the meaning of real work, getting a proper job!"

Crister saw the irony of my words immediately. He smirked. "Well, at least we're not having a mid-life crisis. That's why you got this flashy new bike, right?"

"I'm not having a midlife crisis," I replied indignantly. "If anyone's having a crisis around here, it's Josh. Look at him. A sexual identity crisis!"

With his knobbly pink knees, frizz of red hair, and yellow frock, Josh had the English rose look down to a T. He'd worn the dress for a bet a couple of times earlier in the trip, and by Mount Isa grown rather attached to the thing, wearing it almost daily.

It was a worrying trend.

The Americans were appalled. Unlike the Brits and Aussies raised on a diet of Benny Hill, Dick Emery, and Dame Edna Everage, their cultural frame of reference to cross-dressing was limited to Lou Reed's *Walk on the Wild Side.*

Josh mounted his bicycle and rode away.

"So, this is just great," I called after him. "Here we are, in the middle of the outback, with a teenage transvestite on the loose. What am I going to tell your mother?"

"I'm allowed to have a baby if I want to!" he shouted over his shoulder. "I HAVE MY RIGHTS!"

"Ah shut up, ya' feral trannie."

On this occasion, however, Josh was on a mission. We'd ridden into the aboriginal settlement of Yuendumu the day before, passing a sign that read: "If you bring grog into Yuendumu Land Trust Area, you will have your vehicle taken from you by law. First offence, $1,000 or 6 months jail."

It was like entering The Twilight Zone: burnt out homes with grills over the windows, graffiti and litter everywhere, a thousand stray dogs. Dusky urchins ran alongside, snatching at our handlebars. A pot-bellied aboriginal man sped by in a golf cart, tipping his enormous black cowboy hat at the ladies. It had taken most of the day and the tireless assistance of Wendy, a local teacher, to negotiate an interview with a spokesperson from Warlpiri Media for our Discovery Zone on aboriginal land rights. To kill time, the team hung out at the general store with her husband, Frank, a mid-fifties geologist sitting barefoot and shirtless in the stifling heat of the store office. There was no air conditioning, just a small desk fan paddling feebly at the heat. Outside, two boys were burning a King Brown snake in a can of petrol.

The sight of Josh in his floral dress launched Frank off on a long and colourful account of the cross-dressing history of the Tanami. "There was this one bloke on his way back to Queensland. Had a revelation from God to give up wearing women's lingerie."

Frank's stomach rolled with laughter. Our host clearly relished an audience, planting his cracked heels on his desk and leaning back in his swivel chair.

"So he decides to have one last fling in the bush before burning some of the underwear and burying the rest. Someone finds the clothes and calls the cops. They figure someone's topped their missus and tried to destroy the evidence."

While the team stood in a semicircle, listening, I was sitting cross-legged in the corner, trying to send the day's lesson activities through the defiantly slow Internet connection. Sending them through the satellite phone cost around $60 a day and still took an hour every evening struggling with dropped connections. Today, the process was taking just as long, but at least it was free.

Frank continued: "Eventually, after tracking down the missus in Queensland, they find out the truth—that her husband's a trannie. But in the meantime, this cyclist comes into town looking like an Arab with a sheet over his head and wearing only underpants. Said he was riding up north to find his girlfriend or somethin'."

"What happened to him?" asked Crister, all agog.

Frank paused for effect, turned to Josh, and said theatrically, "Never seen again!" His belly started shaking again. "So, as you can see, the Tanami is quite used to sexual deviants. You guys'll fit right in."

That evening, our land rights interview in the can, Frank handed Josh an envelope as we prepared to leave.

"Do us a favour, young man. Give this to Bruce, willya?"

Bruce was Frank's archrival at Rabbit Flat Roadhouse, three hundred kilometres to the north. The two had been sending abusive messages to each other for more than a decade.

Josh agreed.

"But don't open it before you get there," Frank said. "It'll spoil the effect."

He guffawed and swatted the air. "I've sent messages up there by truck, motorcycle, helicopter. But getting it from a cross-dressing push bike rider, that'll really fix the miserable old bastard!"

YELLOW DRESS FLUTTERING, blue helmet jammed on his head, Josh cycled up to a lone breeze-block building set back from the main track and parked his bike. The room inside was dark and furnished with a few token plastic chairs. In the far corner, a shoebox-sized opening above a gridiron counter offered the only means of conducting trade.

Clutching Frank's note, Josh made his way across the no-frills interior and rang a bell hanging on a red ribbon. A young man appeared with a crumpled face. He'd been asleep.

"G'day," said Josh, nervously patting his frock.

The attendant had obviously seen his fair share of trannies on the Tani; he didn't give Josh a second look. "How're ya goin', mate," he replied.

"Are you Bruce?"

"No. Dan."

"Could I speak to Bruce, please?"

"He's actually tied up at the moment. Can I help?"

"Ah, special orders." Josh tapped the side of his nose, and waved the envelope. "For Bruce."

The attendant gave him a hard look and disappeared.

Chocolate wrappers were taped to the wall, tempting the hungry traveller with the delights that lay beyond the counter—Kit Kats, M&Ms, Cadbury Flakes, and the like. The prices were outrageous: $4.80 for a loaf of frozen bread, $56 for a carton of Victoria Bitter (in Alice Springs, the same 24-pack cost $33). But this was the most remote roadhouse in the country. If you didn't like the prices, you could keep on going.

A few minutes later, Dan was back. "Bruce is actually asleep at the moment. Can you come back in an hour?"

Outside, Git was using a pair of scissors from the first aid kit to give Todd a haircut. "Are you sure you don't want a mullet? This is your last chance. Got a special on mullets today."

As instructed, Josh, Todd, and I went back after an hour. Through the narrow aperture, I could make out the spitting image of Jerry Garcia—beaky nose, greying beard. Seeing Todd's camera, Bruce pressed his mouth against the hole and snarled, "Turn that fuck'n thing off. It's fuck'n impolite to film a man without his fuck'n permission."

Bruce's hatred of the media was well documented. Since moving to the Tanami in 1969, he'd used his pump-action shotgun to ward off many a nosy television crew looking for a scoop on one of Australia's most isolated residents. The no-nonsense proprietor also had a reputation for straight talking, once informing a journalist from *The Australian*, the country's biggest-selling broadsheet, that he refused to deal with the, quote, "shiny-arsed wankers" from the Northern Territory Government over switching to non-sniffable Opal petrol.

Bolstering his resolve, Josh approached the counter. "Um, I've got a note from Frank at Yuendumu."

Bruce glared at him. "Nah. That'll just be another fuck'n letter telling me to get fucked." He took the envelope, clawed it open, and glanced at the contents.

"Fuck'n told ya." He thrust the note at Josh.

For Bruce, it read.

Get Fucked

Frank

THE NAYSAYERS WE'D met since leaving the Queensland coast had told us the Tanami Track was uncyclable. A thousand kilometres of soft sand, they said. Shadeless. Not a drop of water. Unsurprisingly, the truth was something else. The corrugations were indeed punishing, but compared to the week of sand slogging from Hermannsburg, the track was a dream, hard packed and entirely rideable.

Not so for Git, however, who was beginning to suffer from lower back pain.

"This is so frustrating," she said, dismounting and doubling up. "So ridiculous."

Crister raised her handlebars to take the strain off her lower spine, but it made no difference. Git stuck it out for three days, then made an announcement. "You know what, I'll just get in the truck. I can't hold up the group up any more than I am already." She looked utterly demoralized at the prospect. "I'll just have to get creative in the kitchen or something."

On we rode, passing bumpers, bolts, and mangled license plates rattled off by the murderous washboard. The ubiquitous road kill struck evocative poses in death's final throes—open-mouthed roos howling at the sky, their eyes and stomach cavities long gone. Clattering road trains shook the desert still with unnerving violence and infused our lungs with talcum-like bull dust. On windless days, the swirling layers hung in suspension for so long it seemed we might never breathe clean air again. Bell took to reciting Macbeth as we rode:

"Tomorrow, and tomorrow, and tomorrow,

Creeps in this petty pace from day to day,

To the last syllable of recorded time,

And all our yesterdays have lighted fools the way to dusty death."

In the town of Kalkarinji, four hundred kilometres farther up the track, Blue Dog went off in search of the Northern Land Council office to pick up the permits we'd applied for in Alice Springs. We needed a total of thirteen passes to get through the aboriginal-owned properties ahead. The rest of us waited outside the service station, watching life go by.

Scowling aborigines sat on the bench, stabbing at brown envelopes of potato chips bought from the store. A mixed-breed dog with a beer cap stuck to her hind paw sniffed at our feet for scraps. An hour passed. A 4x4 Ute pulled up in a pall of billowing dust, brown hands trailing from the windows stirring the heat. The doors burst open and a posse of jabbering women in shapeless dresses spilled out, breasts hanging to their midriffs. Chaos ensued. Barefoot ragamuffins ran shrieking in dizzying circles, their arms outstretched, faces smeared in snot. A dogfight erupted over a discarded chip wrapper, ending in a convulsion of snapping jaws and high-pitched yelps.

When Blue Dog rolled up with twelve of the thirteen passes in hand, we fled for the sanity of the wilderness.

We were now entering a transition zone between the desert and more tropical Top End. Out were spinifex and sand dunes. In were kangaroo grass, Nutwood trees, round-leafed Bauhinia, gnarled Hakea, and Plains Bloodwood Eucalyptus, home—much to Bell's delight—to mobs of screeching corellas, lorikeets, and custard-headed rosellas.

With the wet season almost upon us, the combination of stifling heat and suffocating humidity became almost unbearable. The strain of living in each other's pockets was also beginning to tell. Tempers frayed easily. Mike threatened everyone with a "slow, painful death" if he missed his flight out of Darwin. Bell taunted Blue Dog over his custard. "*My* custard's better than *your* custard. *Your* custard's crap!" And outside the settlement of Lajamanu, I hit the wall, slumping in the shade of a gum tree during a scroggin break.

"I'm tired of being on the expedition right now." I grumbled to the camcorder in my hand. "For seven years, it's been non-stop, every waking minute, seven days a week, three-hundred-and-sixty-five days a year."

Overland Australia was turning out to be far more demanding than I'd anticipated. During the school week, Monday to Friday, we were on the computers from eleven in the morning to four in the afternoon, the hottest time of the day, when we typically sought respite from the sun. Later, after riding through the evening cool, while the team sat around the campfire chatting or strumming a guitar before turning in, I'd be back in front of a flickering screen being bombarded by insects until well past midnight, editing the updates before sending them to the guys at Video Free America. Four hours sleep a night would be exceptional. Now even that was a luxury. Most nights we lay sweating in our tents, too hot to sleep.

Then there was a feature of the Top End sure to send any reasonable person over the edge.

Flies.

These weren't just your run-of-the-mill houseflies, nervous and jittery, quick to buzz away when shooed. Top End flies were the most assertive and tenacious parasites ever to fly out of Satan's bunghole. Burrowing, crawling, wriggling, gnawing, they launched themselves undeterred into any available orifice—ears, eyes, mouth, and nose— in kamikaze-like forays for moisture. The females were the most aggressive, starved of protein for their eggs. Even as we rode, they swarmed by the thousands, making a head net essential. April discovered this the hard way when a fly breached one of her nostrils and tunnelled into her sinuses.

"I can feel him wriggling in there!" she wailed.

It was our second morning on the Wikham, an old droving track leading north through the escarpment district of Gregory National Park. The rugged terrain made for challenging but thrilling riding. The first day alone we encountered drop-offs, jumps, water crossings, and washouts, requiring all the skills we'd picked up since the Starcke—especially riding one-handed, the other batting at the flies.

April dismounted and tried sneezing out the obstinate creature—to no avail. At Git's suggestion, she used her water bottle to squeeze water down one nostril, then the other, blowing out the contents each time.

"It's like drowning! I don't wanna drown in the middle of the outback."

Git patted her back. "The only direction it can go is down your throat."

April repeated the procedure.

"Is he still in there?" asked Git.

April stood still for a moment. "Well, he's not wriggling anymore. Maybe I drowned him? Do you think he'll eventually make his way out?"

"I dunno. I'd try again."

But it wasn't flies that drove April, usually the paragon of composure, to finally lose it. The following evening we were camped beside a billabong, a "Blue Dog four-and-a-half-star campsite" according to the man himself. The outback guide had certainly surpassed himself locating such an immaculate body of water in an otherwise parched landscape. It was piss and shit free, not a leach or croc slide-mark in sight. Being the hottest day of the trip so far, 107 degrees in the shade, it was like stepping into a refrigerator.

April was the last to sink neck-deep into the deliciously cool water.

She sat with her hair covering her face, dangling in the water.

"Got a little tough out there, didn't it, Ms A?" I said.

"Well, not so much tough, but the heat really got to me. Made it hard towards the end."

"Harder than the Coral Sea?"

Behind us, Mike, Crister, and Todd were splashing and shrieking at each other, and even Blue Dog had ventured in up to his knees. He stood there in his baseball cap and Y-fronts, the chicken-chaser type worn by Australian men, holding a can of Victoria Bitter and watching the team at play.

April shook her head. "Yeah, this doesn't even compare to the Coral Sea. Put me back there any day."

This surprised me. "Really?"

"Yeah, the road and the travelling has been great, but … this probably isn't the time to be talking about this. I'm just tired. Or rather, hot."

"Why, do you regret coming?"

"Oh no, this whole expedition is an incredible gift! I think that's one of the points of frustration, because I feel there are people here who …" Her voice tailed off again. She was crying. "They don't know that," she whispered. "They don't know what a gift they've been given. That's one of the really frustrating things for me, I guess. They just gripe and bitch about all these different things. I feel like telling them you should be happy, because you're *so* lucky to be here."

SINCE YUENDUMU, GIT had spent more and more time in the truck, unable to cycle even an hour before the pain in her lumbar region became intolerable. Now her bike was tied permanently in the back. With characteristic good cheer, she was making the best of a bad situation: preparing food, collecting firewood, writing updates, and so on. But riding in the cab was driving her crazy.

"It doesn't feel like my trip anymore," she complained.

Face beetroot red, hair cropped for the heat, she scowled at the Bitch Cam—the new nickname for the video diary camera set up on the outskirts of camp. "At least when I was biking I felt like I had a purpose. Now my only use is cooking, cleaning, helping set up camp."

Squadrons of flies were taking turns dive-bombing her face. She swatted at them half-heartedly and looked away in disgust. "I'm as close as I've ever come to completely losing my mind. The heat is intolerable. Biting flies are everywhere. The ants bite, too. Even the plants— these wait-a-while plants or whatever they're called—have teeth." She reached down to scratch her knee. "The sand flies are chewing my legs. They don't leave you alone. *Nothing* leaves you alone out here."

Standing up straight, she looked squarely into the camera, and said, "I've had it. I can't take it anymore."

At Timber Creek, the first asphalt since Alice Springs, 2,000 kilometres to the south, Git bought a bus ticket to Darwin. She would be there in eight hours.

Crister presented her with an expedition memento: a "fart can" of baked beans signed by the rest of the team. We then bid her farewell. I was sad to see her go. She was funny and smart, and her positive outlook had served to balance out some of the personality clashes in the group. And even though it was for unforeseen medical reasons, losing a team member had a ring of failure to it.

"It's pretty twisted if you think about it," I said to her. We were standing outside the Wayside Inn roadhouse, waiting for the bus from Broome. "How you escaped that bus trip to Alice Springs, only to—"

She laughed. "Ride in a friggin' truck!"

In contrast to her last video diary entry, Git was smiling and happy. She was eagerly looking forward to all that awaited her back in the US: *Starbucks for a mocha, then to Wild Oats to get about three-hundred dollars of fresh fruits and vegetables, rent enough movies for a week, a big bath, bottle of white wine …*

"You know, it's funny," she went on. "When you first asked me why I wanted to join, I said that I really needed space—from my life back in America and from whatever I was feeling at that particular moment. But I didn't realize how we'd be living in such close quarters. So now I feel that I … need some space from my space."

She paused for a moment. "But I reckon if you can get through three months of this, you can get through pretty much anything."

DARWIN WAS STILL a week away for the rest of us, another five hundred kilometres along the winding tracks of the Victoria River pastoral district. Sod's Law, the rains had come early this year. At the local police post, the officer on duty informed us that the Australian army had been bogged down for a week north of Timber Creek. The alternative was to try making it through the aboriginal-owned station of Innisvale farther to the east. We'd applied for the relevant permit from the Northern Land Council six months before but heard nothing back. It was the only one that had been missing in Kalkarinji.

This was the reason I'd planned the cross-country route to bypass aboriginal land wherever possible. It wasn't aborigines I had a problem with. It was the land councils. Born of a liberal era in Australian politics that saw the federal government handing back vast tracts of the country to its traditional owners (and rightly so, more often than not, albeit the useless parts with little or no water) these quangos had carved a cosy little niche for themselves. The aboriginal owners had to be contacted and consulted, a process that took several months if they'd gone walkabout. Unlike "white" stations that you could just call up and ask permission yourself, everything had to go through the self-approving bureaucrats.

Ironically, Innisvale had until recently belonged to one of Blue Dog's rancher friends from Broken Hill, before being taken over by an elder from the Wardaman Nation. What to do? We called up neighbouring Wombungi station to ask advice. The owner, a white Australian by the name of Alan Fisher, was sympathetic but warned that we faced prosecution if we tried to make it through without a permit.

Blue Dog was sitting in the truck, topo map draped over his knees, satellite phone pressed to his ear. "Yeah, but we've done everything we can," he said despairingly. "I can't understand what the problem is."

"Look," said the voice. "All I'm saying is, you could be prosecuted."

Half an hour and ninety dollars of airtime later, Blue Dog hung up the receiver and stared angrily into the night. "It's ridiculous. If anyone wants to come through my property in New South Wales, then no worries. Just close the gates behind you and have a nice day. But no, no, no, because it's an *aboriginal* property, you might get prosecuted."

He rolled up the map, slapping the bugs off as he did. "I mean, I was born here, too. I didn't have any choice where I was born in the world. What's the big difference whether you're white or black all of a sudden? So much for being an Australian citizen!"

In the end, we decided to barge through en masse in the early hours and hope we didn't run into anybody.

It was daylight by the time we neared the station homestead, following a dirt track that looped around a clutch of buildings and took off north in the direction we wanted to go. Crossing the courtyard, we found our way blocked by a small girl with honey-coloured skin standing astride a mountain bike. She looked curiously at us, her angelic eyes dark like billabongs. Beyond her was a short scruffy man in a cowboy hat. He introduced himself as the owner, Bill Harney.

So much for the element of surprise, I thought.

Face creased and tumefied like the swollen trunks of the baobab trees we'd seen in the Gregory, the old aborigine grimaced at our intrusion. He looked blankly over my shoulder as I gave my spiel, and I was on the verge of abandoning the effort and turning the team around when a glint on the side of his hat caught my eye. It was a silver star with a blue circle in the middle. The crown jewels and letters EIIR looked familiar.

Interrupting myself, I said, "Excuse me, Mister Harney, but is that a police badge?"

He squinted at me. "Where you from?"

When I told him, he smiled. "From your country, mate."

"England?"

"Yeah. My friend, he's a policeman there."

"Which part?"

He took off his hat and handed it to me. The badge was for the Cumbria Constabulary. "He sent me the helmet, too," said Bill.

"A bobby's helmet?" I put my arms over my head.

"Yep, that's it, a bobby's helmet."

A few minutes later, Bill emerged from the main house with the hat perched on his head like a flowerpot. It was so big he had to tilt his head to see where he was going. "Is this what them coppers back where you're from look like, then?" he asked, strutting along, his eyes twinkling.

I looked at the dusty feet, the faded shorts, the frizzy hair, and the tee shirt with a winking kangaroo on the front, and I thought: *No, not really.* But it didn't matter. We'd made a connection, and for the far-flung traveller in a distant land, finding something in common with an indifferent local whose sanction you need is like picking up an "Advance to Go" card in Monopoly. With Bill's blessing ringing in our ears ("No worries, you can get to Dorisvale from here. It's a good track. Be my guest!"), we rode on, waving to the gaggle of women and children who'd come out to smile shyly at us, and wondering at all the nonsense we'd been told about uncooperative Australian aborigines and the certainty of being clapped in irons for setting foot on their property.

BEFORE US LAY a scene of unimaginable horror: scores of dead cattle hanging thirty feet in the air, heads and legs trapped between railings, limbs twisted and horribly broken; others, still alive, struggled to free themselves from the upturned trailers. The idyllic Daly River shimmered peacefully in the background, a bizarre and incongruous backdrop complete with lilting birdsong and gnarled Daliesque trees reflected in the still water.

Riding tail, I was last to come across the pile up. April hurried to meet me as I walked my bicycle the last hundred yards down to the river. A rookie road train driver had apparently fallen asleep at the wheel, and his three-trailer double-decker rig flipped and jackknifed before coming to rest across the river fording point, wheels in the air and dusty red underbelly showing.

A few of the surviving animals had managed to escape. "They're on the fight," April warned, going on to explain that some of them were "scrub" bulls that had never been handled and were mustered for the first time by helicopter two days before. Now each of them was a two-thousand-pound ball of fury bent on retribution.

While the expedition team milled around Blue Dog's cab, three ringers who'd been fishing when the crash happened tried to bring order to the chaos. One, a feral scarecrow in a greasy baseball cap, laid a cattle prod against a bull lying inside the rearmost trailer. The animal sprang to life. Then all hell broke loose.

Like rats streaming up the side of a sinking ship, the young explorers streamed over the bull bars and up onto the roof of the truck as the bull thundered past, scything its horns back and forth. Todd dove underneath. Mike clambered on top of the cab, hollering as he went. The bull rammed the passenger door shut, narrowly missing Bell standing on the running board.

Another bull, a dark russet, came clattering out of the trailer, long ears flopping, neck folds swinging. It slipped and lay there for a minute, panting. Then it was up again, charging up the track to where April and I stood watching.

We turned on our heels and ran. To the left was a steep sandbank covered in thistles. Scrabbling on all fours, we snatched at the stems as the sand gave way under our pumping feet and the sound of thundering hooves drew closer.

Reaching the top, April said, "Wow, that was more of a rush than the King Brown and the crocodile!" Her fingers were trembling as she picked out the burrs from her hair. "'Cos I know what bulls can do."

The day before, April and I had been exploring the Flora River during our afternoon break. A dark torpedo shape emerged from the mud and leaves of a pool we were wading across, giving us the fright of our lives. It turned out to be a freshwater croc, the harmless, narrow-nosed, fish-eating type. Then a little later, walking back to camp, I'd almost stepped on an eastern brown, the world's second most venomous terrestrial snake. A warning shout from April could well have saved my life.

The bull was now at the foot of the bank, pawing the ground and snorting at us. Denied vengeance, the beast swished its tail furiously, then turned and cantered back down to the river in search of easier victims.

The whole team had gathered on the roof of the truck, their legs hanging over the edge like flood refugees. Three more bulls had escaped and were wreaking havoc. One was trying to hook the ringers' yapping blue heelers out from under a pickup. The other two stampeded back and forth before taking their chances swimming the river. Only one made it to the other side. The exhausted survivor stood panting on a narrow shelf, its escape blocked by the vertical riverbank. The unlucky companion had meanwhile disappeared, either drowned or yanked under by a croc.

Shots rang out. The ringers were destroying the bulls that were trapped. Checking that the coast was clear, Crister and I climbed onto one of the trailers and peered through the slats. Forty or so animals were piled inside, their heads, legs, and tails pointing every which way. Those still alive appeared resigned to their fate, patiently waiting for one of the ringers to clamber barefoot over the carcasses and fire a .22 rifle point-blank into their skulls.

Anger and disgust flared in my throat, at the mindless destruction of it all, at the driver falling asleep, at the greedy haulage bosses expecting someone to drive sixteen hours a day, at the snarling ringers, and at the meat industry in general—all of them cashing in on the lucrative live export trade to punctilious Muslims worldwide. The last thing on anyone's mind was the welfare of the animals.

Above us, the clatter of a helicopter announced the arrival of Alan Fisher, the owner of the cattle. He stood surveying the slaughter.

"It's just the animals that gets me," he said grimly. "Don't like to see 'em get knocked around."

Finally, I thought, *someone with a modicum of compassion.* Alan struck me as Old School in his long-sleeved blue shirt, jeans, and short sandy hair, a world away from the bullying ringers with their "fackin' this, 'n fackin' that."

On the kill floor, extermination was complete. A blood-splattered ringer pulled out a hunting knife and began carving out a crude rectangle of flesh from a random torso. "This'll be for me tea," he growled at Crister. His beard was matted and his shirt soaked with sweat. "No good wasting a good feed, eh?"

"He'll have *that* with a cup of tea?" Crister whispered to me.

"No," I replied. "In the UK and Australia tea means dinner."

I remembered the youngster's first day on the Battle Camp road heading inland from the coast. He was standing beside the corrugated track, nursing a nosebleed, his face chalky white. He'd looked so young and vulnerable at the time, I'd wondered if I was being too ambitious inviting teenagers on the expedition. Three months later, the eager-to-please innocence had gone. Crister looked three years older, more grounded and self-assured, well on the way to becoming a man.

"Surreal," he murmured, shaking his head. "Beautiful river. Beautiful sunset. A million dead cows."

BUT THERE WAS one animal we could save. The following evening, while looking for a campsite, Blue Dog came across a lone cow bogged in a waterhole. She was an older "gummer" nearing the end of her life—rail thin, haunches sticking out like a hat rack. She'd obviously been struggling for some time, working herself deeper into the mire, becoming ever weaker in the process. Her head was tilted to one side to keep the putrid water from filling her lungs. Another inch, and she would drown.

The team sprang into action, grabbing planks from the back of the truck to prop her head up. Next we tried pulling her legs out of the mud. The bog was deep, though, and with the animal already exhausted, our efforts proved futile. Blue Dog produced a length of polypropylene rope, tied one end to the tailgate and the other around the cow's hocks, locked in the hubs, and pulled her out backwards.

The cow lay there in a wheel rut, her neck stretched out, tongue lolling. Rolling her right side up, we began working to get her feet underneath her. When she eventually tried to stand, her hindquarters came up only halfway. She just didn't have the strength.

Half an hour of this, and it became too dark to see what we were doing.

"Maybe she'll regain her strength overnight," I said optimistically.

But at five o'clock the next morning, when April and I returned, the old girl was lying in the same position.

Back in camp, I solicited volunteers. Josh, Crister, and Bell were game. The rest of the team kept packing their gear, eager to press on to Darwin, now less than 48 hours away. "I know it sounds cold," explained Mike, pulling on his yellow cycling jersey. "But I really, really don't want to get attached to living things that are in trouble. There have been enough coulda, shoulda, wouldas about people and things in my life already."

A week earlier, he'd broken down sobbing in the Gregory, mourning his beloved canine companion that had died a year ago to the day.

The five of us hurried to the cow and began excavating soil out from under her legs, making it easier for her to stand. Mike appeared suddenly.

"Are you here to lend a hand or what?" I asked suspiciously. Mike and I had been butting heads again recently. He was probably mad at me for holding up the group.

"Yup," he replied, striding over.

Good old Mike, I thought. For all our differences, he was deeply principled, a trait I admired. He just needed to believe in something more than himself. And perhaps, in a way, the old cow symbolized something in each of us we were all trying to save, the reason we'd come to the outback, to be purified by heat and sand and the emptiness of the desert. After the massacre on the Daly, she was a symbol of hope, offering atonement for the heinous things that we'd seen.

April, Mike, and I tried to get her to stand. The old cow grunted as we heaved.

I looked up and saw Blue Dog standing at the top of the rise.

"Is it a go?" he said irritably. "Or are we going to stuff around here all day for the same result?"

I was digging with the long-handled shovel, bug net pulled back over my head. "No," I snapped. "We're just going to stuff around here all day."

The old cow gurgled, tried to get up, and flopped back down again.

Blue Dog had his hands on his hips. "I'm just saying if she's strong enough to get up, she'll get up. It won't make any difference. If she can't hold herself now, she never will."

"We're not asking you to hang around, John," I said. "If you want to go, that's fine. And if anyone else wants to go"—I looked around at the others—"you can go, too."

No one did.

Blue Dog sighed. "Look, we'll just go down there to Dorisvale. I'll call in and tell the bloke to come and check on her this afternoon."

Yeah, I can just imagine what she'd get from him, I thought sourly. *A bullet.*

The old cow groaned, a deep, sonorous bellyful of woe. She was perched on a ridge, the best position yet to get up. While Mike gathered rocks and threw them into the rut, I shovelled some more dirt under her back legs for purchase. She tried again, nearly making it all the way.

"Go on, girl!" I cried. "You're almost there!"

She slumped back down.

"She stopped trying for a second," said Mike hopefully. "But she's getting the idea."

April massaged the cow's haunches to get her blood going. When she lunged again, the cow straightened her front legs first. The near hind came next. She was almost up. Then the off hind faltered. Again, she collapsed.

We switched to scare tactics. While April held her tail to stop her from rolling back into the mud hole, Mike, Crister, and I gathered fistfuls of dry grass. On the count of three, we ran shrieking down the track towards her, shaking the grass above our heads. The cow put her ears back, but didn't budge.

"Hah! Ay ya ya ya ya ya!" Mike flung his grass at her. "On guard, bonehead."

"She's not buying it," I said.

An hour had passed. We'd done all we could. Placing the grass in front of her, the six of us started slowly back to camp.

Crister turned to look at the old gummer one last time. "I really wanna see her get up," he said.

Sunlight was peeking around the bleached limbs of the gum trees. The infectious hip-hop blips and whoops of tropical birds were just getting going. Frogs croaked. Cicadas sawed. Flies buzzed half-heartedly in the cool morning air. Another day in the outback was beginning.

Hard country, I thought to myself. *Hard on people. Hard on the animals.*

"Me, too, junior." I sighed. "Unfortunately, things don't always work out the way we want. All we can do is our best and let the rest go."

CHARCOAL GREY THUNDERHEADS reared in our wake as we reached the Stuart Highway. We'd made it to the sealed road just in time, before the deluge.

"What *is* that?" said Crister, staring at the asphalt. "Hard and black with yellow stripes down the middle."

"It's pavement!" cried Todd, playing along.

"Pavement? I've heard about it."

"What do you think?"

"I dunno. Kinda prefer my dirt." Crister scooped up a handful of bull dust and rubbed it against his legs, a token reminder of the outback.

Then we were flying single file through the Darwin suburbs, our journey's end firmly in our sights. It was like coming off a long sea voyage: eardrums reeling from the sound of roaring traffic, eyes hungrily taking in all the signs. "No Trespassing - Keep OUT! Gift Shop - REAL Crocodile Products. French Lingerie. First Assembly of God - DARWIN WAS WRONG! 5:00 PM."

I brought up the rear, my bike decorated with celebratory balloons tied on by Bell. She was next in line, her bike creaking terribly—she never bothered to oil it. Then again, she hadn't really needed to. Accustomed to her single-speed penny-farthing back in Victoria, she hadn't changed gears once since leaving the Starcke.

In a wrap-up interview the evening before, Todd had enquired whether the trip had lived up to her expectations. Bell flapped her hands and repeated her mantra from the beginning: "No expectations!"

Did she feel like she'd changed at all, Todd asked?

Taking a deep breath, Bell smiled, and said, "I'M A BIT LOUDER!"

Ahead of her was April. She was heading back to Colorado to author an interactive CD-ROM for her school district, making use of the Discovery Zone footage that Reddo Publishing had reneged on. Then came Josh. Of everyone, the youngster had taken the biggest plunge, having never left home before. But he'd seen the job through, finishing something that no one could ever take away from him.

Mike was riding point, where he liked to be. "I've hated this," he confessed in his final video diarrhoea. "I've loved this, I've been wowed by this ... I've asked an awful lot of this expedition, to help me find some sense of self-esteem, some point of continuing on. But I've come to realize through the day to day of it that this trek through the outback was never going to be some magical pill for me, that I still have to do the work. It's not like I'm going to put my foot in the Timor Sea and my life will suddenly be different. That said, I think I'm coming out of this liking a little more who I am."

At 8:50 on the morning of October 21, the eighty-eighth day of the journey, we passed a warning sign for box jellyfish and caught sight of the muddy brown chop of the Arafura Sea. Blue Dog had erected an altar of Victoria Bitter cans part way down the beach. Sitting atop was his namesake, the stuffed blue dog that had ridden on his dashboard all the way from Queensland.

Bell took dead aim.

"I can't believe it!" Blue Dog sputtered after she'd swept past, flattening the lot. "The bitch ran Blue Dog over!"

Then it was a last hundred-metre dash, everyone whooping, riding headlong into a soupy cocktail of seawater, blue-green algae, and cheap champagne sprayed in all directions. The team wrestled and congratulated each other in the surf. Only Bell managed to avoid a dunking, citing allergies to the sea. April was yanked in, wriggling like an eel. Even Blue Dog, still fulminating at Bell's sabotage, was seized and chucked in forcibly like a trussed pig.

DARWIN
BEST JOB I EVER HAD

Rock bottom became the solid foundation on which I rebuilt my life.

—J K ROWLING

*C*ITIBANK *$1,200*

American Express Optima $2,000

I was sitting in front of a cold cup of coffee in Northern Territory's biggest mall, jotting figures on a paper napkin. Earlier, I'd met with the events manager to discuss an exhibit similar to the one at The Pier Shopping Centre in Cairns. In return for the PR draw of hosting *Moksha,* I would be allowed to sell merchandize, repaying the expedition debt $20 at a time.

Sister Julia $2,000

Taking the E*Trade meltdown and Overland Australia costs into account, the expedition was now $106,000 in the red. Nine years of effort, and keeping the project going was still like pushing a turd up a hill using a rubber fork.

American Express $21,000

I looked up from my scribbling and thought, "Are you ready to give up?"

Sony camcorder $5,000

I'd been in Darwin for a fortnight, tying up loose ends and helping Blue Dog clean the truck before he returned it to the Mitsubishi dealership in Cairns. *Moksha* had meanwhile arrived on a barge from Townsville, courtesy of the Swire Shipping Company.

Internal Revenue Service $50,000

My phone rang. The voice sounded familiar.

"Hey, you piece of dog meat. Something to share with you."

It was my old friend Mick Bird. Having rowed the Pacific, he was on track to become the first person to row around the world. I braced myself for the big news. "So, Mick, you finally springing for that sex change, mate?"

"No, brother."

"Just clinched the big sponsorship deal, then?"

"No bro. I'm pulling out."

"Pulling out?"

A few days ago, he'd overheard his wife, Stacia, discussing birthday plans with their two six-year-old daughters. Mick went on to explain: "I realized I couldn't join in the conversation because I knew I wasn't going to be there. That's when it hit me. At first, all I did was change nappies. Now they're older, it's different."

Satellite airtime $20,000

Mick's journey had run its course, helping to clarify what was now most important in his life—raising a family. Steve had voiced something similar before parting ways in Hawaii. "Being on this boat doesn't suit my loves," he'd told me.

Did the expedition continue to suit *my* loves, I wondered?

The idea of a human-powered circumnavigation still put goose bumps on my skin, especially here in the Casuarina Shopping Centre, besieged by the relentless background drone of consumerism. "To travel the farthest a human can go, to the very ends of the Earth itself, under their own steam." Like all good ideas it was elegantly simple and concise enough to scribble on the back of a cigarette packet—as Steve once had, above the words SERIOUSLY DAMAGES HEALTH. But as the journey dragged on, year after year, the Greenwich meridian had proved too distant to sustain the day-to-day grind. My side interests had shifted accordingly, evolving from an early thirst for adventure, to a deeper psychological stripping down in the ocean wilderness, graduating to a more useful raft of educational curricula promoting world citizenship and environmental stewardship. Now, facing the spectre of bankruptcy once again, even these outreach programmes were starting to lose their efficacy. I felt stretched, like elastic ready to tear.

Several lifetimes seemed to have passed since I sat cross-legged on Cerra de Muerto in Mexico and years later kneeled in despair on the beach on Tarawa, laughed at by the girl with the frangipani blossom in her hair. Both times, like now, I'd been ready to throw in the towel. Yet on both occasions, I'd carried on. Why? Deep down, I knew the answer. Underpinning all other motives was the as yet unresolved riddle I'd posed in Paris all those years ago.

Life. How to live it?

Turning the napkin over, I wrote:

Rule #1. Find a way to keep moving forward.

Rule #2. When all else fails, refer to Rule #1.

I thought of returning to the life of a mall rat, whoring out my stories.

There had to be another way.

MERCIFULLY, AN ALTERNATIVE presented itself during a brief visit back to Colorado to have the rods removed from my legs. Hearing of the project's financial woes, Doctor Ken offered me a job on the same ranch that Stuart and I had stayed at six years before. Mountain Pine Beetles were decimating the ponderosas. The diseased trees had to be destroyed to save the healthy ones.

It took three-and-a-half years to claw the expedition back to solvency. I stayed with April in the little mountain town of Rye nestled in the foothills of the Rockies. Since meeting in 1995, the fifth-grade teacher had become my rock, the ultimate one-person support team. She now set to horse-trading with the IRS and American Express. In return for lump payments, both agreed to waive penalties and interest, and even slash the principal, bringing the total debt down to a more manageable $38,000.

After a year of lumberjacking, I took over as ranch manager, responsible for a hundred head of bison and various construction projects, including installation of an underground pipeline and crop-irrigation systems. It was hard physical work, the kind you can look back on at the end of a day and feel like you've actually done something. The key was being connected to the land, giving a sense of place and duty within the natural order of things. There was an unspoken code between the local ranchers largely absent from the white-collar world. The measure of a man, I came to see, lay not in his talk, but in his hands. The more scored, begrimed, and weather beaten they were, the more upstanding the owner.

It felt good to be part of a community again, seeing the same faces, joining in the light-hearted banter, sharing advice and trading insults. Staying would have been easy: settle down, start a new life, do the things that normal people do. But as I often reminded myself, I was there for a reason. Every day I went to work took me one step closer to getting back out on the circumnavigation and one step closer to Greenwich.

In the end, my brief encounter with civilization was just another leg of the expedition, another ocean to cross.

THE TIMOR SEA
AGROUND IN THE APSLEY

After all, Ginger Rogers did everything that Fred Astaire did. She just did it backwards and in high heels.

—ANN RICHARDS

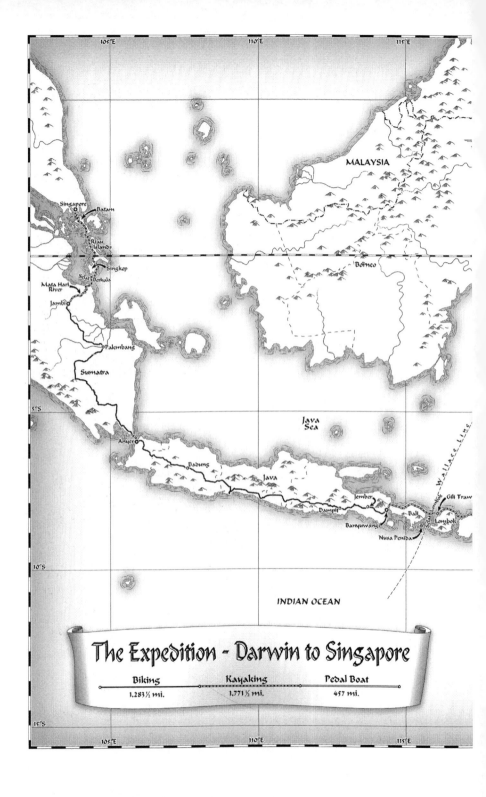

The Expedition - Darwin to Singapore

Biking	Kayaking	Pedal Boat
1,283½ mi.	1,771½ mi.	457 mi.

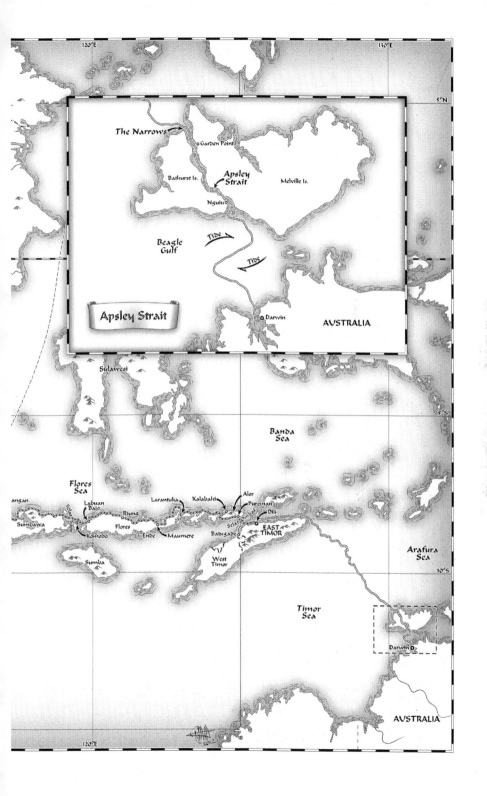

ANTLES OF GREY DUST, scuttling cockroaches, everything spattered in filth—a glimpse into some unborn post-apocalyptic world. Boxes of equipment overturned and rifled through, anything of value looted, the rest smashed beyond recognition. It was mindless vandalism. All the bottles in the first aid kit had been opened, the pills tipped out and stamped on; a box of CDs shattered, *Moondance* in twelve pieces; both lifejackets disembowelled, batteries and radios missing; my bike gear, all of it gone; bundles of tee shirts, precious expedition currency, soiled with human faeces and cast aside.

After a day of detective work tracking down the bozo who'd offered to keep an eye on her during my absence, I'd found *Moksha* in an old storage shed on Fort Hill Wharf.

She was in a terrible state. Cobwebs choked the cockpit. Dirt-encrusted flags hung limply across her deck like streamers on a ghost ship. She'd been ransacked and everything of worth stolen: EPIRB, VHF radio, solar panels, and cameras. They'd even taken the desalinator pump.

I made a list, totting up the total value.

$10,372.00.

A more disastrous start to the Indonesian leg was hard to imagine. Of the $15,000 I'd managed to save after working off the debt, two thirds was already spoken for. Still, I had to be thankful for small mercies. A few days before my return, one of the port authority managers, a belligerent Scot, had apparently proposed burning *Moksha*, claiming that she'd been abandoned.

My plan was to pedal her four hundred and fifty nautical miles from Darwin to Dili in East Timor, then island hop the remaining 2,200 miles to Singapore by kayak. Pedalling any further up the archipelago would be foolish, I'd decided. Too cumbersome for beach landings and ill-suited to swift-moving currents, *Moksha* would likely run aground on one of the many coral reefs surrounding the islands. She would stay in Dili and be shipped to Singapore on a barge once I'd arrived.

That was later. The immediate priority was to find some workspace and bring her back to life. I wandered down the road to the Dinah Beach Cruising Yacht Association, where I was told I could catch the commodore around the cocktail hour. It was early when I arrived, around 10:30 am, but sure enough there was the big man himself nursing a rum and Coke out on the terrace. From his cropped scalp and grimy wife-beater, I suspected Peter Suitor was one of the more down-to-earth commodores I'd meet on my round-the-world journey.

"Fuck yeah!" he yelled after listening to my plea for a corner of the boatyard to put *Moksha* for a few weeks. "That's what this place is all about, mate. Sailors comin' in 'ere, gettin' their boats fixed up, then fuckin' off again." He drained his glass and rattled the ice. "You fellas are welcome. Too many useless cunts around these days, that's the fuckin' problem."

Letting these words of wisdom sink in, I gazed out across the boat ramp, past the mud flats and mangroves of the estuary, north towards Indonesia. My thoughts turned to kayaking. Was it even possible to get to Asia from here? To the best of my research, no one had ever done so. The closest precedent was a group of Special Forces soldiers paddling in the opposite direction, from north to south, in the closing stages of World War II. After a botched raid on Japanese shipping in the Port of Singapore, the twenty-three British and Australian commandos were left stranded by their getaway submarine *HMS Tantalus*, leaving them no choice but to try to reach Australia in their canvas Folbots. The ensuing odyssey, a desperate bid to reach Allied territory through thousands of miles of enemy-held territory, is the stuff of legend. Within three months, all but ten had been killed in action or drowned trying to paddle across the narrow fast-flowing straits between islands known as selats.

The ill-fated Operation Rimau captured my imagination and demonstrated the theoretical feasibility of negotiating the monsoonal weather patterns and sea conditions to reach Singapore in a kayak. Setting off early in the wet season of December 1944, Unit Z Force took advantage of the prevailing northeasterly wind and current to aid their southwesterly flight. They had six months to reach Australia before the pattern was reversed. It was after this switch in May, when the southeasterlies reasserted themselves and the winds and currents flowed northeast again, that I would strike out for Singapore.

As on previous legs, I invited others to join me, though nothing like on the scale and ambition of Overland Australia. April signed up, as did Chris Tipper. Then there was Lourdes, a Californian of Cuban descent and an experienced kayaker, who would accompany me in *Moksha* to Dili. Four would be the perfect number this time, I was sure of it, and the mix of personalities conducive to six months of bicker-free travel.

But of course, there's a reason why they say, "The best laid plans of mice and men …"

"How long have you been in Australia, Andy?"

Trimmed white beard, jug-handle ears, and a gimpy leg, the old Glaswegian had his shirt off, sporting a barrel stomach covered in a thick fleece of chest hair.

"Thirrrty six years," he replied happily.

"You've kept your accent well."

"Och aye. Too tight even tae give that away!"

Belly shaking with laughter, he turned to climb the ladder to his single-hull sailing boat, one of forty or so dilapidated vessels propped up on stilts in the Dinah Beach car park. Having been recently laid off and given the heave-ho by his wife of twenty-six years, Andy had split from Freemantle and made the club his home. Like Alcoholic Rodney in the catamaran opposite, he had absolutely no intention of going anywhere. Rent was cheap. The bar was within teetering distance and sold the cheapest and coldest beer in town. It was the ideal retirement set-up. When I'd asked how much longer he thought it would be before his boat was ready to launch, Andy had pressed his whiskery face to mine, and hissed "Yearrrs!" with hearty optimism.

In the event the club lost patience with the liveaboards and forced them to expedite repairs and return their hulks to the sea, Andy had taken the precaution of drilling a hole through the bottom of his. The aperture was three inches in diameter, guaranteeing his craft never went near water again. And it had another use. At regular intervals throughout the evenings, we'd hear the *Clink! Clink! Clink!* of another beer can clattering into the dustbin below.

Lourdes and I had spent almost a week at our new residence, the thirty-by-fifteen-foot concrete pad next to Andy's. Scavenging local materials, we'd erected a makeshift shelter of tarpaulins supported with driftwood, the corners anchored to car tyres weighted down with gravel. *Moksha* was rolled down the road on her cradle and given pride of place. What gear we'd managed to salvage was spread out on the ground to be inventoried, creating an obstacle course of pots, pans, charts, books, Tupperware containers, and other paraphernalia. At the back of the lot, behind *Moksha,* we pitched our tents between the piles of refuse left by previous occupants.

Such was our new expedition base camp.

It was also an office-cum-workshop. A stack of abandoned pallets served as a desk to order parts, write proposals for replacement gear, and fill out visa application forms. Another stack became a workbench to strip down the wind generator, service the pedal units, and resuscitate all manner of corroded electronics with the help of Australia's answer to WD40, a potent engine spray called Start Ya Bastard. A local supporter, James Walker, loaned us deck chairs and a fridge to preserve food in the tropical heat. We cooked meals on camp stoves.

In spite of the open-air appeal, certain drawbacks of running a business alfresco quickly became apparent. The boatyard was hot, humid, and noisy—birds screeched in the nearby bushes, doves cooed, geese cackled and honked on the adjacent property. From dawn until dusk, our brains shuddered to the sound of sawing, hammering, and chiselling, and our ears convulsed to the whine of power tools. A two-foot-long monitor lizard, mottled brown with primrose yellow underside, shared our tent space, feeding off dead rats poisoned by Andy (and on one occasion a pair of his underpants). And being the wet season, the skies opened like clockwork at two o'clock every afternoon, producing a river running through our camp. During these gully-washers, we dashed around shoring up the tarps, preventing reservoirs of rainwater from collecting on the roof, and doing whatever else we could do to keep our fragile little abode from collapsing.

To our fellow Dinah Beach denizens, the notion of pedalling a boat to East Timor, a shorter but otherwise comparable voyage to the club's once infamous annual race to Ambon Island in the Moluccas, was ridiculous to the point of insulting. "But why?" they would ask, shaking their heads. Some, like Captain Seaweed, a sun-roasted Swede in a permanently affixed captain's cap, even became irate—which struck me as odd. As a haven for those clearly ill-suited to society's norms, giving sanctuary to ex-cons, cons on the run, and misfits in general, the Dinah Beach Cruising Yacht Association seemed to me the perfect home for the expedition.

A few, like Andy, "got" the concept of human power and offered to help. Leon from Darwin Shipstores found cheap used equipment to replace what had been trashed or stolen, including lifejackets from the Royal Australian Air Force. Kris, a shipwright who lived on a Chinese junk anchored in the creek, replaced *Moksha's* spirit guide with a turtle native to the waters we'd be pedalling through. The majority of people, however, treated us with thinly veiled scepticism. As we'd found in the past, it took the endorsement of the media to win over the Average Joe. A current affairs programme, ABC Stateline, ran a story, and suddenly we were worth speaking to.

I was in the club workshop one day, grinding off a pedal rusted to a crank arm, when I heard a voice behind me. "So vot heppens in der rof wezzer?"

It was Captain Seaweed. His breasts were sagging and folds of skin hung from his shoulders like an old bull elephant. He had just two teeth left, and his eyes were cerulean blue and sunk back into their sockets.

Without waiting for a reply, he added, "Ent vot ebout der waater?" He was the type who talked at you, not with you, delivering his sentences in the monotone machine-gun chatter of Scandinavians.

I gave answers, but when I tried to explain our route, I was interrupted. "If ya goin' up dare to Indonesia, oy'd floy der Shveedish flag oy would. Doze crazy facking *baarstards*, dey'll shoot'ya if ya say you're Hamerican hor Heenglish. Floy der Shveedish flag. Dey never done nothin' to nowan!"

He had a point, albeit a paranoid one. Ninety-eight per cent of Indonesia's 220 million inhabitants were Muslim, the highest percentage of any country in the world, and Islam produced more than its fair share of fanatics. A number of these, members of the radical Jemaah Islamiyah group, had recently been turfed out of the Moluccas following bouts of religious cleansing between Christian and Muslim communities. It was this same looney tunes outfit that had slaughtered two hundred and two people, including one hundred and fifty-two foreign nationals, in the 2002 Bali bombings.

From then on Captain Seaweed became one of our biggest allies. An accomplished sailor, he was a wealth of information on the hazards of the Beagle Gulf, the body of water immediately north of Darwin.

Most crucially, he photocopied detailed charts of the Apsley Straits, the narrow sea passage between Bathurst and Melville Islands, which offered the best route to clear the eastern edge of Timor to reach Dili.

AT 6:35 AM, AN hour after first light, the mouth of the Apsley Straits shimmered golden brown like a sheet of stained glass. Daisy-chain clouds bloomed above us. The wind was fitful. *Moksha* bobbed gently in an undulating swell.

I tried the VHF a third time.

"Calling Kenny Brown, this is *Moksha*, come back, over."

Again, nothing.

I looked at Lourdes sitting opposite me. She wore shorts and a white long-sleeved shirt. A straw hat bound by an orange sash fought to subdue a mass of dark curls.

"I wonder where that bloody Scotsman is?" I said, feeling the first twinge of concern.

We'd agreed to rendezvous at the entrance to the straits exactly 24 hours after *Moksha's* departure from Darwin. As part of his ongoing effort to film the beginning and end of each leg, Kenny had chartered a catamaran from one of the more eccentric members of the Dinah Beach clan (which was saying something). Captain Crazy Trousers had two great passions in life: loud juggling attire and sausages. The fee for taking Kenny to the entrance of the Apsley was therefore set at twelve packets of pork chipolatas.

The lead-up to departure had been the usual pandemonium, with everything coming together at the last minute. Replacement marine batteries arrived only the day before, leaving barely enough time to recalibrate the error correction in the bulkhead compass. Vaccination courses for yellow fever, tetanus, hepatitis A and B, typhoid, Japanese encephalitis, meningitis, rabies, measles, mumps, rubella, polio, and diphtheria were completed on the final day. The last thing on my list was to buy Indonesian currency. I walked into Westpac Bank on Knuckey Street with a thousand US dollars in my pocket and walked out five minutes later with my rucksack stuffed with banknotes. At an exchange rate of $1 US to 8,500 Indonesian rupiah, I was an instant millionaire.

The send-off itself was predictably bizarre. An hour before casting off, I'd found myself sitting on a pontoon attempting to blow up a life-sized kangaroo.

"Look!" exclaimed Niki, our most diligent local supporter who'd presented the kangaroo as a farewell gift. "He's getting a smile on his face."

Something was taking shape, but nothing that resembled a kangaroo.

Lourdes was reading from the instructions. "It says, 'Do not attempt to blow out all the wrinkles'."

"Why," I gasped between breaths, "is it a Greater Spotted Wrinkly Kangaroo?"

Niki chuckled. "Yeah, sort of a half-breed roo mixed with a Shar Pei."

I blew some more. Up popped a leg.

"It'll be your life raft!" a voice yelled from the small crowd that had gathered.

With Skippy fully inflated and bungeed to the cabin roof, I'd slipped on my ocean ring, bid farewell to our Darwin hosts, and pushed *Moksha* away from the dock. Chalk-white high-rises caught the sun as we swept out of the estuary on an ebb tide the colour of dishwater. Almost immediately, Skippy started to nod. A quick examination revealed the marsupial had sprung a leak and needed resuscitating. This would have been unremarkable were it not for the top-up valve being located where its butthole should have been. As it was, those watching from shore were subjected to repeated acts of depravity as we strove to keep Skippy from drooping.

Twenty-three hours later, Lourdes and I made it the forty-three miles across the Beagle Gulf, tracking east then west with the tide, arriving an hour ahead of schedule.

But where the blazes were Captain Crazy Trousers and Our Man Brown?

On a whim, I used the satellite phone to call Kenny's mobile. A panting voice answered. *"Sand bar ... Crazy Troosers ... Mad as a brush ..."*

"Kenny, where are you?"

I heard a few garbled words. Then the line went dead.

"Sounds like he's back in Darwin," I said to Lourdes. "Something about shoes, pussies, and ferries, and for us to wait for him outside Nguiu."

Nguiu was the settlement at the bottom of the straits.

"Wow, so he's still on land?"

We had to wait another four hours to get the full story, the time it took Kenny to take the ferry to Bathurst and persuade someone with a boat to bring him out to us.

"So we set off about an hour after you guys." Kenny was standing in *Moksha's* cockpit, chuffing on a cigarette, surrounded by his usual heap of camera bags. He was wearing an pair of battered flip-flops that looked strangely familiar. "Ev'rythin's goin' okay. Crazy Troosers' boat seems to be workin' fine."

But as he went on to describe, things started to go awry when darkness fell. Crazy Trousers took the first watch. Kenny awoke from a three-hour nap to find he wasn't the only one sleeping.

"So I wake him and ask, 'When do we tack?' And he says, *Oh no, I don't tack.*"

"What do you mean he doesn't tack?" I said.

"I don't do corners in the dark, he said."

"Oh my God!" cried Lourdes. "That's priceless."

The catamaran, called *Pussy,* as in cat, had started out life as a canoe, apparently, with bits stuck on willy-nilly like a children's Lego project.

Kenny exhaled a lungful of smoke. "It had these weird outrigger thingies, and the midsection—originally the canoe part, I think—doubled as a berth and a sort of James-Bond-style evacuation capsule."

Realizing Captain Crazy Trousers was even more unhinged than he first thought, Kenny took charge of the situation. He grabbed the tiller and steered *Pussy* in a giant circle back towards Darwin.

"So I says to him, 'What about tides?' And he replies, *Oh no, I don't do tides.*"

Finally, at 5:00 am, they'd spotted the lights of Fannie Bay.

"We were about a mile from shore, going four knots. I thought to myself, I'm gonna survive this, I'm not going to drown after all. Then the boat slammed into a sand bar."

Kenny smiled grimly and took a last drag on his cigarette.

"We both get in the water and try to shove her off, but she's stuck. So Crazy Troosers launches this dinghy, which is like a million years old. We make it about sixty feet before the motor dies—run out of fuel, of course. And there are no oars."

Short on options but a man of his word, Captain Crazy Trousers had made a last valiant effort to get his customer to safety.

"So he puts the rope between his teeth and starts doggy-paddlin' to shore, towing the dinghy half-inflated and leakin' water. I'm in the back, meanwhile, water sloshin' ev'rywhere, bailin' wi' one hand and holdin' me camera wrapped in a dustbin liner wi' the other."

At dawn, Kenny found himself stranded on a random beach with no shoes and no money.

"That's when I realized me sandals were still on that bloody cat'maran."

It had taken him two hours to totter barefoot back to the Dinah Beach car park, where he'd rooted in the dustbin and found my old flip-flops.

Kenny shook his head and squinted into the midday sun. "I'm tellin' ye, the things I do for this shitein' expedition."

WE MADE IT twelve miles up the mud-coloured straits before the tide turned, slipping past twisted pandanus trees, spindly eucalypts, and volcanic rocks of cinder. We tethered *Moksha* to a tangle of mangroves and checked for slide marks before stepping gingerly ashore. It was evening. The top of the steep riverbank where the salties couldn't reach offered a safe spot to cook and eat a meal of pasta and fried veggies. Then Kenny and Lourdes collapsed exhausted in their tents, while I returned to *Moksha*.

In the darkness of the early hours, I woke to the sound of splintering wood and popping metal. The Rathole was listing to starboard. I fumbled for my headlamp and scrambled into the main compartment. *Moksha* was well and truly aground. Two of the four clamps around the pedal unit had sheared. The entire boat was now resting on the centreboard, breaking the waterproof seal around the casing and pushing the timber up into the cabin. The rudder was also in trouble, jammed in the mangrove roots, the pintles in danger of tearing out of the transom. Climbing onto the port gunwale, I was about to jump into the water when a pair of yellowy eyes appeared.

A croc.

Cursing myself for underestimating the tidal range, all I could do was sit there and hope the rudder didn't break. Eventually, the tide turned, and by daylight *Moksha* was once more afloat.

It took the rest of the morning to repair the damage, first drilling out the old bolts, then replacing the locking clamps on the Dogs Bollocks, before reseating the centreboard with Sikaflex, all the while being jeered at by babbling birds and bitten by the vicious red flies that lived in the mangroves. I came away learning two valuable lessons. That dragging a bag filled with miscellaneous nuts and bolts and seemingly useless bits of hardware around the world does eventually pay off. And paddling kayaks from Dili onwards was indeed the right decision given how unwieldy *Moksha* was around land.

Later that afternoon, once the tide turned in our favour, we reached Garden Point, the most northerly settlement on the straits. Kenny hailed a passing fishing boat and bundled himself and all his gear ashore in time to catch the weekly flight to Darwin. This was fortunate. Although the two-day jolly up the sheltered Apsley had been fun with three of us aboard, continuing together all the way to Dili across the open sea would have been dangerous and, frankly, insufferable.

As the light plane banked overhead, Kenny used his handheld VHF to identify the treacherous reefs and shoals around The Narrows, the north entrance to the straits through which Lourdes and I would navigate later that night in the dark.

Timor-Leste
On the Trail of the Rimaus

The atmosphere of officialdom would kill anything that breathes the air of human endeavour, would extinguish hope and fear alike in the supremacy of paper and ink.

—Joseph Conrad, *The Shadow Line*

TIMOR EMERGED FROM THE delicate pinks of the morning like an accusing finger levelled at the east. Wooded hills framed the lower elevations, with gold-tinted storm clouds menacing bold, black, and beautiful hovering above. My pulse quickened. Approaching unfamiliar territory in *Moksha* was always thrilling, but this was a seascape to steal my heart.

To the native Timorese, the island took more the shape of a crocodile swimming in the sea. Like Australian aboriginal Dreaming stories, this widely held notion reinforced the legend of how their homeland was formed by a mythical being, a giant crocodile that once roamed the earth before ossifying into dry land. For as long as anyone on Timor could remember, *Crocodylus porosus* had enjoyed sacred status, fondly referred to as grandfather by those who regarded themselves as progeny.

With the wind blowing a salubrious ten knots from astern, we slid effortlessly past the tiny satellite of Jako Island. Clearing Timor's easternmost tip was a major achievement, avoiding the dreaded Plan B of trying to track around the south coast and reach Dili from the west—a daunting proposition against the prevailing southeasterlies. Now, we could alter course from 330 to 270 degrees magnetic, taking us along the north shore all the way to Dili.

We'd been lucky, admittedly. Thanks to near idyllic conditions, we'd notched fifty- to sixty-mile days since leaving the Apsley five days earlier, chaperoned by turtles, sea snakes, droves of jellyfish the size of tuppenny pieces, and a posse of terns that alternated riding bronc on the rudder. Into this universe of motion, Lourdes had slipped effortlessly. Her love of laughter certainly helped, much of it provided by the deteriorating condition of her hair. Unlike April on the Coral Sea voyage, Lourdes hadn't even tried to wash hers.

"You're beginning to look like the Wild Woman of Kalimantan," I said to her on our last morning.

She was attempting to run a brush through the tangled mass. "Normally I can go for days without brushing my hair," she replied. "But here, look at it." She took her hand away, and the brush hung suspended in mid-air like a handle for her head.

"Serves you right for having so much hair in the first place," I said. "It's so thick. You could stuff a mattress with that thing."

"Tell you what," she said. "Whatever comes out of my hair brush, I'll give to you for a toupee."

"Perfect," I replied. "I'm going to hold you to that. We can use Sikaflex to stick it on."

"It'll be your thinking cap!"

The outstretched arms of Cristo Rei, a statue of Jesus commanding the rocky promontory of Fatucama, beckoned us the last few miles into Dili Bay. We passed gaily coloured fishing boats bucking in the breeze and merchant dhows in the process of being unloaded the old-fashioned way: their cargos of sawn planks tipped over the side and swum to shore by hand. I steered *Moksha* around a floating hotel, one that had been brought in to billet UN personnel during the recent transition to East Timorese independence, and let her come to a bumping rest against the lee side. Lourdes threw a line. A circle of sweating drummers from the Arte Moris School struck up a rousing rhythm, while a rank of smiling faces beamed down at us from the rail. One of these belonged to a handsome East Timorese woman wearing a blue bandana. None of us knew it then, but Ina Bradridge held the key to the expedition's future in ways we couldn't possibly have imagined.

DILI, ITS HOT dusty streets filled with glassy-eyed men loafing aimlessly, was where we picked up the trail of the Rimau commandos. The last two to be captured, Warrant Officer Jeffrey Willersdorf and Lance Corporal Hugo Pace, made it an astonishing 1,860 miles through enemy territory before being captured. A few days away from safety, a village chief had betrayed them to the Japanese. The men were tortured and left to die of their wounds in a Dili prison cell.

The former regional seat of Portuguese colonial power was also our new temporary base of operations for the kayaking leg to Singapore. *Moksha* was stored safely in a port authority warehouse, ready to be shipped to Singapore. Our kayaks, meanwhile, sat in a crate on the wharf, awaiting customs clearance. Like many poorer countries, the wheels of officialdom in East Timor were kept greased through an *I'll-scratch-your-back-You-scratch-mine* policy of muted bribery. "It will take five weeks to clear your boats," I was told by a young customs agent our first morning in Dili. "Maybe six." This was a setback. To keep on schedule, we'd planned to be in Dili only a week. But when I learned that he was a big Chelsea fan, and suggested that my brother-in-law Andrew in London might be persuaded to send him the official blue-and-white scarf of the Blues, I had the documents in my hand the next morning.

Our visas for Indonesia, something the Rimau servicemen never had to bother with, were a very different story. The national coordinator for UNESCO's school programmes at the Department of Education had obligingly agreed to act as our sponsor for a social cultural visa—a Kunjungan SosBud, as it was known. But there was a minefield of conflicting opinion as to whether this was the right visa for a kayaking expedition. An Australian diplomat working at the New Zealand Consulate in Jakarta assured me that it wasn't. A SosBud visa had to be renewed each month at the same immigration point, he insisted, making it impractical for travel. "Your only choice is to exit the country every thirty days, and re-enter via Singapore, or Darwin, on another tourist visa."

This was out of the question. Even without the prohibitive cost of flights, the toing and froing would make the journey logistically impossible.

Another contact, an immigration specialist at the Bali Marina whose job it was to arrange visas for visiting yachties, was adamant we were wasting our time trying to kayak through Indonesia in the first place. *You'll be forced to abandon your boats on the island of Batam,* he wrote in an email, *and fly the last hop to Singapore.*

Ironically, the most confusing advice of all came from the Head of Indonesian Immigration in Dili. A look of utter bewilderment came over Pak Hendarsin's face when we outlined our plans. We weren't tourists pissing it up in Bali. We weren't itinerant yachties. And although UNESCO would be connecting us with schools along the way, we weren't part of any official study or work programme. He scratched his head. What kind of beast were we? Animal? Vegetable? Mineral?

"You may have trouble renewing a SosBud visa at different immigration points," he told Chris, Lourdes, and me, who were sitting in his office. "Or you may not. It depends on the policy of each regional office."

Plus, there was the whole business of trying to get the kayaks into Indonesian-controlled West Timor. The boats were too small to qualify for a cruising permit and too big to be taken across the border as personal effects. What to do? Again, Pak Hendarsin offered his contradictory advice: "You can try registering them with the East Timor Department of Revenue," he said, holding up his hands suggestively. "With a tax identification number, customs might let you take them across the border. Then again, they may not."

It was all smoke and mirrors. We were entering a part of the world where officials were deliberately ambiguous, a safeguard against losing their jobs by giving the wrong advice.

A fortnight went by, and we were still in Dili, beating our heads against a seemingly impregnable bureaucratic wall. And the longer we stayed, the more horror stories we heard about travelling through the archipelago. If we weren't robbed blind, the ex-pats told us, Islamic fundamentalists would bundle us into the back of a van and lop our heads off. "You'll be famous on the Internet!" said one with hearty enthusiasm. Then there were the Indonesian police, army, and navy. "Real bastards," said another, going on to explain that Indonesia was about to build a naval base on the island of Wetar, north of Dili, and regional tensions were riding high. Only a month before, an Indonesian gunboat had opened fire on a dive boat in East Timorese waters. "Even if you have all your paperwork in order," said the ex-pat, "they'll assume you're spies, shoot first, and ask questions later."

On any other leg, I would have dismissed all this talk as the usual fear mongering engendered by tall poppy syndrome, but enough of it tallied with an experience Mick Bird had had dealing with local offialdom. Five years earlier on his Indian Ocean row, he'd stopped for emergency supplies at the south Javanese port of Cilacap. His rowing boat was immediately impounded and $10,000 demanded for its release. The reason? Not having a cruising permit. The penalty was a thinly veiled excuse for extortion; international maritime law decreed a grace period be extended to any vessel experiencing mechanical failure or in need of food, water, or medical assistance. It was at that point, realizing the financial hardship such an expense would put on his family, that Mick had decided to end his row around the world.

The scare stories gave us pause enough to request a meeting with the British ambassador to East Timor, Tina Redshaw. Could she have a word with her Indonesian counterpart, we asked, to raise awareness of our presence in the region? It was the level of the common foot soldier we were most worried about, the nervous, trigger-happy virgin armed with an assault rifle. The ambassador replied that she didn't know anyone at the Indonesian Embassy. This seemed unlikely. It was her business to. "You should go and speak to them yourselves," she added impatiently.

"We do," I replied. "Every single day."

She then fobbed us off with some guff about The UK Mission in

East Timor needing to concentrate its efforts on developing trade relations, not the holiday plans of a few adventuresome tourists, and sent us on our way.

If the threat of being shot or beheaded wasn't enough to put the wind up us, there were the stories circulated by local sailors of the notorious selats, of tidal streams running at twelve knots, of riptides and whirlpools that could suck a boat down in seconds. Even if we succeeded in getting the kayaks across the border, our chances of surviving the first selat crossing to the island of Alor were slim.

The fears, they just kept coming.

A week later

"I'M GONNA TRY to keep to your rhythm," said Chris, air-paddling slowly and deliberately, demonstrating the ideal stroke. "Which basically means you have to have *some* sort of a rhythm, yeah?"

We were in the port authority warehouse, getting acquainted with our beautiful new kayaks: a burgundy Current Designs Libra XT tandem and a green and a yellow single-person Solstice GT. The boats were fast through the water, durable enough to withstand months of being hauled up and down coral sand beaches, and spacious enough to carry food and water for up to a fortnight without resupply. Chris was sitting in the rear cockpit of the double, giving Ina her first lesson.

"You can't kinda, go like that"—Chris took a half-hearted stroke, stopped, and looked gormlessly into thin air—"and then go, 'Oh yeah, I think I'll have another one now'." He took a stroke on the same side. "And go like that, and say, 'Hmmm, I'll have one on the other side now', do you know what I mean? 'Cos that'll be difficult for me sitting behind you. I'll be going like this"—he waved his paddle back and forth in a discombobulated, jerky motion—"Oooh, umm, eerrrr …"

Ina started to giggle. A newcomer to kayaking, the mother of two had volunteered to paddle as far as Kalabahi on Alor, filling in until April arrived. She was the right shape for kayaking—short and muscular—and spoke Bahasa Indonesian fluently. Her language skills would be invaluable for our first critical days in Indonesia.

"It'll be too messy," Chris continued, paddling smoothly again. "We need to be like … one two, one two, one two."

"Like in the army," said Ina matter-of-factly. Most of her early adult life had been spent in the jungle, fighting the occupying forces that invaded her country in 1975. She'd suffered the same hardships as the men. At one point, besieged on a hillside with nothing to eat, she and her platoon had resorted to cannibalizing the body of an Indonesian soldier they'd killed. Ina had been captured, imprisoned, and tortured with burning before independence came in 1999.

"And Ina," said Chris, still paddling, "If you hear this sound"—he made a cracking noise like a whip—"it means you're not doing it properly."

Ina clenched her teeth and looked scathingly at him. "Hey, mongrel, I will kick you in the balls, okay?"

Lourdes and I were both watching. "You've got that drum as well, haven't you, Chris?" I said, winking.

"Oh yeah. The bongo drum." Chris tucked the paddle under his arm and started beating out an imaginary rhythm with both hands. "When I get tired, I'm just going to stop paddling and bang my drum."

"So *I'm* doing all the paddling?" said Ina, eyebrows raised.

"If we need to go faster, I'll start going *boom, boom, boom, boom.*"

Ina smiled thinly and gave Chris the finger.

"And if you see a shark," Chris went on, keeping a straight face. "You know when your heart beats, it goes *boom … boom … boom*. When you see a shark, it goes *BOOM! BOOM! BOOM!* That's the speed." He whirled his paddle like an eggbeater. "Your heartbeat sets the pace for paddling."

Now coming up on three weeks stalled in Dili, such comic interludes were a rarity. Tensions between team members had been rising steadily as we waited for a letter from the Indonesian Embassy, stamped by the ambassador himself, to better our chances of getting across the border. Even after umpteen meetings and bottles of Claymore Scotch Whisky pushed under various desks, there was still no sign of the promised paperwork.

Things came to a head the day before our planned departure. In the morning, Ina informed us that the elusive letter still hadn't materialized. For Lourdes, this was the last straw.

"I've had enough of all this!" she exploded. "I've been waiting around in Darwin and Dili for too long. And to be *completely* honest, I'm used to having my own adventures, so it's absolutely no skin off my nose to go off and do my own thing."

The expedition was already falling apart. To clear the air, we paid a visit to an orphanage set up by Ina and her Australian husband, Isa. Nestled in the foothills above Dili, the Hope Orphanage cared for twenty-six children whose parents had either been killed by Indonesian soldiers pre-1999 or had since died of disease such as tuberculosis.[*] Several of the children themselves were lucky to be alive. Five-year-old Moisses had been left for dead with his head cleaved open after his mother and father were hacked to death with machetes. And Dulcita, a pretty nine-year-old girl, still lived with the emotional and physical trauma of being raped by soldiers when she was only four.

Taking us by the hand, the children led us on a tour of their home, including the vegetable garden where they grew their own food. We learned many things during the course of the day, but one thing in particular was impressed upon us. For these orphans to be as level-headed

---

[*] Amnesty International estimated 200,000 out of a total population of 700,000 were killed between 1975 and 1986, leaving half of East Timor's remaining population under the age of fifteen.

as they were considering all they'd been through, we had absolutely nothing to complain about.

That evening, back in Dili, I received a message from Ina to come to a meeting with the head of immigration for East Timor, a last ditch effort—so I assumed—to contrive the all-important paperwork. I was given instructions to wear a smart shirt, long trousers, and black shoes, and be waiting outside the Venture Hotel at seven o'clock. *Funny time for a meeting*, I thought. *Government offices would have been closed for hours.*

By seven thirty, there was still no sign of Ina's red jeep. I was about to bail when a Mercedes with blacked-out windows slowed to a stop on the opposite side of the street. I waited for something to happen: a door to open, a window to roll down.

Nothing.

A few seconds later, the car pulled away as quietly as it had arrived.

INDONESIA
THE BORDER AT BATUGADE

I get by with a little help from my friends.
—JOHN LENNON

I LIKE THE INDONESIA people, the food, the islands." Ina made a face as she tied her hair up in a business-like bun. "But I *hate* the government."

We were standing in the jungle next to a battered office desk, the only indication we were about to leave East Timor and enter the sensitive, demilitarized zone that denoted the border. A smiling immigration officer opened our passports one by one, thumbed his way to a blank page, and wielded his exit stamp like an auctioneer's hammer.

Chris, looking spectacularly out of place in a flowery blue Brighton-friendly shirt, grinned, and said, "Ina, have you ever thought about getting a job with the Indonesian tourist board?"

For once, I wasn't in the mood for Chris's wry humour. Five security checkpoints over the mile of no-man's land separated us from West Timor, and hidden in our kayaks was enough electronic equipment to raise a giant red flag to journalist-wary security personnel. In spite of this, and the added worry that we still didn't have a letter from the Indonesian Embassy, Ina seemed confident. "Just trust me on this, Jase," she said. "Let me do the talking, okay?"

How could she be so sure, though? The leg to Singapore was forfeit if our boats and gear were confiscated.

Accompanied by an armed escort of three East Timorese soldiers, we started walking towards the West Timor side. Milling goats bleated half-heartedly in the afternoon heat. Cockerels crowed. A gaggle of youths pushing rubber-wheeled carts followed close behind, transporting the kayaks and the rest of our gear for the six-month journey through the island chain: desalinator pump, water filter, saucepans, frying pan, kettle, mosquito domes, sleeping bags, a hundred pounds of dried food and two hundred litres of water (enough for eleven days), laptop, solar panels, master batteries for the electronics, two camcorders, a hundred DV CAM video cassettes, still camera, sixty rolls of slide film, fishing line, epoxy resin, fibreglass sheeting, McMurdo Personal Location Beacons, and eight flares.

After two hundred yards, Ina stiffened. Five men standing beside the track were staring at her. "Militia," she breathed. "These people, they kill my family."

The story of her wedding day was like nothing any of us had ever heard. The year was 1991. Ina had been out buying film for her camera when three truck loads of militia carrying death lists and machetes arrived at her family home in Dili. The bride-to-be returned a little while later to a scene of unimaginable horror. Unable to scale the high walls of the compound, more than twenty members of the wedding party had been rounded up and hacked to death, her brother and bridesmaids among them.

We walked on towards a sign that read, "Selamat Datang di Indonesia." Welcome to Indonesia. Then, our first checkpoint: maritime police. My heart was thumping.

The police just smiled and waved us through.

Next came the army checkpoint. Again, nothing. Just big toothy grins and fluttering hands gesturing to continue.

Something wasn't right. Not a single question had been asked of us. No one had demanded any paperwork, money, or even a cigarette. It was green lights all the way. We sailed through customs, immigration, and arrived at a sign with a fluorescent light strip underneath reading "POS POLISI MOTA'AIN." This was our final checkpoint: the notorious Republican National Police. Three officials in grey shirts and dark trousers lounged behind a wooden desk at the back of a tin shed.

They leapt to their feet upon seeing us. One, "Y, WASAN – POLISI" according to his nametag, reached forward to give Ina a fawning handshake. Another, "FERDINAN DT," offered Chris a cigarette, before insisting they had their picture taken together.

"Wow," Lourdes whispered to me. "That's all I can say."

"I know. Weird, isn't it?"

"Pretty incredible." She laughed nervously. "This whole thing …"

A cringing underling stamped our passports as fast as he could.

"Is it coming good?" I said to Ina.

She smiled. "Yeah, it's coming good. Thanks to Bambang."

"Bang, bang? As in gun?"

"No, Bambang, the president."

"Of what?"

"Indonesia, of course."

I stared at her. "You mean, Susilo Bambang Yudhoyono?"

She shrugged, meaning yes. "Bambang. He make everything easier."

Clearly, there was more to this freedom fighter than she had let on.

Escorted by "FERDINAN DT," and "S. ARIS," we walked the three hundred yards to the beach, palm trees rustling above us in the onshore breeze.

"Well, that was a cinch, wasn't it?" murmured Chris.

By the time we reached the water's edge, now dragging our kayaks, a crowd of inquisitive villagers had gathered. A toothless old woman pushed her way to the front and grabbed our hands in turn, pumping them vigorously. She was jabbering incoherently, bowing deeply, and baring her gums in excitement. When she got to Ina, the crowd whooped with approval.

"Ina," I said. "What's going on? Who *are* you, really?"

"Oh, just someone who is trying to help you guys. Help your expedition."

"But not just anyone gets through a border like that."

She paused. "You remember the night you waited outside the hotel?"

I nodded.

"That was my father in the car."

"Your father?"

"He wanted to see how the guy leading this expedition look like. Make sure he's not a mongrel." She winked at me. "He phone Bambang.

Ask to take care of me."

"Who is he?" I asked. But deep down, I already knew.

PADDLING AWAY FROM the beach and the shrieking people, Ina explained the mystery of the elusive letter from the Indonesian Embassy, including the last-minute refusal. Once Susilo Bambang got involved, the whole affair had become too high level for either Pak Hendarsin or the ambassador himself. If anything had gone wrong, their necks were on the line.

It occurred to me then how this particular border crossing had taken the form of a real-life version of Dungeons and Dragons. Some of the characters encountered in the fantasy role-play game were helpful. Others tried to trick you and take you for all you were worth. From the moment the expedition arrived in East Timor, Ina had held the key to the magic door that allowed us to advance to the next stage of the journey. All we'd needed to do was to close our eyes, surrender control, and step into the abyss of not knowing.

WE'D PADDLED TWELVE miles, almost two-thirds of the way across Selat Ombai, when Lourdes spotted the warship. From a distance, it looked almost triangular, very different to the oil tanker we'd seen earlier with its gleaming white bridge and three tall gantries.

"Indonesian," said Ina, partially lifting her head. She was seasick, slumped over her cockpit in a cloth hat and purple shirt. Shortly after leaving the beach at Maubara, she'd up-chucked her breakfast. The former guerrilla was clearly more at home in the jungle than on the briny.

Chris was in the back of the Libra, holding his paddle to his chest and peering into the glare. "How can you tell?" he asked.

Ina twisted her head to take another look. "The colour. American is one colour: green. Indonesia: camouflage."

Sure enough, as the vessel drew closer, a collage of grey, blue, and charcoal blotches took shape against the cobalt sky. This was alarming. If intercepted, we had some serious explaining to do. To make the fastest passage to Alor, we'd re-entered East Timorese waters illegally, paddling back up the coast to the shortest crossing point at Maubara.

"Okay, guys!" Ina was suddenly upright and alert. "Can we paddle to land, please? If they come this way, we dead."

We'd been lucky up till this point. The conditions were ideal: a gentle rolling swell and the wind light. Averaging two-and-a-half knots, we'd reached the halfway point over slack water and were on schedule to complete the seventeen-mile crossing in the optimum timeframe of seven hours. Aside from one patch of broken water, there was no sign of the half-mile-wide, eight-knot tidal rips that Jim from the Dive Centre in Dili had warned about. "With my seventeen knots," he'd told us, "I can keep going. But in a kayak, you'll be swept east or west, depending on what the tide's doing."

With the appearance of the warship, fatigue vanished instantly. We leaned into our stroke, which itself posed a risk, a random glint off a paddle blade enough to give us away. The coastline of Alor drew near in agonizing slow motion. Bit by bit, emerald curtain folds of impossibly steep valleys emerged vibrant and tropical beneath clouded peaks, spilling down to the water's edge where the surf crashed ominously.

Glancing anxiously over our shoulders, we aimed for one of the smaller valleys with two light-coloured cliffs at the bottom. A rocky beach comprised of fist-sized stones rose up to meet us, beyond which a wall of seemingly impenetrable foliage panned left and right. I saw movement. Naked children ran screaming from the water, pissing themselves with fear. Gabbling women with infants propped on their hips melted into the bush. It was only after we'd made a precarious landfall in the heavy surf, and Ina assured a few hostile-looking men that we meant no harm, that the blinking villagers re-emerged.

The four of us slumped exhausted on the beach and deliberated how we would manhandle the heavily laden kayaks over the rocks without them being damaged. As if on cue, a sea of hands belonging to some twenty whooping villagers appeared, and in one fluid manoeuvre, our kayaks were lifted shoulder high and spirited above the high-tide mark to a bed of black shingle under a splendid shade tree. We followed with our paddles, Ina translating how the little round stones were sorted by the women and sold to the Japanese for 50,000 rupiah a sack, a little under $6. The only other way the village generated money for buying goods was to boil seawater for salt.

Word quickly spread. Within minutes, the entire village, which went by the name of Pureman, had turned out to watch us make camp. Women fingered the fabric of Lourdes's tent and clucked at the wood-less stove that could bring water to boil in a matter of minutes. The younger kids giggled at the sight of Chris blowing up his air mattress and yelped with delight when the poles of his bug hut snapped magically together. For the men, experienced fishermen who'd spent their entire lives on the water, it was our kayaks that caused the most stir. When they weren't craning their necks into the compartments and muttering, "Carga, carga," they were caressing and prodding the fibre-glass hulls. Compared to their wooden dugouts, our plastic boats must have seemed like interstellar spacecraft.

"We're the zoo animals for a change," said Chris, smiling at the ranks of pop-eyed children perched in the branches above our heads. It was true. The conventional image of tourists goggling at locals had been well and truly reversed.

Having inspected how the mysterious rudders worked, the old timers turned their attention to the Admiralty chart I had folded in a map case tied to my cockpit. Each of them possessed an intimate knowledge of their coastline, mental mapping imprinted and refined since early childhood, yet this was clearly the first time any of them had seen a diagrammatic representation of their three-dimensional universe. Taking turns using a pair of grimy spectacles, they pored over the contours, their leathery faces creased in concentration as they mouthed the names of features they recognized: Selat Pantar ... Alor Kecil ...

Suddenly, there was a commotion. The crowd peeled back to reveal a red-toothed man, his charcoal frizz peppered with grey curls, who stood scowling at us. This was the village chief, the kepala kampung. Without more ado, the big man planted himself cross-legged between our tents and pulled out a small woven basket from the folds of his brown lava-lava. When I saw what was inside, my heart sank. The last time I'd tried betel nut was in the Solomon Islands, five years earlier. My throat had swollen so badly I was certain I was having an anaphylactic reaction. But how could I refuse the chief's hospitality without causing offence?

Taking the smallest segment on offer, I slipped the rubbery nut inside my cheek along with a pinch of lime and started to chew. The chief watched intently.

"Mmmmh." I rubbed my tummy theatrically. "Delicious!"

In reality, my tongue had gone numb and bile was rising in my throat. There was none of the mild euphoria I'd been led to expect. I turned to Chris and grimaced.

"How is it, then?" He smirked.

"Can't really speak right now," I mumbled. "The stuff made me gag in the Solomons, and it's making me gag again."

Lourdes tried next. At first, her face wrinkled like a prune, but she kept at it, and soon a crimson residue was forming around her lips, proof that she was doing it properly. She wiped her mouth, leaving a red smear on the back of her hand, prompting chuckles from the chief and shrieks of approval from the villagers. And when she bared her teeth and used her fingers to streak her cheeks as if with war paint, the place erupted.

The chief gave us a short history lesson of the island and made a point of impressing upon us that Pureman was home to the first King of Alor—which struck me as unlikely. A long tradition of headhunting and endemic inter-village violence had made communities in the region suspicious of each other (the reason, presumably, our sudden arrival had produced such hysteria—maybe the villagers thought we were stopping by in our space-age dugouts to bag a few heads?) As a result, villages were entirely autonomous of each other, as indicated by the number of languages spoken in the archipelago, with over seventy on Alor alone.*

We served the chief tea and biscuits and presented him with a handful of incense, fishhooks, and a souvenir card with our names and photographs set against a map of Indonesia marked with our route. Gift exchange would be an almost daily ritual throughout our travels in Indonesia. In return, one of the chief's wives brought us a dozen hens eggs and a small square of traditionally woven tais.

Later, after the villagers had drifted back to their huts, a young man began leaping around outside our tents, a machete in one hand and bow in the other. He had a clutch of arrows thrust through the waistband of his lava-lava, and his head was bound with a purple sash. Meanwhile, three masked percussionists pounded on gongs the size of manhole covers. A full-on ceremonial welcome was underway.

More musicians arrived and set up a row of bronze moko drums, legendary instruments brought from Vietnam in the fifth century BCE. The drums were beautifully engraved with frogs, snakes, monkeys, elephants, warriors, dragons, and other mythical creatures, illustrating how animist faiths had permeated Southeast Asian cultures down the ages. Even today, all social strata from Papua New Guinea

---

* An average of one every fifteen square miles.

to Myanmar privately subscribe to the belief that natural phenomena, including plants and even inanimate objects, are endowed with a soul, a superstition that underpins even the relative newcomers of Christianity, Islam, Buddhism, and Hinduism. Alor was no exception.

The chief was back, barefoot and smiling, and wearing a green floral shirt and a length of tais draped over his right shoulder. He had ten wives in tow, sombre-faced women ranging in age from sixteen to sixty, wearing purple tube dresses with red, white, and black stripes. Taking his place at the front of the line, the chief began a slow, shambling dance, a sort of sideways conga affair. He brandished a switch of dried reeds as he shuffled, his wives tramping after him with their arms linked. They all had red blossoms shaped like dragons in their hair and a miniature basket on their forehead woven with beads hanging down around their necks.

The drummers upped the tempo, and the dancers picked up the pace, hoofing it back and forth. Finding his groove, the chief swatted the air and made occasional frisky leaps like The Pied Piper of Hamelin. The grinning young man—surely one of the chief's sons—continued to prance, drawing an occasional arrow at the sky. And all the while the dancers chanted a high-pitched melody, not unlike the falsetto of the Native American Indians I remembered from the Canton Lake pow-wow in Oklahoma.

As the light faded, the great mother tree cast a ghostly green light over the assembled gathering—the palpitating dancers, the goggling villagers, and us, the toe-tapping visitors. The chief and his wives were working themselves to a frenzied crescendo, crouching to their knees, writhing to and fro, and shaking their tais. It rounded off a thrilling introduction to Indonesia. We'd made it across the border and negotiated our first selat crossing without anyone being drowned or shot. After all the histrionics and derangement of Dili, we'd fallen firmly on our feet.

"INA, IF YOU get really cold again tonight," Chris was holding up his long johns, "you can borrow my thermal underwear, okay?" He twanged the elastic. "Grandpa Grunts Chicken Chasers."

Ina collapsed into giggles. "Keep them for yourself," she replied, " 'cos you're getting to that age, you know?"

We were camped on the southwest corner of Alor before turning north into Selat Pantar. Before us lay a sweeping bay of pristine sand, the first of the trip. Since Pureman, three days earlier, the beaches had all been rocks.

Ina pouted. "Chris, I'm gonna tell my father you sleep with me."

Chris raised his eyebrows. "Oh yeah?"

"If I'm pregnant, that's your problem."

It was another Ina leg-pull. She and Chris were constantly winding each other up.

"The immaculate conception," murmured Chris, sprinkling his breakfast noodles with salt from a film canister. "That'll be interesting. The second time in two thousand years."

I grinned. "What, you firing blanks or something, mate?"

"I'm not firing at all."

"Really? When was the last time you fired one?"

He winced. "Oh God. Two or three months ago? I'm going to have to find a firing range somewhere, I think."

"Maybe they've got one in Kalabahi?" I said.

"Yeah, I think they have, actually. It's called the Hotel Suzie."

Lourdes was meanwhile ferrying camping gear down to the low-tide mark. The biggest challenge so far had been just getting the kayaks afloat, as heavy as they were. First, they had to be dragged partly empty to the water's edge, where the bulk of the food, water, and equipment was staged close by. They then had to be loaded as quickly as possible, either before the tide came in and swept them away or receded and left them stranded. Most crucial of all was remembering where everything went. Every dry bag, saucepan, and toothbrush had its place like a jigsaw puzzle.

By seven, we were packed and ready to catch the flood tide heading north through the selat. All four sets of hands were needed to manhandle the cumbersome Libra into the shallows. Ina hopped in the front, while Chris took a running start like a bobsleigh brakeman, jumping in at the last second. Lourdes and I then launched our own boats, and the group wheeled right-handed out of the bay and into the mouth of the narrow straits.

It was a day after new moon, and the spring tide was at its strongest, with the water flowing at nine knots. After thirty or so minutes of exhilarating progress, something up ahead caught my eye, a body of turbulent water surging off a black, volcanic headland. It was several hundred feet across, spiralling down to a single foaming eye. A whirlpool!

Retreating to a narrow slip of sand, we beached the boats, and Chris and Lourdes took off on foot to scope out the situation. Ina and I stayed put with the gear.

"Jase, do you think we'll get to Kalabahi today?" Ina was sitting with her head in her hands, staring gloomily at the water.

This was likely to be our last day together. Once we reached the principal town of Kalabahi farther up the selat, Ina would return home by ferry. We would miss her teasing, even her bossiness. And she had done the expedition proud getting us plus the kayaks through the border.

"Depends on this whirlpool," I replied. "We have to wait for things to calm down a bit first. Hopefully, though."

Ina lapsed into brooding silence. She was desperate to get to Kalabahi. A week away from her family had been quite enough adventure for her.

Chris and Lourdes reappeared a little while later, arguing as they approached. "No, no, no," Chris was saying. "I don't think we should head out into the channel. I think we can stick to the coast till we get there, 'cos it's really mellowed out, hasn't it?"

Lourdes held up her hands. "You know what? You just decide what you want, Chris, 'cos I'm not interested anymore."

By the time they'd finished quarrelling, the whirlpool was gone. It was now slack water, the transition between high and low tides. We relaunched the boats and continued, passing the dormant volcanic cone of Kabupaten Alor in the middle of the straits, and turned northeast into a lozenge-shaped inlet dotted with bamboo fishing platforms big enough to house entire families. With her journey's end in sight, Ina was transformed, pulling eagerly ahead like a barn-sour horse.

Chris was similarly inspired. "Kalabahi, here we come!" he cried. "We've only been out, what, six days? Feels like a month already."

Sense of time isn't the only thing to be distorted by travel. A week away from civilization, and even the distant *pata-pat-pat* of an outboard motor sounded like an evil, corrupting thing, and the amplified wail of competing muezzins grated horribly. The evening call to prayer came floating out across the water from several steel-domed mosques, the first real indication we were now in the world's most Islamicized country.

At the head of the inlet, farthest from the reach of the tide, the sea was clogged with bobbing detritus flung from houses packed cheek-by-jowl along the waterfront. We aimed for a lone bungalow with a yellow roof to enquire if there might be a cheap place to stay the night.

"Wouldn't it be amazing if it was a losmen," I said to Lourdes, "with somewhere to put our boats?" Losmen were the cheapest accommodation option in Indonesia, costing only a few dollars a night.

This was the downside of arriving in a new town with kayaks. We were looking forward to washing off the salt, knocking back a few beers, and eating different food. But where do you park a twenty-one-foot boat?

Lourdes laughed. "Oh yeah, that would be almost *too* easy."

It turned out to be one better. A few days earlier on the south side of the island, we'd crossed paths with a motorboat skippered by a Frenchman who introduced himself as the regional manager for Médecins Sans Frontières. Jeremy was part of an international team of physicians hosting malaria clinics in remote villages. By happy coincidence, the bungalow was their central office.

"Eez really no problem," said Jeremy, wading into the shallows to help unload our kayaks. "You can leave your boats in the front garden if you want. We have 24-hour guard. No one will touch zem. I promise."

Nusa Tenggara
Zombies, Spats & Sea Serpents

That old black magic has me in its spell.
—Johnny Mercer

L EAVING THE CORRODED TIN roofs of Larantuka and its green-peaked volcano in our wake, we paddled north, past a clanking boat yard, the usual posse of mangy dogs, and children shrieking at us from the beach. The water in the narrow selat was surging south at seven knots, but close to shore the current was more forgiving, allowing us to make slow but steady headway.

I slipped in beside the double. "How do you feel, April?"

"I'm excited," she replied, shivering in the early morning chill. She wore a baseball cap, wrap-around shades, and blue spandex top. "It feels good to get going, get my sea legs under me, as it were."

Two days earlier, she'd caught up with us in Larantuka, exhausted after a gruelling five-day journey from Colorado: two on a plane to Bali via Seoul and Singapore and three more on ramshackle buses across the island of Flores. While the rest of us scoured the town for supplies, the schoolteacher had recovered in the delightful Hotel Rulies surrounded by pink bougainvillea, abundant shade trees, and bad-tempered Dutch women glaring down at her from the peeling walls.

"So, do you think you'll be seasick this time?" I asked, voicing the question I knew was on both our minds.

She wrinkled her nose. "No, I don't think so."

Despite her ordeal on the Coral Sea five years earlier, April was keen to join another waterborne leg of the expedition. She'd spent six months researching Indonesia for the schools following online, compiling a wealth of teaching materials that included the region's volatile plate tectonics and resulting volcanism, the diverse flora and fauna, and the colourful and at times bloody history of the spice trade and colonization by the Dutch.

Around the headland of Cape Matangdu, the sea became steep and confused, giving us the impression of paddling nowhere. It took more than an hour of hard effort to reach calmer water. Then we had a long, sloggy stretch without a break, the crashing surf making landfall impossible. After three hours, April admitted to feeling queasy.

"It's okay." She smiled. "It's all part of the learning curve. I just ate a bit of apple and that helped."

"If it's any consolation," I said, "I've been feeling a bit nauseous myself. It's the swell coming from astern, I think."

We pressed on. The clouds cleared, and the sun took centre stage, glittering off the heaving sea. Another hour went by with nowhere to land, just black volcanic rock and frothing spume, not a grain of sand in sight. April's first day in a kayak was turning out to be another baptism by fire.

"Jason!" Chris called out. "April needs a rest."

"I know," I replied. "But we can only rest people if we can get them to shore safely."

As a stopgap, we rafted up with the Libra sandwiched between the two singles and took a five-minute breather to grab a snack and some water.

"Just from here," April observed, turning to look at the foaming rollers pounding the shore, "there doesn't seem to be much."

Around noon, a slip of yellow appeared beside another headland marked on the chart as Tanjung Kari. I paddled over to take a closer look. As I drew near, the beach disappeared under a series of boomers. One of these picked up my kayak and hurled it forward. By the time I realized that what I'd assumed to be sand was actually light-coloured coral, jagged and deadly, it was too late to turn back. The Solstice hit the rocks with a sickening crunch and bounced over the coral like an aircraft skidding off a runway.

Clearly, it was not a suitable spot to make landfall in the Libra. Twice the surf knocked me down as I tried to turn my boat around and point it back out to sea. Breakers crashed over the hull, slamming the heavily laden mass into my shins. *If I break one of my ankles out here*, I thought, *I'm screwed.* Ignoring the cockpit half-filled with water, I jumped in, secured my spray skirt as best I could, and thrust with my hips and poled with my paddle to push the kayak off the beach. The first wave swallowed the kayak and me whole. The second pushed the bow almost vertical. My stomach did a flip, and the kayak shot forward, slicing through the back of the five-foot roller.

"I've got an idea," said Chris after I'd rejoined the group. "We could backtrack towards that last headland and see if—"

"No," I snapped. The episode on the beach had left me shaken and my kayak likely damaged. Looking around, there was nothing but rollers as far as the eye could see. "We should keep going," I said firmly. "The last thing we need is to go backwards."

Besides, I thought, *April's the toughest person I know. She can handle it.*

For the next hour, either the surf remained too high or the rocky beach was exposed by low tide. The wind picked up, and the swell increased. April, now seasick and enervated, threw up. I examined my chart in growing desperation. Six miles up the coast, a protuberance stuck out like a tiny penis from the belly-shaped contour of the Flores coastline. With the wind from the southeast, our best chance of finding shelter was on the lee side.

By 4:30 pm, we'd been in the boats for more than ten hours. We rounded the nub of land and there, mercifully, the water was calm and a perfect camping spot presented itself in the form of a sandy beach with a large shade tree in the middle.

April was the first to disembark, re-enacting her Lizard Island arrival with a neat pirouette and matching arse plant. The first priority after unloading the boats was to light a fire for hot, sweet, resuscitating black tea. But as was to happen often in the coming weeks and months, we were beaten to it by a smiling local stepping out of the bushes holding a fresh coconut.

"Oh, gosh," said April, raising the football-sized nut to her mouth and drawing deeply. "That is *sooo* good."

The next day would have to be a maintenance day. My crash-landing on the coral beach had torn a four-inch-long gash in the front of my boat, flooding the bow compartment and drenching various battery chargers, including the one for my laptop and the camcorders. Of far greater concern, though, was the damage to my kayak.

"Pretty bad," said Chris, picking at a loose flap of fibreglass with his fingernails, "but repairable."

We had epoxy resin and fibreglass sheeting, but no brushes to apply the resin. With the nearest marine store a thousand miles away in Darwin, Chris set to improvising. He scavenged a few dried-out coconut husks from the beach, tore out the longest fibres, and bound them into a set of single-use paintbrushes.

In many ways, acquiring locally made dugouts after crossing into Indonesia would have been cheaper and easier than importing plastic boats. The thick wooden hulls of indigenous craft were better suited to being hauled up and down rocky beaches, and being made of native materials, they were easily repaired or even replaced outright. The downside to dugouts was they were slow and cumbersome; whenever locals challenged us to a race, we beat them easily. During the planning process, I'd decided the key to reaching Singapore in one piece was to cross the swift-moving selats as quickly as possible, using slack tides to our advantage. This was the trade-off of carbon Kevlar, fiberglass, and a tapered hull. Speed and stability were optimized at the expense of strength and serviceability.

While the sheets of fibreglass soaked in epoxy, we caught up on chores. Using a sailor's palm, an upholstery needle, and dental floss, I reattached a strap on my sandal that had torn while re-launching from the coral beach the previous day. April sat nearby transposing a handwritten update to the laptop, surrounded by thirty or so adrenalized children.

"Eighty-three," she said, holding up a hand. "What comes after eighty-three?"

"Seven," a boy answered confidently. The rest pranced and chattered and took turns wrestling on Chris's sleeping mat. A tiny crab appeared at April's feet.

"Ooooh!" she exclaimed. "A crab!"

The children imitated her. "Cab! Cab! Cab!" they chanted.

The next morning, our twenty-ninth since leaving Dili, we were on the water by first light. The air was cool. Tendrils of smoke rose from villages slumbering in the dense foliage lining the shore. The north coast of Flores was a paddler's paradise. Bone-white beaches stretched for miles without a soul in sight, underscoring a brilliant azure sky broken only by cotton spindles leaking from the rugged crowns of smouldering volcanoes. Sheltered from the southeast trades largely by the island's topography, the sea around us remained tranquil. We slipped soundlessly over a universe of glass, peering down through a pellucid prism at the flitting fish and shimmering coral. Limestone bluffs festooned with creepers rose sheer out of the water, their jagged forms towering for hundreds of feet before dropping away to yet another stunning sweep of ivory sand.

It was at one of these idyllic beaches, overlooking a cluster of giant mushroom-shaped rocks sculpted by the rise and fall of the tide, that we stopped for lunch and to snorkel the reef. For April, this was another first. Lourdes demonstrated how to fit her mask and to practise breathing through the snorkel before venturing into deeper water.

From the beach, I watched this happy interlude with growing relief. After a rocky start, April was enjoying her first nausea-free day on the briny since rounding the western edge of Guadalcanal five years before. And it would only get better, I was certain of it. Unlike blue water crossings where the fabric of daily life changes little, kayaking through an island archipelago promised a steady stream of new and exciting experiences. Each island was like its own planetary universe, with unique shorelines, unique paddling conditions, unique languages, and unique religions. The flora and fauna changed constantly, too, shifting by degrees the nearer we got to the legendary Wallace Line between Lombok and Bali, marking the convergence of the Indo-Australian and Eurasian tectonic plates.*

But, of course, I should have suspected that things were going too well. By the time we reached Maumere, five days later, the expedition was on the verge of falling apart.

CHRIS PAUSED FOR a moment to gather his thoughts before launching in. "I think you're becoming quite headstrong about 'let's get west at all costs'."

I held his gaze. "Oh yeah?"

Chris, Lourdes, April, and I were sitting in the foyer of the losmen closest to the water in Maumere, airing grievances that had been building since Dili. Outside the window, a woman padded back and forth with armfuls of dripping laundry, adding to a line of clothes drying on a metal railing.

"Yeah, which is not a bad dynamic to have, but I think sometimes you have your own idea of how far you want everyone to get." Unshaven and sun burned, Chris leaned back against the wicker couch and crossed his legs. "And I think what you have a tendency to do is make us *feel* like it's a democratic process by sharing the smaller decisions, but actually the big decisions need to be shared as well."

His words had a familiar ring to them, reminding me of what Mike Roney had voiced in one of his video diary entries on the Australian leg: *I think this leadership day is a paper tiger. It really doesn't give me the ability*

---

* A hypothetical line proposed by the English naturalist, Alfred Russel Wallace, the Wallace Line symbolizes the demarcation between Oriental and Australian zoogeographical regions. To the west, Asian animals such as monkeys predominate, to the east, marsupials.

to lead as I'm used to. And it's driving me insane. Perhaps it was true. Maybe
I only gave the impression that decisions were being made democrati-
cally, whereas in reality I was the one always calling the shots. Earlier
in the trip, following a disagreement about whether or not to continue
around a particular headland, Chris had accused me of being "dictato-
rial and bullish," a tyrant who demanded "my way or the highway."

"Like what decisions?" I said guardedly.

"Well, about our itinerary," Chris replied, "and about how far we're
going to go each day."

For the first time, Lourdes nodded. "That's true," she said.

They were correct on this point. I did have my own idea of how far
I wanted the group to get each day. This was an expedition, after all,
not a holiday.

"Look," I said, "our target mileage isn't something I just pull out of
thin air for the hell of it." I went on to point out that every thirty days
we were required to renew our SosBud visas at a preset immigration
point. What was more, the expedition needed to reach Singapore before the monsoon shifted and the winds and currents turned against us.

Chris brought up his next point. "Then there's the whole issue of
filming." He had to raise his voice to be heard above the sound of pigs
squealing in the background. "Two or three times on April's first day,
we sat bobbing around in that huge swell waiting for the wind to pick
up, not knowing what you were up to. I felt that was bad judgment. I
felt, considering the circumstances, that we were potentially in a very
dangerous situation."

This I couldn't deny. In Kenny's absence, I tended to overdo the
filming, falling behind to do a piece to camera or shoot cutaways. Even
when we were together, the decision of what point to switch the camera
off wasn't always clear-cut.

"The thing is," I said, gesturing to the camera April was using to record our exchange. "Often the most engaging footage is when things go

wrong. What do you do when the shit hits the fan? Deal with the situation or film it? I appreciate what you're saying, though, Chris. Maybe my judgment wasn't what it should have been that day."

"No, it wasn't!" he replied sharply, before going on to express how he didn't want to be fodder for my journalistic intentions, which he often didn't agree with, anyway. "If you want to hang back and keep us all waiting in those kinds of conditions, I actually think that's a biggie that needs to be shared with us, like, 'Guys, do you mind?' or 'Do you feel comfortable doing this?' Because if I'd have been asked, I would have said, 'No, I don't'."

"But Chris, don't you think that those decisions will always be somewhat related to your comfort zone and that perh—"

"No! I don't think—"

"Excuse me, can I talk?"

He held up his hands. "Sure, okay."

Lourdes was keeping quiet. Like me, she was more of a risk-taker, and being the most experienced kayaker in the group, capable of long paddling days.

"We all have different comfort levels," I said, "and while I appreciate that decisions should take into consideration the person who is the least comfortable—the lowest common denominator, as I think you called it, Chris—sometimes I feel that you're *overly* cautious."

This really got his goat, and the argument became even more heated. Just when it looked like all was lost and our fellowship was about to implode, Chris managed to pull back from the edge with one of his quips.

"I don't know about anyone else," he said, looking at each of us in turn, "but everything downstairs has kind of shut down." He nodded at his groin. "I've stopped waking up with a stiffy. And that's worrying."

There were no supermarkets in Maumere, only Chinese shops filled with tins of mackerel and sacks of monosodium glutamate (MSG), the universal flavour enhancer used extensively (as we were to find out) throughout the archipelago. Needing to stock up on supplies, we rolled up our sleeves and took to the dusty streets, dodging the honking trucks, beeping mopeds, and jabbering yokels visiting from the hinterland. Local women sat beside open drains clogged with rubbish, presiding over palm fronds buried under piles of cucumbers, carrots, onions, chillies, radishes, pineapples, garlic, tomatoes, bananas, bok choy, eggs, fresh fish, squid, and elegant mounds of spices. This re-provisioning exercise took all day, because everything had to be haggled over (limes 500 rupiah—three pence each), and living in a remote town that seldom saw outsiders, people stopped and gawked at April's blonde hair, further jamming the thoroughfare.

We left the next morning after visiting a secondary school, the SD Inpres Patisomba, to distribute pen pal letters. Following 9/11 and the Bali bombings, the expedition was better placed than ever to build bridges of understanding between children in the West and their Muslim counterparts in the East. The entire school of three hundred pupils came down to see us off, forming a giant Indonesian flag of red-and-white uniforms covering the beach. We finished packing surrounded by an amphitheatre of smiling faces, and it struck me then how very different our reception in Indonesia had been compared to what we were expecting. No crazy fundamentalists. Quite the opposite. We'd experienced nothing but warmth and hospitality since arriving, many people going out of their way in conversation to denounce the extremist element of their faith.

A few miles down the coast, with the voices of the kids still ringing in our ears ("Selamat Jalan! Baye baye!"), we paddled past a ragged stretch of shoreline stripped like a carcass, only the skeletons of palm trees remaining. We later learned it was the work of a tsunami that struck without warning in 1992. The coastline had been completely redrawn, rendering my chart all but useless, and 2,500 people drowned.

We all found this statistic rather unsettling. Not because a natural disaster had occurred—this was the Pacific Ring of Fire, after all, home to ninety per cent of the world's earthquakes and a total of four hundred and fifty-two volcanoes, making the region particularly susceptible to tidal waves. But while the 2004 tsunami that devastated Banda Aceh in northern Sumatra was well familiar to us, none of us had ever heard of this one.

A WEEK LATER, we paddled into the village of Riung to buy provisions, wading the last quarter of a mile to shore through raw sewage, a particular concern for April who had open sores on her feet and legs from scratching sand fly bites. Being a traditional Bugis village with the houses built on stilts, people just shat off the balconies and tipped their rubbish over at high tide, watching it all bob out to sea. Six hours later, when their backs were turned, it all washed back in.

Perched above the high-water mark was a two-storey wooden losmen with orange and green trim and a tin roof. The family lived upstairs, leaving paying guests to take their chances on the ground floor in the event of a tsunami. The rooms were closed, airless, and stinking with mildew. April and I opted to camp outside on the grass.

"Not top flight, by any means," she said, looking around for a clean spot to pitch a tent. "But it's traditional and that's"—she paused for a moment, choosing the words—"kinda cool."

By "not top flight" she was referring to the chicken shit, the cow shit, the gnawed corncobs tossed carelessly, the plastic wrappers, and the festering pools of sewage wriggling with mosquito larvae. Rusty oil drums smouldered with partially incinerated rubbish, giving off the stomach-turning stench of burning plastic. And from the corner of the open-air shower-cum-lavatory—the mandi, as it was known in

Indonesia—a narrow trench led to the mudflats carrying an evil tar-like substance too disgusting for words.

It was against this backdrop of unqualified decay that I had my second row with a group member, this time Lourdes, in the communal kitchen of the losmen the following morning.

Chris and Lourdes were discussing the attitudes of different cultures towards privacy, when I pulled up a chair and commented how it wasn't always clear-cut whether a local was being nosy or just trying to be helpful. "More often than not," I added, "we seem to end up giving people the benefit of the doubt."

"Well, you don't always have to," said Lourdes, giving the example of the young man with tricolour hair who'd followed her behind a bush outside Maumere. "I was trying to go to the bathroom, so I basically told him to get lost with my finger."

As she talked, three scraggy-looking chickens stalked through the open doorway, clucking cautiously.

"Right," I agreed. "But by the same token, the day before yesterday when that guy in the dugout paddled up to the beach just as we were about to have lunch, you didn't tell him to take a hike. As it turned out, all he wanted to do was collect some firewood and light a fire for us—which he did. Then he paddled away again. So it was good we didn't tell him to bugger off."

The chickens were under the table now, scratching for grubs.

"Well, I remember you weren't into him being there, either," said Lourdes.

"I wasn't. But I'm just making the point that it's hard for us to know the correct protocol when it comes to personal space. The locals here don't have the same idea of it as we do."

Lourdes blinked at me and said nothing. What I didn't realize at the time was how personal she was taking all of this, believing I was going out of my way to criticize her. As it turned out, the misinterpretation had rather more complicated origins. Lourdes, like Chris, felt I was becoming overbearing and autocratic, taking slim account for other people's wishes or opinions. The conversation therefore had nothing to do with how different cultures valued privacy. It was about me once again raining on Lourdes's parade.

"Well," she said, "you're not so perfect either, Mister *Around the World Traveller.* I mean, that same day I remember you weren't interested in him being there, and yet you did nothing!"

She was reiterating my point, but I sensed that it would only make things worse to point this out. In the space of a few minutes, the discussion had gone from harmless generalizations to character assassination. Instead, I said, "So what's this whole 'Mister Around the World Traveller' thing about?"

Lourdes rolled her eyes. "Oh no, you're not going to get into that, are you?"

Chris shifted uneasily in his seat, sensing what was to come.

"Well, what do you mean by that remark?" I said, feeling the irritation build in my voice. "If you have a problem with me, Lourdes, let's hear it."

She levelled her eyes at me and curled her lower lip. "Jason, I've had a problem with you since Australia."

This floored me. After all the tension between us in Dili, Lourdes and I were getting along much better—or so I thought. "So why didn't you tell me that things weren't okay?" I said.

"I wanted to give it a go and see how it went."

"Well, I'm getting tired of this shit, Lourdes, and to be honest, tired of travelling with you and your baggage."

The chickens remained unfazed.

Lourdes leaned forward on her elbows, fingers under her chin. "Oh, the feeling is *sooo* mutual, Jason. I've been tired of travelling with you since Darwin."

We'd passed the point of no return, and we both knew it. Slinging words around in the heat of the moment was one thing, but the exhumation of bitter secrets and pent-up grievances were things that couldn't easily be retracted.

"That's too bad," I said, feeling a sudden twinge of regret. "I actually had a good time with you on *Moksha.*"

Lourdes, too, became contrite. "I did, too," she admitted, pursing her lips.

"Well, let's just go our separate ways, then. Why draw out the agony?"

"You know what? That works for me, Jason. Where do you want me to leave the kayak?"

April and I set off that afternoon in the Libra, leaving Lourdes and Chris to paddle separately to Labuan Bajo on the western edge of Flores. Splitting temporarily into two groups was Chris's idea, an inspired solution to allow Lourdes to save face and avoid the bother of having to tow her kayak behind the double. There was a better chance of finding a replacement paddler in a tourist town like Labuan Bajo, where Lourdes could also catch a ferry to Bali.

Steering the nose of the Libra towards the twenty-three islands of Pulau Tujuhbelas marine park, one of which April and I planned to camp on overnight, I took to brooding. Was I really that difficult to travel with? Since childhood, I'd clashed with authority figures, an anti-establishment trait that no doubt led me to lock horns with Steve on the Atlantic, Mike Roney in Australia, and more recently, Chris. But Lourdes was one of the most easy-going people I'd ever met, a true minimalist owning little, entirely self-sufficient, asking nothing of anyone. No, the root of our disconnection had to lie elsewhere.

It was while passing a colony of squeaking fruit bats on one of the outlying islands—the sky was thick with them as they came in to roost, their furry brown bodies swarming the mangroves, bending the branches to impossible angles even as others funnelled into the air like chimney soot—that I worked it out. The logistics, the filming, the media, lobbying embassies for special permissions, all of this palaver made Lourdes deeply uncomfortable. "It's a croc of shit," I'd overheard her say on the beach in Dili, as she surveyed the mound of electronics to be loaded in the boats. If it was just her, she later admitted, she would have purchased a local boat and travelled light. No cameras. No laptop. No satellite phone. For the amount of attention they drew, even our fancy kayaks made her uneasy.

And so, without really knowing what she was getting into, Lourdes had been sucked into the expedition vortex, a multi-headed hydra trundling tornado-like across the surface of the world in all its various forms: education programmes, documentaries, press events, video diaries, blogging, and so forth. Not that it could be any other way. With the shameless self-promotion it took to keep going in lieu of sponsorship, the project had developed an insatiable appetite for recognition, gobbling up lives and attention in every country it traversed. This was what Lourdes had come to resent. It trampled on her most treasured tenet of travel, one that I'd once held in high esteem myself but since lost to the demands of technology.

Keeping it simple.

AHEAD OF US was the most beautiful islet either of us had ever seen, a tiny jut of windswept grass surrounded by pristine coral beaches. The whole thing measured less than a hundred by three hundred feet, an unsullied pearl set in the balmy waters of the Flores Sea. We made a circumnavigation, looking for signs of human habitation. There were none.

"Looks perfect," I hollered from the rear cockpit.

After the confrontations of the past weeks, it would be a quiet spot to decompress for a few days and not have to deal with anyone other than each other. Pulling the Libra ashore, April and I gathered driftwood to boil a pan of water, then clambered to the highest point, a limestone bluff with a three-sixty-degree panorama, and sat drinking our evening tea.

"And all is right with the world again," I murmured happily, gazing at the twenty-two other islands scattered like gems over a bed of blue velvet.

April smiled. "Yes, this is paradise."

We sat there until dark. When I finally rose to my feet, I heard something in the wind. "Did you hear that?" I said.

April nodded. "Like human voices."

"Almost like laughing."

"Yeah. Weird."

We scoured the island—it didn't take long. Were the voices coming from Riung? This seemed unlikely. Riung was eight miles away and the wind blowing in the wrong direction.

Back in camp, we resurrected the fire and boiled some noodles.

"Maybe we can sleep outside tonight," suggested April. "There don't seem to be any mosquitoes."

Nor would there be a problem with security, another reason we usually zipped ourselves in the tent every night, our passports and money wedged safely under our heads.

As we sat in the firelight, taking turns spooning from the pan, I watched a column of ants carry a moth to its subterranean doom. The insect was still very much alive, flailing its legs and fluttering its wings, and seeing its futile efforts I thought of frenzied Lilliputian hordes overcoming Gulliver, prompting a strange sense of foreboding to sweep through me.

After dinner, I fired up the GPS and was about to walk down to the water's edge for a clear signal when something moved at my feet. With its black-and-white-banded flanks, the five-foot snake was identical to one I'd seen while swimming in the Solomons. I pointed my headlamp at the flattened tail. "Banded sea krait," I said.

"Jeepers," replied April. "Are they venomous?"

"Highly. Ten times more so than a rattlesnake."

Flicking its tongue, the serpent slithered past and disappeared into the fleshy-leafed vegetation behind the Libra.

April breathed a sigh of relief. "Well, looks like he's not too interested."

"Rather knocks the idea of sleeping outside on the head, though, doesn't it?" I said.

After helping April set up the tent, I turned my attention back to the GPS. Every 24 hours, I sent our latitude and longitude position to my father as part of a date-time group in a satellite text message. The army protocol had become a nightly ritual, ensuring that if anything went wrong, someone would at least know where to start looking for us.

I heard a shout. "Oh, Jeez, there's another!" A snake with the same black and white markings was approaching from the opposite direction.

April laughed nervously. "What we don't know, of course, is what they eat to get so big."

"And then what eats the snakes," I said.

"Komodo dragons?"

This wasn't as far-fetched as it sounded. The same species of giant monitor lizard that inhabited the islands between Flores and Sumbawa a mere hundred miles to the west had been sighted around Riung. Our little island was too small to sustain a permanent population, but the dragons were strong swimmers and known to visit other islands in search of food.

A third snake suddenly appeared. I grabbed the video camera and began filming. "What is going *on?*" I said. Snakes gave me the heebie-jeebies almost as badly as spiders. "Why all these snakes all of a sudden?"

It didn't make sense. Sea kraits were extremely docile. Moreover, at first sight of a human, virtually every wild animal I'd ever come into contact with had turned tail and scarpered, millennia of extermination rendering them wary of engaging *Homo sapiens.* Why were these snakes taking such an interest in us?

"Third snake over here," I narrated for the camera. "Fourth snake over there." We were surrounded. Our enchanted island was becoming less so by the minute.

"No wonder this place is uninhabited," remarked April.

We found ourselves standing back to back in a defensive position. The snake in my viewfinder had turned away from the water and was now gliding up the shingle towards us.

"Watch to your left," warned April.

"Got it," I replied. "This is starting to freak me out."

"Yeah, I've got a bit of prickly skin. This doesn't make me feel comfortable at all."

I switched the camera to night vision mode to better track the snakes in the darkness.

"Just keep an eye on that one," said April, pointing to a length of black hosepipe slithering off the edge of my screen.

"Yup, there's two of them right here. They're going for the boat."

It was a nightmare. The prospect of trying to extract lethal snakes from our cockpits made my head reel.

"Actually," April said, "they can move a little quicker than you think."

"Yeah, they're beginning to wake up."

The two heading for the boat altered course and made straight for us, their heads raised, crossing and recrossing each other's paths.

"It's like they're working as a team," I said, noting the rising desperation in my voice. "Hunting us in a pair."

April and I began inching down to the water's edge to make a last stand. With our backs to the sea, we had less area to defend. Of course, this was assuming the snakes didn't take to the water, in retrospect a fairly likely thing for an amphibious animal to do.

"Okay, here comes one," said April, pointing to the nearest, now a few feet away.

"Son of a bitch."

"What do we do, kill them?"

As a vegetarian of nine years, one of my guiding principles in life was to avoid killing or eating anything that shat or had a face—both indicators of higher intelligence than, say, a potato. But the situation was getting out of hand. We had no anti-venom. If either of us was bitten, it was a three-day journey to the nearest hospital in Ende.

"I'd say we're getting to that point," I conceded.

"Watch!" April shouted. Even backing away, the snakes were gaining on us.

I reached for a stout piece of timber from the fire and dispatched the lead snake, crushing its head in a cloud of sparks.

"Where's its buddy?" I said.

"Here he comes."

"Very sorry, Mister Snake." Again, I swung the timber. The snake convulsed into a pretzel and was still.

The others were nowhere to be seen. Treading carefully, I picked up the two carcasses and laid them under a tree above the high tide mark. If one of us was indeed bitten during the night, we could take a snake with us to Ende to be identified for the right anti-venom—assuming the victim survived that long. We then slipped the covers over the cockpits and retreated to the safety of the tent.

In the morning, April described her dreams. Snakes featured in all of them: "Hanging off my legs, gnawing at my flesh." It was the Lariam talking, the same lucid dreaming as she'd had on the Coral Sea voyage.

Gingerly, we crawled out of the tent, hoping that no visitors had crept under the groundsheet for warmth in the night. While April took a walk down the beach, I started a fire for tea. A minute later, she was back, her face drained of colour.

"They're gone," she whispered.

"What are?"

"The snakes."

For the first time I noticed a dead tree partially submerged in the shallows, its grey skeletal limbs poking out of the water like the ribcage of an elephant.

"That tree," I said. "I don't remember that tree being there when we came in yesterday."

The hairs on the back of my neck were standing up. April, too, looked rattled.

"Maybe they got washed out to sea?" she offered.

I shook my head. "Impossible. It's only neap tides, and I threw them way above the high tide mark."

LATER THAT DAY, we paddled to the Muslim village of Pota. More than a hundred people crowded around us on the beach, the faces of the women painted ghoulish white with the cosmetic paste that Indonesians used for skin bleaching.* The atmosphere was excitable as we set up camp, lots of laughter and whooping and, "Hello, Meester! Hello, Meesees!" But when the village elders arrived, the crowd regained its composure.

April and I recounted our earlier experience.

"*Sihir!*" one of the elders hissed. Witchcraft.

---

* In Indonesia, skin lightening is promoted as an "opportunity enhancer" and social indicator of wealth, status, and beauty by a multi-million-dollar cosmetics industry. I'd found the same to be true in Central America, where darker skin is considered by the social elite to be inferior, even ugly.

"Dukun santet," said another. Black shaman. This was Haji, a smiling octogenarian in a blue shirt, purple lava-lava, and Peci, a black fez hat. "Indonesia beeple superstitious," he continued. "You break promise in village? You make disrespect? They take revenge with"—he nodded sagely and wagged a finger—"dukun santet."

Translating was his son, a pint-sized forty year old with the flitting eyes of a blackbird. Haji went on to explain how someone seeking retribution could retain the services of a black shaman, a witch. First, you obtained a strand of the intended victim's hair or something they'd been standing on. Then the dukun santet would concoct the spell. The customer had a variety of options to choose from. Fire was one. If the shaman lit a match or a cigarette and pointed it at your enemy's house, within a few days the building was sure to burn to the ground. Another was to cause their crops to fail or livestock to die.

"Or snake," said Haji, raising another finger. Like fire, snakes could be sent long distance and, after eliminating the target, retrieved the same way. Apparently, the most crucial ingredient in any of the methods used was for the client to believe unequivocally in the spell they'd commissioned. Otherwise, it just wouldn't work. This struck me as an ingenious let-out clause for the shaman. If the magic failed—which, presumably, it always did, unless the victim happened to croak or their property be destroyed anyway—the fault ultimately lay in the client's lack of conviction, avoiding the irksome business of having to fork over a refund.

Being the target of a grudge wasn't entirely beyond the realms of possibility. Perhaps I'd offended the owners of the losmen by refusing to pay for a room and sleeping outside on the grass instead. Nevertheless, the notion of black magic being at play, albeit entertaining, was frankly absurd.

"What a load of mumbo-jumbo," I whispered to April.

It wasn't until four days later in Labuan Bajo, another tin-roofed town with an open-sewer policy, that the truth finally revealed itself. According to the "Fun Facts" of the Sea World website I googled in the town's Internet café, sea snakes were attracted to light. That explained why so many of them had entered our camp. The snakes had been drawn like moths to our headlamps.

When I told April, she seemed relieved. After all, the light theory solved a mystery that had been playing on both our minds and had us both badly spooked. Then her face fell, clouding with uncertainty.

"Okay," she said softly. "But where did they disappear to in the night, then?"

With just the two of us, April and I could dig in and make miles. We bought a fortnight's worth of supplies and paddled the Libra—*Queenie,* as April christened her, after the elephantine *RMS Queen Mary*—out of Labuan Bajo on the ebb tide. Chris had already left with Lourdes on the *Tilongkabila Gorontalo,* four decks of grunting, belching, rusting steel bound for the Balinese port of Benoa, but not because he was going home. Two months of hauling *Queenie* up and down beaches had compounded an old motorcycle injury, crippling his back. We agreed to rendezvous in Bali in a month, giving him time to recuperate before the onward paddle to Java.

It wasn't long before April and I were slipping past the Jurassic backdrop of Komodo National Park, a series of stunning island vistas dominated by steep, craggy peaks. Between the islands, the currents were deceptively strong. Rounding one headland, I had the disconcerting feeling of the boat being taken out from underneath us, before losing control of the steering altogether. It was like being drawn into a fast-moving river, *Queenie* careening along at ten knots and spinning in a race of overfalls and eddies. A minute of furious paddling, and we managed to finally regain control.

Although the extra provisions made the boat more cumbersome to manoeuvre, the added weight was welcome, lessening the chances of capsize. We had two dangerous selat crossings coming up: Selat Sape, described in the cruising guide as a "wild body of water" owing to the confluence of wind, tide, and current forced between the islands of Komodo and Gili Banta, and Selat Lombok, the twenty-five-mile deep-water channel separating Lombok and Bali.

And the dangers weren't limited to water. On land, there were the dragons to contend with, growing three metres in length and weighing up to three hundred pounds, their reptilian skin crimped like a pineapple. Komodo dragons were largely docile and rarely attacked humans, but were nevertheless opportunists and fatalities were known to occur. Village children were occasionally hauled off, and all that remained of a Swedish tourist who disappeared in 1973 was a pair of spectacles and a camera. The animals reached speeds of up to fifteen miles an hour over short distances, enough to ambush a wild pig, a deer, goat, water buffalo, horse—or a human. They dispatched their prey by biting and slashing with sabre-like claws, injecting venom and delivering a killer cocktail of septicaemia-inducing bacteria.

That the closest thing to a living dinosaur still roamed the earth in any number (there were 6,000 Komodo dragons at last count) was thanks to strict regulations imposed on a far more dangerous animal. Man. With the exception of one traditional fishing village, no human settlement was tolerated in the park, along with no hunting and no fishing—inspired laws that permitted marine life to flourish. On the first day alone, we saw three whales, a cream-bellied manta ray with a fifteen-foot wingspan that corkscrewed out of the water less than thirty feet from the boat, and a peculiar species of dolphin that buried its head in the water and waggled its tail in the air.

"It's waving at us," said April.

"You mean mooning us," I said. "That's probably dolphin speak for 'bugger off'."

On the second day, we found ourselves traversing Telok Gili Lawa, a wide horseshoe bay spanning the north coast of Komodo. The far northwest peninsula was the preferred point to launch in the morning to Gili Banta, a stepping stone island in the middle of Selat Sape. It was late in the afternoon when I glanced at my watch and realized I'd underestimated the effect of the tide working against us. The time was now 6:15 pm, with only fifteen minutes of daylight remaining, and the headland was still five miles away.

It took an hour and a half to close the distance. With no moon and no stars, we rounded the headland in darkness. Mountainous seas washed over the deck and filled our spray skirts. On the other side there was nothing but rocks and the sound of waves breaking against the cliffs, certainly nowhere to land. The day was turning into a repeat of April's first day out from Larantuka, only now we were paddling blind.

All we could do was head south and keep the crashing surf within earshot. I could just make out April's straw hat in front of me. Nothing else. For the next two hours, there was no sign of anywhere to land. It was looking increasingly likely that we'd be spending the rest of the night in the boat.

"Please," I whispered imploringly, "*please* let there be a sandy beach around this corner."

Then, a faint glimmer off to our left …

"Is it my imagination, April, or is that a thin line of sand over there?"

She bowed her head in relief.

"There is a god," I said.

"Ask, and you shall receive."

"That's a sight for sore eyes. And sore shoulders."

As we drew near, something shambled across the beach and disappeared into the bushes beyond.

"Did you see that?" I said.

"No. What?"

"Never mind."

We unloaded *Queenie* by flashlight, hanging our net bag of veggies on the branch of a tree and spreading out our sodden clothes on bushes to dry. After a hurried meal and fixing a broken tent pole with a makeshift splint and fishing line, we collapsed exhausted into our sleeping bags.

As a precaution, I sharpened one end of a four-foot-long piece of timber and placed it inside the tent.

"Spot to aim for is behind the ears," I murmured before drifting off. "It's the equivalent of kicking 'em in the balls, apparently."

I awoke in the early hours to the *ping … ping … ping …* of our security system and lay there for a moment, listening. The infrared beam surrounding camp had been broken only twice before, once by scavenging dogs, the other by a snooping local. But neither of these seemed likely. Apart from the village on the south side of the island, there were no humans on Komodo and no dogs. I heard the sound of scratching, something trying to force the cover of *Queenie's* main food compartment. Unzipping the tent quietly, I aimed my headlamp and hit the power button.

A yellowy eye glared back, prehistoric-looking and menacing.

"What is it?" whispered April.

"Not sure," I lied.

I hurled a sandal. The monster turned and lurched off into the brush, crashing as it went.

"Wild pig, maybe?"

"Yes, a wild pig."

Three weeks later. Eve of Selat Lombok Crossing
APRIL AND I sat on the highest point of Gili Trawangan, one of three islets off the northwest coast of Lombok, overlooking the biggest and most hazardous water crossing of the entire Indonesian leg.

"So, A, what do you reckon?"

She paused before answering, letting her gaze follow a succession of whitecaps that melded with the haze, beyond which a conical shadow, Bali, reclined on a featherbed of low-lying clouds. Farther still, an apricot sun created a canvas of evening purples and pinks.

"What do *you* reckon?" she replied.

I looked up from the chart resting on my knees and studied the dark tidal streams snaking through the silvery water. Eight hundred miles of paddling from Dili had been leading up to this point.

"Well, it's a long way, but we're at peak fitness." I tugged at my beard, now thick and tangled with four months of unrestricted growth. "If we get going really early and paddle like hell, we should be able to get two-thirds of the way across before the tide changes."

Privately, I put our chances at around fifty-fifty. Ever since poring over the charts in the embryonic preparation stage, Selat Lombok had filled me with the greatest uncertainty. My reservations had been validated earlier in the day when I asked Simon from Blue Marlin Dive whether he thought a support boat would be a sensible precaution. "Absolutely yes," he'd answered before I'd even finished my sentence. However, the cheapest quote from any of the Indonesian skippers was four million rupiah, over $450, nearly half our remaining budget.

What to do?

If we winged it and *Queenie* capsized and flooded, we were on our own. Bobbing out there in our lifejackets, either the sharks would pick us off or the tide suck us down into the dreaded Selat Badung.

This was my biggest fear, ending up in the narrow neck of water between Nusa Penida and the southeast coast of Bali, a gurgling, roiling, saltwater nightmare of contra-flowing currents jostling for space, creating tidal rips, standing waves, and terrifying whirlpools. Every twelve hours during spring tide, at the height of the ebb, a monster vortex formed off the southwestern tip of Nusa Penida. Our bodies would be swallowed by the deep and flushed out the U-bend of the selat, expelled from the archipelago like two insignificant turds into the vast emptiness of the Indian Ocean.

Of all the risks I'd taken since leaving Greenwich, this would be the biggest yet. I'd always counted on the universe mitigating such leaps into the abyss, rising up to meet them halfway. But this time it was different. Surely no quarter could be expected from such a malevolent body of water, and there was the added factor of having another person's life at stake.

The shadow of the tree we were sitting under merged with the night reaching in from the east, and I became minutely aware of the beetles buzzing lazily in the long grass, the birds trilling in the branches, the leaves rustling in the onshore breeze, and the last colours bleeding from the western sky. All the little things that made up the experience of being alive were now enhanced and resonating, as though filtered through some giant psychedelic prism. Time slowed to a crawl, and I was overcome by an almost Samadhi-like sense of *being* in the present. No past. No future. No sense of self. Just a seamless coupling with my surroundings. And with it, the immutable fragility of life fell into sharp focus and a realization of how often I took it for granted.

April spoke up. "Don't you think Magellan once looked at an early map of the world and said, 'Yeah, that's doable', even though the map wasn't accurate, and he had no idea what he was getting into?"

I nodded. "Probably."

"So why not? This is doable, too."

I toyed with my ocean ring. Despite being worn and faded with time and saltwater abrasion, I could still make out each cresting wave forming a wheel of aqueous infinity, and I wondered. After all these years, would it still bring me the same luck?

IN THE DREAM we were camped on a black sand beach, almost identical to the one on Sumbawa where a man with chronic wasting disease had wandered over to bum a cigarette. He had barely any flesh on his body, his face a living skull with glazed eyes set in sunken holes. I'd given him one of the packet of Garams we'd brought with us to hand out, and he'd smoked them all, one after the other. The zombies that crawled out of the sand—hundreds of them, their bony fingers snatching at my arms, legs, and neck—wore the same skeletal mask. With Lariam, you can't tell the difference. The zombies *are* real. The feeling of suffocation *is* real. My throat filled with sand as they pulled me under, drowning me slowly until I awoke screaming in a slough of sweat.

At 4:20 am, we slipped *Queenie* into the water. I felt nauseous, my stomach churning. It was my third day with an upset stomach, and this one-day crossing had me more concerned than any long haul voyage in *Moksha*.

The moon was new, the tide at its strongest, the clock ticking. High tide was shortly after nine, after which the water in the selat would start flooding south. We paddled in darkness, only the long, wavering fingers of light from waterfront chalets reaching us across the black water. To keep from catching a crab and tipping over, we used our inner sense of equilibrium to plant our paddle blades. An eerie glow from a light-house beacon swathed in blankets of spray from the pounding breakers marked the northernmost tip of the islet. Then the protection of land slipped astern, and the ocean swell picked *Queenie* up like a twig and thrust her forward.

Striking out at night into open water in a tiny boat with no land in sight goes against every human instinct, like stepping off a cliff blind-folded. I used celestial points to steer by, occasionally turning on my headlamp to check the deck compass. Our fate, in essence, rested in a scrap of paper, the all-important Admiralty chart, and it occurred to me how cartographers through the ages faced huge responsibility to ensure the area denoting land on their charts was actually where they said it was. People's lives depended upon it.

Just after 6:00 am, two white masthead lights and a red port light appeared out of the north. The vessel—a tanker, perhaps—was over fifty metres long. Could they see us, I wondered? All we had was an all-round white light powered by AA batteries, a Mickey Mouse thing attached to *Queenie's* stern deck with a suction cup.

Peristaltic contractions gripped my gut. Fighting the waves of diarrhoea, I strained into the darkness, desperate to pin down the ship's exact heading and proximity. A minute passed. The red light began to move, slipping behind the two whites. Relief. The vessel was turning to starboard to avoid us.

"Stop paddling a sec, Ms A."

The low *phut-phut-phut* of engines drew closer. A crane loomed, spanning the length of the deck, and a figure peered from the bridge.

After the ship had passed, my queasiness vanished and pumping adrenaline took over. Dawn broke, filling our watery universe with enough light to see how big the waves really were: six feet, much higher than I'd anticipated. A brisk force 4 was gusting from the south, throwing another variable into the mix: a wind-against-tide scenario after slack water, producing large standing waves. *If the wind is this strong this early,* I thought anxiously, *we could be in trouble later on.*

By 6:50 am, it was fully light, but Bali remained shrouded by haze. The southerly wind was whipping the water, sending white horses charging towards us, hissing crests that collided with *Queenie's* port beam with a resounding thud. A twelve-footer appeared by my left elbow. There was a moment of suspended animation as April and I air paddled. Then the wall of water broke, engulfing us in a deluge of white foam and putting *Queenie* on her beam-ends. Teetering on the brink of capsize, our training kicked in. We thrust out our right paddle blades and slapped the water hard, pushing us upright again.

"Son of a bitch!" I exclaimed, more out of fright than anger. "How're you doing, April?"

Her reply was barely audible above the howling wind. "Oh, hanging in there, I guess. It's gettin' a little Western, though."

The near capsize triggered a fresh wave of intestinal cramps, forcing me to focus all my attention on sphincter control. Every time April took a stroke, water came spooning off her left paddle and into my face. *Splat ... Splat ... Splat ...* Rather than being a hindrance, I found this physical taunting actually helped. The rhythmic slapping was like being prodded with a sharp stick, goading me to paddle harder.

At 7:45 am, we stopped for a five-minute break.

"It's like we've been crossing one giant headland all morning," April remarked through clenched teeth. She had her spray skirt in her mouth, scooping out the water that had pooled in her lap.

"The waves are bigger than I thought they would be," I agreed, biting into an apple.

"They're a little high. Feels like I've already got half the selat in my cockpit."

Yet, in spite of the conditions, we were making good progress: nine miles under our belt, fifteen more to go. Gili Trawangan was now a featureless blob in our wake, and the bruised peak of Bali's Gunung Agung was clearly visible ahead. The sight of land was tremendous.

I switched on the GPS while we drifted, looking for the first signs of being taken south. In another hour and a half, the ebb would begin in earnest. At that point we would have to start compensating with our heading to keep on track, veering as much as 45 degrees to the north, which in turn meant longer on the water and the likelihood of even rougher seas as the wind strengthened into the afternoon—as it always did.

For the time being, though, the wind neutralized any southerly drift and kept us north of our clearing line.

The day wore on. Blotches of vegetation took shape on Bali's easternmost volcano, Gunung Seraya, and I imagined at least some of plants being exclusive to Asia, an indication that we'd crossed the Wallace Line. Having taken only one five-minute break in six hours, our arms were weary and our lower backs knotted balls of pain. The saltwater also aggravated a four-inch laceration in my right hand that I'd earned trying to climb a coconut tree two days before.

At eleven o'clock, we stopped to give way to a freighter steaming up the selat and to share a packet of Biskuat, Indonesian malt biscuits. The GPS indicated we'd paddled sixteen miles—only eight more to go. It also showed, however, that we were starting to drift south now that the tide had changed.

A sudden spasm gripped my lower abdomen. Having wrestled the urge since leaving Gili Trawangan, I couldn't hold it any longer. I slipped over the side, yanked off my shorts and evacuated. Instant, glorious relief! I trod water for a while, basking in the post-jettison glow, and was about to heave myself back in when I noticed a brown slick spreading out like the Exxon Valdez spill. The stuff was everywhere, bobbing around my head and getting in my beard.

"Look, dolphins!" April suddenly exclaimed, mercifully oblivious to what was going on behind her.

Two dark shapes slid past. They bore the same white markings on their ventral fins as the visitor that had attacked *Moksha's* propeller on the Pacific. I was back in my cockpit faster than you could say, *Jaws!*

"Those aren't dolphins," I gasped. "Oceanic whitetip sharks. Bloody dangerous, too."

Coming in for another pass, the pair sidled closer, wagging their blunt heads back and forth. I unclipped my paddle leash and reached out to tap the nearest one on the nose. A flick of tails, and they both swirled away.

"Better not tell Chris about this," April said. "He won't want to come back."

The ebb tide was now in full flow, spilling south between the two islands. Using my foot pedals, I turned *Queenie's* nose to starboard, slashing our speed by two thirds but allowing us to maintain a 260-degree heading. It took four hours to paddle the next five miles, but when a cluster of huts took shape against the volcanic slopes, their quaint forms interspersed with patches of neatly clipped grass, red bougainvillea, terraced rice paddies, and the detail of the gaily painted fishing boats on the beach became unmistakable, I knew we'd make it.

The first thing I did on making landfall was to drop to my knees and press my face into the grey sand. Then I stood to address April. "I knew you were strong after the Coral Sea voyage, Ms A, but today you were a real trooper. I wouldn't have wanted to do this crossing with *anybody* else."

Hat stuck to the side of her head, hands clasped under her chin, April teared up. "Oh, no, no," she replied breathlessly, lowering her head. "This is my greatest adventure. I wouldn't have it any other way."

I laughed. "Got pretty hairy out there, didn't it?"

She nodded vigorously. "Yeah, it was full on, *really* full on. Right up until the last half hour where it kinda slacked off a bit. I'm really glad to be here."

The truth was we'd been lucky. The unexpected force 4 from the south had prevented us from being sucked down into Selat Badung.

"Yup," I agreed. "Any selat crossing you walk away from is a good one."

THE SURF HISSED in my ears and sucked at my toes as I dialled my parents' number on the satellite phone. As my first line of support, monitoring sea state and weather conditions and texting me forecasts, my father was living the expedition as closely as it was possible short of actually being with me. The dining room in their Dorset home had long been given over to what my mother referred to as "the operations room," with the dinner table buried under reams of maps and charts.

When he picked up, I said just four words: "We made it okay."

My father had heard me say the same thing many times over the years, but this time the emotion in his voice was palpable. He'd known the risks of this particular crossing as well as I did. "Well done, bwana," he replied. "Well *done.*"

Leaving April to guard *Queenie,* I followed a path leading up through towering bamboo, babbling waterfalls, and pondering Buddhas camou-flaged by canopies of ferns and carefully tended heliconias. Climbing further, electric blue swimming pools shimmered into view, surrounded by linen parasols bedecked with swinging pom-poms and immaculate white villas topped with carmine terracotta tiles. Having earned our passage to Eurasia the hard way, I'd decided we deserved a night in something a little more up market than a tent pitched on the beach.

A smiling Balinese woman in a white chiffon robe appeared sound-lessly before me. "You are looking for a room?" she asked, her voice the embodiment of oriental deference.

Yes, I said, I was.

"It's eighty-five a night for a bungalow. A hundred and five for the beachside ones."

"Great," I replied happily. "We can just about afford a bungalow." In dollars, this worked out to be around $7 a night. "That's eighty-five thousand rupiah, right?"

She looked at me sadly. "No, sorry. Eighty-five dollars."

I suddenly felt rather self-conscious standing there in my rotting straw hat and bare feet, my arms streaked with salt and grey tank top unbe-lievably filthy. *I must smell terrible,* I thought. Then I noticed the woman was staring at something in my beard. I had a pretty good idea what it was and what was going through her head:

Is that what I think it is?

JAVA
A Long Way From Home

I am homesick for a place I am not sure even exists.

—Unknown

O NE OF THE BIGGEST challenges of the Indonesian leg was simply staying in the country long enough to complete it. Visa extensions were an arbitrary affair. The underpaid immigration officer who'd been yelled at by his wife that morning and bitten by a dog on the way to work could turn around at any moment and bark: *"No extension! Must leave Indonesia immediately!"* and our bid to reach Singapore would be sunk. After I'd tracked down Chris in the fleshpots of Kuta ("Blackpool in the tropics," as he described it), we completed our second visa renewal (new sponsor letter from the Department of Education, forms filled out in triplicate, copies of passports, and explanation as to how Indonesia would benefit by us staying another month) and fled for the sanity of the sea.

Sporting an enormous jungle-green hat that doubled as a spinnaker when he tilted his head, Chris was jubilant to be back out on the water. With the exception of brain-dissolving Bintangs (Indonesia's answer to malt liquor), a month's convalescence appeared to have done wonders for his health and rekindled an enthusiasm for kayaking. The north coast of Bali being an easy, low-stress paddle also helped to put our friendship back on track. There were no risky headlands. No scary selat crossings. None of the friction born of misinformation and fear mongering we'd fallen foul of in Dili.

In all other respects, however, the north shore was a disappointment. Naively, I'd pictured crisp sandy beaches dotted with quaint Balinese villages, little chocolate-box utopias like Amed where April and I first made landfall. In reality, every inch of the coastline was crammed with people living hugger-mugger in tumbledown housing. Either that or access to the beach was hindered by seawalls that stretched for miles, keeping us in the boats for long, wearisome days.

Despite April and I fast-tracking it from Labuan Bajo, we were still up against it to beat the monsoon. Our solution was to buy cheap bicycles upon reaching Java and make up time by riding the seven hundred and seventy miles across the island. Comprising a sordid hash of grubby industry and belching oil refineries, there was little incentive to paddle the north coast, anyway. We would travel light, stay in losmens, and eat at roadside food stalls. As well as breaking the tedium of camping, renting a room and feeding on the fly offered respite from what was fast becoming one of the more tiresome aspects of kayaking through Indonesia.

People.

It hadn't started out that way. I recalled fondly our first contact with the villagers of Pureman on Alor. Although rambunctious, they'd been endearingly hospitable, and the fishbowl experience almost flattering. But in the weeks and months that followed, the novelty of having a hundred people sitting a few feet from us gawking for hours on end had worn thin, becoming annoying to the point of infuriating. In the village of Pota, Flores, besieged by waves of locals badgering us with inane questions even as we tried to sleep— *"Hello, Meester! Where you from? Hello, Meesees! Where you going?"*—I'd resorted to the acerbic, "Jangan ganggu kami!" Don't disturb us!

"The thing is," Chris pointed out the evening before we crossed over to Java, "we're the equivalent of a television show for these people, a western reality show they can goggle at, just as folks back home sit in from of the box and goggle at villagers in Indonesia."

It was an astute observation. As outsiders, we offered a living window into a culture they were fascinated by but knew little about. The gear, the gadgetry, the tent poles, the cameras; we were a mobile circus, a compelling curiosity they couldn't pull themselves away from.

For us, though, camping on the beach had become a labour of forbearance, a battle of self-restraint I was beginning to lose. *Their blatant lack of regard for personal possessions, bordering on open thievery,* I journaled angrily the day my shorts were pinched off a bush, *thinking it's okay to help themselves to food, or whatever we have in our kayaks, is unacceptable. Before when locals rolled into camp, it was nearly always positive. Now I feel an instant sense of resentment verging on hostility.*

The thing was, no one had demanded we come to Indonesia. When all was said and done, we were the ones imposing on the local people, not they on us.

Clearly, it was time to switch gears.

Rolling out of Banyuwangi, Java's easternmost town, each of us riding an Indonesian-made Wimcycle costing $60 total for each bike including lights, racks, panniers, tyres, pedals, seat, spare inner tubes, and puncture repair kit, it was quickly apparent that negotiating Javanese roads constituted an exercise in survival in its most vital and rudimentary form. A honking cavalcade of cars, trucks, bullock carts, rickshaws, and a million zinging mopeds wrestled for space on the shoulderless two-lane road that served as the island's main artery, all of them squeezed down the same ribbon of black. With no rules, it was every man, woman, child, duck, pig, dog, chicken, and cyclist for itself. The preferred method of overtaking appeared to be approaching a blind summit in the opposite lane. Why bother waiting for a gap in the oncoming traffic? If they knew what was good for them, anything smaller coming the other way would bail off into the ditch.

Roundabouts offered the best demonstration of Darwin's theory of natural selection in action. For some mystifying reason, vehicles entering traffic circles had the right of way, resulting in a primordial pile-on where only the fittest prevailed.

"I think the trick to biking in Java is to adopt faith in a higher power," I said to April on the second morning, swerving to avoid yet another motorist who'd pulled out in front of us without looking.

We were riding side by side through the town of Jember, the roaring traffic weaving past, missing us by inches in the blinding fumes thrown up by the two-stroke motorcycle engines. April, her hat forced back by the airflow and face wracked in concentration, replied, "I'm just trying to keep out of everybody's way. Like normal!"

For all the chaos, road rage was curiously absent in Indonesia, a reflection of people's tolerance. Road users simply made room for you as you would for them. Truckers were the shining example. Even after jamming on the airbrakes to go around us, an inconvenience guaranteed to trigger an incendiary response from a heavy goods driver in the West, a trucker would draw level with us, give the thumbs up, and smile happily.

"Hello, Meester! How are you?"

Oblivious to the traffic jam building behind him, the driver would then attempt to strike up a conversation in English. There would be no angry toots from the lengthening queue. No obscenities shouted. The long-suffering line of motorists would wait patiently for us to finish what would invariably turn out to be a lengthy and clumsy conversation. Living on Indonesia's most densely populated island, people spent half their life waiting as it was.

Beyond Jember, we swept through coffee and rubber plantations and puffed up ridges of waterlogged rice paddies flashing in the sun like fractured glass. Tan-coloured swifts dipped low over the water, snatching insects in flight, and teams of portly water buffalo coupled by bamboo yokes plodded hock deep through the sucking mud, flicking their tails obstinately at the farmer's whip. We passed gangs of harvesters, frowning men slashing at the mature rice plants with short-handled sickles and gossiping womenfolk slapping fistfuls of freshly cut stalks over slatted frames, the brown kernels of rice drizzling onto squares of canvas below.

On the fifth evening from Banyuwangi, we found ourselves at the Mutiara losmen, the definitive roach motel in the aptly named town of Dampit. At 35,000 rupiah for a room, less than four dollars, our expectations weren't overly high. Nevertheless, the Mutiara, translated as "pearl" from Bahasa Indonesian, took the baseline for squalor to a new level. Room nineteen had no windows and no fan. It was like a sweat lodge, according to April, who made no attempt to conceal her repugnance. Clouds of malaria-bearing mosquitoes orbited a single light bulb that hung from the flaking ceiling, its yellowy light illuminating a multitude of horrors: maps of Africa on the stained bed sheets, suspicious brown streaks down the walls, and a herd of fat, shiny cockroaches migrating to and from the squat toilet, itself unspeakably filthy.

Staring at the bed sheets, April scratched her legs involuntarily. "I doubt they've been washed in a month," she said.

When I asked the old man at the front desk for fresh bed linen, he laughed in my face.

Back in the room, I said to April, "If this were anywhere else in the world, we'd be better off getting ourselves arrested. A prison cell in Mexico would be five-star compared to this place."

She nodded. "If the roaches don't get you, the dengue fever certainly will."

"I'm beginning to wonder if we shouldn't take our chances outside in a rice paddy," I said.

"Yeah, if it weren't for the snakes."

But this was the price for making time, putting in long days that often ended in obscure settlements with scant accommodation options. It took a fortnight to pedal across the island, grinding up and down the long necklace of volcanoes marked on our map. On the penultimate day, I caught up with Chris on a rare stretch of traffic-free road outside Jasinga. He was squirting water over his head and neck with the water bottle he kept behind his seat.

"It's actually quite hot," he said, pouring water in his hand and splashing his face. "But sort of does something. You don't use a cooling bottle, do you?"

"No, mate. I'm cool enough."

Squirting water under his shirt, Chris gave a silent guffaw. "That's hilarious. Maybe at this moment, but you've lost your cool a few times on this cycling trip, wouldn't you say?"

The goat incident a week before had admittedly put me on a short fuse. I'd ridden past a kid goat with its hind legs broken, and before I had time to dispatch the unfortunate creature with a nearby rock, a man appeared holding a blunt penknife, which, after briefly sharpening on the running board of his moped, he used to saw at the animal's neck for a full thirty seconds before finally piercing the carotid artery. It took another two minutes and sixteen seconds (I was counting) for the goat to bleed to death, its human-like cries fading with each breath. The helmet-clad butcher then turned to face Mecca with his blood-spattered hands outstretched, put his head back, and closed his eyes in melodramatic piety.

As one of the most barbaric and inept methods of killing that I had ever seen, the episode left me questioning halal and the cruelty involved in preparing meat for Muslims worldwide. But this was nothing compared to what I witnessed a few days later.

I'd almost reached the top of a steep grade on the dual carriageway from Banjar to Bandung when it happened. A white retriever-mix puppy trotted out into the road, wagging its tail at the oncoming traffic. I stopped, parked my rig, and was about to run out and grab the hapless creature when the traffic caught up, labouring past me in the nearside lane.

Through a gap in the vehicles, I watched helplessly as events unfolded. The puppy was in the passing lane, its ears pricked and wagging its tail. The first car didn't even try to avoid it. The animal rolled twice, bouncing beneath the chassis. Struggling to its feet, the puppy stood there looking dazed and confused. The second vehicle ran over its back. I heard the crack of spinal column and splintering of bone. Lying there, unable to move, guts spilled out on the road, the puppy still patted the tarmac feebly with its tail. A truck finished the job, running over its head with a sickening pop.

Something inside me snapped.

It began as a red-hot ember in my chest, rising in my throat and igniting under my tongue, an uncontrollable rage the like I had never known before. I had an overwhelming desire to take revenge for what, at its core, was a senseless and deliberate act of cruelty to a defenceless animal. None of the vehicles had been going more than fifteen miles an hour; taking evasive action would have been easy. But in Indonesia, as in almost all Asian countries I would later discover, dogs are considered unclean, the lowest of the low.

"Fucking, bastards!" I roared, striding out into the traffic. Cars slowed, swerving around me. One even stopped. The driver poked his head out of the window, looking curiously at me. "Yeah, *you*, you fucking arse-hole!" I stabbed my fingers, willing him to open the door so I could drag him and beat his brains out on the road. But he didn't. He just stared at me in mute bewilderment. Car after car was meanwhile trundling over the carcass, making it twitch and jerk like a meat marionette. Grabbing the tail, I dragged the body to the side of the road and dumped it in the storm ditch.

Later, replaying the episode in my head, I realized that retrieving the puppy was the nearest that I could come to some form of atonement, like saving the old gummer cow from the mud hole in Australia after the road train massacre. Travel makes you a witness, brings you closer to the Earth and its people, and human-powered travel gets about as up close and personal as it's possible to get. You witness the best and the worst in humanity, starting with yourself.

The puppy was just a speed bump in the onward march of human progress, a minor inconvenience to be swept aside. This was the blight of the twenty-first century, the way machines and technologies detached humans from their surroundings and accountability for their actions. Peering through the windscreen of a steel cage, the world "out there" appears different to the world "in here." But, as I'd discovered on the Atlantic, this was a misconception, a falsehood unique to humans.

Differentiating between the subjective and objective world was merely a sleight of consciousness, a distortion of perspective conjured by the warped prism of dualistic awareness.

Running short on time to reach Singapore, April and Chris had to make the western edge of Java their journey's end. Chris needed to get back to his furniture business, April her teaching. Her white bag bulged with treasures to share with her pupils: five different shades of sand for a "Colors of Coral" project, rolls of ikkat, stubs of polished driftwood, and several lumps of igneous rock she'd managed to keep hidden from me in the front of *Queenie*.

Seeing them go made me sad and a little jealous. I was tired of the logistics, the bureaucracy, the chaos, the noise, the grime, and the constant teasing by the locals:

"Hello, Miss!"

"—TER!"

I was travel weary and longed to be going home, too.

"When you go away," Chris observed before leaving, "especially to a place like this, it helps to put your own life back home in focus. Because sometimes you forget how big the world is and how diverse it is, and your local world becomes everything. For me, this trip has been a positive reinforcement of my own life back home and what I've got there."

We were overlooking the marina at Anyer, where the kayaks had been shipped overland from Bali.

"So, what are you going back to?" I asked.

Chris leaned forward in his chair. "A workshop and a whole list of jobs, things I want to get done, a bit of money to earn. I'm going back to my old life, which I actually rather like. Going back to lots of good friends who live not far away, a stove, and a cupboard with loads of cooking ingredients in it."

Listening to him, I realized I had none of these. All I had to show for years of westerly effort was a few yarns already hackneyed to death from fundraising blather.

Chris paused before summing up what I took to be the guiding insight he'd come to Indonesia to find, a prescient truth that I myself would have to reconcile one day: "I feel if I leave my life for any longer than six months, I would have left it almost completely. I would feel like there wouldn't be anything to go back to. I would have forgotten the solidity of home and all that it means to me."

SUMATRA
KEEP PEDALLING &
LET THE PARANG DO THE TALKING

You must not lose faith in humanity. Humanity is an ocean; if a few drops of the ocean are dirty, the ocean does not become dirty.

—MAHATMA GANDHI

I HAD TO FORGE the request letter for my third and final visa renewal, my contact at the Department of Education having left town on a conference. Every day for a week I made the twenty-mile round trip to the tumbledown immigration office in south Jakarta, an Orwellian dungeon of brown-uniformed clerks hunched over desks ten rows deep. Every day it was the same story: another queue, another stamp (Indonesian officials were obsessed with rubber stamps), another "Meester, come back tomorrow." Finally, on October 16, purple visa stamp in place, I paddled away from Java and completed the fifteen-mile crossing to Sumatra in a little over five-and-a-half hours.

I gave myself five days to bike the six hundred and sixty miles to Jambi, where I planned to rent a vehicle, backtrack to Java, load up the kayaks, pick up Kenny and his Kiwi friend, Phil, who were flying into Jakarta, and then head back to Jambi. The three of us would strike out on the last one hundred and fifty miles by kayak, paddling down the Batang Hari River to Selat Berhala, before wending our way through the Riau Islands to Singapore.

At first glance, Sumatra seemed wilder and less overrun by humans than the anthill of Java. It was certainly hotter and more humid, with an abundance of rainfall and bursting with jungly growth. Riding one-hundred-and-forty-mile days, I breezed past swampland and swollen rivers, houses floating on rafts of bamboo, and pairs of fat, happy water buffalo bathing in muddy waterholes lovingly fussed over by their handlers. The locals struck me as friendlier, too. No sullen-faced drivers giving me the finger like they had in Bandung.

But first impressions can often be misleading. The native forest soon petered out, supplanted by ugly swathes of oil palms grown for the lumpy haemorrhoid-like fruit rich in unprocessed biofuel, rendering the fragile tropical soil a barren wasteland. And on the morning of the third day, seven boisterous teenagers strode into view as I pedalled up a steep incline. They were in high spirits, giggling and chattering, strutting along on the opposite side of the road.

"*Mirah BLAY!*" one of them yelled. Look at the foreigner! They all laughed.

Blay, short for bule, translates to albino from Bahasa Indonesian. Despite the dubious reference to skin colour, it was a harmless enough term frequently used by Indonesians to address Westerners—I'd been called it many times and never felt offended. But like any word, its meaning could change with context and delivery. Surrounded by his posse, this boy was being intentionally rude and disrespectful, wielding the word as a taunt.

I carried on cycling. After losing my cool in west Java, I was determined to keep my mouth shut.

"Hey, Meester!" yelled another. "I want smoking."

"Saya tidak morokok," I replied over my shoulder. "I don't smoke."

It was the worst time to encounter these brats, grinding uphill in low gear, unable to make a quick getaway.

"Hey, Meester! There is bomb in next town." More laughter.

This was too much. Three days before, suicide bombers from the al-Qaeda-linked Jemaah Islamiyah group had targeted two beachside restaurants in Bali, killing twenty people, most of them locals.

Laying down my bike and trailer, I turned to the comedian, a seventeen year old in a muscle shirt featuring the American rapper, Ice Cube. "I'll give you a bomb, you little bastard," I hissed. "Right up your fucking arsehole!"

The youth was stunned. On holiday, out of their comfort zone, tourists rarely respond to ridicule. Who wants to make a scene? Even expatriates fluent in the native language usually just grin awkwardly and let such episodes slide. But I'd been travelling long enough to know that people are people wherever you go, and regardless of how unfamiliar the culture is or impoverished the people, an insult is an insult.

Seeing me advance, fists clenched, the younger kids turned and fled. But the ringleader held his ground. *This could end badly,* I thought.

The teenager had been working in the fields. He was carrying a parang, a machete, which he undoubtedly knew how to use. Perhaps it
was the five-month-old beard that finally tipped the balance. Con-
fronted by this hairy, scary albino devil bearing down on him, he, too,
lost heart and bailed.

The Muslim fasting month of Ramadan was in full swing as I
pushed on to Jambi. It was supposed to be a time of self-reformation
and spiritual cleansing, of reading the Koran, performing acts of charity, and do-gooding in general; all noble intentions, but abstention only
seemed to make the locals tetchy. As the afternoons wore on, you could
sense the nation's blood sugar level dropping. People wilted like ne-
glected hothouse flowers, their eyelids drooping and heads nodding.

Because restaurants were closed between sunrise and sunset and
eating in public was frowned upon, I found I was having difficulty obtaining enough calories. Inspired by less-disciplined devotees I spied
snatching sneaky snacks behind buildings or down obscure alleyways, I
took to pulling off the road and snatching a sneaky snack myself.

It was shortly after scoffing two chocolate donuts in a gum tree plan-
tation that the bandits struck. Two young men on a motorcycle fell in
beside me as I pedalled. The one riding pillion had a handkerchief
covering the lower half of his face.

"Hello, Meester!"

"Hello."

"Where are you going?"

"Jambi."

"What is your name?"

"Jason."

The motorcycle moved closer.

"Where are you coming from?"

We were travelling at speed, and the potholes, some of which were
big enough to swallow my entire front wheel, meant I really had to con-

centrate. The last thing I needed was someone practicing their English on me.

"I'm sorry," I said, "but I can't speak to you right now."

As it turned out, I'd unknowingly cut to the heart of their intention.

In the blink of an eye, the passenger reached out and grabbed the strap of the camcorder I had around my neck. The first thing he did was to try to push me over. When this didn't work, he yanked on the strap to break the camera loose.

We were on an isolated stretch of road bordered by palm oil plantations, not a house or a villager in sight. Hanging onto the camera with one hand, I steered with my left. The would-be robber gave the strap another sharp tug, this time hard enough to pull me off the bike. Next thing I was being dragged along the asphalt, on my back, hugging the camera like a rugby ball. We continued like this for another hundred yards, and just when I thought I couldn't hold on any longer, the burden of towing me became too great, and my adversary came tumbling onto the road with me.

The rider promptly brought the motorcycle to a stop, dismounted, and started walking back towards me carrying a large parang.

Is that to use on me or the strap? I wondered.

A bus suddenly hove into view, its lights blazing. The bandits hesitated for a moment, looking from me to the bus, then sprinted to their machine and sped away.

At the police post in Tebing Suluh, I stopped to report the incident. Maybe the thieves could still be apprehended? Two bored-looking officers sat in the shade of a banana tree. They wore brown berets, and their embroidered epaulettes were covered in gold insignia. One of them yawned as I began recounting what had happened.

"You have to go to the police, Meester,"

Was this a joke? "But you are the police," I said.

"No, Meester. You need another kind of police."

"Another kind of police?"

"National police. POLRI. In Tugumulyo."

I stared at them. "So what police are you, then?"

"Traffic police."

This was ridiculous. "This is a road," I enunciated slowly, feeling my blood pressure rising. "I was attacked on the road. You are the police. Don't you think you should do something about it?"

"No, Meester."

It was hopeless. Up until now, the Indonesian police we'd met had been universally polite and courteous, falling over themselves to help.

"They threatened me with a parang!" I protested.

They found this hilarious. "Yes, Meester! You need protection, eh? There are bad mens near Palembang. Very bad mens. You need parang, too."

On their advice, I bought a parang at a nearby hardware store, and from then on I never had problems with banditry on the expedition. Packing sixteen inches of steel turned out to be a highly effective deterrent.

It was dark by the time I reached Tugumulyo, where I'd been assured of finding a bed. I'd ridden two hundred and fifty kilometres since that morning, over one hundred and fifty miles. I was sweating, I was filthy with grease from fixing a chain link, and my arms and legs were bloodied with road rash. I still felt shaky from the attack.

I thought: *If the people in this village are hostile, I might just have a mini meltdown.*

A sign appeared for the Ratu Pangkat Hotel. I entered a floodlit courtyard ringed by green doors, each with a neatly painted number. An old man wearing a brown fez stepped into the light. This was Mawardi, the owner. He looked shocked at my appearance.

"Anda akan aman di sini," he said reassuringly. You are safe here. "Ini hotel saya. Keluarga saya tinggal di sini, juga." This is my hotel. I live here with my family.

I smiled weakly. "No bad mens?"

"No bad mens."

He was a lovely old boy, the living embodiment of the virtue of hospitality as prescribed by the Muslim faith. He sent his wife off for some hot water to clean my wounds.

"Apakah anda rumah makan dekat di sini?" I asked. Is there a restaurant nearby?

Yes, he said, there was, but it was already closed. And without prompting, Mawardi, who spoke almost no English, proposed driving the three miles to the next town to buy food, an offer I gratefully accepted. It had been one of those long human-powered days that felt like a week, reaffirming in my mind how travel is a timeline of extremes, a series of highs and lows that can leave you emotionally skinned, but with a greater appreciation of how there is always good if you look for it, even in the farthest flung corners of the world where at first you thought all was darkness.

KENNY LOOKED SPECTACULARLY out of shape. Having spent four months working on a feature film in New York, he was whiter than lard, chain smoking, and wearing a paunch, calling to mind the crime boss "Fat Tony" Salerno in his black gloves and long-sleeved dress shirt. In contrast, Phil had not an ounce of fat on his wiry torso. They paddled *Queenie*. I was in the yellow Solstice.

Under cloud-studded skies, we paddled towards the sea, slipping past dense jungle on either side of the Batang Hari, Sumatra's longest river, its billowing greens spilling into the water. Hundreds of yards wide at this point, the Hari was swollen, slow moving, and choked with all manner of debris loosened by recent rain—submerged trees, floating rafts of vegetation, bobbing coconuts. It was Joseph Conrad right down to the monkeys blinking at us from the shadows, the geckos burping lazily in the sticky heat and spiders jumping from overhanging branches into our cockpits.

We reached the delta late in the afternoon of the second day and started scouting for somewhere to camp. This wasn't easy. Impenetrable mangroves choked the shore all the way to Cape Jabung. We kept paddling, the light fading, and just when it looked like we might have to climb into the trees or sleep on one of the rickety offshore fishing platforms, a scrap of cleared jungle appeared.

I turned to the others. "What do you guys think?"

It was easily the worst campsite of the trip so far. The jungle lay hacked to pieces, mangrove stumps sticking out of the mud. A foul stench permeated the air, and clouds of insects hummed a few feet above the primordial goop.

"Aye, it has a certain rustic charm," muttered Kenny, wiping the sweat from his brow. He prodded the sludge with his paddle. "Like a homecomin'."

"Godforsaken shite hole, you mean," said Phil, obviously not one to mince words.

It would do in a pinch, and we were in a pinch. Birds screeched. Crickets whistled. Bug-eyed mudskippers whizzed around our paddle blades. Alerted of our approach, a family of monkeys swam across the narrow creek, youngsters riding piggyback, and disappeared into the swallowing darkness beyond. Once we'd unloaded the boats, Kenny lost no time in wading across the muddy creek to take some photographs before the light faded completely. On the return journey, he found himself stranded by the outgoing tide.

"Jason!" he cried. "This place is teemun wi' sea snakes, you know."

I nudged Phil and pointed at Kenny. "That's a strange-looking animal. Any idea what it is?"

The Scotsman was bogged to his midriff in the same shirt and trousers he'd worn on the plane from America. Holding the camera above his head with one hand, he used a loose branch to stop himself sinking further with the other.

Phil squinted into the gloom. "Water buffalo, maybe? One of those albino ones you were telling us about."

"I'm thinking lesser-spotted Sumatran hippo," I whispered. "A rare sighting indeed."

Kenny was puffing and heaving. "The going's a little soft," he wheezed, red-faced and sweating. Eventually he made it back to *Queenie* and planted his camera safely in the rear cockpit.

Our Man Brown hadn't changed. Whether it was hanging off a crane at our sea trials in Devon, tied to a leaky air mattress in the middle of the Pacific, or floundering in Sumatran mire in the company of sea snakes, he still did whatever it took to get the shot.

"Well, that was worth it," he said, crawling on all fours up the bank and clambering to his feet. From his breast pocket down, he was covered in brown sludge, as if he'd been dipped in a vat of chocolate. Below his knees, the mud was tinged a putrid green.

"Fuckin' stinkin' as well," he said, wrinkling his nose. "Have ye got a bit ay rope? I'll just fling ma troosers in th' water an' shake 'em aroond a bit."

Mud squelched between his toes as he padded away, and an evil black substance pooled in his footprints. Only later would we discover that the creek doubled as the sewage outlet for the local village.

We lit a fire with difficulty—the available wood was either wet or too green; only the slashed palm fronds showed any interest in staying alight—and then cooked and ate a simple meal of mashed potatoes and fried veggies. In the distance, wavering over the buzz of insects, the call to evening prayer began.

Faced with an earlier start than usual, we were in our tents by nine. None of us could sleep, though. "Interminable wailin'," I heard Kenny grumble from his tent. "Nae wonder the buggers lie aroond all day doin' nuthin'. They niver get enough sleep!"

At 2:00 am we were up, breaking down camp in the darkness and paddling out of the inlet before our boats were stranded by the falling tide. In the purplish predawn light of Selat Berhala, we tied up to a fishing platform to wait for the tide to slacken, then struck out for a low-lying smudge on the horizon to the north, a stepping stone island in the middle of the straits.

Six hours later, we paddled into a tiny cove lined with brilliant white sand like the lip of a mother-of-pearl oyster.

"I didn't think places like this actually existed," said Phil, laying down his paddle and gazing in wonder at the picture postcard setting before us.

Domed rocks protruded from the tranquil water like the pregnant bellies of dreamtime ancestors. Broadleaved trees and towering palms garnished a saddle of land just wide enough to pitch three tents. It wasn't much, just a toehold in the sea, but it was our own private billionaire's islet for the day. Best of all, it was free. Phil, who'd suffered from lower back pain during the fifteen-mile crossing, stretched out on the beach and smiled a wide, seraphic smile.

It was heaven. But, as April and I could attest, Indonesian islands didn't always turn out to be the utopian sanctums they first appeared.

It was three in the morning when the monsoon hit. I woke to the sound of hissing waves, distant flashes of lightning, and that sense of foreboding that precedes a major storm. Wasting no time to get dressed, I rushed around retrieving the clothes we'd left drying in the trees, the food and water bags from the beach, and secured the cockpit covers on the kayaks. By the time I started unravelling the rain fly for my tent, the storm was upon us, sweeping down Selat Berhala from the west. Kenny's bug hut collapsed immediately. "Fucking thing's *useless!*" I heard him curse in the darkness. A minute later, he was at the entrance to my tent, arms filled with cameras and electronics. "Budge up, willya?" he said.

The wind increased to gale force, tearing at the branches above us. Then the rain came. It was torrential, like air gun pellets fired against our skin. I managed to secure two of the four corners of the fly before the wind tangled the remaining lines into a Gordian knot. Kneeling on the windward side of the tent, I extended the fly up and out with my arms, forming a crude lean-to for Kenny to shelter the gear as best he could.

"At least we might get a coconut out ay this," he shouted over the shrieking wind and flapping fly.

Thunderclaps rent the air. The flashes drew nearer, lighting up an awful scene. Waves were now surging up the beach, sweeping under Phil's one-man tent. The poor New Zealander lay spread-eagled inside, desperately trying to stop himself and his tent from being washed away.

"You doing okay, Phil?" I yelled.

Only a pitiful wail reached us through the thrashing darkness.

Kenny chuckled. "I tauld him it was gonnae be a once-in-a-lifetime experience in a tropical paradise. He wouldn't hae come otherwise."

Face squashed against the muslin weave of the tent, loose cords lashing at my back like a cat-o'-nine-tails, I held my crucifixion pose. For the first hour, I had *Three Times A Lady* by The Commodores looping in my head. Then the wind chill kicked in, and my core temperature began to drop. I turned my attention instead to the sensation of cold air flowing in through my nostrils and warm air flowing out, and visualized the sun on my skin. After four of the longest hours of my life, the storm departed as quickly as it had arrived, moving eastwards down the selat.

It took a day to dry out all the gear and seal a hole in *Queenie's* bow caused by a piece of driftwood flung by the pounding surf. Then we pushed on. With the monsoon in full spate, the race was on to reach Singapore before the wind and current turned against us.

At Dabo, on the island of Singkep, we stopped for supplies and to charge camera batteries. This was where we recrossed paths with the ten surviving Z Force commandos of Operation Rimau, paddling our kayaks under the same concrete pier that the men were unloaded on after being captured by the Japanese in December 1944. The prisoners were held in the local police station for a month awaiting transfer to Singapore's Outram Road Prison, where, on July 7, 1945, just eleven days before the Japanese surrender, they were subjected to a bogus trial and then beheaded.

The tragedy of their story, and the appalling manner in which they met their fate so far from home, made me pensive and moody. I paddled the next few days in silence, lost in the swirling nimbus of my thoughts. *Would I ever see home again?* Eleven years was a long time for anyone to be out in the world, and I still had so many thousands of miles to go, so many unknowns to face, so many potential hazards before completing this seemingly endless journey. I remembered finding *Moksha* abandoned the first day in Darwin, everything trashed, and the struggle to get her shipshape and launch the expedition through Indonesia.

Seven months on, everything again was trashed. The fibreglass on the underside of the kayaks had worn almost all the way through, and *Queenie* had a deep crease amidships from being dragged over one too many uneven beaches. Most of the electronic equipment was ruined— laptop, battery chargers, camcorders. All but one of my tent poles had sheared, and my sandals had collapsed weeks ago, leaving me barefoot. Contemplating all of this and how Singapore would be another penniless arrival, I felt a deep sense of weariness, and my various aches and pains screamed for attention. My knees were swollen from hauling kayaks up and down beaches. My hands were blistered and calloused. The soles of my feet had been lacerated by coral and speared by the leaves of wait-a-while plants. I had salt sores on my backside and a middle-ear infection.

When I reach the Asian mainland, I thought, *will I have it in me to carry on?*

It was while I was having a private pity party on the morning of November 7 that Kenny reminded me to check the GPS. At 2:21 pm, in sight of a cluster of stilted bamboo huts and sarong-clad women scrubbing laundry on platforms tilted into the water, I recrossed the equator. The expedition was now officially back in the Northern Hemisphere, headed home.

I'd spent six long years in the Southern Hemisphere, the price of hitting the second antipode in central Australia. When people asked me how long the circumnavigation was taking, often they'd be amused by the answer, as if I was dragging my heels, taking my own sweet time. What they didn't see, of course, in addition to the mishaps and money problems, were the added challenges of travelling through the predominantly aquatic Southern Hemisphere. Compared to a mile travelled over land, a water mile took triple the time, effort, and money to complete by human power, amounting to big differences when you considered that the Southern Hemisphere is comprised of eighty per cent water, whereas its northern counterpart is dominated by the vast landmasses of North America and Eurasia. It was for this reason, in addition to an antipodal circumnavigation being almost double the distance of an exclusively Northern Hemisphere effort, that a bona fide around-the-world journey through all four hemispheres was taking so long.

It was also what made antipodes so important. Passing through two diametrically opposite points on the Earth's surface brought a traveller as close to the geometric ideal of circumnavigation as he or she could get. Antipodes allowed no shortcuts, no glorified variations of trotting around the North or South Pole. Their beauty was their simplicity. There was no wiggle room, no scope for argument.

⟁⟁

UP TO FIVE hundred vessels a day pass through the Singapore Straits, making it the busiest shipping lane in the world, a twelve-mile-wide feeding tube by which China happily fulfils the West's insatiable demand for stuff, cramming it down the narrow throat as fast as the Traffic Separation Scheme will allow. Marshalled by the marine equivalent of air traffic control, vessels line up nose to tail and pass through the bottleneck at an alarming pace, roughly one a minute. If this wasn't intimidating enough to a kayaker, the day of my last selat crossing fell on a new moon, when the tidal stream was running at six knots.

With high tide at 10:33 am, it was imperative to be away from Batam Island by 8:15 to complete as much of the crossing over slack water. In spite of this, I was still in the Waterfront City Customs Office at 9:45 am. The red carpet treatment we'd received all those months ago entering Indonesia from East Timor had come back to bite me in the backside. With no entry documents for the kayaks in my possession, I'd been forced to hire a local customs agent to work some eleventh-hour magic with his pals, putting us behind schedule.

Now there were added complications. To free up Kenny and Phil so they could film the arrival, two members of the Singapore Paddle Club had come over to paddle *Queenie*. As soon as she stepped off the ferry, Esther, a native Singaporean with long black pigtails, was seized for questioning. "She's on a blacklist," barked the grey-haired head of immigration. It took fifteen minutes of interrogation to establish a case of mistaken identity, but confusion remained over the switch in paddlers.

The officer turned to me, and said, "So the two men here yesterday, they are not paddling with you now?"

"No, these two are," I said, indicating Esther and her friend Stuart, a muscly American in a Lycra sports top.

"So where are the other two?"

"They took the ferry to Singapore yesterday."

"And they came back today?"

"No, these are different people."

Ten minutes of frantic phone calls, and Kenny and Phil's departure record was finally tracked down—from a different ferry terminal, as it turned out, Sekupang, a few miles up the road.

At 10:10 am, our kayak clearance paperwork and exit stamps in place, we were finally free to go. But just as we were pushing our boats into the water, a plainclothes official appeared, flashed a badge, and told us to unload everything.

"This is a great honour," whispered the head of immigration, who'd accompanied us down to the water's edge. "Antiterrorism Branch."

Perhaps I was a little distracted by the upcoming crossing, but the privilege of being chosen to turf out all our gear, ostensibly in search of guns, drugs, or whatever it was that long haul kayakers typically smuggled to Singapore, eluded me. All I could think of was the time racing by, as the water in the straits would be if we delayed any longer.

The antiterrorism agent poked one of my biceps and grinned. "Meester, you start from Timor-Leste, eh?"

Yes, I said, I had.

"You big man!"

"Not really. Can we go now?"

"Okay, Meester. You can go."

But not before the agent had his picture taken beside our kayaks, striking a heroic pose holding my paddle.

It was now 10:30 am, bang on slack water. On any other day, I would have postponed the crossing until the following morning; by the time we paddled the six miles to the start of the shipping lanes, the tide would be well on the ebb. But we were already stamped out of Indonesia, and a full-blown media reception had been arranged for 2:00 pm at Sentosa Beach, the southernmost point of Singapore. The event was my one chance to make a big splash and hook the financial backing needed to finish the circumnavigation. After the financial Mecca of Singapore, it was an economic wasteland all the way back to Europe.

Stuart and Esther set a blistering pace in *Queenie.* We rendezvoused with Kenny, Phil, and Louis, a skipper from the Singapore Yacht club, waiting in a Zodiac motorboat at the north entrance to Sambu channel, then pressed on, reaching the shipping lanes a little after 12:45 pm. The tide had very obviously turned. A massive container ship swept by, six stories of rusting steel containers stacked above decks. An oil tanker followed close behind. We now had to wait for permission from the Maritime and Port Authority (MPA) to cross the two-mile separation zone. The rubbly outline of the world's largest city-state was visible through the haze to the north, its Legoland skyscrapers glinting in the sun.

Singapore was tantalizingly close.

Half an hour later, though, we were still waiting for clearance through the Zodiac's VHF. The straits were now in full flood, the water ripping eastwards. To slow our drift, we paddled due west, parallel with the shipping lanes. Even then, the GPS lashed to my cockpit indicated we were going backwards at three knots. Less than a mile astern, tall waves were building around Batu Berhanti, a red-and-white pyramidal tower marking a hidden shoal.

1:30 pm. Still nothing from the MPA. I was beginning to get that sinking feeling of events spiralling out of control. I glanced over at Stuart. He was well familiar with these treacherous waters, having negotiated them many times in a dragon boat, but even he looked worried. "What we're doing right now is going to kill us," he protested, arms bulging to keep *Queenie* from slewing broadside to the current. A container ship, the *Mekong Vision,* flew past, propelled by the current. I felt the Solstice plunge and my stomach squeeze with apprehension. We were entering the unstable water of Batu Berhanti.

For a few seconds, we managed to hold our own. The kayaks pitched and lurched, tossed between seven-foot standing waves and frothing white caps. It was like kayaking a series of white-water rapids, working

our paddles furiously to stay upright. Then I heard a cry and looked up
to see *Queenie* capsized.

A head finally appeared. "Oh, my sandal!" Esther gasped.

She was in the water without a lifejacket, hanging onto *Queenie's* upturned hull, being sucked into a raging cauldron. Her sandal was the
least of her problems.

"You okay?" I hollered.

She nodded, hair plastered across her face.

Stuart surfaced a moment later, his expression confused. Treading
water, he first turned the Libra the right way up. Next he tried bailing
out the rear cockpit with a loose Tupperware container. It was pointless. The waves were filling the boat quicker than he could empty it.

"There's a pump in there, Stuart," I said, "on the left side of the
cockpit."

All three boats were bucking in the swell, Stuart's shaved head bobbing in and out of view. After a minute of hard pumping, he tried
climbing back in. *Queenie* rolled sedately towards him and began shipping more water. The sealed compartments were also waterlogged.

"Do you have any ropes?" I asked Phil.

"Yeah."

"Get a couple out here will you?"

Esther had meanwhile lost her handhold and was floundering in
open water. It occurred to me then that in the confusion of leaving
Batam, I'd forgotten to ask if she could even swim. This was bad. We
had two people in the water, the current raging at six knots, and a
partially submerged kayak stranded in the busiest shipping lane in the
world.

I felt a deep throb in my ears and turned to see an enormous oil
tanker, *Sunrise IV,* bearing down on us. Esther had now managed to
reach the bow of my kayak and was clinging on for dear life, even as
waves crashed over her head. With every deluge, she spat out a mouthful of seawater, coughing and sputtering.

Grabbing one of the lines trailing from the Zodiac, I secured it to my bow rope with a sheet bend.

"Esther, see if you can pull yourself up the rope to the support boat."

"Okay."

Phil pulled her the last twenty feet. "You ready?" he said. Leaning over the side, he grabbed the back of her shorts and yanked her aboard like a gaffed fish.

Stuart was still out there, trying to secure the second line to *Queenie's* prow. The stricken kayak was almost completely submerged, wallowing submarine-like with waves smothering her deck. It happened in a blink of an eye. The bow lifted briefly in the swell and came slamming down on his head.

Sunrise IV was closing fast. Without a lifejacket, Stuart was as good as dead. I cursed the immigration officials at Waterfront City, the customs agents, the antiterrorism officer, and the Maritime and Port Authority of Singapore. Most of all, I cursed myself for allowing this to happen. Stuart had only been trying to help. Now he was gone.

Movement in the water caught my eye. A hand. Then he appeared, looking badly shaken.

"Stuart!" Phil yelled. "Get in here, mate."

Phil was keeping a cool head in a tight spot. With Louis busy at the helm and Kenny filming the disaster as it unfolded, the plucky Kiwi had taken charge of the situation.

"I'm going to try and pump," said Stuart.

"No, get in here, mate. We can pump her alongside the RIB."

The tanker was making my brain shake with the thrum of its engines. I was still furious at myself for not insisting on a proper routing plan before setting out. "Stuart," I shouted. "Get to the *fucking* support craft will you."

We were suddenly cast into shadow. The grin of the tanker's bow wave was less than fifty yards away, topped by towering steel. As Stuart pulled himself hand over fist along the rope, Louie brought up the slack to tow *Queenie* out of the tanker's path. The kayak barely moved. She was dead in the water.

For me, this was cutting it too fine. It was time to save our own skins. "Let her loose," I instructed Phil.

Louie shook his head. Having spent his entire life around shipping, the old hand knew the margin for error better than I. He turned his EMINEM cap backwards, upped the revs on the Zodiac, and maintained his northerly course with implacable calm. *Queenie* followed like a stubborn mule in the Zodiac's wake, yawing from side to side.

As the tanker shuddered past, I was close enough to feel the wall of air pushed ahead of the ploughing mass.

Five hours later. Pulau Subar, Indonesia

IT WAS DARK by the time I paddled into the small horseshoe bay belonging to one of the low-lying islets south of the straits. I was back where I started—in Indonesia—but at least no one had drowned. After the fiasco in the shipping lanes, the day had continued on the same deranged course. *Queenie* had been towed to sheltered water on the Singapore side, pumped out, and paddled on to Sentosa by Stuart and Esther. I elected to use slack water over low tide to return to Batam, camp overnight, and try the crossing again in the morning.

Not surprisingly, the press reception had been a complete flop. Unaware of the drama unfolding in the straits, more than a hundred journalists had waited patiently before giving up and going home. My one chance to impress potential sponsors was gone.

Right now, though, this was the least of my worries. Stamped out of Indonesia and yet to enter Singapore, I was effectively persona non grata, trapped between two countries. As the narrowest point between the Indonesian archipelago and Asian mainland, the Singapore Straits were heavily policed by the authorities on both sides, looking to control the inevitable drug smuggling, gun running, marine piracy, and trafficking in exotic animals—Sumatran orang-utans were a favourite, apparently. If the Indonesian navy spotted me, I could expect to be jailed and deported. The seven-month effort from Australia would be all for nothing.

At least there was no moon tonight. Under cover of darkness, I hauled my kayak up the beach into the dense vegetation above the high-tide mark and lay down to rest from the day's exertions. I was ravenously hungry, but even if I found wood dry enough to make a small fire, I had no matches and no food; all my camping gear had gone across on the ferry with Kenny and Phil. Fumbling in the stern compartment, I found an empty rice sack and a can of warm Heineken thrown in before leaving Batam. I flipped the pull ring and inhaled the tepid fizz gratefully. Heineken wasn't my usual beer of choice, but tonight I was its biggest fan.

Around 9:45 pm, I heard the low grumble of thunder, and the irradiated sky above Singapore turned a menacing shade of black. Intermittent flashes freeze-framed the straits in swathes of white-hot light. This would be interesting. I had no tent, no sleeping bag, not even a waterproof jacket.

Crouching under a pandanus tree with my back to the jungle, I cut holes in the rice sack and slipped it over my head. The tropical storm came in low and fast, beating the water along the shore into a muddy froth. The wind thrashed. Giant leaves slapped around my head like sodden washcloths. The downpour was relentless, lasting nearly six hours. By four in the morning, I was shivering uncontrollably. I pumped my arms to ward off hypothermia, danced a jig on the beach, and even tried masturbating in a desperate attempt to generate heat.

With the inkling of dawn, clouds of mosquitoes came flogging out of the bushes. I had no long trousers, no long-sleeved shirt, no DEET repellent. The insects descended from their nocturnal roosts and began to devour me with ravenous gusto. I heard the long premonitory blast of a foghorn and looked up to see a dense pall of fog rolling into the straits.

At 7:15 am, it was still spattering with rain and the visibility poor, only vague suggestions of ships passing in the ghostly murk. High tide was at 11:15 am, which meant I needed to be away no later than 9:00 am to avoid a repeat performance of the day before. But what if the fog didn't lift?

The prospect of paddling through the busy shipping lanes in thick fog—the confusion of engine noise, foghorns, whistles and whoops ricocheting off the swirling banks of grey, vessels materializing out of nowhere—was utterly terrifying. *Without radar, it'll be too dangerous to cross,* I thought anxiously. That being said, I was gripped by an even greater fear. If I delayed another day, how would I explain the two-day hiatus in my passport to Singapore immigration? Famously paranoid, they could very well refuse me entry, and the leg from Darwin would again be forfeited.

No, I thought, *it's today or never.*

And there was something else. Sitting there in the dripping mist, soaked to the skin, straining to make out the ships in the straits, my thoughts returned to the men of Operation Rimau. The island I was crouched on, Pulau Subar, was the same one that Lt Bobby Ross and Able Seaman Andrew "Happy" Huston had crouched on sixty-one years earlier, peering out over the water through their binoculars, monitoring Japanese shipping in Singapore harbour. After an enemy patrol boat blew their cover, they had crossed the straits in darkness without electronics or support, sunk three enemy ships, and made the return crossing before daylight.

Their example had inspired me to set out for Singapore in the first place, and having chased their shadows for thousands of miles, their courage inspired me to finish the job, regardless of the risk. The forgotten heroes of Z Force never made it home. In the weeks and months following the bungled rendezvous, they were either drowned or hunted down—the remaining six lay in unmarked graves along the trail I had just paddled. And although the hands of time could never be turned back, I felt a duty as a fellow paddler to try to make things right. For I, too, was trying to reach a far country, and perhaps by making it back safely I might finish their journey by proxy and in some small way help to bring them home, too.

SINGAPORE TO CHINA
HELPING HANDS & SIMPERING SMILES

It does not matter if lightning strikes from above, if the earth caves in from below, if the land and sky crash together like mighty cymbals, if your head is ablaze, if poisonous snakes crawl on your lap, whether you have time or are busy, are hungry or well fed, happy or sad; whatever happens you should not give up.

—ZHABDRUNG NGAWANG NAMGYAL, *Founder of Bhutan*

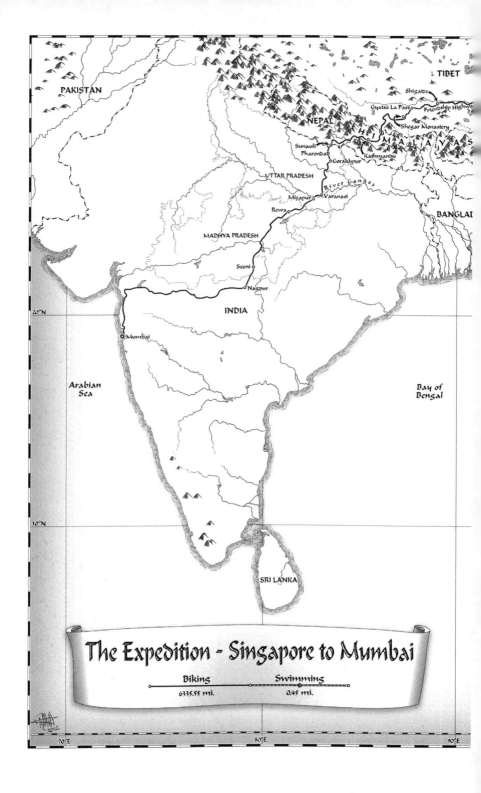

The Expedition - Singapore to Mumbai

Biking — 6335.55 mi. Swimming — 0.45 mi.

Pulau Subar, Riau, Indonesia. November 17, 2005

A T 8:30 AM, THE SKY over the shipping lanes began to clear, honing the shapes drifting through the fog into recognizable ships. I rendezvoused with the Zodiac at 10:00 am. Louie already had his EMINEM cap turned backwards, ready for action.

"Alright, Louie?" I said. "Good to go?"

He frowned in disapproval. To preserve the integrity of the circumnavigation, I'd insisted we return to the tow point from the day before, making for a longer crossing.

"Start from there?" he asked gruffly.

"Yep," I replied. "We're aiming for The Sisters, right?" These were a pair of islets south of Singapore.

Phil handed me an apple and a Mars Bar, and away we went. Today, we didn't even bother to radio the MPA for permission to cross the Traffic Separation Scheme. We just kept going, and after three hours of dodging ships, Louis calling the shots—"This one will go ahead of us, this one behind"—the shipping lanes were safely behind us.

In the lee of The Sisters, I cleared Singapore customs and immigration and paddled the last few miles under an overcast sky to Sentosa Beach, a surrealist's canvas of immaculate sand and neatly choreographed palm trees.

"How yer doin', Jason?" said Kenny, standing beside two other photographers. They were the only media present.

Realizing that something was expected of me, a symbolic gesture to mark the completion of the Indonesian leg, I levered myself out of the Solstice and held my paddle above my head, feigning a victory pose. Except that victory was the last thing on my mind.

"Good to be here," I replied. A wave of emotion welled up, and the beach collapsed before my squinting eyes. "It's been a long trip. Feels good to be finished."

But Indonesia wasn't finished with me. A fortnight later in a hostel in the Indian quarter, I awoke in the early hours drowning in sweat. The fever cycle fluctuated between burning heat and freezing cold.

When I clocked a temperature of 106 degrees on the seventh morning, I knew it was time to see a doctor. "Malaria," he announced, reading off the results of a blood test.

How ironic was that? I'd worn a long-sleeved shirt and trousers every morning and evening for seven months, slept in a tent, and lathered myself regularly with one hundred per cent DEET. Yet all it took was one bite from an infected mosquito my last night on Pulau Subar. Even the Lariam hadn't stopped it.

I took a concentrated course of Malarone and spent the weeks of convalescence planning the overland leg to Mumbai. With Myanmar closed to independent travellers, I would have to take an 11,265-kilometre detour through Malaysia, Thailand, Laos, China, and cross the Himalayas before winter. The biggest unknown was eastern Tibet, 1,600 kilometres of rugged track scaling a series of 16,000-foot passes controlled by police checkpoints. As the historic setting for violent clashes between native Tibetans and Chinese security forces, the region had been closed to outsiders for decades. Various renegade travellers had attempted the journey illegally over the years, but only a handful made it to Lhasa, travelling mainly at night when Public Security Bureau (PSB) officers could be found napping at their posts. The overwhelming majority were arrested, imprisoned, and deported.

My chances of making it to India were further decreased by something that had plagued the expedition from the beginning: money—or rather the lack thereof. The $15,000 I'd earned in Colorado was long gone. The idea of putting Moksha in a shopping centre and returning to life as a mall rat, whoring out my stories to hard-boiled Singaporeans, made my head swim. In February, I suffered a relapse of malaria. *Plasmodium vivax* could reside in the liver indefinitely, I was told, and recur without warning. Not for the first time, I asked myself: *Are you ready to give up?*

Then, out of the blue, an email arrived from the head of Aberdeen Asset Management Asia, inviting me to discuss possible sponsorship of the upcoming leg through Asia and beyond. Hugh Young was a large, jolly Englishman who'd read about the expedition in *The Straits Times*. For eleven years the project had teetered on the edge of extinction, falling insolvent too many times to count. Now, with the help of this self-made man, who had left London around the same time as us and built a financial empire from the ground up, I could finish what Steve and I started.

IT'S INCREDIBLE THE difference it makes to your morale knowing you can keep going, that you don't have to stop every few months and grub around for the means to get a little farther on down the road. In the spring of 2006, I rode north, with three hundred pounds of gear divided between four panniers and a trailer. Most of it was for filming, editing, and sending back daily video blogs (vlogs) via satellite modem, catering to the shifting appetites of online followers living vicariously through the adventure. The thought of lugging the whole lot over the Himalayas was appalling, but once across the Johor-Singapore Causeway into Malaysia, I forgot about the weight, the heat, the humidity, and my lack of fitness. On the Asian mainland proper, Greenwich seemed almost palpable.

Part of the agreement with Aberdeen was to use the journey as a conduit for the company's humanitarian outreach. In Kuala Lumpur, I teamed up with their regional office to visit Rumah Solehah, a halfway house for HIV-positive women and children abandoned by their families. It was a chance to invite media, raise awareness of the plight of the sufferers, many of whom didn't have long to live, and for the managing director of Aberdeen to make a donation. A similar event was planned for Father Joe's Mercy Centre in Bangkok, consisting of an orphanage, kindergarten, and hospice for mothers and street kids living with AIDS. Like the Hope Orphanage in East Timor, the long-term goal was to provide children with the means, most notably an education, to survive in the real world without resorting to drugs, violence, or prostitution.

"Passport, please," said the immigration officer at Bukit Kayu Hitam, the easternmost border crossing between Malaysia and Thailand. The woman wore a green jacket and her black hair was cropped. She looked about forty.

I handed over my passport.

"First time you come to Thailand?" She began leafing through the pages.

"Yes, first time." I smiled at her through the little window. "I wonder, is it possible to get any longer than thirty days?"

"You—Stay—Thirty days. You—Out!" She waved her hand. "Then come back."

It was 1,700 kilometres to the Lao border. I needed at least ten days in Bangkok to secure visas for Laos, Nepal, and India, and to organize the event at Father Joe's Mercy Centre. Time would be tight.

"Do you mind if I film?" I asked, indicating the video camera I was holding.

She wagged a finger. "Just cannot film me nude, okay?" She giggled and bared her teeth at me.

"I'll bear that in mind," I said. "You'd be famous on the Internet, though. Maybe even get your own TV show?"

She batted her eyelashes. "Me? Ya. Ha! Ha! Ha!"

"We could call it 'The Booty Guard' or 'Thai Me Up at the Border'—or something."

She frowned at my gibberish.

If Malaysia had been the Land of Helping Hands, Thailand was the Kingdom of Simpering Smiles. Avoiding the separatist hotspots of Yala, Pattani, and Narathiwat in the southeast, I rode up the irresistible-sounding Isthmus of Kra, the narrow neck of land separating north and south Thailand, passing gum plantations and lush, tropical rainforest. Unlike the scenery, which changed little, I found myself totally at sea reading road signs in an alphabet rooted in the Brahmic family of scripts from the Indian subcontinent. For someone brought up with the Latin writing system, it was like drowning in hieroglyphics. The spoken language was even more of a challenge, each sentence a jaw-twisting meal of yips, gargles, and barks. This made my food orders at roadside stalls a constant source of amusement for the locals and a frustrating lottery for me. On one occasion, believing I'd ordered a fried egg, a slice of bread, and a cup of tea, I was presented with a bowl of hot water with grass floating in it. From then on, I resorted to barging into kitchens and jabbing at vegetables, a survival strategy that worked all the way into China.

In Bangkok, I caught up with a young woman who'd buttonholed me in Singapore and persuaded me to let her join for a section. Melissa's initial email announced her ambition to ride through Africa. As an Outward Bound instructor, she explained, it had always bothered her that she'd never actually been on an expedition. "What about Thailand?" I suggested when we met over coffee. At least if we didn't get along, she could take a bus or a train to the nearest city and fly home, impossible in the middle of the Sahara Desert.

Now, in the arrivals hall of Bangkok airport, seeing her round bespectacled face peering over the top of a trolley piled high with biking equipment, I was quietly amazed that she'd even turned up. By the end of my time in Singapore, I'd come to the conclusion that the inhabitants were largely compliant, few questioning the preset path laid before them. They went to school, got a job, bought a house, and then married and started a family. Yet here was this twenty-five-year-old woman, a secure and promising future ahead of her, about to go gallivanting off into the depths of Asia with a total stranger.

"So, is this typical behaviour for women your age in Singapore?" I asked her back at the guest house in Banglamphu.

"Noo." Melissa shook her head and contemplated the bike pedals in her hands. "Noo, not at all. But ... like with the kids I teach on the ropes course, there's always a safety net. So maybe it's time to throw it aside for now. I used to be a worrier. But I thought, noo, it's time to stop worrying. Why worry?"

Her compatriots, almost without exception, were marching to the beat of a different drummer, Lee Kuan Yew, a self-professed social Darwinist and the nation's prime minister from 1959 to 1990. Lee's autocratic legacy lived on in his son, Lee Hsien Loong, the current prime minister.

"I thot it would be pupossful to see," Melissa went on, using the sing-song vernacular of her fellow Chinese Singaporeans complete with glottal stops, "wot it is like for the people to live in these places. Nothing beats being there, seeing it wid your oon eyes. Different to reading about it in a magazeen."

Everything worked in Singapore. Everything was clean. It was the perfect place to raise a family, people said. And when I'd asked these same people—Chinese, Indians, Malays, and expatriates—whether they minded living in what was essentially a one-party state, every one of them had responded that as long as the streets were safe and their kids received a good education, they could do without political pluralism.

Clearly, though, not everybody was happy. Melissa was the first Singaporean I'd met who dared question the status quo, an act of defiance that impressed me enough to let her come along.

I said, "So what did your father say when you told him you were going on this trip?"

Melissa looked off into a corner of the room, twisted her face, and uttered a Hokkien wail: *"Aiya! Wah ca' you stay hom' an' watch TV wi' meee?"*

"And the rest of your family?"

"Brother says hooray. Sister thinks I am crazy. But she is crazy about roller coasters, so she's no better. My mum thinks I should be doing this before I get too oold."

Next morning, a Sunday, we left the hostel at first light to beat the traffic.

"I never felt my bike so heavy!" Melissa complained, wheeling it out the front gate. She wore a yellow jersey, a CamelBak, and a blue helmet jammed over a white bandana advertising Thompson Island Outward Bound. She stepped over the frame and pushed off.

"Ookay! Ookay!" She hopped on one foot. "I think I got it!"

The blue waterproof bag behind her seat began to wobble. Then the bike tipped over, taking Melissa with it. A car following close behind swerved around the tangle of limbs, missing her by inches.

By the time I caught up, Melissa was already on her feet, delivering a staccato commentary on the speed implications of her load. "So instet of operatin' at eighteen km per owa, I'm gonna do somethin' like ten km per owa."

Then she was off again, weaving back and forth, struggling to maintain balance.

"Just be careful when a bus is coming," I shouted, hearing a dull rumble behind me. "Like one is now."

An hour later, we were slipping towards Laos in the shady cool of an overpass, passing orange-clad monks, droves of cyclists, their front baskets groaning with potatoes and other produce, and skyscrapers draped with giant tapestries of King Bhumibol Adulyadej. The sight of an emaciated dog stretched with scabby pink skin reminded me of one of the more distressing aspects of travelling through Southeast Asia. Man's best friend was considered as much a pariah in Thailand as it was in Indonesia, which struck me as a puzzling paradox for the predominantly Theravada Buddhist population. The rubbish-choked canals known as klongs lined with rambling shacks, and the children in rags scampering in stinking filth, afforded us glimpses of the ever-present poverty, the one common feature of the majority of people's lives.

But we were moving and, shameless though it was, the very act of leaving these wombs of suffering in our wake was liberating in a twisted sort of way.

By 9:00 am on the morning of the third day, we had summited a ridgeline fifty kilometres east of Saraburi. The temperature was already 102 degrees. We snatched a ten-minute breather, scoffed a bowl of noodles from a roadside stall, and began the long downhill descent into Pak Chong.

The gradient was steep, and we quickly gathered momentum with our heavy loads. I remembered thinking: *This is the kind of hill you can pick up too much speed too fast—a front blowout, and you're toast.* My odometer was nudging 37 kmph when it happened. Ahead of me, Melissa's bike started to wobble. The front wheel carved out an exaggerated S. Then—*WHAM!* She pitched head first over the handlebars, slammed into the tarmac, and skidded down the hard shoulder on her face.

When I arrived on the scene a few seconds later, she was lying motionless, trapped under her bike frame, blood pouring from the side of her head. The way her neck was twisted, the first thing that ran through my head was: *She must be dead.* The horror of the situation was unfathomable. How could I explain this to a family at odds with her leaving home in the first place?

Taking care not to move her spine, I removed the bike and fished in her mouth for broken teeth. That was when she let out a faint moan. Relief! Despite the blood, the lacerations on her knees and thighs, and the peach-sized swelling around her left cheek, she was alive. I removed a large chunk of gravel from her right temple, marvelling that she hadn't landed in one of the lanes of traffic and been run over.

Motorists stopped. Someone with a mobile phone called for an ambulance. Paramedics arrived, scooped her body onto an orange stretcher and disappeared in a flurry of lights. Fortunately, the nearest hospital was only thirteen kilometres away. A friendly police officer took her bike in the bed of his pickup. I followed behind.

In the emergency room, Melissa was already knocked out on morphine. The senior nurse showed me the x-rays and explained the prognosis in halting English. Thanks to the helmet there were no fractures to her skull or facial bones. Aside from a torn shoulder ligament, a black eye, three stitches in her cheek, and extensive road rash, she'd escaped serious harm.

How long before she could ride again was another matter. Next morning, when I arrived to escort her to a local guest house, her face had swollen to the size of a pumpkin, and her eyes were closed nearly all the way. She squinted at me despondently from a wheelchair. Her legs and arms were swathed in bandages leaking serum, and her face was covered in bite-sized wads of cotton wool.

"You know you should really go easy with those marshmallow fights," I said. "Someone's going to get hurt one of these days."

She attempted a smile. "If only it was just a marshmallow fight. I look like a stuck pig!"

"Don't worry. People don't care what you look like."

She shook her head. "My skin is prone to scarring. I think I will need plastic surgery."

You're lucky to be alive! I wanted to say.

For the next three days, I fetched food and medicines, and then rode north before my Thai visa ran out. Melissa took the bus to Khon Kaen, the last big town before the border. When we rendezvoused in the Charoenchit House four days later, her shoulder was still bad, and her knees remained bandaged, scabs yet to form. The hardest thing of all, she said, was keeping up morale.

"Being stranded in these roach motels in the suffocatin' heat is twisting my het," she said.

Then, displaying the upbeat attitude and determination I already admired in her, she informed me that if I tried to stop her from getting back on her bike, I'd have to shoot her.

———⟨∭⟩———

ELEGANTLY FRAMED BY what the English travel writer Norman Lewis described as "haze-dimmed mountain shapes," the flower head of northern Laos rests in a saucer-like plain fanning out from the Mekong River. Melissa and I entered this kingdom of limpid paddy fields and monoliths of jutting rock after taking a wrong turn leaving the capital, Vientiane. It was a happy mistake, putting us on a longer but more picturesque back road to the once-religious centre of Buddhist Laos, Louangphrabang. With the sun on our faces, we skimmed through a dreamy water world of wallowing beasts, conical hat-wearing rice farmers up to their elbows in cloud-mirrored paddies, and children heaving on bamboo poles connected to box-shaped nets, fishing for sprats.

Pedalling on the level proved to be no problem for Melissa. Apart from her still-bandaged left knee, the road rash was crusting over nicely, some of the scabs even coming loose, revealing tender new skin underneath. The question was whether her torn shoulder would be strong enough to pull the long mountain grades in the days ahead. More than running out of money, being robbed, attacked by dogs, or her bicycle breaking down, Melissa's biggest fear was to have to walk all the way to China.

Riding ahead, I came to a tributary of the Mekong, muddy and turbulent from monsoonal rain. The river was littered with branches and tree trunks flushed down from the mountains. It was also bridgeless. The only way to cross was by one of two pontoon-style ferries: one for cars, the other for passengers and motorcycles.

This posed a problem.

The distance was only three hundred yards, a tiny fraction of the total circumnavigation. It would have been easy to slip across on the ferry and keep quiet about it. Deep down, though, I knew I had to do it. Swimming the river was symbolic of the larger effort to reach antipodal points, ensuring an unimpeachable around-the-world journey. *You either do it right,* I told myself, *or not at all.*

I was busy studying the river and how the ferries crabbed across, angling upstream to compensate for the current, when Melissa rolled to a stop beside me.

"What are you thinking?" she said, following my gaze.

"That I need to swim this bloody thing."

She laughed. "You're kidding, right? Wot about a safety net?"

I glanced around but there was none, only a lone canoe tethered to the far bank manned by a father and his two sons. They were just sitting there, fishing, perhaps. The likelihood of me winding up at the mouth of the Mekong, spat out into the South China Sea along with all the other refuse, suddenly struck me as rather high.

"I'll swim perpendicular to get across as quickly as possible."

"Are you a strong swimmer?"

"I can doggy paddle."

Melissa's eyes widened, and she gave one of her Hokkein wails. "Aiya!"

"Only joking. I wonder if there are any crocs left in this river?"

While Melissa went across on the passenger ferry with all our gear and my shirt and shoes, I limbered up on the bank. Then, heart racing, I waded into the river. The current immediately took me downstream much faster than I was expecting. The ferry ramp on the far side quickly disappeared. So did the canoe. I kept lunging at the filthy water, thinking of my near-fatal swim to retrieve the sail bag mid-Atlantic and the hypoxia-induced hallucinations. No blood in the water this time. Only branches and other obstacles threatening to yank me under.

After what seemed like an eternity, I reached the halfway point. Here the water was roughest, the waves breaking over my head, forcing me to stop and cough out the water. The bank still seemed so far away and my arms were screaming. Where was Steve when you needed him? I imagined him now sitting on the far bank, dorado fish cradled in his arms, staring at me with that implacable expression of his. *Typical Jason, taking his own sweet time as usual!*

At last, a low curtain of overhanging trees darkened the water around me, and a bamboo cane as thick as a scaffold pole appeared, jutting into the river. I grabbed it and pulled myself up the bank, a climb of thirty or so feet. Standing there at the top with my hands on my hips, panting heavily but otherwise feeling rather pleased with myself, I turned and noticed three pretty Laotian girls sitting under a banana tree. They stopped nattering briefly to glance at me, at the same tight-fitting Lycra shorts that had once induced horror and disgust in a French lorry driver, and then went back to their gossip, as if the river offered up half-naked farangs every day. It was only when I was well down the riverside path to where Melissa was waiting that the inevitable peel of giggles caught up with me.

As I hobbled, carefully placing my feet to avoid stepping on anything sharp or poisonous, the music of their laughter grew fainter until it blended with the murmuring of the water and the two became one, giving the river a new song to sing as it tumbled its way to the sea. Listen to a river long enough and beneath the gurgling chatter you start to pick out other sounds, voices and melodies that tell of long-forgotten secrets gathered on its journey through the ancient land, mysteries and magic that make up the story of a continent and its people, their myriad wars, catastrophes, and triumphs played out through the millennia. All of it was there in that venerable old waterway, whisked and blended into one, like the energy compressed into the mortar of an old house, encoded messages chronicling past lives that resonate in the floorboards and haunt the corridors, waiting to be discovered.

THE SAME OPPRESSIVE topography that once dogged the early French colonialists, the invading Imperial Japanese Army after them, and the Americans fighting in Vietnam after them, now conspired against us as well. Riding up and down these sheer inclines was good training for the Himalayas, but for Melissa, accustomed to the gentle undulations of Singapore and her shoulder still in considerable pain, it demanded an almost super-human effort. Since the backpacker retreat of Vang Vieng, she'd had to walk nearly every major climb, pushing her laden bike up to seven hours at a stretch. The reward of freewheeling down the other side was invariably short-lived, faced as she was with another tortuous climb at the bottom. Her nightmare scenario of walking all the way to China was fast becoming a reality.

"How are you doing?" I asked her part way up a thirty-six kilometre, 2,300-foot climb from Kasi to Phou Khoun. We were sitting by the side of the road, taking a breather. Melissa's hair was plastered across her face with sweat.

"I'm getting irritated easily," she replied glumly. "When someone honks, I have this crazy idea to just scream at them. But I don't. Because it's a waste of my bref."

I knew how she felt. I would have happily dragged the driver of every madly honking bus and 4WD out of their cab and pushed them off the mountain.

Before us, beyond a latticework of terraced paddy fields, a string of smoky peaks punctured the sky, their tabletop summits jagged and hewn like the ramparts of mountain fortresses. Mist poured down the jungly slopes, swirling like dry ice all the way to a ribbon of silver, the Mekong River, snaking its way south.

Travelling through such vertiginous terrain, we found that the clouds migrated up and down the mountains with us. One minute we'd be floating on an island hovering in space, gazing down onto the milky canopy below. Next, we were in a real pea-souper and getting drenched.

"Do you have any water left?" Melissa asked.

I handed her my spare bottle. "Not much, I'm afraid. It's mainly backwash. But you're welcome to it."

She wiped the nozzle with the hem of her shirt, lifted the bottle to her lips and took a gulp. This would have been unthinkable a week earlier—Singaporeans were fanatical about hygiene. But clearly even the most ingrained cultural habits were dispensable when needs must.

Pushing on, we passed glowering granddads in green Mao caps shouldering homemade rifles, lethal-looking things with five-foot-long barrels and a pistol grip instead of a shoulder stock, like something cobbled together in a garden shed. We later learned these men were the same Viet Minh guerrilla fighters who had harried the French, ambushing convoys sent from Vientiane to supply the northern provinces, before booting out their colonial overlords in 1954.

Not everyone was hostile, though. When we reached Phou Khoun, the owners of the guest house where we stayed asked us to join them for a family meal. It was the first time in Laos we'd been invited into someone's home.

"So, what is it we're eating?" I asked part way through a mouthful of mystery meat. Although vegetarian, I tried to eat whatever was offered in a stranger's house so as not to cause offence.

A lad of about eighteen, who'd travelled from Vientiane to set up a computer shop for his uncle, spoke a little English. "Vogs," he replied.

"Frogs, really?" It surprised me that Laotians would continue such an iconic gastronomical legacy from their former French masters. "Where do you get them?"

He laughed. "They everywhere. So easy find!" He waved a hand at the rain-splattered street in front of us. "Look, so many."

I looked, but all I saw were roadside stalls selling pineapples, bananas, dragon's eye, and other fresh produce. "I don't see them."

He pointed underneath one of the carts.

"Oh, you mean *dogs?*"

Melissa stopped eating and stared at her bowl.

"Yes! Yes! Good eat!"

"Cats, too?" I asked.

The lad frowned. "No." He then embarked on a long rambling story about how a cat had once escaped the protein-starved highlanders' pot by befriending a holy man, amnesty that was eventually passed on to the rest of the feline kingdom.

"It brings a whole new meaning to being Chinese," Melissa commented the next morning. We were in another village, eating noodles, watching three dogs being pushed into hessian sacks. The rain was pouring down, making for a thoroughly pathetic scene. The doomed animals—one black, two tans—whimpered in fear as they were trussed up against the side of a motorcycle.

"There's a statement that Chinese can eat everything." Melissa looked into space and rattled off something in Chinese. *"Things that can fly, that can walk, can swim, we can eat everything."* She hung her head. "But I cannot eat that. It's too cute!"

When we finally reached Louangphrabang, Melissa made the shock announcement that she'd decided to go home. "I don't want to hold you up any longer," she said, referring to my deadline to cross the Himalayas by winter.

We were sitting in her room, the contents of her panniers laid out on the bed.

"Let's first try getting rid of some of this kit," I suggested. "Lighten your load."

This was easier said than done. Another Singaporean trait was their love of gadgetry.

"What about that mosquito coil holder?" I pointed to a metal box that resembled a small cake tin fitted with a hanging clip. "You don't need that."

She clasped the contraption to her chest protectively. "Noo. That's staying."

"It's useless, though. What do you need a holder for?"

She looked at me like I was an idiot. "For holding mosquito coils?"

"Which you can quite easily do using a penknife, or the little stand they come with. Come one, Melissa, do you want to get up these hills or not?"

"I'll get rid of the books if I haff to, but this is staying."

I picked out other non-essential items: calamine lotion, shoe bag, selection of Triangia pans, AA batteries, and a pair of socks.

Melissa held up a plastic bottle. "I will lose haff a bottle of my precious shampoo that I brought specially."

"If you shaved your head," I pointed out, "you wouldn't need shampoo."

She gave me an icy look.

"*And* you wouldn't need to spend money on haircuts."

"Bite me," she replied, picking out a compass and a pencil case and laying them on the To Go pile. "Right. That's it. Everything else is staying."

I nodded at her computer. "Laptop ..." I whispered in a brainwashing voice. "Must send laptop home ..."

"Noo! I can't be sure it will be secure. It's too costly to replace."

"Fair enough. But what about all these wretched mosquito coils?" I picked up a plastic drum of them, pried off the lid and threw most of them out. "You've got about twenty in here. Just buy them as you go."

Melissa scrunched up her face and clenched her fists in frustration.

Breaking open the remaining packet, I fished out the little aluminium stand and waved it in her face. "And there's a support, so you don't need your fancy blummin' mosquito coil holder." I grabbed the cherished item off the bed and flung it on the pile.

"Noo, it's staying!" she cried, snatching it back. "It's staying. It's staying. Ookay?"

Now, several pounds lighter, we reached the Chinese border a day earlier than expected. As we meandered through no man's land, the potholed Laotian track morphed into a brand spanking new road with a gloriously smooth finish. Unruly creepers gave way to a manicured grass verge planted with zigzagging bonsai hedges. Elegant street lamps and shrubberies prettified the surrounds. It was Disneyland in the tropics, down to the twittering birds.

Melissa was flushed with excitement. As a second-generation Singaporean, this was the closest she'd ever got to her native China. "I can finally eat something I knoo," she said happily. "Like roast duck! No more buffalo meat swimming around in my noodles."

My blood was pumping, too, but for a different reason. Hidden inside my trailer was an arsenal of electronics—cameras, laptop, satellite phone, hard drives, high-speed modem—all of it synonymous with undercover journalism. Conscious of its less-than-exemplary human rights record, China was neurotic about filmmakers sneaking in and shooting unauthorized documentaries. I also had a historical account of Tibet written by the Dalai Lama's elder brother, Thubten Jigme Norbu, containing valuable background information on the region I'd be passing through. I'd torn off the front and back covers, but it wouldn't take long for a nit-picking official to leaf through and figure out where I was going. The book alone was enough to get me barred from entering China.

Fortunately, the customs officer wasn't the least bit interested in our panniers. Being on his lunch hour, all he wanted was to go back to sleep on the wooden bench behind his desk. The immigration people were a different matter, though. Three officials took turns scrutinizing my six-month visa. Superiors were consulted, phone calls made, and alternative forms of identification demanded. Eventually, thanks to Melissa's Mandarin, they stamped our passports and waved us away.

Walking our bikes down Main Street, our first glimpse of China proper was an avenue of grandiose shops with gaudy roofs, like a toy town plonked in the middle of nowhere. All the buildings were vacant.

There wasn't a soul in sight. Maybe the shops hadn't officially opened? The real reason soon revealed itself. Past the agricultural bank at the bottom of town, the pristine road dissolved into ankle-deep mud.

"Where's our beautiful road?" I said to Melissa.

She chuckled. "That is the Chinese way. It's all about show, displaying wealth and progress, giving a good impression to visitors arriving at the border. Did you see behind those shop fronts? It was like a film set. Nothing there."

Another peek into the Chinese psyche was provided by the new road being built from the north, the G213, a 2,827-kilometre trade corridor linking China with the rest of the Indochinese Peninsula. The four-lane artery sliced through the heart of the Xishuangbanna National Nature Reserve, home to a quarter of China's animal and plant species, including golden-haired monkeys, wild elephants, leopards, tigers, peacocks, hornbills, gibbons, slow loris, and spotted civets. It was a miracle of engineering, people said, and this much was true. A procession of concrete pillars supporting the road above the rainforest canopy cleverly negotiated the precipitous terrain by marching down the middle of the Nanmuwo River. But the highway was also a harbinger of things to come, a bold statement heralding China's great leap forward into the twenty-first century complete with large swathes of the country smothered in tarmac and concrete.

Restricted to the old road, we caught only glimpses through the trees of this architectural marvel in the making. The rain continued unabated as we pressed on to Mengla. The mud got so bad at times and the track so rutted, often it was easier just to wheel our bikes through the jungle. Three days of this, and Melissa's newfound love affair with China was showing signs of strain. The rain, the mud, the obnoxious drivers leaning on their horns, the suspicious body parts bobbing in her bowls of soup (there was no sign of her beloved roast duck noodles at the roadside stalls) all added up to a rather less-rosy picture than she'd imagined.

And our trials were only beginning. Riding up a twenty-kilometre incline out of Mengla, my joints started to ache. By the time we stopped for something to eat in Nalong, I felt feverish and my head was pounding. The restaurant had an upstairs guest room. I spent the rest of the afternoon swaddled in my sleeping bag, wearing every item of cold weather clothing I had for the Himalayas and still shivering with cold.

By nightfall, my body temperature had soared to 107 degrees. With the nearest hospital in Jinghong, a day's ride in a decrepit bus, we resorted to one of the self-test malaria kits we'd brought with us. These little plastic cassettes basically told you whether you had malaria, and if so, whether it was the most severe form, *Plasmodium falciparum*, or one of four other strains. They weren't as specific as a clinical lab test, but they were better than nothing. Melissa took a drop of blood from my thumb, and within ten minutes we had a result. Two red lines indicated it was *falciparum*.

For more than a million of the world's 250 million people infected each year with *falciparum*, this same result would have been a death sentence. Left untreated, cerebral malaria can develop in days, even hours, leading to seizures, coma, and death. For me, however, lucky enough to be armed with a cure, the diagnosis was actually a relief. A bigger fear was coming down with dengue "breakbone" fever that shared the same symptoms as malaria but was untreatable. Sufferers were immobilized sometimes for months, enduring the excruciating joint and muscle pains that gave the illness its name. Contracting it would have almost certainly meant missing my window to cross the Himalayas.

I immediately started a concentrated course of Malarone, four tablets three times a day, and combined it with artesunate, a derivative of qinghaosu, a plant-based substance used by Chinese herbalists to treat *falciparum* since AD 341. With Melissa on nurse duty, I rode the rollercoaster fever ride for the next 48 hours, from the broiling peaks to the icy troughs. Peace and quiet would have been nice, but after dark the restaurant below became a roistering karaoke bar with locals getting drunk on rice wine and butchering Jackie Cheung into the early hours. When I begged Melissa to go down and tell them to put a sock in it, she just laughed. "In a nation of shouters and noise lovers in general, what do you expect?" she said.

The fever broke on the evening of the third day. Facing another night of Jackie Cheung, I opted to push on to Jinghong.

It takes weeks to build cardiovascular fitness, but only days to lose it, especially if malaria parasites have been using your red blood cells as incubation pods and caused them to rupture, a condition known as haemolysis. In just seventy-two hours, the condition I'd gained in Laos had all but disappeared; even carrying my gear down one flight of stairs had me gasping for breath. For the first time since taking on the highlands of Guatemala with a Raleigh 3-speed in 1997, I had to get off and walk.

So now we were both pushing our bikes up the hills, cursing as we trudged. As much as I wanted to backtrack to a guest house in Mengla and recuperate properly, we had to keep moving to try to claw back some of the time lost in Thailand and Laos. The travel gods, naturally, had other ideas. Three days out of Nalong, Melissa baled off into the bushes and threw up. Her lower spine was in agony, she said. We dug out the thermometer and clocked a temperature of 103 degrees. Malaria seemed the obvious culprit, but one of the self-test kits said otherwise.

The public hospital in Jinghong was like walking onto the pages of *Oliver Twist:* dingy wards echoing with bodiless wailing, filth everywhere, overpowering toilets, and no running water or hand washing facilities. In the corridors, doctors stooped Fagin-like over cigarettes, their faces lit in twitching flashes by lone fluorescent tubes that blinked idly from the ceilings. It was one of those terrifying places where, unless constantly harried or palmed money, the medical staff avoided patients at all costs, and someone without a family could die unnoticed.

Melissa was ushered to a hospital bed still warm from its previous occupant and immediately put on a saline drip—at forty yuan a bag, the equivalent of two days' pay for many patients. Black turbaned men reeking of wet tobacco tramped in and out, their haggard wives wearing magnificent headdresses of coloured beads, pom-poms, and silver coins followed behind. These were the ethnic Hani people, indigenous to the Xishuangbanna region, their skin sun-roasted and chiselled.

Five bags of saline and a blood test later, Melissa was diagnosed with a severe bacterial infection.

If it had just been that, she could have started a course of antibiotics, and we would have been on our way. But another complication had emerged. Two-week tourist visas couldn't be extended, according to the local PSB office. Her only option was to fly to the nearest consulate in Hong Kong, apply for a sixty-day visa, then re-enter the country. As well as the prohibitive cost, the extra time the detour would take was less than ideal. Might an exception be made just this once, we asked the boot-faced official sitting behind the counter?

He looked up from his scribbling, puckered his lips like a cat's backside, and said, "Bù!" No!

Melissa was furious. "I'm going to go to the office three days before my visa ends, and I'm going to kick up a big ruckus until they extend it. I don't give a damn. They give me shit? I'll give them shit back! It's fine if they deport me. I don't want to come back to China."

This was the first time I'd seen Melissa throw her toys out of the pram. Usually the model of restraint, she continued for the next day and a half to rail against Chinese officialdom. But when her own relatives working for the PSB in China told her even they couldn't help, the vast monochromatic face of Sino bureaucracy closed in on all sides, and she became resigned to her fate.

"It's been a big change for me," she said before leaving for the airport. She was squatting on the pavement outside the Galan Guest-house, taping up a large rectangular box containing her bicycle. "The nomadic life. I like that. Don't get to do that very often in reality. Maybe I will get into healthcare? Work for the World Health Organization and come back to China and sort out their hospitals."

Like Git in Australia, I felt bad for Melissa having to leave the expedition prematurely. Her determination walking up every hill in Laos had quietly amazed me, and her refusal to be herded along with the rest of the Singapore sheeple, lured by the promise of Shangri-la, would doubtless inspire other young men and women to question the linear trajectory of their lives. The city-state was an economic miracle, certainly, but where was the edge? As the poet and former UNESCO director general Frederico Mayor pointed out, "Only rebels are beacons for the change that the human condition demands." A free spirit and a lateral thinker, Melissa had the kind of innovative chutzpah that to my mind her compatriots could do with a little more of.

"What's the first thing you'll do when you get home?" I asked her.

She looked away, and squinted through her glasses at the motorcycles sputtering by. "Eat roast duck!" she said finally with hearty confidence.

THE HIMALAYAS
SEVEN WEEKS IN TIBET

There is a saying in Tibetan, 'Tragedy should be utilized as a source of strength'. No matter what sort of difficulties, how painful experience is, if we lose our hope, that's our real disaster.

—HIS HOLINESS THE 14TH DALAI LAMA OF TIBET

ACH DAY I RODE north under the benevolent Yunnan sun, passing fields of golden stooks shaped like the local houses, their thatched roofs tapered into spires to slick off the rain, I gained a few hundred feet in elevation and a little of my former strength. It was August and the rice harvest was in full swing, fuelling a festive atmosphere in the surrounding paddies. I was witnessing the completion of a life cycle that began in Laos with the planting of fledgling rice seedlings.

I stopped between villages to watch a row of barefoot women laugh and crack jokes as they worked, doubled over, scything a stand of mature rice plants with their short-handled sickles. One of the men threshing the stems waved me over.

"How ... ode ... are ... you?" he asked. He was using both hands to beat a bundle of stalks against the inside of a wooden box. The grains ricocheted around the inside and bounced down the slanted sides.

"Thirty-eight," I replied.

In spite of the hot sun and the back-breaking toil, it was all smiles. Bringing in the harvest was the highpoint of the year for these people, knowing they'd get through another winter.

I picked up a sheaf myself and whacked it into the box. They all thought this was hilarious, the foreign devil playing at Chinese peasant. "Okay, okay! Ferry guda!" And I laughed with them, because it was a glorious day and the sun was shinning and the landscape stunning, and in spite of the limited communication, I was enjoying the rosy-cheeked scene of pastoral bliss.

Sadly, such cultural breakthroughs were turning out to be a rarity in China. In spite of Melissa's daily lessons in Mandarin, my grasp of the language was still abysmal, limiting social interaction. The only thing I could say with any degree of competency was, "Wǒ xiǎng jiān jīdàn." I would like a fried egg. Even then, every few hundred kilometres regional inflections would change sufficiently for my attempts to be rendered ineffectual, and I'd be reduced once again to marching into kitchens and stabbing at ingredients.

In Kunming, a city of four million, I stopped to track down an over-size printer. There were plenty of reasons to be apprehensive about travelling through Tibet—the risk of landslides on the steep mountain trails, vertical drop-offs, rabid dogs, and falling sick with no hope of medical treatment—but the thing that worried me most was the where-abouts of the police checkpoints, making accurate maps essential. My father had emailed digital versions he'd found on the Internet, avoiding the risky business of smuggling them across the border from Laos. Now I had to find a way of converting them to hard copies to use in the field.

As a provincial capital, Kunming afforded a glimpse of the new China everyone was banging on about, the rags-to-riches story that hogged the covers of international business magazines with headers like *China Rising, New Powerhouse of the East,* and *Red Dragon Apparent.* As the publications indicated, I could have been in London or New York going by the trendy shops with kitschy English names selling everything from the latest Paris fashions to Double Choca Mocha Frappuccinos, all presented with a designer's flare for complementary colours, slick lighting, and subtle techno pulsing in the background. But I couldn't stop thinking of Jinghong Hospital, its medieval hygiene standards, and the farmers less than a day's ride away bringing in the harvest with their bare hands, not a machine in sight. The disparity was so marked, the urban fantasy so out of synch with the harsh realities of Chinese rural life, that future dissent from the impoverished many seemed almost in-evitable.

But hey, what did I know about China? I found my oversize printer, had twenty-two large-scale maps printed on durable silk, and spent the next two days holed up in a cheap guest house working out the exact location of the checkpoints. The maps were 1:200,000 Russian military topos, the only ones my father had managed to find marked with latitude and longitude. Working backwards, I first had to marry the place names and key features—prominent peaks, rivers, and bridg-es—to those on a Chinese road atlas, translating the Cyrillic script into

Chinese Hanzi and Tibetan uchen characters. Next, a list of essential odometer readings compiled in English, including the checkpoints
themselves, had to be transposed to the Chinese atlas, and then to the
Russian topos. Finally, I entered the latitude and longitude fixes of the
checkpoints into my GPS, shaved my head and beard, trading the hairy
foreigner look for that of a Buddhist monk, and struck out for Dêqên,
the last legal town before the Tibet border.

The first topo I slipped into the map case on my handlebar bag
was dominated by three parallel scars gouged by the Mekong, Salween,
and Yangtze rivers, each of them full-blooded torrents spilling off the
Tibetan Plateau. Between them, and over millions of years, these engines of attrition had produced the most demanding topography I had
ever faced. The road to Benzilian involved a fifty-six-kilometre climb
between the Mekong and the Yangtze. It took all day snaking up 7,800
feet of cobblestone switchbacks, leading to stunning views of tumbling
glaciers and saw-toothed peaks capped in snow. Ten kilometres before
the pass, it started to rain, which turned to sleet, then to hail, causing
my wheels to lose traction and sending me sprawling. The air was so
thin I could barely think straight, my breath coming in shallow, ragged
gasps.

It was a preview of what lay in store over the coming weeks: rugged,
merciless terrain, and the road spiralling through the roof of the world.

2:45 am. Three kilometres south of Yanjing
THE BEEPING OF my watch alarm woke me. I rolled up my sleeping bag
and air mattress, slipped out from behind a partially collapsed wall
above the road, and scrambled down to the dusty track, dragging my
equipment behind me.

There was just enough moonlight to ride by, if I pedalled slowly.
Keeping the thundering Mekong to my left, after forty or so minutes a

yellowy ball of light appeared, hovering in the darkness ahead. I dismounted and began walking my rig, tyres crunching on the loose gravel. Drawing near, I saw the light was from a household bulb suspended by a naked wire from the eaves of a low building: the first of two checkpoints either side of Yanjing.

Fifty yards short of the guardhouse, I stopped and listened. *Will the guards be asleep yet?* I wondered breathlessly. Only the wind whistling through the sleeping town made any sound. The shadows of the surrounding mountains crowded in, adding to the sense of claustrophobia gripping my throat. I pressed the night light on my watch. Usually an inoffensive glow, the green luminescence seemed to light up the entire valley. I cursed myself. Any moment there'd be a shout, the clatter of boots, searchlights probing the night.

Nothing. Just the gusting wind.

I crept closer, my breath sounding horribly amplified. A pole barrier materialized from the blackness with a sign written in English and Chinese. DO NOT ENTER, it read. Keeping one eye on the guardhouse, I steadied my bike and trailer and ducked underneath. Suddenly, a dog began barking. The night erupted as others took up the cry, baying and howling in a frenzied cacophony.

Still there was no movement from the guardhouse. I vaulted into the saddle and pushed away, the canine chorus following me in a rolling wave.

Three kilometres later, the second checkpoint loomed. Again, I got off and tiptoed the last hundred yards towards the barrier. The guardhouse was set back from the road and dimly lit by another solitary bulb, this one affixed to the top of a pole. Once on the other side and around the first bend, I pedalled as fast as my headlamp beam would allow, aiming to put as many miles between Yanjing and me before daylight. What a rush! Punch-drunk with nervous exhaustion and relieved at negotiating my first checkpoint, I stopped only once to fill my water bottles from a stream crossing the track.

The Mekong in this part of the world had a different name, the Lancang Jiang, meaning the river kingdom of a million elephants. It was young and peppy, a boiling cauldron of whirlpools and swirling mud. The valley floor, more a sharpened V, was stifling even in the shadowy dawn light. Animal trails criss-crossed the sheer slopes, and only scant vegetation and the hardiest of creatures prevailed—the odd feral donkey, sure-footed sheep, and black goats that scrambled nimbly along the lips of dizzying precipices, sending mini-avalanches of rocks clattering onto the track. I even saw a lone cow up there, perched hundreds of feet in the air, eking out a precarious existence between the vertical bluffs of rock.

Averaging six kilometres an hour, I started up a thirty-eight-kilometre series of switchbacks to the next pass. Time slows to a crawl on long mountain climbs. As the river below receded in microscopic slow motion to a loop of sepia braid, my mind began to wander. What were the chances of being apprehended between the checkpoints? Maybe I should ride only at night and hide in the day? But at night, going slower, would I still get over the Himalayas before winter? And was that tinkling bells I could hear echoing off the canyon walls?

Around the next bend, a dozen mules appeared with plaits of red wool wound in their leather halters. They teetered stiff-legged under the weight of the sacks slung across their backs—barley flour, I assumed, the only cereal capable of growing at such altitude, producing the regional staple known as tsampa. Three weather-beaten herders brought up the rear, their mahogany faces creasing into smiles as we passed. When I greeted them in Chinese, "Nǐ hǎo," they scowled and responded with, "Tah-shi de-leh. Keh-rahng kah-bah phe-geh?" Greetings. Where are you going?

I knew then for sure that I'd made it to Tibet.

AT THE TOP of the pass, the sun was already clipping the peaks to the west. A herd of yaks came shuffling up the track in the twilight, their straggly black-and-white tails swinging like pendulums, keeping time with their plodding gait. Five nomads in wide-brimmed hats walked beside them. If it had been earlier in the day, I would have stopped to soak in this classic Tibetan moment. As it was, having ridden for fifteen hours straight, I was dog-tired and longed to camp, so I kept going. I also felt queasy—from the altitude, perhaps, or from the stream water I'd collected earlier in the day but hadn't had a chance to filter yet.

After jouncing down fourteen kilometres of switchbacks, I looked for a turn-off near a small hill. Another kilometre up a steep sandy track, according to my notes, I could expect to find a monastery, one that was home to a friendly English-speaking monk called Jamanbo, and ask for sanctuary.

The square-roofed monastery was snugged up against the mountainside. It had slab-sided walls that were freshly whitewashed, and the entrance to the inner courtyard was sumptuously framed like a gilded mantelpiece, its stepped eaves painted with elaborate flowers and mythical beings—dragons, demons, and goddesses—brought to life with earthen pigments of reds, blues, and radiant gold. At the centre of the cast iron gates was the monastery's emblem, a bouquet of fiery eyeballs tethered like balloons to their optic nerves, the flames alluding to the modus operandi of the establishment: the raising of spiritual heat, kundalini, leading to moksha, the final release from the cycle of rebirth and worldly pain.

At least that was my assumption. Once inside the courtyard, I found little evidence of devotional pursuit. The place was shambolic, abandoned, as if invaded by gypsies. There was litter everywhere, a beat-up dump truck parked in a corner, and two men tinkering with a motorcycle. Chinese pop music blared from an upstairs window. Where the heck were the monks?

A woman holding a snotty-nosed child appeared before me. When I repeated the name Jamanbo, she just giggled, and the child shook a packet of instant noodles at me. Feeling too sick and exhausted to backtrack and find somewhere else to camp, I made the international sign for sleep. One of the tinkering mechanics seemed to understand and led me out of the compound to a walled garden filled with fruit trees and purple flowering plants. It was the ideal spot, just what I'd been hoping for, hidden from the road and the PSB.

The hinges on the wooden doors collapsed when I pushed them, but no one seemed to mind. Assisted by two filthy, grinning children, I wheeled my bike inside and set about erecting my tent under a leafy apple tree. It took forever, my fingers fumbling with fatigue, guts gurgling. As I was finally pegging down the rain fly, I heard whistling, and turned to see an old woman whirling something over my head, a rattle-shaped prayer wheel inlayed with colourful stones and Sanskrit letters. She hobbled around the tent, spinning her wheel, her exquisite face lined with compassion. Was this a blessing? An exorcism? I didn't really care. Five minutes later, I was curled up in my sleeping bag, riding out the stomach cramps until sleep finally came.

The sound of padding feet and low voices woke me. It was late, the sun on my face. Encouraged by how much better I felt, I stretched contentedly, unzipped the fly, and peered outside. A monk in magenta robes was helping a woman stuff dry grass into the branches of a nearby apple tree. Beyond them, past the far wall of the garden and partially hidden by trees, I noticed another whitewashed building, one that I'd missed the previous evening. *That must be the actual monastery,* I realized. Two monks were sitting with their backs against the outer wall, glancing furtively in my direction. Maybe they were having second thoughts giving me refuge and getting ready to alert the PSB?

Seeing that I was awake, one of the monks got to his feet and hurried through a side door. I was considering breaking camp and making a run for it when the same monk reappeared with a thermos of hot water and three steamed dumplings wrapped in a cloth napkin. I was delighted. Two nights before, the fuel line on my stove had cracked, leaving me unable to cook food or heat water. Having a replacement part shipped to Tibet was out of the question. So was lighting a fire or stopping in towns. To keep as low a profile as possible, I'd resigned myself to soaking instant noodles in cold water until Kathmandu, 2,300 kilometres away.

I made some tea, rehydrated a packet of noodles to go with the dumplings, then sat slurping my breakfast, watching the monks shyly finger the fabric of my tent and contemplating where I was: an apple orchard in eastern Tibet, home to one of the last great cultures that had managed to preserve its identity and traditions from the homogenizing onslaught of globalization.

Not for much longer, I feared. Reading Thubten Norbu's *Tibet - Its History, Religion, and People,* I was surprised to learn that Tibetans were once a warlike people, thrashing the Chinese in a series of military campaigns beginning under Pu Gye, one of their earliest kings and a national hero ever since. But after Buddhism was introduced in the seventh century AD and the people eschewed fighting for peace, the Chinese reversed the tide with a series of punitive invasions, culminating in full authority when the present Dalai Lama fled to India in 1959. The last nail in the coffin of subjugation was the recently completed railway from Beijing to Lhasa. Having endured centuries of humiliating defeats, China was poised to deliver the ultimate act of vengeance by turning Tibet into one giant amusement park overrun with goggling Han Chinese tourists.

Only one thing is more damaging to a culture than tourists: their money. The chattering sightseers and shutterbugs would leave, but their dollars would stay, fuelling the appetite for more. Tibet had remained unique for as long as it had in large part thanks to almost impenetrable geography, something I could attest to. But people are people, and with the railway acting like a giant hypodermic needle, mainlining the country with cash-rich holidaymakers and extracting its soul one trainload at a time, a way of life that took centuries to evolve would almost certainly be gone in a few years.

"Ho! Yes! Look at me! Ha-ha!"

It was four days later. I was passing a low wall between the villages of Chadang and Chongquig when a pirate captain beckoned me over. The farmer wore an eye patch, a knotted red bandana around his head, and all his front teeth were missing. When I dismounted and produced a camera, he sprang into showbiz-mode, snatching fistfuls of yellow barley straw and flagellating himself.

"Whoa! Look at me!" He whooped with glee as he whipped himself over one shoulder, then the other. *"Look at me working like a Trojan while you're swanning around on that bike!"*

At least, that's what I imagined he was saying. His wife, teenage son, and daughter were working close by, bent over their sickles, whirling the shorn bunches of barley like batons before binding them with loose stalks. Even in the heat, the two women wore purple long-sleeved shirts, folds of dark cloth on their heads, and ankle-length dresses as heavy and dour as blackout curtains from the Blitz.

I then experienced something that happened on several more occasions and always with men, some as young as twenty. The father quit playing the goat, glanced nervously up and down the road, and fished out a pendant hidden inside his smock. Inside was the faded black-and-white photo of a young man, his face open and guileless, looking studious in a pair of thick-rimmed glasses. It took me a moment to register who it was: Tenzin Gyatso, the expedition's patron and the fourteenth Dalai Lama. This made sense. The Buddhist leader had fled Tibet forty-seven years ago, aged just twenty-four.

The piratic farmer then became distraught, gabbling in Tibetan and gesturing between the photograph and me. Was he trying to solicit something? Money perhaps? I caught the Chinese words for English and American governments—Yīngguó zhèngfǔ and Měiguó zhèngfǔ—and then I twigged it. As a Westerner, able to leave Tibet, could I please ask the British and American governments to put pressure on the Chinese to allow their beloved leader to return?

The wife and children had stopped working and were sitting cross-legged on the stubble, listening intently. It was a heart-wrenching scene, this little Tibetan family huddled together in their barley field in the high Himalayas, tears streaming down the old woman's face, the father wringing his hands, imploring me to do the impossible and reverse the inexorable tide of Han Chinese expansionism. I was moved to tears myself, by how endearingly naïve they were of the size and complexity of the world beyond their borders and at the bravery of the old boy to keep such a photograph in his possession—anyone caught with an image of the Dalai Lama could expect to be beaten and imprisoned. Above all, I was touched by their loyalty to a man who'd done a bunk nearly fifty years ago. Where else in the world could you find such devotion to a religious figurehead who hadn't already been dead a thousand years?

The older Tibetans I met in the coming weeks were respectful and courteous, but the children, bar a few exceptions, were little shits. I grew wary of the effusive smiles and hearty salutations approaching a village. As soon as I'd passed and my back was exposed, the rocks would come zinging. In the village of Yaka Luo, a dozen tykes with hoes and other digging implements tried to jam my wheel spokes as I rode by. The bolder ones even ran alongside, snatching at the water bottles and camping equipment strapped to my rear panniers. By this point in the journey, I carried a long piece of timber sharpened at one end to ward off attacks by rogue Tibetan Mastiffs, a powerful breed traditionally kept by mountain nomads to protect their livestock from leopards and wolves. I now used this to great effect on the children.

Appeasement was useless. Tormenting the foreign devil was obviously a national pastime for the youth of Tibet, whose parents stood idly by, clucking proudly as their beloved offspring took aim. I quickly learned to bury any scruples and play them at their own game. Detecting an ambush, I would dismount, pick out a few choice missiles from the arsenal of rocks in my handlebar bag, and use my longer range to lay down covering fire, scattering my pint-sized assailants long enough to slip past.

Equally obnoxious were the white Land Cruisers schlepping Chinese tourists to Lhasa in double-quick time. Every day a convoy would roar past in a barrage of beeping horns and volleying gravel. One vehicle would typically pull over, stopping long enough for a lens to poke out of a window and snap the lone cyclist at his toil, before tearing off in a cloud of choking dust. None of them ever asked permission or, more to the point, whether I needed anything, food or water—a given rule of the wilderness road elsewhere in the world.

In truth, though, I wasn't that surprised. The way drivers hogged the road tallied with the male personality traits Melissa and I had observed since entering China: loud, overbearing, and just plain rude for the most part, chain-smoking men wandering around with their shirts rolled up, bellies pressed against the face of the world. They reminded me of the bullies you find in any schoolyard, pushy fat kids competing to be the noisiest, the most ostentatious, jostling for attention with exaggerated shows of excess, starting with their gut size.

Of course, these were all simply snap judgments born from the lazy traveller's tendency to generalize and create fiction, rather than bother to stay long enough in a place to actually learn the language and the customs. Nevertheless, I hated the white Land Cruisers.

The monsoon season was officially over, but it still rained every afternoon. It was raining when I pushed my bike off the road sixteen kilometres south of Mangkam, a crossroads town known for its vigilant checkpoint, and looked for a hidden spot to camp in the folds of the surrounding hills. It was raining when I awoke at 3:00 the next morning, broke camp in the freezing darkness, and rejoined the track.

It was raining still as I entered the outskirts of town, soaked to the skin, wheels sloshing through the mud. The sound of arguing drunks echoed from the shadows as I wound my way through the empty streets, eventually arriving at the junction with the Chengdu road, another muddy track coming from the east. Fifty yards to my left was the checkpoint, this one floodlit. A PSB officer was standing beside a truck parked at the barrier, talking to the driver.

It was 4:47 am, the rain hammering down harder than ever. The guard stepped back from the cab, waved, and lifted the pole barrier, allowing the truck to rumble past, then lowered the barrier and ran through the slashing rain to the shelter of his guardhouse. I agonized over what to do next. Chance it tonight, or try again in 24 hours when the guards would hopefully be asleep? The latter carried the risk of my campsite being discovered in daylight by an inquisitive local. I leaned my bike up against a low wall, slipped off my crackly jacket and SPD sandals with their noisy clips, and crept barefoot to the office window.

Standing on tippy-toes, I could see the top of the policeman's cropped head through the ornate bars. He was sitting at a desk, writing in a ledger. Seizing my chance, I hurried back, grabbed my rig and started walking briskly across the glare of the floodlights, the hissing rain drowning out the sound of the crunching tyres. *What if he steps out to pee?* I thought suddenly. This was not the time for having second thoughts. I reached the barrier, ducked underneath, and slipped into the darkness beyond.

Four checkpoints down, seven to go.

A FEW NIGHTS later, I neared the checkpoint at Zuogong, again in the
rain. Like at Mangkam, I planned to dismount well before the barrier
and reconnoitre on foot to make sure the guards were asleep or otherwise distracted. With two hundred yards to go, however, something
large and hairy emerged from the shadows and gave chase. A short
distance later, another appeared. Then another. Soon, a whole pack of
Tibetan Mastiffs was in hot pursuit. By the time our little posse reached
the barrier—which was raised, thank goodness—we'd reached terminal velocity, blazing past in a muddle of legs, teeth, and flying fur.

At the edge of town, the road started up a steep incline. My speed
dropped to six kilometres an hour, and I could hear my pursuers gaining on me. It was time to deploy the secret weapon I'd been carrying with me since Kunming, recommended by a veteran cyclist who'd
made it to Lhasa.

Sausages.

Chinese sausages are really no different to any other sausages, but
the Schwinway brand was particularly disgusting, apparently, making
them irresistible to Tibetan Mastiffs. I reached into my handlebar bag
and threw a couple over my shoulder. The pounding of feet stopped
immediately, and a furore followed me into the night as the pack turned
on each other, fighting over ground up tits, lips, and arseholes.

For the next hundred ragged kilometres I shadowed the Oi Qu, a
tributary of the Salween, before reaching the junction at Bamda. Here
the track split. The left fork took me to the next checkpoint, which I
crossed in the early hours and started climbing to the next pass.

At the summit, it was snowing hard. The trademark streamers of
flapping prayer flags that adorn all Himalayan passes were virtually
obscured by swirling fog. Originally, I'd intended to fire up the satellite modem and send a video clip back to the website, but this clearly
wasn't going to happen. My knock-off Chinese waterproof jacket was
no longer waterproof. My fingerless gloves were useless. My feet felt like

two blocks of ice wearing sandals. Finding shelter before I succumbed to hypothermia was the order of the day. I did a quick whinge to the camera and was about to push off when a white van with black-tinted windows pulled up. When the passenger window rolled down, my heart sank.

Inside were three PSB policemen.

I'd been so careful up until this point, doing everything not to be caught. The police generally kept to the towns, secure in their strongholds. Running into a vanload of them out in the boonies was plain bad luck.

The driver, who looked to be the ranking officer, leaned forward to address me. "Nǎlǐ shì nǐ de xǔkě?" he barked. Where is your paperwork?

He was referring to the three permits I should have had with me: a Tibet Travel Permit provided by the Tibet Tourism Bureau, an Aliens' Travel Permit issued by the PSB, and a Military Area Permit for sensitive areas like eastern Tibet.

I had none of them, of course, so I just shrugged and feigned simple-mindedness—not difficult in the circumstances. The heat generated from the climb had already dissipated, and I was shivering uncontrollably.

"Nǎlǐ shì nǐ de xǔkě?" the officer shouted again.

"Wǒ bù míngbái." I shouted back. I don't understand.

The weather was deteriorating, the snow coming in horizontal globs, melting against my neck and trickling inside my jacket. The driver yelled some more, too fast for me to catch this time, and his two subordinates sank up to their noses in their greatcoats.

I hunched my shoulders and offered him my palms. "Sorry, mate," I said this time in English. "But I have no fucking idea what you're talking about."

It was one of the few occasions on the expedition when a communication impasse might actually work in my favour. After all, how much longer were the policemen prepared to keep the window open, losing the heat from their cab, trying to get the stupid foreigner to understand?

"Nǎlǐ shì nǐ de xǔkě?" shrieked the PSB officer.

"What's that?" I cupped my ear.

"Nǎlǐ shì nǐ de xǔkě?"

The junior officers inched closer to the heater vents as the charade continued. Finally, one of them leaned in and muttered something to the driver, who shook his head in disgust. The window then rolled up and away they went.

A deluge of icy runoff had washed deep furrows across the track. With no suspension and in danger of breaking a spoke (worse still, cracking the frame), the twenty-kilometre descent took nearly as long as the ascent. My hands, which had long lost all feeling, rested on the handlebars like frozen claws. To change gears, I had to stop and use my right sandal to depress the lever.

After four hours of this, a raised water tank materialized in the blinding sleet. Beside it was a tiny shack fabricated out of flattened forty-gallon drums with smoke leaking from a makeshift chimney.

I poked my head inside. A man and a boy wearing a lime green New York Yankees cap were huddled against a wood-burning stove. Seeing me, the man smiled and gestured to a kettle on the hob.

"Cuppa cha?" he said.

What was this, an East London chai wallah in the middle of Tibet? Thinking I'd misheard, I said, "Cha? You mean tea?"

The man nodded, a cowlick of black hair falling across his broad forehead. "Cuppa cha?"

He was thirty, maybe, wearing grey trousers, a grease-stained cardigan, and the serene expression of someone who accepted life's privations with humble equanimity. For him and the boy, this consisted of eking out a living in this roadside hovel, filling the overheated radiators of Chinese Dongfeng trucks labouring up to the pass.

Feeling hypothermic and my legs caked in freezing mud I needed little persuasion. Elbowing my way inside, I planted myself next to the stove. The man found a plastic cup and filled it with steaming yellow liquid from the kettle. Yak butter tea is oily, pungent, and difficult to choke down at the best of times, having the consistency and flavour of unsweetened motor oil. But being high in fat and energy-releasing calories, it is the ideal beverage for life in the arctic Himalayas. It was also the first hot fluid to pass my lips since the monastery, ten days before. Reaching for the cup like it was the Holy Grail, I inhaled the contents greedily and felt instantly revived. The storm meanwhile continued to rage outside, banging on the flimsy walls and slamming the sheets of the tin roof.

"Cuppa cha?" The man poured me a refill.

"Cuppa cha," I parroted, just happy to be there. "And a very good cuppa cha, too, if I may say so."

The man beamed with pleasure, and the three of us sat grinning at each other, bobbing our heads.

The sleet and snow gradually slackened to a light rain. My core temperature now stabilized, I pushed some yuan into the palm of my host and continued my descent. The river valley below was spectacularly prehistoric: barren and hostile, not a blade of vegetation growing. The Salween itself was a roaring livid thing the colour of chocolate milkshake, churned by the fresh run-off. I grew anxious about landslides. Composed of shale and pebbles embedded in sandstone, the canyon sides were hopelessly volatile. A Belgian cyclist had been killed on this particular stretch in 2002; the same year an entire Land Cruiser filled with Chinese tourists was buried. I put on my helmet. Not for fear of coming off the bike but of loose rocks falling from above.

Exhausted and dreading yet another early start in the rain to cross the checkpoint at Baxoi, I opted for a layover day. Hiding my tent below the track on a concealed bend of the river, I took the opportunity to rest up, clean my bike, and attempt to dry at least one set of clothes by wearing them inside my sleeping bag. My feet had swollen and turned white from the constant damp. *Another cold camp, everything drenched,* I scribbled in my journal. *Even if I thought I could risk it, there's no chance of a fire—all the wood is wet.*

I lay on my back and dreamed of a hot meal. Now, well into my second week in Tibet, food was becoming a serious issue and hunger my constant gnawing companion. Every morning and evening, I soaked a packet of instant noodles in a pan of rainwater to try to soften them, before adding the little sachet of monosodium glutamate for taste. Even then, the noodles were barely edible cold. So, when a lone restaurant appeared the other side of Baxoi the following morning, I thought: *What the heck, it's safe here, surely.*

Propping up my bike outside, I hurried in and ordered two portions of egg with tomato and rice, one to eat on the spot, the other later. Feeling chuffed at making myself understood, I pulled up a chair and watched the orange fish bob in the aquarium, while my mouth puddled with saliva at the smell of frying egg batter. When the food arrived, I realized I hadn't paid yet. I stepped out to retrieve some money from one of my panniers and noticed a blue and white sign with Chinese writing on the building opposite. "Police Station," it read.

How did I miss this?

Dashing back inside, I slapped a ten-yuan note in the hands of the bewildered restaurant owner and then fled, riding away as fast as I could. Ahead of me lay a twenty-two-kilometre climb to a 15,000-foot pass. I was ravenous. My stomach was empty and rumbling. I thought: *There's something seriously wrong with this picture. I'm pedalling away from two hot meals I've already paid for.* But all it would have taken was for a policeman to stick his head around the corner and see my bike, and the balloon would have gone up.

By September 13, I'd been in Tibet exactly three weeks. To celebrate a mini-milestone and break the monotony of my daily routine, I decided to camp early near the town of Tangme. It was also my birthday.

Scouting random footpaths, I stumbled upon an old road-construction camp, since grown over and hidden from the road. I set up my tent and settled down to enjoy what had become the highlight of each day: wearing the one piece of gear that remained remotely dry, my sleeping bag, and thawing my fingers on the one part of my body that remained remotely warm. Lying there, staring at the roof of my tent, hands clamped around the family jewels, I marvelled at nature's genius. Ergonomically shaped to the human palm, perfectly positioned at arm's length, and suitably apportioned with one for each fist, testicles make the ideal hand warmers.

Fingers duly defrosted, I got up, cleaned my bike, and prepared my birthday dinner. This didn't take long. Unable to face cold noodles for the umpteenth time, I opened a packet of "Good Taste Biscuits" instead. I'd found these between villages in a remote kiosk, a rudimentary affair knocked together with rough-cut lumber and run by a woman with red-and-blue woollen braids twisted into her hair and all her own teeth—a rarity in Tibet. Inside, hunks of fat dangled from the ceiling and freshly flayed animal skins shared wall space with posters of torpid Buddhas and strutting Chinese rock stars. The shelves were virtually bare, just biscuits, rice whisky, a few packets of instant noodles—all of which I bought—and stacks of high-tar cigarettes.

The Good Taste Biscuits were stale, oily, and tasted of paraffin, but I managed to choke a few down with frequent swigs from a bottle of ninety-proof whisky. The pitter-patter of rain began on the outside of the tent. Of the twenty-one days I'd spent in Tibet, rain had dominated all but three of them. I'd given up cursing at the sky, saving my breath for scaling the mountain passes. Every day felt like a month, and although Lhasa was only six hundred kilometres away, less than twelve days' ride, it might as well have been an eternity for the dawdling rate that time passed.

"Today, I am thirty-nine years old," I grumbled to the camera, taking another pull from the bottle. "I've been fucken around doing this expedition for …" I had to think for a few seconds. "Twelve years, now."

Egged on by the whisky, I was soon on a roll, sinking into that slough of preoccupation and self-pity that afflicts the long-distance traveller in times of loneliness and despair. The beauty and mystery of Tibet that had once so captivated me was fading fast. Riding through villages, I was becoming more and more grouchy and bad-tempered, surprising even myself at how I snapped at the children: *"Don't touch my bike, you little bastards!"* Cold, wet, and starving, all I cared about was getting to Lhasa.

The gut-rot whisky set my belly on fire, sending a wave of nausea into my throat. Unzipping the rain fly, I scrambled out just in time and upchucked my birthday dinner at the foot of a nearby tree. Standing there, retching, I felt a stabbing pain under my left ear. A hornet! Having taught me a lesson, the enraged insect returned to a swarm that was busy flogging around a rugby ball-shaped nest hanging from a branch above my head.

I was stung two more times before making it back to the safety of my tent, which had been invaded by mosquitoes in my absence. After conducting a purge, I inspected my face in the LCD screen of the video camera. It was already swollen, making me look ten years older. I was about to comment on this, and how I *felt* ten years older, when something moved in the corner of the viewfinder. Another uninvited guest, a leech, was in the process of attaching itself to my kneecap.

Flicking it off into a corner of the tent, I watched with interest bordering on morbid fascination as the parasite reoriented itself and began the long journey back to my leg. Every time I pulled it off and flicked

it away, the leech picked itself up and tried again with undeterred enthusiasm. It was the most entertainment I'd had in weeks, distracting
me from what was undoubtedly my worst birthday on record. But there
was also a lesson to be had here.

My knee was Lhasa. I was the leech.

Three days later. Fifteen kilometres west of Nyingchi
A LINE OF colourful umbrellas appeared beside the track, the reds, pinks,
yellows, and greens more colour than I'd seen in a month. When I saw
the produce underneath, I had to pinch myself. Boxes and boxes of
apples: green Granny Smiths, yellow Golden Delicious, crimson Galas.
None of them had obviously been grown in Tibet, which I took to be a
good sign. It meant I was getting close to Lhasa and its markets.

"Five," I said to the girl, holding up my hand. "Wǔ."

She was in her late teens, wearing a trench coat with synthetic fur
lining the hood. I pointed to a mound of Granny Smiths.

The girl giggled as she picked out the apples and placed them in
an orange plastic bag. "Wun … Chew … Free …" Her friends crowed
with delight as she regaled me in English.

A kilometre up the road, I pulled over beside a willow and retrieved
one of the apples. It was huge, the biggest I had ever seen, so big it
barely fit in my hand. Pausing to savour the moment, I sank my teeth in
all the way to my famished gums. The flesh was white, succulent, and so
crunchy I thought I might lose a tooth. Then something quite wonderful happened. Through a gap in the clouds, the sun appeared for the
first time in weeks. I turned to face the warmth and closed my eyes in
ecstasy, feeling like a worm peering out from under a stone on the first
day of spring. I took another bite and smiled. The last checkpoint was
in Bayi, the next town. Like the ten before it, I would rise in the early
hours of the morning and slip across. After that it was a straight shot to

Lhasa, only three hundred kilometres away. I allowed myself to say the words I hadn't dared to until now.

I'm going to make it.

LHASA TO KATHMANDU
THE ROAD OF OPEN PALMS

There's one element that's even more corrosive than missionaries: tourists. It's not that I feel above them in any way, but that the very places they patronize are destroyed by their affection.

—TAHIR SHAH, *House of the Tiger King: The Quest for a Lost City*

THE HIGHLIGHT OF MY short stay in Lhasa was seeing a cat sharpen its claws on an ornate curtain in one of Tibet's most sacred temples, the seventh-century Jokhang. This quintessentially Buddhist gesture, encapsulating the impermanence of all things, even the holiest of relics, lifted my spirits. Lhasa up until this point had been a disappointment, one ginormous Chinese shopping mall selling imitation artefacts—thangkas, sutras, masks, and prayer wheels—amounting to one of the biggest copyright infringements in history, robbing Tibetans of their cultural heritage. But the apparent ease with which this common tabby sliced through the ancient fabric reminded me to take it all with a grain of salt. In time, as Shelley foretells in "Ozymandias," the entirety of man's efforts turn to dust:

Round the decay

Of that colossal wreck, boundless and bare

The lone and level sands stretch far away.

I spent a few days recuperating in an overpriced guest house that reeked of mildew, sleeping and eating and regaining a few of the thirty-two pounds I'd lost since entering Tibet. Then I ventured out. In a camping shop near the Barkhor, I found a new stove. Not a Chinese copy, to my surprise, but an authentic model offloaded by an American tourist. Next stop was the PSB office to apply for an Aliens' Travel Permit to the Nepalese border, one thousand kilometres away. When the police officer on duty asked how I'd got to Lhasa, I told her the train.

She smiled condescendingly. "Did you enjoy?"

"Loved it."

The Friendship Highway, or The Road of Open Palms as I called it, didn't bode well for the rest of Tibet. Everyone was mad for the money—children, adults, grannies, and grandpas. Parents shooed their offspring to the road when they saw me coming.

"Money! Money! Money!"

Outside Shigatse, a man and an older woman made a beeline for me on their donkey cart. Their intention was so transparent, I had time to remove my video camera from a rear pannier and have tape rolling as they came to a halt. In perfect choreography, they stuck out their palms together.

"Money! Give money!"

Another time I was squatting under a bridge, taking care of business, when three women dressed in black marched up with their arms outstretched.

"Mister, Money!"

To preserve at least a fragment of the integrity and charm I'd encountered in the east of the country, I shifted my attention to the surrounding landscape instead. Brown, barren, and lifeless, the stunning austerity of the hills reminded me of the Soda Mountains in California's eastern Mojave Desert—just sand and rock, cracked and scored by time. A wide open plain rolled out before me, dotted with fluttering stands of aspens already turning chestnut brown in the autumnal breeze. Staggering ponies ploughed the waterless sod, and mobs of farmers stabbed at heaps of barley straw with medieval-looking rakes, flinging the chaff high into the mountain air.

So far, I'd been lucky to avoid mechanical failures, but in Lhatse, a cracked wheel rim had me backtracking to Shigatse in a shared taxi squashed in with three ripe Tibetans. The town's bike shops sold only Chinese-made rims with thirty-six spokes. Mine had thirty-two. I was directed down a narrow alley to the best mechanic in Shigatse, so I was told. The run-down premises when I found them inspired little confidence, but what the bike monkey lacked in presentation and precision tools he made up for with ingenuity and the can-do attitude of someone living in the middle of nowhere who has no choice but to fix everything. With his wife pinning the wheel under her high heels, the no-nonsense mechanic took a cordless drill to the rear hub and added the four extra holes it needed to accommodate a thirty-six-spoke rim.

Back in Lhatse the next day and keen to make up time, I immediately set out for Gyatso La, a 17,125-foot pass. This was a mistake. It was already past 2:00 pm when I set out. Even forgoing acclimatization breaks, another no-no, there was only an hour of sunlight left by the time I reached the summit. The rule of thumb at altitude is to sleep no higher than 1,000 feet above your last night's camp. Shigatse was 4,400 feet lower than the summit. This meant I needed to lose at least 3,400 feet, descending to around 13,725 feet above sea level.

Against a backdrop of madly flapping prayer flags and snow-capped peaks, I started my descent. The south side of Gyatso La is more a gentle meander than a steep drop-off, and I was still at 16,000 feet when darkness fell. I slipped on my headlamp and continued, picking out the ruts, corrugations, and fist-sized rocks in the dancing beam. The nausea hit first, followed by the headache. My skull felt like it was being cloven in two with a dull gardening implement. Afraid I might lose my balance and hurt myself, I pulled off the track and set up the tent. This ended up taking a full forty-five minutes, five times longer than usual. Finally, I collapsed in my sleeping bag and took to coughing—more a dry rasping wheeze—and to cursing myself. After seven weeks in Tibet and negotiating numerous passes over 16,500 feet, I'd become complacent in assuming there was no chance of contracting altitude sickness.

Brought on by fluid in the lungs, high-altitude pulmonary oedema (HAPE) can be fatal. If the migraine got worse and I started bringing up blood or frothy sputum, I would need to get off the mountain as quickly as possible—a tall order on my own. Sapped of energy and feeling completely debilitated, I had the self-sufficiency of a newborn. So I just lay there, hacking away, furious at my late start. After three hours the nausea subsided enough for me to sit up and make some hot food.

I'd been lucky.

Before leaving Tibet, I took in Shegar Chöde Monastery, partly to satisfy a notion I'd had as a young twenty-something year old of becoming a Buddhist monk. Built in 1296, Shegar "gompa" was an architectural marvel of whitewashed buildings clinging to the side of a mountain. For six and a half centuries, the rambling structure had weathered the elements—freezing winters, roasting summers, with torrential rains in between—before being knocked flat in a matter of weeks by Mao's Red Guards. Only freestanding walls remained and a few buildings restored in the 1980s that now housed some forty monks, a fraction of the eight hundred before the Cultural Revolution.

A stone staircase, scooped and polished by millennia of shuffling devotees, took off from the base of the mountain, climbing past bell-shaped stupas ringed with blackened prayer wheels and stacks of yak horns etched with uchen script. It was a sheer drop to the river below, where clouds dappled the valley floor with their shadow play. Strati-fied slopes, creased and folded by time, formed a caramelized backdrop to meet the humped skyline, calling to mind a camel sleeping in the landscape. Farther still, the unmistakable north face of Mount Everest sizzled radiant gold in the afternoon sun.

After several hundred feet of elevation, the path levelled out. Kicking aside the empty Red Bull cans and sweet wrappers, I arrived at a set of stout crimson doors centred on an impressive brass knob.

SPLAT! Something red and wet landed at my feet, coating my legs. I looked up. A man with a saucepan was perched above me on the out-ermost wall, his face scrunched with laughter. He was short and fat and wore loose-fitting tracksuit bottoms and a tee shirt plastered with blobs of red and white paint.

"Hallo!" he cried.

"Hello."

"Nǐ shì nǎli rén?" Where are you from?

"England."

"Nǐ yào qù nǎlǐ?" Where are you going?

"Nepal."

He tried a little English. "Me." He grinned and poked himself in the chest. "Me, monkey!"

It took me a second to work out what he meant. I then asked him what a monk was doing up there in such a dangerous place—the wall was held together with mud and looked capable of collapsing at any moment.

"Huà!" he replied, pointing to a row of paint-splattered figures on another, even higher wall. The monks were precariously balanced, handing a milk churn down the line. When the container reached the last man, he crouched, filled a silver tea kettle with red paint, and flung the contents down the outside of the wall in a great slashing arc.

The monastery was getting a new lick of paint. I was told later this was done every October after the rains, in the monastery's trademark colours of red, white, and black, the same earthen hues I'd seen garnishing the walls of houses in the nearby town of New Tingri.

The monks sang as they worked, their voices echoing shrilly across the valley. There were no safety lines. No hard hats. If any of them fell, it was easily a hundred-foot drop. Paintbrushes were also notably absent. Armed with only pots, pans, and kettles, the monks were getting as much paint on themselves as the walls—half the idea, I suspected. The atmosphere was one of hijinks, an excuse to cut loose from the restrained regimen of monastic life. Every time an unwitting victim like me wandered under the main entrance, they, too, became the target of a kettleful of paint and a source of merriment for the frolicking monks.

The fat man clambered down a dilapidated pole ladder, tracksuit bottoms sagging dangerously, and introduced himself as the abbot. This rather blew the image I had of an austere, elaborately robed cenobite wearing a magnificent tagdroma hat with canary yellow crest arching over his head.

"Can I take a look around?" I asked.

He waved a hand. "Méi wènti." No problem.

Even the ruins were getting a fresh coat. Sort of. I watched a pair of young monks trying to paint a fifty-foot wall using a rolled-up bath towel strung between two ropes. One stood at the bottom yanking on one end, while his friend lay on top yanking on the other. Together they tugged and heaved, and the towel slapped feebly against the wall, barely making a mark. It didn't matter, though. The two were obviously having a wonderful time.

Nosing around, snapping pictures, I ran into the fat abbot again. He was brandishing a garden hose, mixing up more paint in a basin of red earth. He gave me a quick tour of the buildings, including the long drop, basically a shed built over a precipice. Then, needing to get back to work, he waved me away, but not before inviting me to join them for breakfast the next morning.

This was what I'd secretly been hoping for, a sneak peek into the everyday life of a monk. Maybe it wasn't too late to take vows? Settled in one place, meditating regularly, I could return to the mindfulness that had eluded me since stepping off the boat in Miami. This was the great irony of the expedition. What started out as a bid to escape the stresses and complexities of modern life had become the very opposite.

I thanked the abbot and took off to find somewhere to stay in town—and got nailed by a bucket of paint on the way out.

At first light, spurred on by the chill, I hurried back up the mountain and was ushered into a rudimentary dining chamber where the monks were already gathered. As the only guest, I sat beside the fat abbot on a low bench reserved for the higher-ranking lamas. On the floor in front of us were the novitiates, squatting cross-legged. Some wore jackets and baseball caps. Others the maroon robes of the Gelugpa sect. All of them had their heads shorn. The mood was chipper, being another painting day, the monks jabbering and laughing.

Yak butter tea was served in small wooden bowls. I took my cue from the abbot. He drank half his cup, leaving room for tsampa, which he mixed into a doughy ball and placed in his lap, ready to pinch off chunks during the next course of mutton stew.

Lacking an eating implement, I was given a section of ribcage to use as a spoon. The "tooba," as the abbot called the stew, was utterly foul, all fat and gristle and sinew. Along with yak butter tea and tsampa, it was never going to put Tibet on the map as one of the world's great gastronomic destinations. But with every eyeball in the house trained on my bowl, I attached smile clips and forced the stuff down.

Meanwhile, the fat abbot was teasing the young monks, calling out their nicknames and nudging me to repeat.

He pointed to a young lad and said what sounded like "Een-gee."

"Inji?" I looked to my host for confirmation. The abbot chuckled at my pronunciation, and the whole room erupted with glee, all except for poor Inji who sat there looking miserable. Someone at the back then called out the abbot's nickname: "Pàngzi!" Fatso! And the laughter dried from his lips.

Looking around at the happy smiling faces, hot food settling in my stomach, a sense of inner peace and contentment stole through me. I thought: *I could stay here for a day or two, but for years?*

I recalled the conversation Steve and I had had in a pub in Dorset before leaving in 1994. Sounding me out, he'd asked if I thought I would ever quit the expedition. No, I replied, at least not for physical reasons. I felt I could handle almost any hardship. But one scenario did enter my head.

"In two years, when we get to Tibet," I'd said, "if we end up visiting a monastery and there's some brilliant Buddhist teacher to study with, I could see myself hanging up my travelling shoes for a while."

To my surprise, Steve was unfazed by my confession, perhaps because it echoed the underlying reason he'd dreamt up the expedition in the first place—to win freedom from what he described as "an unquestioning obligation to society."

We'd then made a pact. If the expedition became anything less than wholehearted for either of us, we agreed to pack it in. And five years later, Steve had done just that, renouncing the surface skim of travel for the deeper engagement of collaborative community.

But for me, twelve years had passed. The accidents, the mishaps, the dead ends, the illnesses, the continual grind of fundraising, all of it had added up. I was no longer the young upstart hungry for enlightenment, pedalling out into the Atlantic blue. Freezing my arse off in a monastery in Tibet might have worked back then, but not anymore. No, sir! I'd since discovered that while cloistered isolation may be the ideal environment for stripping away the illusion of consciousness and an independent self, having attained insight, the question still remains … so what? Only in sharing does knowledge become useful, and that means living in the real world, around real people, propagating your learnings through art, literature, music, mathematics—whatever field suits your truth. Otherwise, wisdom remains a hermetically sealed gob of introspective bullshit.

That was really what the expedition boiled down to—for me, at least. All quests by definition start with a question, and the one I'd posed at the beginning of ours had only been partially resolved through meditative contemplation. *How to live your life so you're part of the solution to a sustainable future not part of the problem?* The final piece of the puzzle didn't reside in a monastery in the snowy Himalayas, I was sure of that. In whatever shape or form it might eventually reveal itself to me, the answer would only come through my chosen koan of planetary plod.

INDIA
SWIMMING THE GREAT TIKKA STEW

The first condition of understanding a foreign country is to smell it.

—TS ELIOT ON RUDYARD KIPLING

FROM THE CHAFED, ASCETIC beauty of the Tibetan plateau, the road to bustling Kathmandu drops 12,800 feet over one hundred and twenty miles, making it the longest downhill in the world. The transition to the lush indulgences of the Nepalese rainforest was so sudden it reminded me of reaching land after three sensory-deprived months at sea. An orgy of sights, sounds, and smells jostled and aroused the senses: damp earth, tropical birdsong, chattering crickets, cascading waterfalls, and rich velvety greens that felt like satin compresses to my tired eyes, dry and scratchy from the windblown dust and dour browns of the Himalayas. All around me crops were flourishing in the glorious sunshine. I looked back at the frosted peaks piercing the clouds behind me and thought: Did I just come from *there?*

An even greater transformation in people would be difficult to imagine, the kinder climate playing out in the soft eyelashes and delicate features of the Nepalese, a very different breed of cat to the mooching, stone-hurling highlanders. *Tibetans are the toughest people I've encountered on the expedition so far,* I wrote in my journal while sitting outside the Fish Fry Restaurant in Dolalghat, less than a day's ride from the capital. *Human reflections of the merciless landscape that shaped them.*

Generalizations aside, the Nepalese were friendly and almost painfully polite. Old people stood and bowed as I passed, and gangs of kittenish girls giggled shyly as they lollygagged back from school. Children shouted "Hallo!" but never swarmed or fingered my gear when I stopped in a village for biscuits or a cold drink.

To mark the end of the "tricky" section through Tibet, I ordered a bottle of Tuborg beer and sat watching the village scene at dusk. Groups of young mothers were taking the evening air with infants wrapped around their necks. Farmers with hoes slung across their shoulders trickled home from the fields, some with an urgency to their stride, others just sauntering and holding hands in the touching display of friendship characteristic of the Indian subcontinent.

A man with wild hair sidled up and started jabbering in my face. To appease him, I offered the packet of Bourbon biscuits I'd just bought from a kiosk for twelve rupees, and off he went, holding it to his ear like a telephone, muttering. Some of the shopkeepers smiled, but no one laughed or poked fun. A screw loose, maybe, but the man was still a local, a resident of the village, and Dolalghat wasn't a very big village.

"See, the fing is, mate, Indians are nin'y nine point nine per cent the same as the Nep'lese."

It was a fortnight later. I was sitting outside the pink immigration shed in Sunauli, waiting for an exit stamp to cross into India. The eyebrows on the Nepalese immigration officer standing in front of me twitched when he heard this, but he kept his mouth closed and gaze averted, exhibiting the modesty and decorum I'd come to associate with the Nepalese.

The expatriate was in his forties, originally from Sussex, with dirty blonde hair and a business in Goa exporting cheaply made clothes to the UK. He was on his way back from a visa run to Kathmandu.

"I've lived in India for seven years, mate."

"You must have seen quite a bit of the country, then."

"Oh, yeah. Know it back to front, mate. Back to front."

This seemed unlikely. Even the nomadic tribes of India—the Chitrakathi, the Kasi-Kapadi, and the Masan-Jogi—see only a fragment of their homeland. The smorgasbord of terrain and culture is just too vast to digest in one lifetime.

I looked down at the ex-pat's hemp sandals and bandolier-style man purse and thought, *Why do Westerners who go native always look so scruffy and hopelessly out of place?*

Pulling out my map, I asked, "Could you show me the quickest route to Mumbai?"

"No worries, mate. I've been all over India. This is my country now."

But running a grimy finger over the network of roads criss-crossing the northern part of the country, my fellow countryman couldn't even find Lucknow, the capital of the province we were about to enter, Uttar Pradesh. And I knew he was a bullshitter for sure when, later that same day, I was nearly mugged outside the town of Gorakhpur. With less than six hours in India under my belt, I could see that the people were a breed apart from the diffident Nepalese. Inquisitive and sharp, falling over themselves to help, Indians could also be pushy, aggressive, and ruthless, sticking to you like glue. They were the most full-on people I'd ever met, and stepping over that border into the heaving mass of humanity was like being tossed into a giant blender. Add heat and dust, colour and spice, screeching air horns, sweat, excitement, gagging stinks, choking fumes, grasping fingers, limbless beggars entreating you at every turn, then top it off with a hefty dollop of sexual repression, and you're a double-whipped latte of frayed nerves in no time.

I was on a tight deadline to reach Mumbai for a press event, which meant riding 1,900 miles in nineteen days, doable as long as the roads remained roads. What I hadn't counted on was the sleeping arrangement in India. Wild camping is almost impossible, especially in Uttar Pradesh, home to some two hundred million people. Nearly every square inch of the state already had a human being living on it. Just when you think you're alone, cooking up some food or squatting behind a bush taking a poo, up pops a head and announces, "Hello, sar!"

Two miles south of Purandarpur on the shoulderless Highway 29, I was looking for somewhere to camp. A stand of trees appeared to the east. I pulled over, switched off my blinking red taillight, and plunged into the semi-darkness, wheeling my rig towards the trees. The path led to a small clearing, the perfect spot to set up a tent. I began unfastening my panniers.

"Hello, sar!" A figure stepped out of the shadows.

"Jesus, you scared me."

"You have cigarette?"

"Err, sorry, no, I don't smoke."

Two more figures materialized, gliding through the trees. Alarm bells began ringing in my head. Bumming a cigarette is the classic precursor to a robbery, a way to draw your victim in close before springing the trap. Abandoning any plans to sleep there, I reattached the panniers and started walking back to the road.

The men followed. "Sar! Come back. You have pen?"

A pen? What the fuck would anyone need a pen for at this time of night? "No," I called over my shoulder, "I don't have a pen."

When I walked faster, they walked faster. When I ran, they ran. Realizing they would outpace me before the road, I stopped and turned to face my pursuers, trembling with fear. At the same time I fumbled behind my bike seat for the sixteen-inch kukri I'd bought in Kathmandu to replace the Indonesian parang.

"Come any closer, you fuckers," I screamed, holding the blade high above my head, "and I'll cut your fucking heads off!"

The thieves froze, wide-eyed at the kukri's curved silhouette, and then backed away, melting into the darkness. I gathered up my sleeping bag and air mattress (in my haste to unsheathe the kukri I'd sliced through the bungee cords securing them) and continued on to the road.

With my first lesson in India Survival 101—No Camping—lodged firmly in my head, I was ready for lesson number two. In the next town, Pharenda, I asked a frizzy-haired boy sitting on a street corner if he knew of a place to stay. Was there a guest house or cheap hotel? The boy was the first fat kid I had seen since Singapore. He shook his head. "But there is temple," he replied. "Hindu temple with room for VIP. My father, he is manager."

The temple turned out to be a building site filled with asphyxiating concrete dust, and the VIP room a windowless cell, stiflingly hot and reeking of fresh paint. There was no running water or fan. The room's sole furnishing comprised a filthy mattress lying on the floor.

Nevertheless, I was grateful. After my experience earlier in the evening, a locked gate and a high fence had to count for something.

Before leaving, the boy motioned to the bolts on the inside of the door. "Please, lock," he whispered. In the next room, four painters lay sleeping in their dusty work clothes.

The boy was back a few minutes later, an older man in tow.

"Your father?" I guessed.

"No. Driver."

One of the challenges facing the lone traveller is separating truth from fiction in a very short amount of time. Sensing something a little off but unable to put my finger on it, I asked, "Where did you learn English?"

The lad looked down at his feet. His expression turned miserable. "School," he mumbled. "But cannot speak wery vell, sar."

"You speak fine."

He looked shyly at me. "Cannot afford school anymore."

This intrigued me. After all, every child in the UK was entitled to free primary education.

I asked, "Why, how much does it cost?"

The boy glanced furtively over his shoulder. "Five hundred rupee, sar."

"For one term? A week?"

He shook his head uncomprehendingly and said something in Hindi to the old man. There was definitely something fishy going on, but I was still thankful to be safe in a room I hadn't had to pay for. I rummaged in my panniers and picked out a five-hundred-rupee note, the equivalent of around ten dollars. "Here," I said. "This is to help get you back to school."

The moment the money touched the boy's hand he was gone, into the night. I started unpacking my things and rolling out the air mattress on the dusty floor.

Fifteen minutes later, I heard a gentle rapping. "Sar!"

It was the boy. He was sobbing, face hidden behind a chubby fore-arm.

"What's the matter now?" I asked.

"I need one hundred more rupee."

"What on earth for?"

The boy sobbed some more. "School books." He peered at me through moistened eyes. "From the market. Please, sar!"

It was then that I saw what marvellous actors Indians can be and the ease with which an eight year old had tricked me into thinking that I was actually contributing to his future. Egged on by the strutting gods of cinema, the great tikka stew of Indian culture is suffused with melodrama, making life bearable for the five hundred million living on less than a dollar a day, the faceless horde fated to endless grinding pov-erty. Histrionics kept the population entertained with everything from ear-splitting religious festivals, of which there seemed a never-ending supply, to volatile domestics. Public-facing India was, for the most part, cordial; the lid only really came off behind closed doors. On a more pragmatic level, the art of the masquerade sharpened people's business acumen and helped them become wily negotiators, as I was now find-ing out.

"Please, sar. Give one hundred more rupee." Again, the wracking sob, the forearm over the eyes. It was a performance worthy of Best Actor in the Bollywood Movie Awards.

I smiled. "You seem like a resourceful fellow. Now you have the tuition fee, I'm sure you'll get that hundred rupees from somewhere."

"But my family has no money. We are so poor!"

The boy was taking the piss now. "But you have a driver," I pointed out. "No more money, okay?"

Seeing that he'd pumped me for all I was worth, the lad's eyes dried miraculously and off he went.

Having learned my second lesson in India survival—never accept an offer of help, no matter how unconditional, without first fixing a price—I pushed south into the fertile floodplain of Ganga Ma, the great Mother Ganges. Plodding Brahma oxen, fatty humps swaying, hauled trailers laden with hay across a tan, sun-roasted landscape of spindly trees. Gangs of women squatted beside the green murk of temple pools, their arms rising and falling against the red splash of lotus flowers, beating soapy bundles against the polished rocks. On the road itself, wiry granddads strained tortoise-like at carts piled high with bricks, while young men in white cotton shirts with oversized seventies collars raced me on their single-gear clunkers, first drafting, then pulling out to overtake.

"Vhere going?"

"Mumbai."

Legs whirling like eggbeaters, the riders would shake their heads, pearly whites gleaming. "Cannot. Too far!"

This from someone who pedalled forty miles every day to and from work, school, or the fields.

But for a culture that regarded bicycles as purely utilitarian devices, it made sense. I saw flotillas of these sit-up-and-beg Heros being pedalled sedately to market by gaunt, hollow-cheeked men, the frames groaning under mountains of unripe bananas. Whole families would appear as teetering circus acts, dad cycling bow-legged, mum sitting side-saddle on the parcel shelf behind, and the kids perched like roosting birds on the centre frame and handlebars. Bicycles in India were used for almost everything except leisure.

I liked Indians for their instant warmth, enthusiasm, and insatiable curiosity, their eagerness to jump in and assist at the drop of a hat. And I loved the way the whole place clanked along at a chaotic, free-for-all pace, maddeningly inefficient at times, subtly endearing at others. But the truth was that as an outsider, making friends could be time-consuming and expensive. Alone and exposed on two wheels, the only way to keep solvent and moving forward was to be polite but firm around crowds. I hated to do it, but I started to adopt the same disinterested expression I'd seen on sacred cows, a kind of contrived detachment, gazing over people's heads as if they didn't exist. Make direct eye contact, and I was dead meat. Someone would be in like Flynn.

"Shoeshine, sar?"

"No, thanks. I'm wearing sandals."

"Same price, sar!"

As a coping strategy, a degree of feigned aloofness served another purpose. Look too closely at anything in India, and the truth can turn your stomach. Riding through villages in the early morning gloom, I passed shadowy figures crouching by the roadside, shitting. South of Saidpur, I glimpsed a young girl, six perhaps. As soon as she'd finished defecating, a black hairy pig moved in and wolfed the whole lot down, reaffirming my allegiance to a plant-based diet.

Malamūtra, or excrement, is so intrinsic to life in rural India that for some it constitutes their sole reason to be. I saw a thirteen-year-old boy who should have been at school squatting under a cow's backside instead, his job being to wait until the thing shat. When it finally did, he caught the deluge in a rudimentary baseball mitt fashioned from an old grocery bag. Like an expert pastry chef, he mixed in some straw and spanked the steaming matter into four dung patties before laying them out in the sun to dry for fuel.

It wasn't long before I, too, was using the road as a lavatory. Hygiene standards were scant in the truck restaurants where I stopped to pick up samosas and dhal. After a few days, I could last barely an hour in the saddle before having to dive off into a field and yank down my shorts. But the most distressing part of biking through Uttar Pradesh wasn't so much the lack of sanitation as it was witnessing the pitiful value placed on human life: grannies with shovels loading enormous gravel trucks by hand, cheaper than renting a loader, and young men squatting on farm harrows being jerked around the fields behind a tractor, their lives worth less than a block of concrete.

When it came to suffering, India was like nothing I'd ever encountered: stray dogs covered with open sores, maggots eating them alive from the inside out; beggars with hideous deformities, arms shrivelled and legs missing, using sticks to manoeuvre themselves between lanes of traffic. A puppy was flattened before my eyes, followed by its mother, her teats heavy and swollen, trying to reach her stricken offspring. Destitute men, very obviously mentally ill, wandering naked, their hair filthy and matted, going ... where?

And just when I thought I'd seen it all, I rode past some hessian sacks dumped in a drainage ditch. Looking closer, I saw a face, shrunken and cadaverous, hidden in the folds. It was ten in the morning, already blazing hot. Had anyone noticed the man was dead? Did anyone care?

Coward that I am, I rode on.

It was scenes like these in 534 BCE that shocked a local prince, Siddhartha Gautama, into renouncing courtly life to seek insight into the root cause of suffering. On a rare outing from the confines of his palace, he observed for the first time the horrors of penury, including disease, malnourishment, and death. Moved deeply by what he'd seen, the twenty-nine-year-old aspirant embarked on a spiritual quest, living first as an ascetic, before settling for a more moderate path between self-mortification and material indulgence. After meditating for forty-nine days under a pipal tree in what is now southern Nepal, he attained enlightenment. The rest of his life he dedicated to refining and disseminating a self-help programme for others, the so-called Middle Way of Buddhism.

I was also deeply moved by what I'd seen, but as an outsider, just breezing through, they were not my problems to be concerned with. This had been firmly impressed upon me after witnessing a head-on collision between two buses on the road from Kathmandu. One of the drivers was pulled from the wreckage, unconscious and drenched in blood. When I'd stepped forward to give cardiopulmonary resuscitation, the crowd, now hysterical with grief, pushed me away, shouting: "Not your problem! Not your problem!" And the man had died at my feet.

The more horrors I encountered on my way through India, the more I came to see how elevating the gaze an inch above the horizontal was an option available only to foreigners, another baffling privilege of the antiquated class system. For the scheduled castes, immersed in hardship 24/7, a very different means of detachment had been prescribed by the Buddha. At the heart of the Middle Way was a methodology that allowed a person to keep functioning, a set of tools to keep from turning to emotional mush every time life put the boot in. The key lay in addressing the nature of true Self. Was the sum and substance of a person defined by flesh, blood, and bone, their senses and personality? No. In India, this version of reality was too grim and depressing. What was needed, according to Gautama, was a shift in consciousness, achievable through meditation, the same cognitive control technique I'd used myself on the Atlantic. By exercising One Pointed Attention, the phenomenal appearance of worldly existence, the layers of illusion, could be stripped away to reveal, at its innermost core, true Self, impervious to circumstance. For Hindus and Buddhists this was the Atman: the Supreme Reality inherent in all things.

Divine being or not, the Buddha was certainly a cracking shrink for his time. Equipped with this early form of cognitive behavioural therapy, Indians living at the time of Christ could bring some semblance of peace and composure to the gut-wrenching mayhem of their everyday lives. Furthermore, from all that I had seen, the Middle Way was as relevant now as it had been 2,500 years ago. Contrary to the success story on everybody's lips, in particular the two-percenters hoarding ninety-eight per cent of the nation's wealth, India's great leap forward meant precious little to the average farmer, of whom more than 17,000 committed suicide each year over crop failures and compounding debt.

"India is best for everything!"

A short, pompous man had buttonholed me on the banks of the Ganges. "Natural resources," he sniffed confidently. "Spiritual base for major religions. Economic growth. Yes, India is definitely best."

His name was Bose, or Boss, and he had the common trait you find in many Indian yuppies and politicians of monopolizing the conversation with their interminable speechifying. Letting him ramble, I took in my surroundings. It was still early in the ancient city of Varanasi, centre of the Earth for Hindu cosmology. The sun hovered low over the glassy water, taking the form of a copper coin that burned in the ethereal mist, projecting wraithlike silhouettes of boats that seemed to hang in suspension. Around us on the ghats, digital-watch-wearing sadhus were tucked into the lotus position, fingering loops of prayer beads, their saffron robes shining resplendent in the golden light.

I turned to Boss. "Then why is it," I asked, finally getting a word in edgeways, "that with all this economic development, you still read in the papers about people dying from easily preventable diseases like polio and bubonic plague?"

To further illustrate, I could have pointed to the man in front of us dragging his young son into the microbe-laden river, water that had been officially declared septic by the Indian government, or the other chattering pilgrims, men stripped to their sagging underpants and fully clothed women, holding their noses and dunking in the holy water before scooping the stuff eagerly into their mouths and swallowing. A few miles upstream, bodies wrapped in white sacking were cremated on the riverbank and tossed in, the charred remains joining the emissions of 240 million who used the river both as their drinking supply and sewage outlet.

I added, "And isn't it true that over twenty thousand Indians die each year of rabies?"

Boss waved his hand dismissively. "Yes, yes, of course. We are not yet like Europe. But mark my words, in a few years time you will see."

"See what?"

"That India is best for …"

South of Mirzapur, the main arterial road running north-south through the middle of the country, the National Highway 7, dissolved into a farm track. It stayed that way for another one hundred and sixty brain-shuddering miles, earning me a snapped chain and five broken spokes. Just when I was beginning to think I wouldn't make it to Mumbai in time, the asphalt resumed at Rewa.

On I rode, entering the Seoni District of Madhya Pradesh where Rudyard Kipling drew inspiration for his precocious jungle waif. In 1831, a case was recorded of a "wolf boy" found living in the forest. Only a fraction of the trees now remained, and most of the tigers were also gone—grimly appropriate, I thought, given that Shere Khan met his end in nearby Waingunga Gorge. Yet, for all the land clearing, or more likely because of it, the locals still looked on their arse end.

Harried by six months of travel and rubbed raw by India, my spirits sank like they always did towards the end of a leg. It was the familiar anticlimax before switching gears to a very different frame of mind required for the discombobulated turmoil and stress of preparing for an ocean crossing. Turning west at Nagpur, I spent long, brooding days in the saddle. Only the road safety signs offered respite from my enervated thoughts.

"Safety On Road Is 'Safe Tea' At Home."

"Drive Slow. Avoid Blow."

"Your Hurry May Make Bury."

Some of these riddles were easy to decipher. Others required an imaginative leap in butchered linguistics. But they all made me smile with their playful charm and old-fangled quirkiness, the antithesis of dull utilitarian road signs in the West. And by the time I reached the outskirts of Mumbai, they'd joined the growing number of reasons I was beginning to fall under India's spell.

At first, I'd been overwhelmed and intimidated by it all: the noise, the confusion, and the pulsating horde. But over the days and weeks, something seductive and mysterious had seeped into my soul, taking root as it had in others before me, including members of my own family who'd served under the British Raj. For all its historic pandemonium and more recent bourgeois ambitions, India remains a tonic for the world-weary, its restorative qualities serving to rekindle the life force, the longed-for connection to the deeply familiar. *I feel like I've been here before*, kept running through my head as I pressed on to the coast.

Which was perhaps why, on the morning of day one hundred and sixty-five from Singapore, after riding in the predawn darkness to beat rush-hour traffic, past rows of people shitting beside the tracks at Thane and the hurrying commuters streaming out of the Victorian Gothic Chhatrapati Shivaji railway terminus, I arrived at the entrance to the Royal Bombay Yacht Club, an iconic colonial building crowned by wheeling pigeons, and glimpsed a familiar face through the crowd, a beautiful woman with eyes blacker than forest pools and hair cascading in a waterfall of darkness, and I felt like I was home.

THE ARABIAN SEA
INTO PIRATE WATERS

There comes a time in a man's life when he hears the call of the sea. If the man has a brain in his head, he will hang up the phone immediately.

—DAVE BARRY

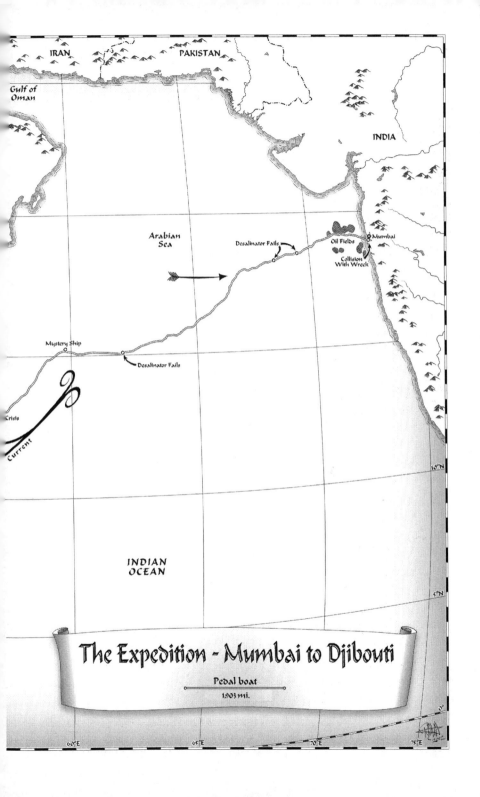

A CHORUS OF TRUMPETING and chanting came booming across the water, from a temple perhaps, or yet another festival, or one of the bullying marches by the Hindu extremist party, Shiv Sena, simmering with orange hate. I'd spent two and a half months in Mumbai, battered by car horns and choked by smog. Now, back aboard *Moksha,* I was looking forward to clearing out my ears and lungs before Africa. "Welcome aboard, Sher!" I had to holler above the racket.

"Thank you." My friend stepped cautiously over the gunnels and worked his way aft into the pedal seat. At six foot two, average height for a Sikh, it was like watching a gorilla jam itself behind the wheel of a Mini.

"How are you feeling this morning?" I asked.

Sher had upheld expedition tradition the night before by leaving Henry Tham's, a local bar, at four in the morning. He smiled ruefully. "I'm awake. I'm alive. It's about seven thirty in the morning, Sunday morning. Quite excited to get rolling."

Astern, the morning sun struggled to pierce a gunmetal curtain of murk draped over the still water, its feeble rays turning the Gateway of India a grubby orange. The conditions were perfect for setting out. A light easterly breeze complementing an ebb tide would help us clear the harbour limits before the tide turned. Once free of the Indian coast, the wind would blow a steady force 3 from the northeast, according to the pilot charts, expediting our crossing to Djibouti, 1,800 miles to the west. If we could manage forty miles a day, a conservative estimate, we should reach Africa before the monsoon transition and the winds reversed.

"And how's the pedalling?" I said.

"Doing pretty good." Sher narrowed his eyes at the compass and shoved the left steering toggle forward. "Err ... Doing pretty good peda—"

"Left a bit," I interrupted.

I'd first met Sher a decade previously in California, where he worked as a software engineer. During sea trials of *Moksha's* new propulsion system down the coast from San Francisco to Monterey, I'd taken him out for a spin in Santa Cruz harbour. Almost immediately, we'd become entrapped by sea kelp, fronds of the stuff wound round the propeller.

"Feels good to finally be off," Sher said cheerfully. "And the conditions seem to be pretty ideal for pedalling right now. It's cool, and we're moving along pretty smoo—"

"More to port," I corrected him.

"Without any kind of—"

"Left!"

"Without any kind of err ... hindrance. So, hopefully we can keep this up for anoth—"

"Okay, straight ahead now."

"Couple of hours, bef—"

"Straight!"

"Before it gets too warm."

A seed of doubt was taking root in my mind. How would my new crewmate keep *Moksha* on course if he couldn't even read the compass? Spotting for him the entire way to Djibouti was out of the question. And what about ships?

"See that building over there?" I pointed to the seven-storey Taj Mahal Palace a few hundred yards off our starboard beam. The luxury hotel was the size of an oil tanker, as clear as day against the Mumbai skyline.

Sher squinted through the starboard window. "No, not really. But I'll be fine."

"Straight ahead, now," I said.

But Sher wasn't listening. "It's just great to finally be out of Mumbai." He sighed contentedly. "Looks like at this rate—"

"Straight!"

"We'll be in Djibouti pretty soon."

As well as being blind as a bat, Sher was a pathological optimist, a quality that would put him in good stead for the rest of the voyage, as it turned out. He was also very brave. For a deskbound techie who'd never been to sea before and could swim none too well, either, taking to the high seas in what some had dismissed as a glorified coffin took a lot of balls. In all honesty, I was surprised he'd even turned up, especially given his atrocious track record for being on time for anything.

A mile south of the Prongs Reef Lighthouse that marked the southernmost edge of the peninsula, a floating fishing net fouled the propeller. I was in the process of unclipping the latches on the pedal unit to pull it free and clear the tangle, when—

KERRUUNNNCH!

Water began flooding in through the old crack in the centreboard housing, forced open by the centreboard driving upwards and backwards like an axe. Sher stared at me wide-eyed from the passenger seat, his aquiline nose emphasizing the horror in his face.

"We've hit something?"

"Apparently so."

Another sickening thud shook the hull. I tried to appear calm, but my head was reeling from the sight of water filling the cockpit. Reaching for the breadboard, I began pounding the top of the centreboard, returning the timber most of the way before it stuck fast with three quarters of an inch remaining.* The worst of the flow had been stemmed, but water still slopped intermittently into the battery compartments.

I grabbed my mobile phone. Land was still close enough to pick up a faint signal.

"Cyrus? Hi, it's Jason here. Bit of a problem."

A Parsee and fellow adventurer who'd once sailed to Muscat and back in a twenty-one-foot open boat, Cyrus Heerjee had arranged for

---

* A wooden breadboard is one of the most versatile pieces of equipment to have aboard a small vessel, serving as a mallet, chart table, saucepan lid, and rigid surface for writing up diaries. You can even cut bread on it.

Moksha to be parked in the yacht club garden while I prepared her for the voyage. The honorary sailing secretary had been unfailingly supportive, sticking his neck out for us on more than one occasion.

"Tell me," he said gruffly.

"We've collided with something here south of the Prongs."

"Ah, yes, that sunken trawler. Didn't you know about it?"

"How could we? There's nothing marked on the chart."

"No, it's probably too recent."

"How long has it been there?"

"Three years or so."

"Three years?"

"Hmm. Someone should have told you."

Limping back to the Gateway of India, every fishing boat we passed knew of the sunken ship. It was nearly always exposed, one skipper said, except for an hour either side of high tide.

Sher shook his head. "Every Tom, Dick, and Harry in Mumbai seems to know about this damn thing apart from us."

Back at the wharf, a mobile crane was waiting to pluck *Moksha* from the harbour. I knocked the centreboard back into alignment using a block of timber and was about to signal for the boat to be returned to the water when I noticed the rudder. It was shattered with only a flap of fibreglass holding the composite pieces together. The wood around the pintles was also rotten, rendering the rudder irreparable.

It was the Sunday before a two-day Muslim holiday—little chance of getting anything done. Such delays were usually maddening, but on this occasion my frustration was mitigated by a tinge of anticipation. Since meeting in November, Meenakshi and I had grown close, spending nearly all our free time together. For me, this was after it became too dark to work on *Moksha* under the old banyan tree, with its ribbed and fluted trunk, and canopy dangling with creepers and home to a festival of flapping, crapping crows. Every evening, Meenakshi would wait for me under the cloisters, and together we would disappear into the wild, untamed night.

We would be back together. For a few days, at least.

She was a dangerous woman to fall in love with, though. Our romance was considered taboo by the xenophobia prevalent throughout Indian society. Women were expected to remain behind closed doors, the property of Indian men to do with as they wished. "No Indian girlfriend," hissed the guest house managers, wagging fat, sanctimonious fingers at me from behind their desks. Not that it would have made much difference. The popular Colaba district was in a permanent accommodation crisis, its overpriced rooms booked weeks in advance. Since arriving in Mumbai, I'd stayed at the Salvation Army for 150 rupees a night, a little over two dollars. And when that was full, I'd resorted to sleeping outside on the cobbled streets, wrapped in an orange tarpaulin smelling of cat piss, alongside the homeless and destitute of Mumbai.

"You're a fool!" Meenakshi had reprimanded me. "They'll rob you and kill you."

But what other option did I have? If the night watchman caught me sleeping inside *Moksha*, the club committee would haul Cyrus over the coals and likely give the expedition its marching orders.

With her extensive knowledge of Mumbai, Meenakshi tracked down a timber merchant open on the Monday, one that could sell us a length of seasoned Burmese teak the same dimensions as the old rudder—four feet long, ten inches deep, and two inches wide. The club shipwright, Razzaq, forwent his Muslim holiday to come and help, braving a four-hour commute by bus and train from his home in north Mumbai. Using only hand tools, he whittled a new one in less than a day, and with the old fittings reattached and paint still wet to the touch, we were ready to roll within 48 hours of hitting the sunken trawler.

Before leaving, Sher and I sat in *Moksha* to make sure he could read the compass properly with his new minus twos I'd insisted he buy from one of the emporiums on Colaba Causeway. The club tindals then slipped garlands of orange and white flowers over our heads, and it was time for another round of ghastly goodbyes, made even more so this time because I knew we wouldn't be coming back. Cyrus came out in the tender with two tindals, Margit and Isaac, who I'd become good friends with. I would miss Margit especially with his toothy, betel-stained grin, his indefatigable goodwill and unconditional willingness to lend a hand, epitomizing the very best of India. We shook hands. Then it was Meenakshi's turn. But I'd had my fill of farewells by this point. I was so very tired of it all. The constant flay of long-haul travel, belonging to no one and no particular land. Stopping in foreign towns. Waltzing into people's lives. Knowing I'd always be leaving. I thought: *What kind of life is that?* And I knew that if I looked into those eyes one more time, eyes that had danced with merriment and mischief and now brimmed with so much sadness, I might not have the strength to carry on and finish what I'd started. So I didn't, because I'd been here once before at the edge of the sea, two hearts breaking. And maybe, just maybe, by keeping the chapter open, the story could end well this time.

"You want some Marmite?" Sher asked.

He had the chopping board on his knees, arranging the leftover scraps of bread like a jigsaw puzzle. As with all previous voyages, the only thing we were able to stomach until the queasiness subsided was Marmite on bread or crackers.

"No," I replied. "You go for it."

"There are still a lot of crumbs here," he said. "So what I'm going to do is just hand you the packet."

"So I eat crumbs, and you get to have actual slices of bread?" I was joking, of course.

"There are no slices left. I'm just going to join these pieces together."

Sher began kneading the overlapping edges to form a complete slice. The result looked like a variation on the many examples of flattened road kill I'd seen since leaving Greenwich.

"So you're gonna have the nice bits then, eh?"

He smirked and reached for a knife from the port side netting. "Yes, that's the plan."

It was the morning of the fourth day. We'd made good progress since rounding the Prongs Reef Lighthouse, without incident this time, picking our way through the oilfields west of Mumbai, avoiding the spoil areas, oil rigs, and numerous wrecks marked on the Admiralty chart. Every night, our southern horizon burned with the lights of ships coming and going, and oil platforms spouting columns of fire. Sher found this blaze of activity particularly disconcerting, unversed as he was yet to reading navigation lights and the direction that ships were heading.

He looked up from spreading Marmite on his mangled creation. "So, what would you like for breakfast today?"

I smiled thinly. "Just crumbs. That's more than enough for me, thanks."

My pointed remark was lost on him. "We're having the last slice of bread," he said cheerfully and to no one in particular.

"No," I interrupted. "*You're* having the last slice of bread. *I'm* having crumbs, remember?"

He grinned. "That's right. I'm having the last slice of bread—"

"Greedy bastard."

"And you're going to have the leftover crumbs."

"Well, just remember to save all your toe clippings," I said.

Sher blinked. "Okay."

"You might need them later in the voyage if we run out of food."

"I will? What do they give you, vitamins?"

"Mainly they just give you the sensation of eating food. You can add them to a soup or grind them into a pâté."

"Right."

"Any flakes of skin? Stick 'em in the skin box. Toe jam? That stuff can be a lifesaver."

"Skin box. Okay. And where is that kept?"

Our electric watermaker failed later that day. I'd spent over a thousand dollars on parts and countless hours working on it in the club garden, replacing the motor and all the seals. It was working perfectly when we left. Now it was refusing to build pressure.

Two days later, the primary hand pump also died.

This time it was my fault for lashing the unit too tightly to the starboard side oar. Sher was using it to pump water when it happened. He was standing in the hatchway, talking while I pedalled and tried to read a book. Being Indian, Sher asked a lot of questions. And being Sher, he asked questions no other Indian wouldn't think to ask: *Why is the sky blue? Why is the sea salty? Why do onions make you cry?* The day was insufferably hot with no fresh air reaching the pedal seat, and Sher was chewing my brain with his interrogation.

"So, the plastic housing on this watermaker, is it important?"

Keeping my nose firmly in the book, I grunted, "Nope."

A second later, there was a loud crack. I looked up to see water gushing from the pump casing. The unit was eight years old. The combination of plastic fatigue, my indifference, and not keeping enough slack in the binding had caused the housing to rupture.

"Slight problem," said Sher.

No problem, I told him. We still had the emergency pump in the grab bag. It was brand new, never even been opened. The same model had kept Steve and me alive for thirty-nine days pedalling from San Francisco to Hawaii.

But the next day, it, too, died, leaving us with eighteen gallons of emergency drinking water in canvas bags. Even on half rations, this would last us only twelve days, nowhere near enough to reach Djibouti.

Many things can go wrong on a voyage, but two in particular really get the pulse going. One is hitting a submerged hazard and watching your craft begin to sink. The other is running out of fresh water. Both have the effect of producing a lot of stress very quickly.

"I'm thoroughly, thoroughly fucked off," I fumed. "Fucked off with how fucking useless these fucking watermakers are. Fucking crap, fucking engineering. They've *never* fucking worked properly."

We needed something rigid, ideally sheets of metal, to try to reinforce the fractured casing of the primary hand pump. The closest anything came to fitting that description was our kitchenware. Retrieving a hacksaw blade from the tool bag, I proceeded to saw my father's treasured mess plate from Korea into three-inch square pieces and secure them to the outside of the housing with stainless steel screws.

"I am quite confident that the work we've done on this watermaker is going to be good to Djibouti," said Sher, giving it a trial run. He pumped the handle slowly for ten strokes, then waited to let the pressure stabilize. A few seconds later, he did another ten strokes. His gentle touch and patience impressed me. And it produced results. After two hours of pampering, we had half a gallon of potable water.

The watermaker worked for another thirty-six hours before stress cracks began appearing. My father's mess plate was made of tin, a relatively soft metal, allowing too much movement. Next to be sacrificed was the aluminium Primus saucepan lid.

Once the deed was done, I looked wistfully at the butchered portions in my lap. "That's a shame," I said. "I really liked that lid."

Sher held up the cannibalized carcass and peered through the gaping holes. "I did, too. I am very, very sad to see it go."

"I've had it since the beginning of the expedition, like my dad's mess plate. We used to use it for frying veggies."

"This one?"

"Yeah."

"It was an effective lid," Sher announced, as if giving a eulogy. "Especially when applied to a saucepan."

One of the joys of having Sher aboard was listening to his precise turns of phrase. As with many other aspects of British culture, Indians had done a better job of preserving the English language than the English themselves.

"It trapped the moisture," he continued, "but let the steam out. And it was easy to unfasten. I was pretty sad when you had to slice and dice it."

Our predicament served to remind me how different human-powered travel on land was to water. On terra firma, if you forget something or a piece of equipment breaks, you can pick up a replacement in the next town or have it sent ahead. At sea, you have to make do with what you have. The smallest glitches can escalate into major dramas, as we were about to find out.

AFTER A WEEK, the wind backed to the west, straight on the nose. For some reason, El Niño perhaps, the seasonal high-pressure system usually centred on the Arabian Peninsula had shifted abnormally far south. The breeze was light, only five to ten knots, but enough to reduce our daily average to fifteen nautical miles. It had also become unbearably hot ever since the fans stopped working. With zero cloud cover and the relentless sun scrutinizing our efforts from horizon to horizon, every day was a sweat fest until the cool of evening finally came.

Another week of being slowly boiled alive was all we could take. We switched to a south-southwest heading, aiming to slip beneath the high by dropping from eighteen to fifteen degrees north and slingshot ourselves into the Gulf of Aden. It was a huge gamble, though. The five-hundred-mile detour would take us into Somali waters, considered the worst in the world for maritime piracy. Dozens of ships were hijacked every year, the crews typically ransomed along with the cargos. In 2007 alone, thirty-one cases of piracy were recorded off Somalia's 1,880-mile coastline.

"No breeze at all now," Sher observed the morning of the seventeenth day. "The swimming pool in your backyard has more wave action than this. It doesn't even look like we're on water."

It was an accurate description. The haze hanging limply over the mirrored surface made it impossible to tell where the sea ended and the sky began. The effect was a panorama of silvery blue rolling out in three dimensions—north, south, east, west, above us, and below us— giving the impression of being suspended in a void, the eerie silence and spatial bewilderment of outer space.

Free of the crippling headwind at last, our average speed increased to one and a half knots. Slowly, incrementally, we clawed our way across the glassy plain, every mile earned with sweat and aching knees. Using my Leatherman, I cut ventilation holes in the Perspex windows on either side of the pedal seat, although with no wind there was hardly any point. *This is an alien environment,* Sher journaled that evening. *Not conducive to human survival. All that separates us from half a mile of water is half an inch of wood. How fragile our condition is.*

In spite of his growing appreciation for our tenuous mortality, my partner was adapting to life aboard more readily than any previous crewmember. After just two-and-a-half weeks at sea, he said he barely remembered what his life on land had been like. The lesson he'd picked up the quickest, apparently, having smashed his head more times in the first 48 hours than either of us dared count, was to hold on with one hand at all times. *Every movement has to be carefully choreographed,* he wrote, *each action rehearsed in the mind. And the steps required to execute each action have to be completed in a methodical and sequential manner.*

In many ways, Sher was turning out to be the perfect travelling companion, good-natured and seldom grouchy—like I could be. He didn't take anything or anyone too seriously, least of all himself. Harbouring misgivings wasn't his style, either; he hadn't once brought up the water-maker incident, for example. Most importantly of all, he had a sense of humour.

"You know what I think the problem is?" he said the next morning, referring to our disappointing progress. "During your stay in Mumbai, you were given too many gods."

"What do you mean?" I replied.

He nodded at the statuette of Ganesh behind the passenger seat. "Like that elephant. If we offload a few of those, then things might turn around for us. Stuff will stop breaking. The wind will pick up. We might actually get somewhere."

"So you think Lord Ganesh should be given the heave-ho?"

"Well, put it like this. From what I've seen, he hasn't done a whole heck of a lot. Do you have any more gods and goddesses on board?"

I thought of the many icons and amulets we'd been given over the years, usually from supporters hoping to solicit divine protection for our ongoing journey. If nothing else, these farewell tokens were a reminder of the myriad efforts that had been made to advance the expedition a little farther around the world.

"The whole boat is stuffed with them," I admitted. "From every continent. It's like a witchdoctor's broom cupboard back there."

Sher bit his lip and stared at the kettle. "You see, I think that's the problem right there."

Sensing that we were about to embark upon a prolonged and ulti-mately inconclusive debate on the workings of the supernatural, I sug-gested my crewmate practise his diving instead. The tranquil condi-tions were perfect for it.

"Okay, it's basically head first, right?" Sher was standing naked on the roof of the Rathole, squinting at me for confirmation.

"Yup. Point your arms above your head, and when you dive, try to touch the water with your fingertips."

"So let's see how this turns out."

He landed with a great crash, soaking everything within a twenty-foot radius, including me.

"How did I do?" He was treading water and grinning.

"Bellyflop," I said.

"Better than this morning's dive, though?"

"A little better than this morning's dive, which was a total disaster."

He laughed. "Right."

"You were still flat on entry."

"How many points would you give me on a scale of one to ten?"

"Three."

"What about if this was the Olympics?"

"If this was the Olympics, you wouldn't get any!"

He blinked and said nothing.

By day twenty-two, having pedalled eight hundred miles from Mumbai, we were nearing our clearing line of fifteen degrees north. The wind kicked in, force 3 from the east-northeast, lifting our spirits. Then the watermaker stopped producing again. The repetitive motion of the handle had enlarged the screw holes enough to render the reinforcing plates ineffective.

The only metal left on the boat was a pair of brass plaques secured to the bulkhead behind the pedal seat. One was *Moksha's* nameplate. The other acknowledged the early benefactors instrumental in her construction. I removed this, drilled a dozen or so pilot holes, and screwed the now perforated plaque to the bottom of the watermaker.

Fresh water began flowing a minute later. Breathing a sigh of relief, I turned to Sher and said, "Well, at least we're not drinking each other's urine just yet."

———— ⚏ ————

THE VESSEL MADE a beeline for us over the northwest horizon, as if they knew where we were. It was also travelling fast, another bad sign.

"Just keep heading straight," I said to Sher, quickly stashing the cameras, satellite phone, and binoculars in the Rathole. "Act like everything's normal."

Sher nodded stiffly as he pedalled. "Okay."

I removed the rocket flares from our RAF lifejackets and placed them within easy reach under a compartment cover. If things got nasty, they were our only defence.

"And if these guys hail us on the radio," I said, "can you do the talking?"

"Sure."

As well as fluent Hindi, Sher spoke some Urdu. With a sixty-mile range on our VHF, I suspected an English accent might draw unwanted attention from eavesdroppers. Since entering pirate waters, we'd seen several suspicious-looking craft, open dories with high prows and dual outboard engines but no nets or other fishing gear in evidence. Often the boats were just drifting, two or more rafted up together manned by five or six crew, their skin blackened to the colour of pitch, killing time, chatting. So far only one had taken any interest in us, a light blue skiff that came bouncing over the water to check us out, two crewmembers standing in the bow for stability. But when they saw the dirty laundry hanging limply and Sher's legs pumping away, they'd laughed and taken off, probably thinking: *Poor bastards can't even afford an engine. We can't take anything from these guys.*

Clearly, they were after bigger fish. Nevertheless, as an added precaution, we'd taken down the radar ball and switched off the Ocean Sentry. Other anti-piracy measures hadn't progressed much beyond our imaginations. My father emailed an excerpt from Joshua Slocum's *Sailing Alone Around the World,* in which the author described sprinkling tintacks on the deck of his sloop *Spray* to deter would-be marauders in the Straits of Magellan. However, as Sher pointed out, while this might have worked back in the late eighteen hundreds when pirates went barefoot, the 21st century variety probably wore designer combat boots for boarding vessels. Another idea was a variation on the theme that had worked unwittingly well for Steve and me pedalling through Cuban waters in 1995: giant beards and bollocky naked with suppurating sores. This time I'd envisioned taking things one step further, smearing our bodies in Marmite and taking the guise of two deranged fools who'd resorted to using their own excrement as sunscreen. No one in their right mind would come near us, surely.

The vessel, a filthy great jalopy, was now just a few hundred feet astern, belching a tail of black soot as it chugged through the water. Our VHF sprang to life with a strange gargling sound. Sher unclipped the microphone and fired off something in Urdu.

More strangling noises, then a high-pitched, heavily accented voice said, "Yes! Yes!"

Sher spoke again in Urdu.

"You want fiss?" the voice said in English.

Sher pushed back a lock of his greying hair. "No. No thank you. We're fine."

"You like fiss?"

"We are vegetarian," Sher replied. "We don't eat fish."

"You like fiss, no?"

Until now, I'd kept myself hidden, assuming the less they saw of a Caucasian the better. Reassured by the inane conversation about fish, I peered around the edge of the cabin and examined the vessel. It was around a hundred feet long, with a high freeboard, no masts, faded green trim decorated with fish symbols, and a grass matt awning spanning the deck. Was it a pirate mother ship? Not by the look of the forty or so people standing at the rail, goggling at us.

Sher repeated himself. "We are vegetarian. We do not eat fish!"

"Why not?" the voice demanded.

Sher squinted and put his glasses on. "Because we do not eat meat."

"Very tasty fiss, eh!"

Sher nodded and chuckled. "That's true. It probably is very tasty."

There was more unintelligible gargling, this time something about shark fish. The vessel was now level with our starboard beam.

"Where are you going?" Sher asked, changing the topic.

"I am going in da sea." Someone giggled in the background. "Finding fiss going in da sea."

"And where are you coming from?"

"Iran."

"Iran? Where in Iran? Tehran?"

There was a pause. They were obviously tiring of Sher's questions already.

"What *your* country?" The voice finally asked.

Sher looked at me questioningly.

"India," I mouthed.

"We are from India," Sher replied. "Mumbai."

"Mumbai. Oooooh! How are you, Mumbai? Speak Hindi?"

Sher laughed. "Hāṁ, maiṁ cāhatā hūṁ!" Yes, I do!

Over the next 24 hours, we were taken another eighteen miles south. This shift in current would have been welcome a week earlier, but now we needed to be going in the opposite direction. North. The closer we were to the Horn of Africa, the greater the likelihood of being attacked, according to the International Maritime Bureau. The trend continued the next day. And the next. Soon we were two hundred miles below our clearing line with the pirate refuge of Socotra Island a mere one hundred and fifty miles to the west. There, the current split, a portion of it heading northwest into the Gulf of Aden, the rest curling southwest along the East African seaboard. The awful prospect of missing the gulf altogether and being swept along the Somali coast towards Mogadishu loomed with every mile lost south. News had just reached us of a UN cargo ship, the *MV Rosen,* being hijacked close to Raas Xaafuun in the northeast region of Puntland and the crew taken hostage for ransom. This most certainly was not a part of the world to linger in any longer than absolutely necessary. We'd been fortunate so far thanks to Sher's language skills and *Moksha's* peculiar appearance. But how long would our luck last?

At four o'clock every morning, the person on graveyard shift would clamber wearily from the pedal seat and wake the other. Day twenty-four was Sher's turn to leave the comfort of the Rathole and pedal through the early morning hours until dawn.

"I've realized there are two stints that I do." Sher was slowly coming round, rubbing the sleep from his eyes and fumbling for his glasses. "Virtual pedalling and actual pedalling. The virtual pedalling is when I'm here, in my dreams, and you wake me up. I think I've been pedalling, and now it's time for me to go to sleep."

"Nice try, mate. Out you get."

He reached for the handrail above his head and heaved his upper body into the main cabin.

"Seriously, as weird as that might sound, it's true. Because when you wake me up, I actually think it's time to go to bed." He pulled his legs out of the Rathole and swivelled around on his behind, unfolding his frame like an insect. "Okay! Let's try this whole drill again."

When fatigue set in and he felt himself nodding off, Sher found inspiration in my iPod shuffle. There were more than a thousand songs to choose from, but the only one he ever listened to was *Dancing Queen* by Abba. According to the playlist, the song had already been played two hundred and eighty-nine times since Mumbai.

The watermaker failed again later that morning. The time had finally come to requisition *Moksha's* brass nameplate, a last resort and a difficult one to have to take. After all she'd been through, the thousands of miles of turbulent ocean, the near misses and near sinkings, it seemed almost sacrilegious to take away her name, to pepper it with holes and attach it to some ramshackle piece of equipment on its last legs. I had to remind myself that while *Moksha* could keep going without her title for a few weeks, we couldn't do the same without water. At the end of the day, as Steve had once pointed out, she was just a boat. If we wanted to survive, we couldn't let sentimentality creep into our decision-making.

Sher and I had been getting along remarkable well until this point. We hadn't even come close to having an argument. Yet, despite regular doses of *Dancing Queen,* tensions between us were beginning to mount. What with our water woes, constant threat of piracy, and the current still pushing us south towards Somalia, we were both getting tetchy and fed up. Fed up of the heat, fed up of the grinding pedals, fed up of each other's farts, fed up of trying to type updates on a donated laptop fitted with a Flemish keyboard.

Food and sleep had become highly prized commodities with the crossing taking so much longer than expected. Sher made his first pointed remark of the voyage—the first since I'd known him, in fact—when he commented on our dwindling supply of biscuits and how few he felt he'd personally consumed. From then on, you could cut the air with a knife whenever someone opened a new packet, its wrapper crackling. And when, on our sixth day of being taken south by the current I decided enough was enough and started pedalling north, Sher ignored my cue at the next shift change and continued pedalling west. Heading north halted our southerly drift, but it also meant no more miles nearer to Djibouti—we'd be pedalling on the spot, essentially. For Sher, westerly progress was everything.

He blamed his rebellious streak on his grandfather, a Sikh guerrilla fighter. But from what I'd gathered, passive disobedience was a universal trait in India, popularized by Mahatma Gandhi in the lead-up to independence from the British in 1947. *Never take no for an answer* seemed a fitting national motto. The art of nonviolent resistance also came in handy when dealing with modern-day officialdom, as Sher had demonstrated in Mumbai when he was told by the French Consulate it would take a minimum of two weeks to get a Djibouti visa on an Indian passport, no exceptions. At the time, needing to leave within 48 hours to catch our weather window, this had presented a serious setback. So Sher had stood his ground and argued, and argued, and argued, until, desperate to go home, the staff had grown weary and told him to leave his passport and come back in the morning.

After all my run-ins with team members on previous legs, I'd made a point of emphasizing to Sher before leaving Mumbai my right of veto when it came to crucial decisions on the voyage. I now reminded him of this and asked him politely but firmly to change his heading to north. "I'm afraid this one is non-negotiable," I told him.

He finished his afternoon shift in a sulk, muttering things like "no mileage west," and "waste of time heading," and "useless current, just absolutely bloody useless."

By the next shift change, I'd had enough. "Well, I'd rather it take an extra week to get to Djibouti," I said irritably, "than get any nearer to the Somali coast!"

A stony silence descended between us. Sher was now standing in the hatch, making water as I pedalled. Nettled by his defiance, I demanded to know if he had any better ideas. His reply was cut short by a resounding crack. The watermaker had split completely in half. There would be no repair this time. With around twenty-two days remaining to Djibouti, a conservative estimate, the eighteen gallons of drinking water in canvas bags would still fall short.

Our disagreement was instantly forgotten, superseded by the latest crisis.

"I can refrain from drinking water the last few days," offered Sher.

"Nah, that's not a good idea," I replied.

"I'll drink seawater, then."

"No you bloody won't!"

That night, hoping to prove that westerly progress was still possible on a course of 330 degrees, just shy of due north, I let Sher sleep and pedalled through the night. By 3:00 am, the current had slackened enough for me to bear away to 315 degrees and maintain the same latitude. By daybreak, I was pedalling 290 and making ground west.

The southerly trend in the current had broken at last.

"WE'VE GOT SNOW on the ground here in Falmouth."

I pressed the satellite phone closer to my ear. "Snow, really? How much?"

"Six or seven inches."

I tried to imagine it, not easy with the temperature well over a hundred degrees in the Arabian Sea. "We could do with some of that right now," I said. "It's pretty toasty out here."

"We'll do a trade," said the voice. "You send us sunshine. We'll send you snow."

"Sounds like a deal."

Andy, an operator at the Falmouth Maritime Rescue Co-Ordination Centre (MRCC) in the UK, was in the process of trying to divert a nearby ship to bring us some water. This wasn't easy. Far from the shipping lanes in the Gulf of Aden, we were effectively in a dead zone. The alarm had been raised by Rajan, sailing coordinator at the Royal Bombay Yacht Club, who'd been reading our weblogs. Upon learning of our watermaker failing for the last time, he and my father had taken the initiative to contact the Mumbai Coast Guard.

Andy went on to ask some routine logistical questions: wind strength and direction, sea state, and the amount of daylight remaining.

"We'll have a sunset in about fifteen minutes," I told him.

Three hours later, at 9:07 pm, a sing-song voice came bouncing over the VHF airwaves. *"Moksha.* You are in need of drinking water? We are heading towards you. Can you relay your exact position, please, if you have GPS?"

This was the skipper of the *MSC Eliana,* a container ship that had kindly changed course to come and help. Our latest coordinates put them twenty miles away.

"Ooh, alright, I did not get your latitude wery vell, but we are on same meridian. We are heading south at twelve knots, proceeding to your position. I repeat. We are proceeding towards your position. I will call you again on the VHF when we are closer to you, in around one hour."

At 10:13 pm, a blister of twinkling lights formed on the north horizon. Individual deck lights soon became visible, along with the red and green running lights. "It's like a ballroom dance hall," Sher remarked as the *MSC Eliana* hove to. We closed the distance, pedalling the last half a mile in the shelter of her leeward side and edged alongside a vertical wall of steel towering into the night.

Leaving Sher to man the helm, I crawled onto the bow and threw a line to the waiting deckhands.

"Take a stern line also," called a voice, Indian by the sound of it.

"Okay."

A rope came dangling down with a tennis ball attached to the end of it. "You can make fast our line on your boat."

Two white hard hats appeared beside a blinding spotlight. One was holding a digital camcorder.

"Can't speak Hindi?"

"I can," said Sher, appearing in the hatch.

"Okay. Acchā!"

They explained their route: "From Colombo. Containers, only containers—"

"Fine night to fuck up!" a voice interrupted from the darkness, loud enough for us to hear.

The hard hat with the camcorder giggled nervously. "Don't listen. He is just a … a silly man."

Down came the first of eight five-gallon containers secured to an old jute hawser slick with oil. It didn't take long for the central compartment to fill up.

"Do you think we'll be able to stow all of them?" Sher asked doubtfully.

Four of the containers ended up on the cabin roof, bound hastily together with rope. Before parting ways, I sent up a canvas bag containing a John Grisham, a Robert Harris, and a Paul Theroux, books we'd already read and which the skipper informed us were the only things we could offer in return. I slipped a $50 bill inside the cover of *Archangel* with a note apologizing for the inconvenience and requesting the money be spent on the crew when they reached port. The books were gone when the bag came back down, but the $50 remained.

"Please, accept this," I shouted to the deckhands.

"God has given us enough already," came the reply.

As we pedalled off into the watery darkness, feeling euphoric and slightly overwhelmed by the whole encounter, two of the canisters rolled off the roof with a muffled splash. They were gone in an instant, swallowed by the black water that glinted with the lights of the departing ship.

"Never mind," I said to Sher. "Including our ballast bags, we have, let me see … around forty-seven gallons on board. More than enough to reach Djibouti, anyway."

Our water woes were finally over.

The following afternoon, I reached under the bunk in the Rathole and pulled out a bottle of red Zinfandel I'd been hiding since Mumbai.

"I was going to crack it open at the halfway point," I said, pushing in the cork with my thumb. "But there wasn't much to celebrate back then."

We were now 51 degrees east of Greenwich, officially inside the Gulf of Aden and at the three quarter mark of the voyage. I rooted for the slab of cheddar cheese wrapped in foil and packet of crackers I'd also been hording. The wine, a Sula, was like red ink, but it was the best domestic wine available in Mumbai. I handed Sher the bottle.

"How is it?" I asked, watching him take the first swig.

He grimaced briefly before baring his pearly whites. "Fabulous. Then again, anything would good taste good at this point."

I looked closer at him, at the black hair matted and plastered over his forehead, the month's growth of raggedy beard and eyes sunk back into their sockets. Covered in a light sheen of sweat, he looked almost in shock.

"You feeling okay?" I asked.

He shrugged and shook his head. "The thing is, usually we know exactly what we'll be doing at any moment of every day. This feels *radically* different."

The act of deviating from the norm elicited a horror of letting go, of losing grip of the reins and not being able to regain control.

"Do you think we'll make it to Djibouti?" I asked, more to sound out his eternal optimism than anything.

He laughed. "Absolutely! I thought we were going to make it to Djibouti before we even started the voyage."

"What happens if we don't, though?"

He paused before answering. "I haven't thought about that, actually. So it's a moot point. I have no idea."

The wind freshened to a ten-knot easterly over the next 48 hours, sending us scudding across the gulf towards Yemen. This was where I'd hoped to be by this point in the voyage, as far from the Somali coast and its pirates as possible. Although, as we were to learn, nowhere in the gulf was really safe. Unbeknownst to us, a convoy of yachts taking part in the Blue Water Rally was being tailed by two pirate boats less than fifty miles from our position. The skiffs began harrying the startled sailboats in an attempt to separate the weakest one from the pack. Alerted by a distress message, a coalition warship operating in the area had arrived in the nick of time and driven the raiders away.

Back on 270 degrees and with the waves pushing us from astern, the drudgery that had plagued the voyage evaporated, and the mood aboard rallied with the exhilarating conditions. The new threat was avoiding the deluge of shipping funnelling in and out of the narrow entrance to the Red Sea: empty oil tankers heading for the Persian Gulf, container ships bound for Europe crammed with consumer crap stamped Made in China, and car carriers shaped like giant shoe boxes stacked with BMWs and Mercedes going the other way, to the Far East.

Approaching the port of Aden, fifteen miles south of the Yemen coast, Sher woke me in the early hours.

"Err, Jason?" he said anxiously. "You might want to take a look at this one."

This was our agreement. Any time he wasn't sure of a ship's heading, Sher would wake me immediately. The seas had roughened with a fifteen-knot east northeasterly. I looked out of the Rathole to see a green and red light bearing down on us. The freighter was on collision course, two hundred yards and closing.

"Turn to starboard!" I shouted. At the same moment, the ship cut its engines. A powerful spotlight combed the water and trained itself on *Moksha*.

Keeping his head, Sher pedalled like hell to get out of its way.

The next morning, we passed through an oil slick that blackened the side of the boat, an unpleasant reminder of the ecological consequences of burgeoning global trade. The water eventually returned to its pristine state. The wind dropped, and the sea became tranquil again.

Sensing that time was running out before Djibouti, now only two hundred miles away, Sher took the opportunity to practice his diving.

He launched himself off the foredeck this time, drenching the entire boat including me sitting on the passenger seat, plotting our latest coordinates on the chart.

"When I first started diving," he said breathlessly, pulling his dripping torso onto the stern deck. "When I knew jack shit, it seemed like the dives were better. Now my head is taking a huge hit every time I go in."

Setting aside the soggy chart, I started on our afternoon tea, the most refreshing and eagerly anticipated part of each day. A dwindling supply of stove fuel made it all the more so—we had to ration ourselves to one mug every 24 hours. This was the glittering prize at the end of each sweltering afternoon. For Sher, it was when his day ended and the next one began.

"I have to admit," I said, opening one of the last of the biscuit packets for us to share. "I haven't seen much of an improvement the last couple of dives. Blame the coach if I were you."

Sher chuckled. "It's okay. We've got a couple more days between now and Djibouti."

I reached for the kettle, a lovely old fangled thing with ornate spout and fluted lines bought from the bazaar in Mumbai. "You need to impress Nathalie when she gets here," I said. Nathalie was Sher's girlfriend, flying out from Belgium to meet him. "It'll be like sports day at school. Show off your best dive!" I began decanting two mugs' worth of water into the kettle from a canvas bag hanging from the side of the hatch. "We've got a bit of a way to go yet before the double flip with a triple somersault, though, haven't we?"

"I can try that right now," said Sher, his expression deadly serious. "Man, that'll be painful if it doesn't work out right."

"You'll probably end up smacking your head on the gunwale," I said.

"Yeah, that'd be a disaster. I'll do that closer to the end, shall I?"

I nodded. "When we're in helicopter range."

"Right!"

I lit the stove, spooned tealeaves into both mugs, and added milk powder and sugar. Sher, meanwhile, tried another dive. It was the same result. If anything, worse. He was back to landing testicles first.

"You know, just looking at this boat and the water all around." My crewmate was treading water, goggles pushed to the top of his head, barely a riffle around him. "It's an interesting perspective. There's water everywhere, and the only thing breaking the monotony is this tiny little boat. That's it. It's amazing looking at it from a fish's point of view."

For Sher, a nine-to-fiver, the voyage had amounted to a quantum shift, allowing him to step back, see the bigger picture, and help clarify what he really wanted in life, a vocation that would hopefully provide more satisfaction than "The Sty" as he referred to his cubicle at Hewlett Packard.

"Small things lift your spirits out here." He was talking to the horizon now, as if by thinking aloud he was less likely to forget the lessons he'd learned once we made landfall. "On land, since we have so much stuff, you don't even notice these things. But out here, down to a very basic existence, small details like the sun, the wind, the size of the waves, fresh water, they all take on a great significance. The odd bird that you see ..."

And there were other insights. Earlier, over our morning porridge, we'd talked about cooperation. "Getting along," Sher pointed out, "helping, camaraderie, things which one reads about and gets talked about, but on the boat, the sense of cooperation is very real and immediate."

He was right. Apart from two minor altercations over biscuits and the northerly heading in the countercurrent, we'd worked together extremely well.

"At night, for example, when you're asleep, depending on your partner to be alert and making sure there are no ships bearing down. It's a dangerous environment, so faith and trust is key. The goal is doing this crossing, and you have to cooperate to make it happen."

Pedalling on the spot in the countercurrent had also taught him how the goal wasn't always so clear-cut. "The action was the same," Sher noted, sitting with his porridge bowl in his lap, "but the outcome entirely different. Maybe that was the lesson the sea was trying to impart, to focus on the task at hand rather than worrying about results. The final outcome, whatever it may be, should not be the focus."

I'd smiled wryly at him. "You can take that philosophy a little too far, though. Don't you think?"

Sher had looked at me nonplussed.

"Like your porridge?" I scooped up a dollop and let it splatter back into my bowl. Much like his diving, Sher's porridge had deteriorated the farther we'd travelled from Mumbai. This morning's effort had been the worst so far: runny, lukewarm, with uncooked lumps floating in it, enough to spark an uprising in a Siberian gulag. "Maybe there should be a little more focus on the outcome?" I'd teased.

Joking apart, I was in total agreement with all that he'd said. His commentary on the inner journey particularly impressed me, reaching conclusions that took other seekers, myself included, years if not lifetimes. That Sher was getting as much as he was out of his time on *Moksha* delighted me. Having other people aboard wasn't always easy—the lack of space, the lack of sleep, the smelly feet, the lumpy porridge— but seeing them profit from the experience always outweighed the negatives. And listening to Sher wax lyrical on the merits of stripping down to basics supported a theory of mine, that exposure to extreme simplicity and the raw elements is a gift, washing away the paraphernalia of human trivia that abounds in the modern world, elucidating all that is still real and good and true in it.

For myself, this would be the last major voyage in *Moksha*. I would miss the three-hundred-and-sixty-degree ocean vista. No buildings. No people. No obstructions whatsoever. And the sky. No light pollution. A thousand miles from land you can see every star that's out there. And even though it was a grind on the pedals at times, and I would cry out, "This is such a *ridiculous* way to cross an ocean. What the *fuck* am I doing here?" I knew that when all was said and done, I would look back on the years of struggle and know that my time on *Moksha* had been the most rewarding, bringing into focus what really mattered. And I would say to myself: *She's more than just a boat. She's a teacher of wondrous things.*

Sher completed his final dive for the day, pulled himself aboard, and clambered into the cockpit. As I handed him his tea, something landed on the back of my wrist: an orange gnat, borne on the wind from Africa.

Land was close.

March 16
10:00 am. 140 miles from Djibouti
"Good morning, Kenny. How are you?"

"Pretty gud, and you?"

Our Man Brown was in a Djibouti hotel room, preparing to document our arrival. He was just over the horizon from us, but the thousands of miles his voice had to travel via satellite made it sound squished and garbled.

"Not too bad," I replied. "How's the hangover?"

"Light to moderate."

"Rather like our sea state, then."

"Aye, lookin' out the window here, it dunnae seem too bad."

But this was about to change. I relayed our position and filled him in on the forecast. The wind would continue to blow for another 48 hours in our favour, from the east-northeast, then veer around the compass to come from the northwest and strengthen to force 6. The timing couldn't have been worse. Nearing the end of the tapered gulf, we were running out of ocean in which to manoeuvre. If we didn't make it to Djibouti before the northwesterly kicked in, the wind would blow us onto the south shore of the gulf. From its border with Djibouti, the Somali coast extended in a long sweeping curve to the first safe harbour at Berbera, one hundred and forty miles to the east. All along its length, the beach was shallow and pounded by heavy surf. There would be no hope of refuge, according to my father, who had emailed a detailed description from his memory of being posted there with the family from 1959 to 1960, when the region was still a British protectorate.

Kenny outlined his plan for hiring a support boat to come out and film. "It's an awld clunker," he said. "Not very fast."

"How fast?" I asked.

"Top speed eight knots, more like six."

"A bloody Ferrari compared to what we're driving, then."

"Aye, costs about as much as one, too."

"How much?"

"Eight hundred."

"Francs?"

"Dollars."

"Fuck."

It was a race against time. We had to pedal seventy-five miles a day for the next two days, a tall order considering our average daily mileage until now had been around half that. I cursed our luck. After pedalling more than 2,000 miles through pirate-infested waters, the end of the voyage was shaping up to be another Coral Sea debacle.

March 17

05:00 pm. 61 miles from Djibouti

To MAINTAIN A minimum speed of three knots, we reduced our shifts to one and a half hours, upped our RPMs from fifty to fifty-two, and abstained from taking any more shared breaks. No time for diving lessons now! The person coming off shift would rest their aching knees in the Rathole for five or ten minutes, then keep the pedaller plied with food and hot sweet tea until it was time for them to take over again.

Even with this last-ditch effort, the best we could average was two point seven knots. The latest six-hourly report from my father detailing wind strength and direction brought more depressing news. The northwesterly blow had been brought forward eight hours, arriving sometime before midnight. It had also been upgraded to storm force 8 to 9.

All we could do was keep pedalling. The wind dropped as the sun burned a dull orange through the clouds gathering in the west, and the ocean settled to an eerie calm—the deep breath before the plunge.

"Hard to imagine there'll be any wind," said Sher, a river of sweat running down his chest as he pedalled. His knees were badly inflamed, but he showed no sign of flagging. His legs kept pumping like pistons.

We switched at dusk, hurrying to change the towels lining the pedal seat. Sher produced the spare he'd been saving since Mumbai, a full-size bath towel still fluffy and smelling lovely compared to my stinking thing. A squall came bustling across the water suddenly, chilling the air and giving us our first shower in forty-six days.

"Give me the pot!" Sher cried, scrambling onto the foredeck.

The saucepan was full of leftover porridge, so I handed him the kettle. Using our laminated sheet of emergency contact numbers as a funnel, he offered the teapot to the sky. Naked, bearded, grimacing at the heavens, he struck a classic pose, like the protagonist of a Greek play petitioning the gods for water.

"We might even get a free cup of tea out of this!" he said joyously.

I realized then how unfazed my partner was, being completely un-aware of the gravity of our situation. He had no way of knowing the mariner's worst nightmare, being blown onto an exposed shore. But what did it matter? As long as he kept pedalling like a demon, bursting his bubble would be pointless.

March 18
04:00 am. 30 miles from Djibouti
THE FORECAST PROVED accurate. The gale started shortly before mid-night, fluttering through the open hatch as shallow breaths before steadily building. By 3:00 am, the sea was boiling and the wind whining through the generator shrouds. Hissing white caps pummelled the star-board beam, sending volleys of spindrift into the cockpit and causing *Moksha* to shudder with each collision.

When the red compass light died, Sher wedged his headlamp inside the chart netting and focused its beam on the ten-degree markers.

Earlier, I'd drawn a pencil line on the chart. If we ended up south of it, the chances of clawing our way back around the reef systems south-east of Djibouti were virtually nil—next stop the Somali coast with its devastating boomers. The clearing line was now only three miles off our port beam, and Djibouti was still thirty miles away. We could com-pensate by veering from 260 to 270 degrees, or even 280, but it was a catch-22. The closer we brought *Moksha's* nose into the wind to stop her from being pushed south, the slower our speed, the longer we were out there, and the more chance of being taken south.

Our only hope was to make a dash for the islands east of Djibouti, Iles Moucha and Ile Maskali, and seek shelter until the storm passed.

March 18

06:15 am. 25.5 miles from Djibouti

IN THE PREDAWN light, Kenny's voice came crackling over the VHF, trying to make contact.

"*Moksha,* this is dive boat *Eos,* come in, over."

I responded with our most recent position.

"*Moksha,* I have eleven degrees, thirty-nine minutes, decimal fifty-nine north, and forty-three degrees, thirty-four minutes, decimal thirty east. Is that correct, over?"

I confirmed it was.

"My position is eleven degrees four one, decimal two, and forty-three eleven decimal seven. I'll plot you on the chart. Stand by on sixty-nine, over."

A minute later, he was back. "Okay, so you're not being blown south anymore."

"No, we're managing to maintain."

"That's gud, 'cos we've got a slight glitch our end. *Eos* has broken down—the water pump's gone out or somethin'. There's a wee motorboat thingy, but it can't go out in heavy seas."

So, we were our own. And what could the "awld clunker" have done, anyway? In the end, it was *Moksha* that pulled us through. The waves slipped effortlessly beneath her rounded hull, and we were able to hold our 260-degree heading without losing further latitude, reaffirming what an incredible design she was. Four hours later, a tremendous boom shook the air from one of the French or American jets stationed in Djibouti, and a band of dark grey underlining an overcast sky appeared to the north, giving us our first glimpse of Africa.

Kenny arrived in a filthy white motorboat streaked with rust, its bow inscribed with red Arabic script. I recalled our first and only day of sea trials in Salcombe, when Steve and I had pedalled out of the estuary on the outgoing tide, intending to spend a full night at sea. Within the hour, we were back in the Kings Arms, getting the beers in. Partly, it had been the tedium of pedalling ("Fucking boring, isn't it!"). But even more so was the sense of doubt, unspoken yet hanging heavy in the air. *This boat will never make it across an ocean,* I'd said to myself. *She's too flimsy and unstable. Why drown any sooner than we have to?*

How wrong I'd been.

DJIBOUTI TO EGYPT
BETRAYAL ON THE LAKE

Avoiding danger is no safer in the long run than outright exposure.
The fearful are caught as often as the bold.

—HELEN KELLER

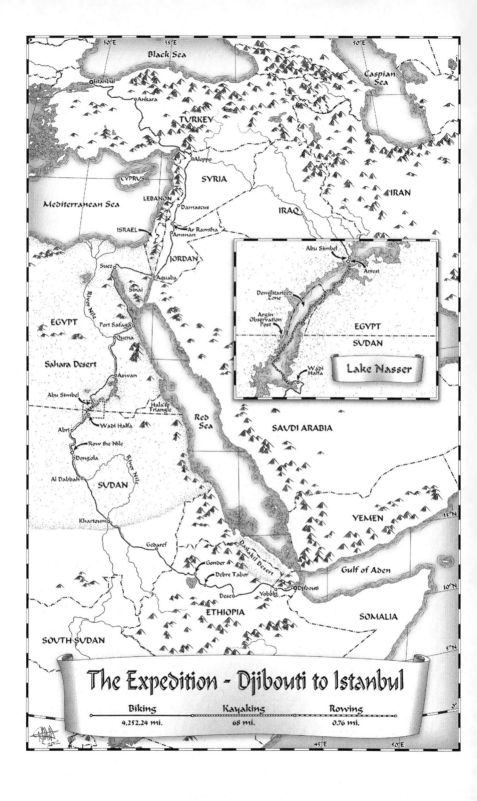

The Expedition - Djibouti to Istanbul

Biking	Kayaking	Rowing
4,252.24 mi.	68 mi.	0.76 mi.

Djibouti, March 31, 2007

A SWARM OF SMALL boys ran to the roadside to mooch for money as Kenny and I laboured up the steep incline out of town. When I refused, one of them jumped onto my trailer, shrieking and waving to his friends. *"Hey, look at me riding the foreigner's cart!"* I roared at him to get off, and a stone whistled past my ear a moment later. Soon, the air was filled with missiles, and being Somali goat herders, their aim was deadly.

Kenny was behind me, riding the red Cannondale he'd brought with him. I saw a rock the size of a man's fist sailing towards his shaved head.

"Incoming!" I hollered.

The projectile curled at the last second and collided harmlessly with his handlebar pannier.

"That'd be the perfect way to start the trip," the Scotsman chuckled once we were out of range. "Laid oot cold in the middle of th' road, a bunch o' thievin' African kids runnin' off wi' awl me camera gear."

At the very least, the incident prepared us for how much more violent Africa could be compared to Asia. Enslaved, tyrannized, and burglarized since year dot, Africans were poorer, more desperate, and quicker to fight than your average Hindu or Buddhist. The cantankerous Somalis and Afars certainly were, eking out an existence in a barren quarter of the continent bursting with refugees from neighbouring Somalia and Eritrea.

Even before the stone throwing, there had been little going for Djibouti to endear itself to us. The place was a hot, dusty hellhole, devilishly expensive from the artificial economy created by the large Western military presence and as dependent on its neighbours for food as they were for its port. Once a week, a dozen clapped-out boxcars came wheezing down the narrow-gauge line from the Ethiopian Highlands, supplying the million or so inhabitants with vegetables. In exchange, every day at noon, the country ground to a halt as eight tonnes of khat leaf touched down at the city's airport, paralyzing the population for the rest of the afternoon under the stunning properties of an amphet-amine-like high.

Its one redeeming feature had been Bruno Pardigon, a charismatic Frenchman who'd befriended the expedition the moment Sher and I stepped off *Moksha*. A mover and a shaker, Bruno had his fingers in many local pies. He found us somewhere to stay and arranged for *Moksha* to be stored until I reached Europe. From Djibouti, I would ride 6,500 miles north through Ethiopia, Sudan, Egypt, Israel, Jordan, Syria, Turkey, and Europe to the French coast, where *Moksha* could be launched across the Channel to England. Another seven months, and the journey would be done. The light at the end of the tunnel, dim for so many years, was now comparatively blinding.

A few unknowns still remained, including a large expanse of road-less desert in North Sudan and the Bosphorus Strait of Istanbul, which I planned to swim or paddle in a kayak. By far the biggest obstacle, however, was crossing Lake Nasser. A long-standing dispute between Sudan and Egypt over the Hala'ib Triangle, a 7,950-square-mile tri-angle of sand backing onto the Red Sea, forced overlanders to take the weekly ferry from Wadi Halfa to Aswan—something I couldn't do. The borders with Chad and Libya were both closed, and crossing the Egyptian border at any other point was prohibited, as was navigating the lake by any other means than the ferry. Nevertheless, my circum-navigation bid rested on traversing the lake by human power. I either found a way, fair means or foul, or faced having to backtrack to India. Leaving the rackety tyre shops behind us, the swilling piles of rubbish and glassy-eyed locals squatting in the heat, Kenny and I took a short-cut to the town of Yoboki. This seemed like a good idea huddled over a map in a comfy hotel room; the desert detour would save us more than twenty miles and take in a point of geological interest, Lac Assal, at five hundred and eight feet below sea level the lowest point on the African continent and the second lowest on Earth after the Dead Sea. But once past the lake with its moonscape sculptures and ghoulish salt-encrusted skulls peddled by desperate windblown locals, the tarmac petered to a 4WD track, which in turn petered to a camel track, and then petered out altogether. With no landmarks to speak of, we were soon lost. The temperature nudged 119 degrees, a pleasant winter cool according to the odd nomad we encountered. These were the bushy-haired Afars, tough looking and austere, the men brandishing staves for driving live-stock, leaving the women to do all the carrying—crude bundles slung over their shoulders and plastic jerrycans sloshing with water.

The wind howled. A few forlorn camels nibbled half-heartedly at the tops of thorn trees or mooched despondently beside dried-up wa-terholes ringed with dead cattle. The land was parched and broken, the sand and gravel tiresome to pedal through. The nickname of The Devil's Playground fit the region perfectly. This was extreme country, barren and inhospitable, the only thing to prosper a billion black me-tallic rocks. We reached the shores of an old lakebed turned biscuit brown and fractured like pumpkin bread. With the wind behind us, we skimmed across, reaching Yoboki two days later.

Relieved to be back on tarmac, we pushed on to Addis Ababa where Kenny could catch a flight back home. We entered a shallow basin of low scrub dappled by clouds. Domed shelters stretched with ani-mal hides appeared by the roadside and sacks of charcoal set brazenly against rusting signs prohibiting tree cutting. It was more heat and dust, the landscape dominated by desert browns with only the occasional green acacia to ease the eye, and the women, tall, beautiful, and asser-tive, proudly flaunting their ornate jewellery and brilliant beadwork even as they buckled under impossible loads. They smiled and laughed as they held my gaze, confident in their sexuality, making for a refresh-ing change to the acquiescent Muslims I'd encountered in Asia.

A 6,500-foot rise in elevation, passing caravans of pitiful donkeys tottering under boulders lashed to their saddle frames, and we reached the Ethiopian Highlands. Here the air was fresher, the temperature cooler, and the rainfall more reliable judging by the amount of agriculture and frequency of villages. The cattle herders carried AK47s instead of walking sticks, another powerfully symbolic glimpse into conflict resolution African-style.

"YOU COULD BE stuck here for a while," remarked the British Embassy official on hearing my plan to cycle through Sudan. "We had some guys from the army waiting three months for a visa. The Sudanese are tricky. You might even want to go home and come back again."

She meant home to England, where people waited even longer, anything up to six months, for permission to enter the ancient land of Kush. I'd spent three weeks in Addis as it was, holed up in the Wanza Hotel where, for seventy birr a night, $8, I had a room with clean sheets, a compact desk for writing, and a squat toilet area that doubled as a kitchen for preparing meals on my camp stove. Every morning, I tramped to the Sudanese Embassy, passing the capital's limbless, deformed, and crippled, many of them lying corpse-like under horsehair blankets in the blazing sun, the only evidence of life a mutilated foot or prosthetic limb jutting next to a begging bowl. Every morning, Mr. L. Waheed, holding court in his office at the end of a long dark corridor, informed me politely there was still no word from Khartoum.

"Come back tomorrow, Mister Jason!"

On a separate matter, I was paying a visit to the British Consulate to seek help in obtaining permission from the Egyptians to cross Lake Nasser. My primary contact in the embassy section was sympathetic but ultimately pessimistic of my chances of gaining support. She went on to tell the story of a young British cyclist who was recently imprisoned in northern Ethiopia for accidentally colliding with a pedestrian. Despite the local resident sustaining only cuts and bruises, the cyclist was jailed and ordered by the local police commissioner to pay $800 in compensation—a thinly veiled attempt at extortion.

"So he called us, and the consulate people said, 'What can we do about it? We're too far away, with him all the way up there'. I said, well, we have to do *something.* That's what we're here for, isn't it? And it was us, not the consulate, that eventually got him out."

This didn't surprise me. In thirteen years, every request I'd made to a British Consulate for assistance with some bureaucratic hurdle had been stonewalled. *We're here to protect British trade interests, not some independent expedition* was the usual response. In East Timor, running out of options to get our kayaks across the border into West Timor, it was the Americans who had put in a good word with their Indonesian counterparts.

Wearying of the wait, I decided to continue riding to the Sudanese border and backtrack by bus if and when my visa came through. The rough-as-guts track to the town of Gondar, once Ethiopia's Camelot, alluded to the country's declining fortunes since the golden era of the Aksumite Empire, a vast, rambling kingdom that at its height in the first century AD stretched to Saudi Arabia and rivalled China, Rome, and Persia as an economic powerhouse. The research I'd done in the Wanza had filled my head with irresistible tales of the Queen of Sheba, the Ark of the Covenant, and black Falasha Jews fleeing the tyranny of Egyptian pharaohs. However, the sight of twenty-first-century farmers tilling nothing but dust and rocks and lashing demoralized oxen with twenty-foot-long bullwhips revealed another, less-glamorous story. The land looked exhausted, nibbled to the bone or ploughed up for the tiny-grained teff that Ethiopians grew for their sour-tasting injera, spongy crepe-like bread the width of a steering wheel. It was a snapshot of the world to come if *sapiens* continued on its current path; all the trees gone, no wildlife left, and the countryside scalped.

"Zis is my raison d'être here, if you like," a German land-management specialist, Doctor Richard, told me in Debre Tabor. "To prevent Ethiopia from vashing into der River Nile."

I'd sought out Doctor Richard to ask permission to stay in one of the huts run by his non-governmental organization, sparing me from the local sleeping establishments that doubled as brothels—prostitutes knocking on the door at all hours, affording little sleep. Once the nation's capital, Debre Tabor was now a tumbledown village filled with blaring music and horse-drawn buggies driven by pop-eyed men high on khat. Doctor Richard had kindly agreed to my request and then invited me to his house for dinner. Being the only outsiders in Debre Tabor, he and his Algerian wife would be glad of the company, he said.

Over fried eggs, roasted potatoes, and beetroot salad, the agronomist complained of the work ethic of his Ethiopian staff. "Zey do zer bare minimum," he grumbled. "Ent often less than vat is required!"

Earlier, waiting in his secretary's office, I'd heard him bawl out two field technicians. The men had failed to fulfil the minimum weekly hours on their contract, yet they were still arguing. "Zere is no discussion!" Doctor Richard slammed his fists on the table. "No discussion!"

But towards the bottom of a Spanish Rioja, he became confessionary.

"I like zer isolated life, but after sirty years working on erosion-control measures around zer vorld, I heff become, how should I say ..." He paused, reluctant to continue.

Disillusionment had clearly taken hold. With the world population rising exponentially, he finally added, land management programmes like his made little difference, especially in Ethiopia.

"Another fifty years, ent we vill be in real trouble."

"We, as in?"

"Zer human race. Vat to do, though? I heff four kids in college at five sousand euros a month."

I asked him whether he thought adopting a plant-based diet might help. Ethiopians were devout carnivores, chowing down almost exclusively on lamb, mutton, goat, and beef. And yet, it took thirteen pounds of perfectly edible grain to produce just one pound of beef.

He nodded. "Yes, I sink so."

Toughing it out on the sharp end, the lone crusader off the edge of the map, at least Doctor Richard was honest, unlike the charity bosses I'd seen hobnobbing with government crooks in the foyer of the Five Star Sheraton Hotel in Addis, a brand new $70,000 Land Cruiser parked out front. Maybe he'd just been at it for too long?

"My idealism is not so much anymore," he admitted, going on to describe how he was becoming more irritable and quick-tempered. I replied that I could relate completely. After a month and a half of biking through Ethiopia, I was on the verge of committing an atrocity.

It was the kids. I'd come to loathe them, the sound of their piercing voices as they caught sight of my bicycle and abandoned their sheep and goats and ran shrieking down the hillsides to intercept me.

"You! You! You! You! You! You! You! You!" Followed by: "Give money! Pen! Highland! Jacket! Give! Give! Money! Pen!"

They made the rug rats of Tibet seem almost cherubic.

On the level, I could usually outpace them, but slogging uphill, I was a sitting duck. First, the "You! You! You! You!" Then the begging palms outstretched. When I ignored them and kept pedalling, the stone throwing would start. Through Nefas Mewcha, I counted more than fifty of the screeching rascals, some trying to jam sticks into my wheels, others hurling rocks. Even between the villages of circular mud huts with thatched roofs and bomas of green thorns, it was impossible to avoid them. Just when I thought I'd found a concealed spot to bolt down some food, I would hear the patter of feet and ten snotty faces would appear. "Give money! Pen! Highland! Jacket! Give! Give! Money! Pen!" Carrying only enough provisions for myself, I became guilty and resentful seeing the undernourished faces waiting for a handout and took to eating in sullen, furious silence.

"The children, they are free," explained Guben Biru sitting in the bar of a jiggy motel in Gasay. As head of the Department of Education for North Wollo District, Guben was suitably qualified to offer an opinion. He was travelling on school business with two of his work colleagues.

I said, "But why do they always shout, 'You! You! You!'?"

We were drinking St. George Beer, named after the patron saint of Ethiopia.

"Because your name is You," Guben replied, as if stating the obvious. He was picking at the yellow label on his bottle that portrayed the dutiful knight sticking the fabled dragon. "Really, they are excited, that is all. They mean no harm."

One of the supervisors, whose name was Mazengia, added, "They are just happy to see a traveller."

"So happy they throw stones?"

He laughed. "You are on a bicycle? So, yes, they like to have a little fun."

"Because I can't get away fast enough like the faranjis in four-wheel drives?"

"Yes!"

"So they use me for target practice?"

He smiled.

I considered this for a moment, trying to make sense of it. They made it sound almost a privilege to be pelted.

"Will they grow up to be the same way?" I asked. "Behaving like hooligans?" I was thinking of the impeccable manners of the older men and women I'd encountered, bowing slightly and muttering "Selam, Selam" as I passed.

"No," said Guben. "They become responsible. It is our culture."

DROPPING OFF THE western escarpment into the desert, passing abandoned tanks and other ordnance, rusting reminders of Ethiopia's sev-
enteen-year-long civil war, I entered the town of Shedi, sick as a dog. I'd
made the mistake of ordering encoulad fit-fit at a roadside restaurant,
egg stew, which, served on a shower mat of injera, bore an uncanny
resemblance to a dirty nappy. My guts gurgled. Every so often, I had to
leap off my bike and fertilize a bush.

Stopping for a cold drink, I saw a baby lying out in the sun covered
with so many flies I thought it was dead. *Filth and flies everywhere,* I wrote
in my journal. *How can people stand it?* Feeling even worse, I continued in
the scorching heat, jouncing along the worst road I'd encountered since
arriving in Africa, a collection of pitted ruts blazed by the double-trail-
er tankers hauling oil from Sudan. At Koki, another flyblown shithole,
I checked into a jiggy motel to rest and hack my lungs free of bull dust.
A prostitute called Dusdas with the tattoo of a crucifix on her forehead
made unambiguous gestures and pointed to one of the bedrooms, a
pungent tin shed filled with scratching chickens. I declined the offer,
thinking: *At least none of the Christian guilt here!* Weaned on a lusty diet of
Old Testament texts chronicling God's chosen few dispatching their
subordinates left and right so they could shag their widowed wives, Or-
thodox Ethiopians were obviously unabashed when it came to sex.

My room was tiny, scarcely big enough to perform the needful,
and rented by the hour. I handed over the equivalent of a dollar and
a quarter, enough for the night, and lay on the bed watching three
men dismember a goat outside my door. The sight and smell of spilling intestines turned my stomach further. Dusdas, meanwhile, started
evening chores. Like most women in impoverished countries, she did
the lion's share of the work—washing clothes, keeping the fire going,
baking injera on a broad clay plate known as a mitad, serving drinks,
and so on. That she was expected to bone the same drunken slobs she'd
been waiting on hand and foot all night illustrated the depths that some

men will sink to in pursuit of profit and how much better off the world would probably be if women were in charge.

At the border with Sudan—I now had the elusive visa in my passport, having backtracked from Gondar to Addis—I felt so grim I hired a local fixer, one of the idle young men kicking around the Ethiopian border post. For twenty birr, David agreed to run me through the bureaucratic hoops. The nearest hospital with a lab for diagnosing disease was in Khartoum, apparently, three hundred and seventy miles away.

A mere one hundred yards inside Sudan, I received my first unsolicited act of hospitality. This was something the country was renowned for in travelling circles, but having read the Darfur horror stories, I'd assumed it to be a myth. What I hadn't fully appreciated was just how big Sudan was: Africa's largest country, comprising five hundred and ninety-seven tribes conversing in over four hundred languages and dialects. Darfur and its problems comprised only a fraction of this multiethnic pie. Upon seeing my weakened state, the tall Nilotic customs officer volunteered his string bed parked under a shade tree in the border compound, and there I lay for the remainder of the afternoon, chugging bottled water and swatting feebly at the pestilent flies.

At one point, the officer, whose name was Chriz Logii, stuck his head out the door of the customs office and said, "You need change money?"

On any other occasion, I would have declined the offer, suspecting a ruse from a poorly paid government official looking to make a little backsheesh. But slumped on this man's bed, wondering if the sickly Sudanese visitor arriving at Heathrow could expect similar treatment and be tucked up with a hot water bottle in the immigration officer's house in Hounslow, I trusted him. My diarrhoea was now streaked with blood, and I was badly in need of rehydration salts—LemLem, as it was called locally, available only on the Ethiopian side, where I'd just come from. As an agent, free to travel back and forth across the border, David said he could retrieve it.

My hunch turned out to be right. Chriz secured the local exchange rate of twenty-two Sudanese pounds to one hundred birr, a considerable improvement from the tourist rate of fourteen to one hundred, and David brought my LemLem.

At first light, I continued, but after a quarter of an hour, the nausea kicked in again, and I threw up. The sensible thing would have been to backtrack to the compound and get more rest, except that I only had two days left to register with the passport police in the town of Gedaref, one hundred miles to the north. So I pressed on, into a crushing headwind that kept my speed below six miles per hour, and took solace in my surroundings. The beehive-shaped houses—still adobe, but neater, with tapered roofs and small rectangular windows—and the tractors ploughing the dark fertile soil suggested Sudan was altogether better off than Ethiopia, which had looked universally on its hind end. The landscape also looked kinder, undulating with low-lying hills sprinkled with leafy acacia and topped by a milky haze that lasted well into the morning, dulling the savagery of the sun.

What will the kids be like? I wondered with some trepidation. A mob of them wearing ankle-length jalabiyas and white taqiyahs, prayer caps, ran screaming to the roadside. I steeled myself for the "You! You! You!" the stones and the grabbing hands. Instead, the children stopped a feet from the road and just stood there, mute with curiosity.

After fifty miles of severe stomach cramps, I was having difficulty staying upright. I wheeled my rig into one of the flood tunnels under the road, laid out my air mattress, and collapsed. Outside, two rotting donkeys grinned at me. When the wind blew from the north, the smell was unbelievable. The gurgling in my gut worsened. I thought: *Nothing has changed since the beginning of this expedition. I'm still living like a troll under the road.*

At least the tunnel was cool, and unless someone looked directly into it, I was hidden from two- and four-legged predators. It was times like these, I reminded myself, that travelling alone had its drawbacks; no one to fetch meds and water or to call for help. *If I die here like those poor wretched donkeys,* I scrawled in my journal, *no one will know for weeks, possibly months.*

I lay there for the next thirty-six hours. On the morning of the second day, feeling rested but still shiteing through the eye of a needle, I wobbled on to Gedaref, arriving shortly before noon. I made my way straight to the passport police office to register within the mandatory three-day limit and to hand over the equivalent of $66 for the privilege. The cashier took one look at my Ethiopian birr and winced like I was holding a turd.

"Change money!" he said brusquely and gave directions to the Sudanese French Bank on the opposite side of town.

The day was another scorcher, 116 degrees Fahrenheit. When I arrived at the Sudanese French Bank, the exchange clerk also winced at my Ethiopian birr. With a sweep of his hand that took in most of North Africa, he ushered me back to the part of town I'd just come from. There, he said, in the souk, the bazaar in the centre of town, a money changer known as Mohammed El Git had a kiosk. By the time I got there—head reeling, stomach churning—I was seeing double. The souk was packed with hustling merchants and elbowing customers. I pushed my way into the scrum of white-turbaned men and black-clad hijab-wearing women, assaulted by the smells, noise, and confusion. No one had heard of El Git. The sight of a dangling camel haunch carpeted with black glossy flies put me over the edge. I lost all sphincter control and my bowels exploded.

Thank god for spandex, I thought.

When I finally tracked him down, El Git was courteous and kind. He gave me the local rate for the birr, a bottle of cold water, and directions back to the passport police.

It was now 2:00 pm. I staggered into the office, reeking to high heaven.

"You are sick?" One of the officers grimaced at my dramatic smelling entrance.

I nodded. "Five days now. Diarrhoea. Vomiting."

He couldn't process my application fast enough. "There is hospital here," he said, stamping my passport and handing it to me.

"In Gedaref? Really?"

"Yes."

"With a laboratory?"

"Everything. It is near." He shooed me away.

Ten minutes later, I came to a stop outside the entrance to Gedaref Hospital and deliberated on what to do with my bike and trailer. Another disadvantage of travelling solo is having to keep sight of your gear at all times, not easy when you're buying supplies in a supermarket, eating in a restaurant, or, like now, in search of a doctor hidden in the bowels of a hospital. As I stood there in my soiled spandex, an inquisitive crowd gathered.

"No problem, you can leave it here!" A short, beady-eyed man snatched at my arm. This was Abdullah, the admissions clerk, fortyish with receding brown hair and evidently energetic. "No one will touch it. You will see."

Feeling in no state to dispute this, I let myself be dragged away by the no-nonsense Abdullah and marched to the front of a queue of people waiting to see the doctor.

An enormous man as black as pitch, a native Dinka from the south, kicked up a fuss. *I was here before this khawaja. He can wait!*

Abdullah, who was half the man's size, shouted him down. *Hey, bonehead, can't you see he's crapped his pants?* And within half an hour of walking into the hospital, I'd seen a doctor, had the results of a lab test in my hand, and taken the first course of treatment for dysentery: metronidazole, two four-hundred milligram tablets three times a day for five days, and ciprofloxacin for any incidental bacterial infection.

Wondering what my chances would be of receiving the same level of care from a National Health Service hospital in the UK, I thanked Abdullah, who stubbornly refused a tip, and hurried outside to see what was left of my gear. Amazingly, the bike and trailer were still there, surrounded by the same crowd of people gawping with their arms crossed. Nothing had been touched or tampered with. I asked Abdullah if this was thanks to sharia, the canonical Islamic law that prescribed amputations for theft—amongst other things.

He shook his head. "No. It is older custom."

I spent three days convalescing at the Aamir Hotel, another flophouse run by a grumpy slug-like man who reminded me of Jabba the Hutt, and then rode north. That first evening, I pulled over beside a verdant orchard, the perfect spot to camp, and followed a dirt track that led me past a man and a boy walking—the farmer and his son, I guessed. I made the universal sign for sleep, resting my head on my hands, and the man smiled and signalled to a nearby stand of lime trees, its branches filled with fruit and chattering birds. I set up my bug hut under the blissfully cool canopy and began humming.

I was happy. I was healthy. I was heading for home.

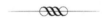

UNTIL NOW, I'D thought there was no more heart-rending sight in Africa than a mule or donkey staggering along in the heat, woefully overladen with rocks. Their benign, long-suffering expressions and melancholic honking made them the saddest, most oppressed creatures on Earth. And from what I'd seen on my travels, they were the hardest working creatures on it, too, sustaining two or more families by hauling water and firewood and transporting produce to market. Many looked whipped and mistreated, and almost all were desperately thin and malnourished. So, when I saw a dun-coloured mule with its back broken left to die by the side of the road, tossed aside like a piece of rubbish after years of loyal service, a wave of anger rose in my throat, and I pulled over.

A man in a white robe was sitting in the shade of a thorn tree. I hailed him. "Hey, Mister!"

He sauntered over. "Hey, Yiaou." He waved and glanced at his wristwatch.

"Yeah? What about this animal, then?"

"Esh. Eshe." He swept his hand in a slicing motion. "Siara."

"So, it's finished?"

He shrugged. "Finis."

A boy in a white tee shirt, black trousers, and beanie hat ambled over to take a look.

"It's not very humane, though, is it?" I said. "Letting it die here in the heat. We should put it out of its misery."

The man squatted so he could better hear me.

"Kill-e?" Using his finger, he made the throat cutting gesture of halal. "Hita?"

The animal made a feeble attempt to get up. It could barely lift its head and neck.

Another man joined us. He frowned like the others, unable to understand what I was saying. *Even if he did,* I thought cynically, *I doubt that animal welfare registers high on his agenda.*

The man in the white jalabiya stood and shouted at the boy in the beanie. I got the impression the kid was being blamed, perhaps in an act to pacify me.

"You need a knife?" I said. "I have a big knife." I retrieved the kukri from its hiding place in my trailer. Since entering Sudan, I'd felt safe enough to keep it concealed so as not to cause offence riding through villages.

When he saw the curved blade, the man became nervous. "No finis … speakin' ah … moni … sidu." He rubbed his fingers.

"Money?" I said. "Faloos?"

He nodded. "Faloos!"

"What for?"

He pointed to the desert, and then I understood. If I killed the mule, the farmer who owned the animal would demand compensation, believing that I was to blame.

"So, because someone else owns it"—I was saying it more to myself than the assembled gathering—"we can't kill it?"

By now, a crowd had gathered. People were gabbing, using the diversion as an excuse to down tools and busy themselves with some roadside drama. A nosy parker rolled up on a bicycle pimped out with lights, mirrors, and antennas to see what all the fuss was about. The situation was hopeless. The mule made another feeble attempt to stand, almost getting its front legs underneath it this time before slumping back down. I was about to explode with frustration. Not so much at these people, or even at the careless driver who'd hit and run in the first place, but at myself for not acquiring at least a basic grasp of Arabic before entering the country, as I had other languages on the expedition.

I'd just spent a week in Khartoum, running around trying to get permission to cross Lake Nasser. The British Consulate, unsurprisingly, refused to get involved. On hearing my appeal, the official I met with quickly changed the conversation to the actors Ewan McGregor and Charley Boorman, who were riding motorcycles from John o' Groats to Cape Town for their *Long Way Down* series. The pair was expected to arrive in Sudan any day, presumably with the blessing and support of the consulate.

"You might even bump into each other!" gushed the official.

Cursing the world of bureaucrats, I rolled up unannounced at the Egyptian Embassy. A soldier sat dozing in the guardhouse looking overheated and bad-tempered. "Can you please make sure the ambassador receives this?" I asked, handing him an envelope containing an expedition pamphlet and accompanying letter. "It's *extremely* important."

The soldier didn't say a word. He simply took the envelope, threw it on a desk already buried in paperwork, and went back to sleep. Had he understood? Would the letter ever find its way to the ambassador? And if by a miracle it did, what were my chances of receiving a response?

Eager to know where I stood before committing to the wilds of North Sudan—it was six hundred and fifty miles of desert tracks to Lake Nasser—I waited another five days in Khartoum, staying in a fan-less room that was so hot I slept naked under a sheet doused regularly from a tap in the communal lavatory. During the day, I scoured the city for a kayak or canoe to cross the lake with. The Blue Nile Sailing Club seemed the obvious place to start, although getting to it proved well-nigh impossible. In a fit of patriotic zeal following the defeat of the Mahdist forces in 1898, Lord Kitchener had decreed the shell-torn city be rebuilt in the shape of the Union Jack. The idea was a clumsy but effective way of reminding the residents of their subjugation to British rule, imposing an indelible stamp on the nation's consciousness. But as the blueprint for a capital, it was hopelessly flawed. At key intersections around the city, anything up to six streets converged, resulting in the most ungodly bottlenecks.

Then there was the business of circumventing the Republican Palace. The official grounds took up four city blocks that cyclists were forbidden to go anywhere near. The reason? Three months earlier, a local had ridden past the palace clutching a chicken, which promptly escaped and hightailed it through the front gates and into the ornate halls. It took the entire palace garrison to corner and oust the recalcitrant fowl, after which the mere sight of a lone cyclist was enough to send the guards into hysterics.

In the end, it was a stranger who helped solve my kayaking dilemma. Having drawn a blank tracking down a suitable craft in Khartoum, I'd decided to take up Sher's offer to have his collapsible canvas kayak sent from India. The problem now was how to transport it from Khartoum to Lake Nasser while I was riding north on my bike. Through a series of lucky connections, I found myself in the office of Midhat Mahir, an avid cyclist who promised to retrieve the boat from the post office and load it on the Kitchener train. His brother, Mazar, who worked as a tourist guide in Wadi Halfa, would take delivery of it at the other end if I didn't get there first.

The likelihood of this was high. North of Khartoum, the rambling scrubland gave way to never-ending horizons of sand, and the wind blew like an oven exhaust fan in my face—always from the north. By eight in the morning, it was already hot. The temperature climbed steadily, settling in the lower fifties by mid-afternoon, around 125 degrees Fahrenheit. Fortunately, the road was paved to Al Dabbah, allowing me to ride at night. Setting off after dark once the wind had dropped, I would pedal by moonlight until three in the morning, then pull off the road, stretch out on a mattress of cooling sand, and sleep until dawn, hoping not to be awakened by any snakes or scorpions. I'd get a few more riding hours in until ten or eleven, before looking for a flood tunnel or shade tree for the rest of the day.

Darkness was the key to navigating this desolate, sun-scorched terrain, now officially the Sahara Desert. There was less traffic, I could cycle with my shirt off without causing offence, and I consumed half as much water as in the day, which meant less weight to carry and time saved filtering water from roadside wells. After Dongola, though, the road dissolved into bone-jarring corrugations interspersed with stretches of ankle-deep sand, impossible to ride at night without risk of falling and injuring myself. It was back to riding in daylight hours and breathing through my nose to cut down on moisture loss. More than three lungfuls by mouth, and my throat would burn horribly. A day of this, and all I could think about was water. Little roadside shelters appeared in the villages housing rows of clay pots filled with well water, the contents kept ingeniously cool by means of evaporation through the porous clay. Panting dogs lay in the dripping pools, and birds perched in the rafters, beaks ajar.

I could only muster the strength to write two words in my journal: *Stupidly hot.*

Between settlements, these shelters were fewer and more rudimentary, just palm fronds thrown over a rickety frame of hewn branches. But they still offered luxuriant shade, and occasionally there'd be a string bed in the corner, one of the many little touches that gave the weary traveller cause to fall in love with the Sudan. Another was the Nubian people, the most hospitable I had met on the expedition so far—which was saying something. In the village of Tombos, passing one of the exquisitely decorated Nubian homes that resembled gingerbread houses, I stopped to ask a group of white-robed men if they knew of a restaurant nearby where I could get some tea.

No restaurant, said one, shaking his head and laughing, but did I care for some tea, anyway? This was Salah Mohamed. A table and chair were mustered from the whitewashed compound and two cups of shai leben, milky tea, served with homemade biscuits. And there I sat, Lord Muck, the nineteenth-century explorer catered to by his retinue, surrounded by the bleached sands. I had many similar experiences in North Sudan, like the lovely old man who flagged me down in the village of Arduan to offer me some dried dates—he was furious when I offered him money. And more than once at a roadside kiosk, when I got up to pay for my meal of ful medammes, mashed fava beans, I was told that a stranger had already picked up the tab and taken off.

Why is it the nicest people always have the worst governments, I wondered? Countries like Iran, Zimbabwe, Turkmenistan, North Korea, Myanmar, and Sudan all had thugs in charge, licensed thieves, racketeers, and gangsters. Yet, the inhabitants, especially the villagers, were some of the kindest, most forgiving people you could ever hope to meet. Perhaps that was the problem. The average hardworking local was just too good-natured, too ready to let themself be bullied and intimidated. They needed to take a few leaves out of books written by feisty French and American revolutionaries: get themselves organized and boot the buggers out.

Salah Mohamed and his brother took me to see a nearby stele, a sunken relief depicting the sack of Kerma by Thutmose I in 1504 BCE. Then it was on to a granite quarry where the Nubian Emperor Taharqa lay face down in the dust, his head split in two like the statue of Ramesses II that served as the inspiration for "Ozymandias." The immediacy of the ancient past was something I found sobering, but even more impressive was how these irreplaceable relics were just lying out there in the desert, abandoned, used as scratching posts by sheep and goats, and getting pissed on by the shepherd boys. It is widely acknowledged in archaeological circles that Sudan is home to even more antiquities than Egypt, the vast majority of which still lie buried in the desert.

North of Abri, the settlements thinned, and the landscape became even more bleak and desolate. Keeping sight of the Nile in such unforgiving terrain meant the difference between life and death. After Delgo, I took a wrong turn, unaware of my error until I looked up and noticed the slender ribbon of life-giving green had disappeared and I was completely surrounded by desert. Taking in the shifting sands and shimmering mirage dancing off into oblivion—there was nothing else, not a drop of water in sight—I was gripped by a rising sense of panic. Without the river, I felt naked and exposed. A quick GPS fix put me back on track. Still, the experience taught me a valuable lesson: Never lose sight of the green.

Part of the problem was no longer having a clearly marked trail to follow, just a muddle of random wheel tracks blazed by the Toyota Hiluxes known locally as "bokasi" snaking off into the Never-Never. A general Sudanese incomprehension of maps didn't help, either. Presented with my Russian topo, the men would gather round and gaze at it in wonderment, murmuring and sucking their teeth. Asking directions to a specific village produced even more confusion. Eager to help, they would start windmilling with their arms and go to great lengths to describe what I was likely to see along the way—people they knew, whether these people were good or bad, the animals they owned, and the frequency of wells. But did the track actually lead to so-and-so village? They would shrug. Not the faintest idea.

At Argo, I needed to cross the Nile to connect with the track leading to Wadi Halfa, which meant swimming the river, then backtracking on the little ferry for my gear. However, when I freewheeled the last hundred yards past a caravan of grumbling camels and saw how far it was, nearly half a mile across, I began to have my doubts. The water was muddy and fast flowing, and according to a group of people waiting to cross, Nile crocodiles were known to inhabit the islands immediately downstream, where I would likely be taken by the current. For once, a sensible voice inside my head said: *Don't do it. Swimming would be suicide.*

Scouting in the reeds next to the slipway, I chanced upon a homemade rowing boat. It was short, twelve feet long, perhaps, comprised of six forty-gallon oil drums beaten out and nailed together. The contraption was clearly a death trap: primitive paddles had been cut from the lids and lashed to branches, the rowlocks were fashioned from an old car tyre, and there was no caulking to seal out the water. Nevertheless, it presented an infinitely more attractive alternative to swimming. *Bloody marvellous,* I thought. The only thing missing was the owner to ask permission to use it.

Two hours later, Osman and I were pushing away from the bank. He was a local fisherman, tall, softly spoken, and noble looking, his pitch-black skin contrasting sharply against a brilliant white turban. Tracked down by a disembarking passenger who knew him, Osman had grasped the concept quickly—"*The khawaja is on a pilgrimage using only his legs, so he cannot use the ferry"*—and without hesitation he'd agreed to let me row his boat. Only once we were underway did he let slip that he'd just come from burying his uncle, an important family occasion that he made sound almost inconsequential, leaving me once again humbled by the readiness of strangers to help a traveller in need.

I pulled on the creaking oars, sending us scudding across the brown water, while Osman described to me in halting English how he'd once taken a similar boat all the way to Wadi Halfa, nearly two hundred miles away. This latest model was nine years old and going strong, he said. We passed the islands downstream, and he pointed to where the crocs lurked. A fourteen-footer was the largest he'd seen.

When we bumped up against the far bank, I unloaded my bike and trailer, and handed Osman the equivalent of $25 in Sudanese pounds for his trouble. He baulked.

"Think of it as a life insurance payment," I insisted, pushing the money towards him. "You almost certainly saved my life."

But he was already off, rowing back upstream, a bed sheet strung between two bowed branches harnessing the north wind to make purchase against the current.

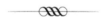

ADIL BARED HIS teeth for effect and turned his fingers into claws. "Wolves," he whispered theatrically, "with long teeth!"

I was in the El Fagre Hotel, just a row of string beds facing the stars in an open courtyard. Adil owned his own boksi and was using scare tactics to convince me not to carry on alone.

"Wolves in Sudan?" I replied. "What rubbish."

But Adil wasn't easily dissuaded. "No! A few years ago, a tourist tried to take a picture of one." He narrowed his eyes and curled the corners of his mouth as he leaned towards me, spewing halitosis fumes. "It ripped him to pieces. Only bones left!"

The story ended almost exactly the same as one I'd heard on the island of Komodo in Indonesia, of a dragon devouring a Swedish tourist. The last photo in the camera found next to the body showed "the animal, about to devour the victim."

Regardless of whether wolves actually roamed the desert north of Abri (or maybe he meant hyenas?), employing Adil to transport water for the riverless section to Wadi Halfa, one hundred and twenty miles away, made a lot of sense. Rumour had it there was an oasis, El Beer, around the halfway point. But what good was a rumour in the Sahara Desert? And "El Beer?" It had to be a joke. Assuming the worst-case scenario, that I could manage only thirty miles a day and there was no El Beer, I would need at least sixty litres to make the journey, enough for fifteen litres a day riding in the heat. That was an extra one hundred and thirty-two pounds to carry, upping my total load to nearly four hundred and fifty.

Even so, his asking price of $250 would leave me with precious little to complete the circumnavigation. So, I loaded up with water bottles, stacking them behind my seat and on top of the trailer, and pressed on, entering a region known as The Belly of Stones. It was dust and rubble as far as the eye could see, and the corrugations of compacted sand were barely rideable without suspension. The only way to pedal was standing up, using my legs as shock absorbers. Or to walk.

The wind blew so hard that first night out of Abri, I gave up trying to erect the bug hut. An east-west crevice in the rocks offered a bolthole to squeeze in far enough out of the wind. I slept fitfully and woke an hour before first light, my ears filled with sand.

By the end of the second day, I was beginning to wonder whether my conservative estimate of thirty miles a day was conservative enough. With the heat, the headwind, the long stretches of sand where I had to get off and push for miles at a time, my average speed dropped to a mere two-and-a-half miles per hour—the same as walking. On the morning of the third day, a lone tree appeared in the distance. So, it was true. El Beer did exist, although its real name turned out to be El Bierr, just a collection of ramshackle buildings either side of the track. It was a dismal set up, the lone outpost blasted by heat and sand, but compensated by a congenial owner who had addis for sale, lentil soup, and—best of all—a pile of watermelons.

Five miles on, the sun shrank to a yellow tennis ball and disappeared behind a smouldering carpet of gloom pouring over the northeast horizon. The wind accelerated, and the air filled with flying debris. I looked around for shelter, but there was none. The only option was to crouch behind my panniers and keep my eyes tight shut and fingers jammed in my ears until the sandstorm passed.

An hour went by. The wind finally dropped. I shrugged off a mantle of sand and continued. Over the brow of the next hill, two motorcycles hove into view and slowed to a halt. The lead rider was bearded and wore a full-face helmet fitted with a camera. His eyes were hidden behind wraparound shades.

"Mister McGregor, I presume?" I said, borrowing from Stanley's famous greeting of the errant David Livingstone—appropriate for a fellow Scot, I thought.

"No, I'm Charlie."

Charlie was clearly the more confident rider of the two, blazing a trail for Ewan, who pulled up a moment later, looking dusty and disgruntled.

"Terrible road, isn't it?" said Charlie, going on to explain that it was their first day of off-road riding since leaving Scotland. One of their cameramen, Claudio, had already broken the suspension on his bike.

A cavalcade of vehicles joined us: two locally hired bokasi and a pair of Nissan Patrols with decals of tyre treads and logos emblazoning the sides.

"Where did you start?" Ewan asked, resting against his zebra-striped fuel tank.

I gave a thirteen-year rundown of the expedition in thirteen seconds, rattling off the continents, oceans, and modes of human power. It made the whole thing sound rather fanciful as I said it. But it was the hottest day yet, 134 degrees Fahrenheit, too hot to be standing around nattering.

Ewan wasn't really listening, anyway. He was staring at the water bottles behind my seat. "Is that Nile water?" he asked.

I replied that it was.

"And you drink it?"

"Yep. Just add a few drops of iodine to each bottle. It's quicker than filtering, and my plumbing seems to prefer it."

I sensed that both riders were rather taken aback meeting a lone cyclist out here in Bumfuck Sudan, perhaps because it undermined the experience of striking out into wilderness proper (if there is one thing guaranteed to dampen the spirits of the intrepid explorer, it is the sight of another face from home). The thing was, though, there was only one north-south track through the Kingdom of Kush, the miserable one we were on, and running into another traveller at some point was inevitable.

Russ Malkin, the UK producer, fetched me a bottle of mineral water from the fridge in the back of his truck. Unlike my Nile water, which was browner than mud and hotter than bathwater, it was crystal clear and ice cold. I unscrewed the cap and took the best tasting gulp of water I'd had in a long time.

Charlie had the same useless roadmap for Sudan as I did. He pulled it out, and we traded information about the road conditions in either direction.

"What's it like up ahead," he asked, "more corrugations?"

"Afraid so," I replied, tracing my finger down the Nile. "Same shit all the way to Dongola,"

Ewan pursed his lips and looked even glummer. Dongola was three hundred and seventy miles away.

Keen to make miles before sundown, Ewan and Charlie took off, leaving me to chat with the crew. "We'll catch 'em up," said Russ.

We talked about our projects, the filming aspect, and how difficult it was to secure sponsorship from the UK. Even with celebrity talent and a TV commission in place, Russ said it had been a struggle. Then we parted, heading north and south respectively. A minute later, though, I heard a rumble of wheels and loud beeping and turned to see Russ pulling up in his Patrol.

"Sorry ter 'old you up," the Londoner said, climbing out of his cab. "But we've got summin' for yer."

Walking around to the back, he pulled open the doors and started rummaging. "We were drivin' down the road finkin' 'ow 'ard it is for you ter get sponsorship. Then we fought, 'ang on a minute, we can sponsor 'im!' We wanna see you finish this fing."

He handed me a wad of banknotes. "There's a fousand quid there. We 'ope it 'elps."

Indeed, it would. With the Aberdeen money dwindling fast, the likelihood of running out completely before making it back to Greenwich grew with each passing day. The irony of the sudden windfall wasn't lost on me, either. After the hundreds of sponsorship proposals submitted to British companies over the years, none of which had come to anything, our biggest financial backer from home would turn out to be another UK expedition.

June 14
THE VOICE ON the other end of the line was barely audible. "Welcome, Mister Jason."

"Good morning, Hadija. Is His Excellency the ambassador available, by any chance?"

The voice mumbled something.

"I'm sorry, could you repeat that?"

More mumbling.

"Okay. So, I need to call Mr Mustafa at twelve o'clock. Same as yesterday."

It was my eighth morning in Wadi Halfa, and like Bill Murray in *Groundhog Day*, I was reliving the same day over and over. Every morning at eleven o'clock, I used the satellite phone to call Hadija, personal assistant to the Egyptian ambassador in Khartoum. Every morning, I was put on hold for twenty minutes and made to listen to the same merry-go-round synthesizer music. Every morning, the same answer came back: still no word from the Ministry of Tourism in Cairo on my request to paddle the lake.

This morning, I knew, would be no different. The monotony of the wait hadn't been helped by the novelty of Wadi Halfa wearing off within the first minute of arriving. *A dreadful place*, I scribbled in my notebook, *the arsehole at the end of all arseholes*. The place had a derelict, falling-off-the-edge-of-the-world feel to it, which, if you looked at the map, wasn't far from the truth. The road ended here, as did Kitchener's railway and the weekly ferry from Aswan. The wind bullied. The sand drifted. The donkeys brayed that mournful and utterly dispirited bray that summoned all the hardships and sufferings of the African continent in one breath. Rubbish billowed from behind a row of decrepit one-storey flophouses catering to travellers stranded until the next ferry, drifters, traders, and vagabonds confined to stark, joyless rooms, twiddling their thumbs. One of those vagabonds was me. Except it wasn't the ferry I was waiting for.

Logistically, everything was ready to go. Sher's kayak had miraculously made it all the way from India, a testament to the postal service in both countries. My bicycle, panniers, and trailer had already gone ahead on the ferry with three overlanders: Tom Wilson, a ginger-headed

Brit backpacking from Cape Town to Cairo, and Dorothee and Kurt from Germany and Switzerland, who'd been cycling for nine years and notched up an impressive 87,000 miles. The only thing preventing me from setting off was the nod from Cairo. After getting off the phone with Hadija at noon—no change, as expected—I called Mazar to ask what he thought was the worst that could happen if I just winged it.

"They will shoot you," he said matter-of-factly. He was in his early twenties, eager, efficient, bordering on a little pushy. "The Egyptians, they don't care. If they don't kill you first, they will arrest you, and they will beat you, and then send you to jail in Aswan or Cairo."

There was a surveillance post either side of the lake, he explained, on the 22nd parallel. The Egyptians occupied the one to the east, the Sudanese the one to the west. The lake narrowed to a width of three and a half miles at this point, giving the security forces a clear view of anyone trying to sneak across. Even local fishing boats were ordered to steer clear. The only vessel permitted to enter the eighteen-mile exclusion zone was the weekly ferry.

"You *must* wait for permission," insisted Mazar, adding that more observation posts were staged at strategic points up the lake. The Egyptians were also known to have at least one patrol boat.

Later, Mazar met me outside the Deffintoad Hotel where I was staying, one of several lodgings on the verge of a cholera outbreak. The wind was gusting as usual, and the dull orange orb of the sun was setting over the lake. In the distance, pinned loosely around the dark green of date palms, a smattering of low-lying houses extended eastwards and melded with the desert's evening hues.

Mazar told me he'd passed on my request to the local authorities for a trial on the lake to test the kayak and get some exercise—I hadn't paddled a stroke since arriving in Singapore, a year and a half earlier. However, the reply from their superiors in Dongola was an unequivocal, "No."

"They are afraid you might go near the border," Mazar said. "And the Egyptians, they may suspect something and cause trouble."

"But I have a GPS," I said. "I'll know exactly where I am."

Mazar shook his head. "It won't make any difference with these people."

"So what happens now?"

Mazar thought for a moment. "I will speak to my brother, Midhat, to try to find a solution for you. But it is getting harder."

I, too, had my doubts. Perhaps it had been a mistake to take the front door approach. Over the years, I'd learned that asking permission to do something from officials in rinky-dink parts of the world often created more problems than if you just went ahead and did it. No one wanted to take responsibility if things went wrong.

Back in room number thirty, which I shared with a flourishing population of cockroaches, I sat on the bed, staring at my feet, and considered my options. Although Mazar had been helpful, I suspected he was struggling with a conflict of interest. On the one hand, he had a duty to me as a paying client, reliant as I was on his knowledge of the local geography and access to the right people to get things done. On the other, his tourism business depended on maintaining healthy relations with the authorities. And there was an even darker scenario that had crossed my mind: *Maybe he's playing both ends of the stick? Keeping me happy, but also working as an informer for the police, making sure I don't do a flit.*

An added complication was my non-renewable Sudanese visa had now expired. If the police showed up and asked to see my passport, I would be summarily detained and deported—bundled on the next ferry to Egypt. This was the scenario I feared the most. With no hope of acquiring another visa and the continuity of the journey broken, I would be forced to backtrack to Mumbai, India, and find an alternative route home.

Mulling all of this and how each additional day spent in Wadi Halfa posed a potential risk to the circumnavigation bid, the right course of action suddenly became clear.

"Fuck it." I started packing my gear.

Leaving behind a few non-essential items to give the impression I was coming back—books, redundant maps, water bottles, and so on—I grabbed my camping equipment and locked the door behind me.

"Just going for a spin," I told the attendant idling on the front steps and handed him enough money for two additional night's stay. "I'll be back. Tomorrow, maybe."

"Where you go?"

"Just around." I gestured vaguely. "Need to get some exercise."

I flagged down the next boksi that passed and readily agreed to the outrageous sum of $10 to have Sher's kayak transported the half mile to the lake. Normally, I would have haggled, but the clock was ticking. I loaded the kayak on the roof and gave "Mister Ali" instructions to drop it at the shoreside.

I walked, sand trudging in the boksi's wheel tracks. Once free of the town, I pulled the room key from my pocket and hurled it as far as I could into the desert.

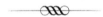

Saturday, June 16

FOR THE NEXT 24 hours, I camped on one of the uninhabited islets on the west side of the lake, taking observations: wind patterns, celestial points to navigate by (the Southern Cross, I noticed, only stayed above the horizon until two in the morning), and whether the moon would betray me by throwing up the glint of a paddle blade or the shadow of my kayak against the lake.

I also called Mazar.

"Are you at the hotel?" he asked suspiciously.

"No, out and about." I was being deliberately ambiguous. "Exploring." Then I dropped the call. Even if they suspected I was out on the lake, I was pretty sure the Sudanese authorities would be loath to come out and look for me. The word on the street in Wadi Halfa was the resident patrol boat was currently out of fuel.

Next morning, I tried Hadija one last time, in case the ambassador had heard from Cairo and I could still cross the border legitimately.

Nothing doing.

I set off at dusk on the evening of the second day, aiming thirty degrees east of Polaris, the North Star, which would serve as my primary compass so long as the sky remained clear. I daren't use my headlamp, and the silver sliver of moon, less than a quarter full, was too weak to illuminate the compass fixed atop my cockpit. The shadow of land off my port beam provided another point of reference, faintly visible for an hour or so, after which it would be completely dark.

The only sounds were the splotch of my paddle and the nervous meter of my ragged breath. The time was 8:05 pm. By the time I reached the 22nd parallel, six miles to the north, I was relying on it being pitch black, the moon having slipped below the western horizon. At this point, I would veer to the middle of the lake and cross the border equidistant between the two observation posts. If either side had infrared surveillance equipment, I would dead in the water. Literally.

It wasn't long before my arms were burning and my palms throbbing with the now unfamiliar effort of paddling. The wind freshened to fifteen knots from the northwest, making the going even harder. This wasn't part of the plan at all. At night-time in the Sahara, the wind usually dropped as the desert cooled. The light canvas kayak bucked and plunged with each passing wave, stopping dead in its tracks and sending lake water slapping in my face. I had to stop at regular intervals and pump out the water streaming under my spray skirt.

All I could do was keep paddling, implore the wind to subside, and visualize the waves getting smaller, willing a flat, glassy calm. Shortly before midnight, lights appeared in the west, blinking behind the waves. This was Argin, the Sudanese surveillance point. Voices came glancing over the water, snatches of muffled conversation and the odd hoot. On the Egyptian side, there was only the night.

Two hours later, I entered a rocky inlet on the east side of the lake. As long as there were no lights, I reckoned it was safe to land. A felucca loomed, cradling a sleeping fisherman wrapped in a blanket. I paddled a little farther, tied up to a jutting rock, and levered myself out to stretch my legs and eat the leftovers of my evening meal by starlight.

Continuing on, my supplications were finally answered. The wind dropped to a predawn whisper, and by 5:20 am, the sky was beginning to lighten in the east. I now had forty minutes of low light conditions to find cover and hide all my equipment before sun-up.

Lucky for me, Lake Nasser was ideally suited to the needs of the fugitive. Like the convoluted intestines of some giant ruminant, the periphery was a labyrinth of tiny islands, inlets, and barren coves leading away from the lake, making it easy to disappear. Within minutes, I'd found the perfect spot: a tiny bay set back from the water, hidden by a row of evergreen bushes choked with cobwebs. A sheer bank prevented detection from the east—only by looking directly over the edge could someone see me. By 6:15 am, having ferried all my dry bags and pulled the kayak up the beach, I was out of sight.

Feeling pleased with myself for having crossed the border without getting shot or arrested, I cooked a meal of porridge and honey and tried to sleep. By seven thirty, though, it was already too hot and the flies incessant. I rigged up some basic shade using the flysheet of my bug hut and disconnected paddle ends and lay there sweating, listening to the birds whistling and giggling in the bushes.

Hours passed. The temperature climbed steadily. I dozed, waking to the *cling-cling-cling* of shepherd bells. Peering through the bushes,

I saw a herd of goats migrating slowly up the beach from the south, nibbling at the greener shoots along the water's edge. The bleating drew closer. A boy in a white jalabiya suddenly appeared less than fifty feet from where I sat. I held my breath as he stopped to urinate. When he turned to make his way back to the herd, he must have glimpsed me in his peripheral vision. He took off running.

Do I stay put or make a run for it? I thought anxiously. A little later, I heard dogs barking. *Shit, here we go ...*

Led by the whistle-blower, three boys traipsed into the clearing, one carrying a wooden staff. I shook their hands in turn. Then a bearded, bucktoothed man in a red shirt and white prayer cap breezed in.

"Assalamu alaikum," he muttered. Peace be with you.

"Wa alaikum assalaam,' I replied, reaching for his hand. And upon you be peace.

"Sam leer?" he asked.

I had no idea what this meant, so I just smiled, and said, "Tamam." Okay.

The man uttered something else unintelligible and pointed to the lake.

I took a wild guess. "I'm going to, err, Wadi Halfa." I lied, at same time wondering, *Are these Nubians or Egyptians?*

The man put his hands behind his back and said nothing.

To fill the silence, I chuckled nervously and offered, "Alhamdulillah," exhausting my knowledge of Arabic.

Another figure with the face of a fox stalked into the clearing. He wore a baseball cap, magenta shirt, and black slacks—definitely not Nubian.

"Hello," I greeted him.

"Okay," he grunted, slapping my hand.

The two adults stood with their arms crossed, contemplating my kayak. Then, as solemnly as they'd arrived, they all trooped out of the clearing in single file, murmuring to each other. Before they disappeared from view, I saw one of the men raise his hand to his temple and make the universal sign for a telephone call.

WITH MY POSITION compromised, it wouldn't take long before the authorities arrived. I broke camp as fast as I could, dragged everything back down to the water and loaded my kayak in double quick time. The kid who'd grassed me up stood a little distance away and watched. He sauntered up as I struggled and handed me a mobile phone. The screen was dead. He pointed at the power socket.

What's this, I thought, *a stalling tactic?*

"No, no charger!" I shook my head and took to the water. The time was now 4:30 in the afternoon of the second day. I paddled hard for fifteen minutes, then ducked out of sight behind an islet and listened for the sound of approaching motors. When night fell, I resumed my northbound journey. The second night's objective was to complete the twenty-three miles to Abu Simbel, the first town north of the border, and find another hiding place before daybreak.

Kayaking in total darkness was utterly mind numbing, compounding the lack of sleep and adrenaline fatigue. Around midnight, I awoke disorientated with my head and torso underwater—I'd nodded off and capsized. Luckily, an island was close enough for me to drag the boat to and pump out the water. Intermittent squawks from the darkness alerted me to roosting birds. Otherwise, the place was deserted, just a few abandoned nests and mounds of stinking guano. Pressing on, I managed only an hour before my head once again began to nod. I reached for my iPod, scrolled to Green Day's *American Idiot,* and scoffed a couple of Twinkies. *Food in your stomach will help you stay awake,* I told myself.

Invented in Illinois in 1930, Twinkies are an American junk-food legend, best described as a mini sponge cake filled with vanilla cream and enough preservatives to last a million years without refrigeration. Bizarrely, I'd found boxes of them in the stores in Wadi Halfa, sold under their Arabic name. Not exactly the energy bars I was looking for, but as a psychological carrot to paddle towards during the long night-time hours, the sugar-laden snacks were turning out to have their use.

It was after one of these refuelling stops that I detected something large, furry, and multi-limbed crawling up my right leg. I have a long-standing phobia of spiders. This one had obviously crept into my cockpit when the boat was pulled up on shore. To make matters worse, my spray skirt was secured tightly with Velcro, preventing me from reaching down and brushing the creature off. When I tried dislodging it with my left knee, I felt a sharp, stabbing pain. This was too much. I tore at the Velcro, grabbed the hitchhiker, and threw it in the water.

There was one upside to being bitten. The pain kept me awake for the rest of the night, and at four in the morning, the yellow and white lights of Abu Simbel finally shimmered into view. I crossed to the west side of the lake, chased by the milky grey light bleeding in from the east, and took a GPS fix. An inlet emerged with boats moored inside. I ducked beneath a gangplank connected to the rocky lakeshore and paddled the last few feet to land. Just then, the yellow beam of a flashlight cut the darkness. A night watchman! The light flickered, died, and sputtered to life again, probing the night. Fortunately, the shaft of light was too weak to penetrate the shadows where I sat, paddle frozen in mid-air. The flashlight then died completely. Taking care not to make a sound, I backed out of the inlet.

Hugging the coastline, I paddled north, looking for cover. There was none. Dawn broke, and with it full daylight. Crossing an open stretch of water between two headlands, I heard a motorboat sputter to life and begin heading in my direction at full throttle.

This was not good.

As it drew closer, I could see that it was a fishing boat with a flared bow, for'ard-pointing outriggers, and blue trim around the gunwales. Egypt's answer to the Artful Dodger stood amidships, his trousers at half-mast and a dirty tea towel wrapped around his scrawny head. Beside him was a bulbous, barefoot thug in a red tee shirt—the one in charge judging by the way he ran to the bow and starting yelling at me.

"Awaya! Ena fesh kabeer." The skipper flapped his arms and gestured to his sagging stomach.

I recognized one word, which meant great, or big. "Kabeer?" I repeated.

"Kabeer. Kersh."

I had no idea what "kersh" meant.

"Se mcfesh." The fat man signalled in the direction I was heading.

"Fish?" I said. "Big fish?"

He extended his arms like an angler exaggerating his catch. "Aya. Mcfesh." A third fisherman in a torn shirt and green trousers squatted in the stern, manning the outboard motor and watching the demented game of charades with bemusement.

"Timsah?" I suggested. Crocodile?

The skipper stabbed at me and then to his mouth. "Aiyo, timsah!" He nodded. "Timsah. Ya. Yoklet."

So, according to these guys, I would be eaten by a large crocodile if I continued. It was true that over 5,000 specimens of *Crocodylus niloticus,* Nile crocodile, inhabited the lake. Only two days earlier, paddling away from Wadi Halfa, I'd seen a brown snout take a fish from the surface in broad daylight. Nevertheless, something seemed a little off.

"No." I laughed. "I don't think so."

"Yolaheh!" The skipper fluttered his fat fingers and stomped his enormous feet. "Anstrophe." He pointed to the island he and his comrades had just come from and gestured for me to follow.

Not on your nelly, I thought, and continued paddling.

"No! No! No!" The skipper became even more agitated. "Timsah kabeer."

Then again, perhaps they were genuinely trying to be helpful. Maybe there was an observation post around the corner, or a patrol boat, and the croc story was just a diversion to prevent me from being caught. Or, being fishermen, they thought my kayak wasn't seaworthy enough.

I cursed myself again for not learning Arabic.

The fishing boat did a big loop and came alongside. The Artful Dodger reached over and snatched the grab line on my port side bow. Sensing events were about to take a turn for the worse, I pulled the video camera from the dry bag between my legs and rolled tape. I'd found on my travels that people were less likely to act rashly if they knew they were being filmed.

"Let go of my boat, please." I pointed the camera at the skipper who had also taken hold of the line. "And I will paddle to shore myself."

Their island was a dump. Tin cans and partially submerged fishing nets slopped in the shallows, trapped by carpets of green gunge. Oil drums lay tossed on the beach, leaking some unknown and unimaginably foul effluent. I pulled in between two fishing boats and hoisted myself out, taking care not to step on the broken glass poking out of the sand.

A ragged character in a green tartan cap escorted me to a brick hut at the top of the beach. Bunches of nets and coils of blue nylon rope were laid out inside. Two dazed-looking fishermen sat in the corner next to a hookah pipe and a box of black tea. Sports bags hung from the ceiling, and a lone window graced the miserable hovel with its only light.

"Alright!" I said, trying to appear upbeat. "Home from home, eh?"

Secretly, my mind was racing, desperately trying to work out what was going on. Were these guys really trying to be helpful, or were they in league with the authorities?

I'll hang out for a bit, I decided, *try to pick up some clues, and then get going.*

The fisherman in the tartan cap was now sitting on the dirt floor, knees tucked beneath him, using a netting needle to mend one of the nets. Another, younger man with a shaved head offered me a cup of tea.

I took a sip and gave him the thumbs up. "Good. Tamam."

After twenty minutes of waiting with no one talking and nothing happening, I'd had enough. I got to my feet, pushed past a silhouetted figure in the doorway, and walked as calmly as I could down to the water's edge. As I neared my kayak, I noticed the boat with the blue trim was heading back to shore.

That's strange. I thought they'd gone fishing for the rest of the day.

Hands suddenly grabbed me under both arms. Next I was on the ground, my legs and arms pinned, and a knee driven into the small of my back. Lying there, face down in the putrid slime, I knew I'd been betrayed. The fat skipper and his friends hadn't gone fishing at all. They'd motored far enough out to get a mobile signal and called the security forces in Abu Simbel.

"WHAT CONTREE YOU?"

I blinked at the mesmerizing eddies of smoke swirling towards the fluorescent ceiling tube. "UK," I replied. "I'm English."

Mid-forties, hair thinning and cheeks pitted, my interrogator sat behind a large wooden desk, cigarette smouldering between his fingers, leafing through my passport. He looked coldly efficient in his narrow framed glasses, yet so far the major had been courteous, disproving Mazar's assurances of being beaten on sight by the Egyptian military. Perhaps he was just treading carefully. Egyptians were famously paranoid about their tourism industry.

Three hours earlier, a white motorboat had pulled up on the beach where I lay being used as a mattress by the fishermen. Major Hassan and two henchmen jumped out, revolvers drawn. The fat skipper immediately began yammering, boasting of his ruse. *No doubt the bastard will be handsomely rewarded for this,* I thought bitterly as the henchmen bundled me into the launch along with my gear. After a short ride down the coast, we disembarked in a little harbour below the Mubahath el-Dawla detention centre, General Directorate of State Security Investigations. I recognized it as the same inlet I'd paddled into earlier under cover of darkness, where the night watchman had very nearly seen me.

The major's English was marginally better than my Arabic, which wasn't saying much. With no translator available, he'd resorted to a Windows translation program on his desktop computer. As he fiddled with the mouse, I studied the inside of the room. The curtains were drawn and the air conditioning turned up full blast. For the first time since crossing the Himalayas, I was freezing. My gaze came to rest on the leather whip coiled on the major's desk. How many prisoners had been coerced into giving confessions by this instrument of torture, I wondered?

The major put my passport down and turned to me. "So, going round Egypt?"

This was what I'd communicated to the fishermen: that I was sightseeing. The problem with this story was that my passport contained neither an entry stamp for Egypt, nor an exit stamp from Sudan. All I had was an expired Sudanese visa, leaving me in political limbo. The major would find this out soon enough, of course. My only hope in the meantime was to play the dumb tourist card.

"Yeah, just paddling around," I replied. "I think I might have got lost, though. Is this Sudan or Egypt?"

The major raised his eyebrows and stared at me. "You choking?"

"No, I'm not."

"Dis Egypt."

"I thought it was Sudan?"

"No, no!" He stabbed the desk with his finger. "Egypt!"

"Oh dear, then I really am lost."

He turned his attention back to my passport. "Where is—" He made a stamping motion with his fist, a reference to the missing visa and entry stamp for Egypt.

I took a deep breath. "Well, I was in Sudan, doing some kayaking around the lake—for tourism—and I must have gone too far north. So, this is definitely not Sudan?"

Major Hassan shook his head in disbelief. This idiot tourist had somehow strayed across the border, the border it was his job to prevent anyone from going near. He hammered on his keyboard and read from the screen. "How did you cross the border?"

"No one stopped me." I replied truthfully, although I chose not to mention that I'd paddled at night. "But I am still confused"—I reached forward to the map on his desk—"exactly where the border is."

Using the ring finger on his left hand, the major traced the 22nd parallel. "Up from here … is forbidden."

"And where are we now?"

The finger travelled forty miles north to Abu Simbel.

I pretended to only now comprehend. "Oh, I see. I suppose that means I'm in trouble, right? I'm just glad you didn't shoot me!"

Major Hassan said nothing. No smile. No laughter. He took a deep drag on his cigarette and went back to scrutinizing my passport. In a corner of the room, one of his henchmen was going through my equipment, pulling out the contents of the dry bags and placing them in different piles. Electronics was already the biggest.

The major glanced over at the growing mound of gadgetry: laptop, GPS, satellite phone, EPIRB, video camera, cell phone, RBGAN satellite modem, digital still camera, solar panels, memory cards, video cassettes, power adaptors, leads, extra batteries, and two compasses—one handheld, the other from my cockpit. He pointed and rattled off something in Arabic, whereupon the orderly retrieved the laptop-sized satellite terminal I used to send video footage back to the expedition website.

"What this?" he asked.

For a moment I considered trying to pass it off as a battery pack, but the compass embedded in the casing would give it away. I told him the truth.

Up until this point, the intelligence officer had been tactful and diplomatic, introducing himself politely ("Hello, my nem ees Major Hassan") and asking routine questions. Now his demeanour was starting to change. His eyes narrowed to reptilian slits as he stared at me through the swirling galaxies of silvery smoke. "I do not be leaf your story," he said, fingered the whip ominously.

"What part of it?" I replied.

"Any of it!" He leaned forward and pointed to the last page of my passport. "Your family name, Levi?"

"No, Lewis."

"You work for ... who?"

I shook my head; I was beginning to see where this was going. In its written form, Lewis bore a loose resemblance to the Hebrew name of Levi, potentially confusing to someone unfamiliar with the Latin alphabet. Egyptians hated Jews even more than the Sudanese, a long-standing hostility stretching back to pharonic times exacerbated more recently by repeated military defeats at the hands of the Israelis since 1948.

"I don't work for anybody," I protested.

The major tightened his jaw and nodded at the pile of electronics. "Then what these? I ask you again ... who you work for?"

A flunky appeared carrying a sheaf of papers and a mug of coffee on a saucer. He placed them in front of the major, who was now speaking rapidly into a telephone, one of several lining his desk. *This is bad*, I said to myself. The inventorying of equipment meanwhile continued.

Lists were made. Then yet more lists. The orderly going through my gear handed the major a burgundy booklet he'd found in my waterproof money belt. This was my back up passport, one free of Israeli stamps that would hopefully get me into Syria.*

Still barking at the phone, the major took the passport and placed it with the other. How would I explain this?

Hours passed. Phones rang. Major Hassan had up to three handsets on the go at once, working them like a telemarketer. Who was he talking to? I lost all track of time. During lulls in the interrogation, I found myself nodding off, having barely slept in three days. A commotion snapped me to my senses. The orderly had cut himself unsheathing my kukri knife, slicing his thumb to the bone. Seeing an opportunity to ingratiate myself in what appeared to be increasingly dire circumstances, I asked the major permission to dress and bandage the wound with supplies from my first aid kit.

I estimated that I'd been sitting in the same chair for around eighteen hours when an orderly brought me a glass of water and escorted me to a bunkhouse. I was allowed to sleep for an hour. Then I was roused for more questioning.

Back in the interrogation room, an exhausted Major Hassan was still working the phones. Cups of cold coffee cluttered his desk. A marble ashtray overflowed with cigarette butts. My cameras and GPS were laid out in a row in front of him.

He signalled for me to sit, then swivelled the LCD screen of the camcorder so I could see. The display was dark, but I could hear a voice, my voice, whispering to the camera. I was describing crossing the border and congratulating myself on avoiding detection. "I'm now heading north towards Aswan," the voice was saying. "So, I really, really hope the Egyptian security forces don't see me."

---

* Several Arab countries, including Syria, automatically refuse entry to anyone with an Israeli stamp in their passport.

The lights of Argin, the border surveillance post, were clearly visible. I'd even filmed the GPS coordinates of the 22nd parallel. My dumb tourist card was well and truly played out. Major Hassan began fast forwarding through the footage.

"Where," he said, stopping to play a section, "Sudan or Egypt?"

A procession of white-robed boys was trooping into shot, the goatherds who'd stumbled on my position the first day.

"Sudan. I think."

He listened to their conversation. "No. Massri. Egypt boyz. Dey say you make reconnaissance."

I noticed my Russian topographic maps were spread out on a table adjacent to the major's desk. Covering the entire lake to Aswan, the maps took in a wide swath of southern Egypt, including the sensitive border region.

Sher's kayak had also drawn attention.

"We use dis for special operations." The major nodded at the boat parked along the back wall. He then handed me my GPS. "Now. Show me."

There were no more "pleases." No more "never minds."

I pressed the power button and the waypoints shimmered into view, revealing my precise route up the lake.

And all the while equipment lists were being made. Then more questions:

"Why are you here in Egypt?"

"What are you looking for?"

And again: "You work for … who?"

It was time to come clean about my intent to cross the border illegally. I explained about the circumnavigation and my plan to kayak Lake Nasser at night. At the end of the confession, I motioned to the map case on the major's desk. "Can I show you something?"

I pulled out a laminated letter and offered it to him. Glancing at the letterhead, Major Hassan grunted, "Ah, the UNESCO." Written in 1994 by the serving Director General, Frederico Mayor, the letter appealed for people, organizations, and governments to assist the expedition on its way around the world. This was my ace in the hole, the ultimate Get Out of Jail Free card. UNESCO had been instrumental in saving two temples built in thirteenth century BCE by Ramses II, relocating them stone by stone to Abu Simbel, before the Nile was flooded to form Lake Nasser.

"But dis name." The major pointed to the first paragraph. "Pe-dal-for-the-Pla-net. Is not the name you give me?"

This was true. I'd given the name Expedition 360. "I can explain," I pleaded. "You see we changed the name in 1999—"

The major wasn't listening. He was back to yelling at his phones.

He left the room a little while later, leaving me in the care of the list-making orderly nursing his bandaged thumb. Perhaps still aggrieved at his injury, the man sidled over to where I sat, raised a hooked finger to my face, and whispered, "Jew spy!" He crossed his wrists, the sign for imprisonment, and bared a gold-capped tooth at me. "Forrrteee yearrr!"

Tens of thousands of innocent people languished in jails around the world, forgotten victims of politic crossfire, attempted extortion, or just mistaken identity. If you were lucky enough to come up on the political radar screen, thanks either to friends in high places or a media campaign launched on your behalf, there was reason to believe your government might get involved. Otherwise, that's where you would stay, potentially for the rest of your life. I pictured the response from the British Consulate in Cairo on hearing of my arrest, especially after warning me not to cross the lake without permission. *Serves the idiot bloody well right!*

As the nightmare prospect of spending my remaining days in prison began to sink in, my disbelieving gaze came to rest on a photograph propped on the bookcase beside the major's desk. A serious-looking boy and a smiling girl gazed back, the major's children, I guessed, and my thoughts turned to my own family. With the height of summer drawing near, the days would be long, stretching well into the evenings. My parents would be sitting outside on the lawn, enjoying the last of the sun before it dipped behind the beach trees to the west. Trilling birds would be settling in for the night, roosting in the hawthorn bushes. The air would be suffused with the aroma of freshly cut hay and lingering traces of honeysuckle blossom. At the local Spyway Inn, Tim's patrons would be lounging in the beer garden getting quietly sozzled on IPA, the rolling green flanks of Eggardon Hill peppered with puff pastry sheep rising up behind.

Will I ever see any of this again? I thought miserably.

On the afternoon of the second day, some thirty-six hours after being seized by the fishermen, another military official entered the room. He was exceptional in that he was in uniform; in all other respects, he looked like the orderlies—dead hamster moustache, pinched expression, and smoking feverishly. The major brought him up to speed on the situation, gabbling in Arabic and going over the lists of gear. It was at this point I twigged what was going on. I was about to be handed over to a different branch of the Egyptian military and transferred to another detention centre, presumably in Cairo, for further interrogation.

Sitting there, contemplating the ramifications of this latest turn of events, I heard a fax machine in a nearby room whir to life. The same orderly who'd been plying the major with cups of coffee entered holding a sheet of paper. Major Hassan took the dispatch and read it slowly, glancing up every few seconds and eyeing me through the cigarette smoke. My pulse quickened. What was this, more bad news?

"Meester Jason." He twirled the page at me. "Ees from Cairo. You ask to cross the lake?"

I nodded. "Six weeks ago. But I heard nothing back."

For the first time since the whole ordeal began, something approximating a smile took shape on the major's face. "Yes, well, never mind. Application ees approved. Seems you tell trooth."

Of course, I wasn't out of the woods yet. Entering Egypt illegally was still a serious enough offence to get me thrown out of the country. But at least the permission showing up in the nick of time staved off the grim possibility of rotting away in an Egyptian cell. And with the arrival of the fax, Major Hassan was a changed man—probably because his own neck was also off the block. Gone was the icy demeanour. He began laughing and joking, asking me about my family and telling me about his.

"Eef you come Cairo, ees my number. You meet my wife and cheeldren!"

Escorted by two orderlies, I was sent off to complete formalities with five other security agencies: Public Security, National Guard, State Security Service, Tourism and Antiquities Police, and the army. The whole process took seven hours. At one thirty in the morning, I was finally ushered back into the Mubahath el-Dawla compound.

"I have good fren Aswan immigration," the major said, rising wearily from behind his desk. He was drunk with fatigue, as was I. "My men will take you now, while still dark."

His contact would be standing beside the road leading into Aswan, the major explained, waiting to stamp my passport with an entry stamp "borrowed" from his own office. Major Hassan didn't have to pull in a favour like this, I realized. He was going out of his way to help. Stirred with gratitude, I fossicked in my pile of gear and presented him with the Nepalese kukri.

"I want you to have this, major. If it wasn't for you, I'd have to backtrack to India."

Observing ritual, he politely refused.

"Please," I insisted, pushing the knife towards him.

As per Arab custom, the major was obliged to reciprocate. He reached for the camel whip on his desk. "Dis here, very useful." He pointed to a small indentation in the end of the lash. "Bedouin put poison. Keel enemy more quickly."

"Very handy," I agreed, thinking of the more obnoxious children in Ethiopia and Tibet I could put it to good use on if I ever found myself back in those countries.

Then the major shook my hand and smiled. "I weesh we could haff meet under better circumstances, Meester Jason. But go now, and feenish dis great joorney."

THE MIDDLE EAST
THE BELLS OF ALEPPO

Travel has no longer any charm for me. I have seen all the foreign countries I want to see except heaven and hell and I have only a vague curiosity as concerns one of those.

—MARK TWAIN

I T WAS MIDNIGHT. A mile to our left, a string of yellow lights blinked in the desert, marking the first checkpoint north of Abu Simbel. Voices echoed faintly through the darkness and our breaths rasped out their steady metre as we trudged. Otherwise, the cooling desert was silent. A three-quarter moon scaled the dunes to the south, casting its frail, crepuscular luminescence on the occasional vehicle that passed, red taillights glowing as it slowed for the checkpoint.

"The sand is quite soft in places," said Sher. "Quite a slog, actually."

I was pushing my bike in his wheel tracks. "I don't know what you're complaining about. You've got hardly any gear."

Two days earlier, Sher caught up with me in Aswan. *The Sty is killing me,* he'd written in an email. *I needed a shot of real life.* Together we'd smuggled our bikes onto a bus to Abu Simbel and set off under cover of darkness from the farthest point I'd reached kayaking. Terrified of a repeat of the 1997 massacre in Luxor of sixty-two tourists by Islamic extremists, the Egyptian authorities prohibited individual travel along the 178-mile section of road between Abu Simbel and Aswan. Visitors were herded onto buses, shipped in convoys to the temple complex, and returned the same way. For us, this wasn't an option.

The detour around the checkpoint took a little over an hour. Back on tarmac, we brushed off the sand and pressed north.

It was 3:00 am by the time we neared the second checkpoint at Toshqa. The buildings were dark. No guards in sight. We rode blind through an obstacle course of oil drums and were almost in the clear when a pack of dogs came spilling out of the darkness. With the baying cacophony hot on our heels, we put our heads down and rode like the wind, hoping beyond hope that no one stirred. An irrigation canal emerged and beyond it open desert. We bailed off into the sand for a few hours of sleep before sun-up, our bodies blanketed by a billion shimmering stars. Then we rode on, through the heat of the day, reaching the third and final checkpoint by late afternoon.

The original plan had been to wait until dark and sneak around it. The other option, with Aswan only four miles to the north, was to try to bullshit our way through. What were the police going to do, send us back to Abu Simbel?

"Sod it," I said to Sher. "Let's go for it."

Beehive-shaped huts whizzed by and pink sentry boxes mounted on stilts. Streetlights. Trees. Red hibiscus framed by desert browns. The road narrowed to a chicane, and a maze of blue-and-white oil drums forced vehicles to stop. Two men in khaki uniforms turned, astonished to see us, and patted at the ground for us to stop.

"Hallo!" I called out cheerfully as we swept past.

One of the soldiers managed to gargle a reply, but Sher and I took no notice. We looked straight ahead and kept pedalling.

"The last checkpoint!" Sher exclaimed once we out of sight.

"Yup," I agreed. "Should be a clear run to England from here."

WELL, NOT EXACTLY.

After freewheeling down from the Aswan High Dam, we neared the old dam built by the British in 1902. A young national serviceman with a pencil moustache and a red beret stepped out of the shadows and waved his machinegun at us.

"Shall we just keep going?" suggested Sher, who was even more gung-ho than me about checkpoints, especially after our recent coup.

Darkness had fallen. A red security light illuminated the scene: two soldiers guarding access to the road running across the top of the dam. Being a potential terrorist target, guard posts were set at regular intervals all the way across.

"We'd better stop," I said. "These guys might panic and open up on us."

Both soldiers looked about ten. Their bayonets were fixed.

Sher rolled to a stop in front of the first one. "Can we just? We'll just—" He made as if to carry on.

The soldier smiled goofily and wagged a finger. "No. No."

He flagged down the next vehicle that passed, a beat-up Toyota Hilux, and signalled for us to load our bikes in the back. He looked delighted with himself.

Sher nodded towards me. "He cannot do that."

The soldier smiled some more and mumbled something in Arabic. His partner, obviously less patient, tut-tutted and flapped his arms. Sher began to argue. A minute of this, and the pickup driver grew tired of waiting, honked, and took off.

"See, he." Sher pointed at me. "He's come round the world." Sher twirled his finger and smiled. "Full world, by"—he patted his thighs— "walk and bicycle. Now, for this bridge, to go in car." Sher smiled again and shook his head. "Not good, see? So, we need to cross the bridge by bicycle, understand?"

The soldiers stared uncomprehendingly at him.

"Uh? Good." Sher wheeled his bike around and started across the bridge.

One of the soldiers dashed after him. "No! No!"

We were getting nowhere fast. At the lowest rung of decision-making, conscripted soldiers were never going to let us cross the bridge.

One of them began jabbering into a radio. He turned to me. "Contree?"

"England," I replied.

His face lit up. "Ah! Foot-boll! Good! Arse-hen-hole!"

And so, until the men's commanding officer arrived, we talked clumsily about football and their lives outside military service, which was mandatory in Egypt. Nusim was a lawyer, Husani a teacher. As white-collar professionals, they had to serve only twelve of the thirty-six months required of other less-well-qualified servicemen. Both men seemed apologetic, their cringing expressions saying: *If we had it our way, we would let you cross!*

Second Lieutenant Arifa was a different story, however. A dour-faced career soldier aggrieved at being dragged from his cosy office by bothersome tourists, he lost no time in telling us that we were wasting our time.

"I haff speaks with brigadier. He sez you will be here forever."

"That's fine," I said, resting my bike up against a railing. "We'll just set up camp here."

Sher pulled the mosquito dome off the back of his bike. "Yeah," he said coolly, "we'll stay here for a couple of years, or until you let us cross, whichever comes first." He rolled out his ground sheet beside the sentry box. "You see, Jason here has been doing this expedition for thirteen years." He snapped one of the aluminium poles together and grinned. "So another few waiting here won't hurt."

The lieutenant's eyes bulged at what he was seeing. "No, you cannot!" It was a nightmare for him. Drivers slowed and gawked as the tent took shape. Some of them began laughing and jeering at the soldiers.

"Look," pleaded the lieutenant, "even the president himself isn't allowed to cross this bridge by foot or bicycle."

What a load of bollocks, I thought, remembering what someone had told us earlier. We'd stopped for lunch at a lone restaurant between Abu Simbel and Aswan. The owner, a business-savvy entrepreneur with two polite, hardworking sons, offered a different take on the security situation in Egypt. Much of it was a scam, he claimed, a way to fleece tourists. For each bus travelling to and from Abu Simbel, the government charged tour companies a $1,000 security fee that bought them a teenager dozing at the back with a rifle. Ten years had passed since the Luxor attack, yet they claimed terrorists were still out there in the desert, waiting to ambush convoys.

The proprietor laughed. "The money is good, so why kill cash cow?"

He'd also given us valuable advice on how to deal with Egyptian security forces. "The best thing to do is shout," he said. "Tourist is king. If you don't shout at them, they will treat you like dogs."

So, the arguing continued, which for Sher was like breathing. "If you just wear them down with arguing," he'd told me in Mumbai after persuading the French embassy to give him a visa for Djibouti, "something will happen eventually."

To help expedite this, I offered to pay for an escort across the bridge. This was met with stony silence from Lieutenant Arifa.

Finally, I lost my patience. "For god's sake man, how hard can this be to arrange?"

"Look," he replied indignantly, "if I was in your country, and I was told that I was not allowed to do something, then I would have to just accept it."

"Yes, but if you were in *my* country, the commanding officer would show some initiative." I was on a roll now. "That's why officers are officers. They think of creative solutions to problems. But I can see that here in Egypt the officers are neither helpful to tourists nor able to show any initiative!"

The lieutenant looked as if he'd been slapped. *Perhaps that wasn't so wise,* I thought, *criticizing him in front of his men.*

"Just a minute," he said, raising a hand and walking away.

After speaking to his men, Lieutenant Arifa was back. "First," he said, addressing me, "I am very ashame you offer money." His voice rose with emotion. "This is not right. You have shown me bad things!"

"I wasn't trying to bribe you," I said. "Where I'm from, if it costs the taxpayer money—"

He cut me off. "Second, I will find a solution for you. Please wait for police car."

The combination of shouting and accusation of ineptitude had apparently worked. While Sher and I waited for the escort, the lieutenant told us he planned to stay in the army only if he was promoted, and soon.

"Well, from the leadership you've shown here today, lieutenant," I said, hoping to reinstate some of his dented pride. "It will happen very soon. I am sure of it."

His chin lifted a fraction.

Half an hour later, still no police car in sight, Second Lieutenant Arifa took matters into his own hands. Hailing a white Peugeot 504 diesel, he leapt into the passenger seat and cried, "Follow me!" and away we went, following the orange blinkers along the narrow two-laner, revelling in the knowledge that even President Hosni Mubarak himself wouldn't be allowed to do what we were doing: riding bicycles across the Aswan Dam.

WITH NO MAJOR obstacles to prevent me from finishing the circumnavigation, I could now pick a completion date to ride towards. The final 4,500 miles involved cycling through the Middle East and Europe, then pedalling *Moksha* across the Channel and up the River Thames to re-cross the prime meridian at 10:37 am, high tide, on Saturday, October 6.

Feeling suitably recharged by his sabbatical from The Sty, Sher returned to California, leaving me to push north up the Nile Valley. There were eleven checkpoints between Aswan and Qus. I rode through every one of them at full tilt. The soldiers shook their weapons at me and shrieked from their pink sentry boxes. Seriously, though. Were they really going to shoot the person they were there to protect?

By the time I reached Qena, I'd grown weary of the Nile locals, their snatching fingers and minds twisted by tourist dollars, so I hung a right to Port Safaga on the Red Sea and took the coast road to the seaport of Suez. Here, at the gateway to the Suez Canal, I sensed a shift. To the north, Christian Europe beckoned. To the south lay the Orient. Retired seamen sat in the narrow streets sucking on hookahs, and hairy Copts proffered their sweaty crucifixes for me to kiss. East of the Ahmed Hamdi Tunnel, my wheels pointing west, the headwind I'd been shouldering all the way from Djibouti became a tailwind. What joy! I flew across the Sinai, clocking one hundred and sixty miles in a single day, and presented my passport to a baby-faced immigration officer at the Israeli border. She was nineteen and flirtatious, which suited my purposes. I needed her to stamp my second passport, conspicuous for its newness.

I asked her, "Why is it everyone in this part of the world hates the Jews?"

She looked at the map of the Middle East I was holding. Nearly every one of Israel's neighbours was openly anti-Semitic, many of them vowing to destroy the Jewish state and its people. "I don't know," she said sadly, stamping the passport. "They just all want to kill us."

I carried on, bit between my teeth, legs pounding like pistons. The sooner I reached France, the better my chances of a fair-weather window to pedal the Channel before the European winter set in. But in Amman, Jordan, fate stuck its oar in again. An official at the Syrian Consulate informed me that my visa application had been denied.

"You should have got a visa in the UK before travelling," the man grunted from his cage.

"I left the UK thirteen years ago," I said.

"Doesn't matter. Application ees refused."

With nothing to lose, I went to the border anyway. At the arrivals building at Ar Ramtha, I met two American backpackers who'd been there all day. "They've faxed all our details off to Damascus," said Andrew, a freelance journalist from New York. "We're hopeful, but I guess nothing's for sure yet."

Dripping with sweat from the morning's ride—daytime temperatures were nothing like the Sahara, but still in the low hundreds—I approached the window reserved for foreigners and handed over my original passport, now battered, creased, and crammed with stamps from thirty-five countries.

"Can you *please* help me?" I said, stooping to address the beetle-browed official sitting behind the counter. "I've been travelling for a long time, and I don't have the time or the money to go to London for a visa." I turned and pointed. "Look, there's my bike if you don't believe me."

He glanced up at the heavily laden rig parked outside the entrance, then went back to leafing slowly through my passport, flicking the pages back and forth, trawling for evidence of an Israeli stamp. "I will try," he muttered.

Five minutes later, I was walking out the door, Syrian visa in place.

The poor Americans were still sitting there.

THE PEALING BELLS of Aleppo, one of the oldest continuously inhabited cities in the world, were the first church bells I'd heard in over a decade. They struck an achingly familiar cord from a past life, evoking memories of green fields and sleepy hamlets, a world away from the caterwaul of the imam. Sentimental longing welled up as I walked from the Al-Gawaher Hotel to the Concord Internet café. My stride was purposeful. I nimbly dodged cars, children, dogs, and market traders hawking their wares. I was monitoring everything around me with three-sixty degree awareness, anticipating likely dangers and opportunities, especially people and their intentions. *This one will ask for money. That one will rob me given half a chance.* All the while reading their eyes. *The old timer sitting in that café over there looks honest. He can probably be trusted.* Any information that could see me safely through another minute, hour, day of the expedition. I thought of the bumbling amateur full of bravado who had left England all those years ago, and wondered: *What kind of person has he turned into?*

Physically, I was honed, at the peak of fitness, notching a hundred and twenty-five miles a day, week after week, month after month. Professionally, I'd acquired a wide-ranging skill set. I was now good at what I did, fully adapted to expedition life.

Mentally, though, I was on a hair trigger.

If someone smiled, I smiled back. But if they shouted, I was ready to shout back—and then some. A week earlier, a Jordanian immigration officer had demanded to see a customs form for my bicycle. I'd ridden obediently back down the hill to the customs house, only to be told that I didn't need one. Slogging back, I found the same official waiting for me arms crossed, expression deadpan, minions smirking in the background.

"Where eez paper?" The officer gestured with fleshy fingers.

I was panting. I was sweating. "They said I don't need one for a bike."

"They wrong. Go back and ask again."

When I heard a noise like air escaping from a balloon, one of the flunkies holding in the giggles, I knew I was being mocked.

"Listen!" I snapped. "I'm *not* going back down that hill. You can call them and sort it out yourself."

The officer winced. "Okay, okay. Why you crying?"

"I'm not crying. I'm just hot and pissed off." I grinned manically at him. "And I'm not going up and down that hill another five times just to entertain you and your mates, alright?" I was marching on the spot now, swinging my arms and wobbling my head, laughing in his face like a deranged fool. "I'm not a clockwork fucking toy!"

Smiling uneasily, the immigration officer waved me on.

I'd grown intolerant of people who were mean, greedy, and cruel.

I had no patience for those who took advantage of the oppressed and the vulnerable—the poor, the elderly, children, and animals. As a solo traveller, I'd developed a hardened exterior to ward off human predators, calling for a level of emotional detachment that had also proved effective against the near-constant stresses, frustrations, and disappointments of the expedition. But such a demeanour cut both ways. As well as fending off the shysters, it sabotaged many potentially enriching encounters with sincere, well-meaning people, putting distance between me and the very thing, the world, I had set out to better understand.

"You're a machine," I said out loud as I passed the old clock tower of Bab al-Faraj, "an efficient, well-oiled machine. But you've been out here too long."

Most expeditions set out to climb a mountain, walk a river, or cross an ice cap, and were completed within six months. Expedition 360 had involved sixteen major expeditions set back to back, making it one of the longest journeys in history. With nearly half my life spent on the road, the casting off of geographical moorings was largely complete, lightening my cultural baggage and broadening my mind as a global citizen. But there was a price to pay for this so-called liberation. Completing this thing had taken total dedication, harnessing me to a dream that allowed precious little time for anything else, least of all what came next. Now, utterly consumed by it, I'd unwittingly traded my Englishness for a new set of walls, the walls of the expedition, and the great unknown was no longer what lay out there in the world, but what lay beyond Greenwich.

One thing was certain. Everything I'd done in the last fifteen years had been connected in some way to heading west, and when I woke up on the morning of October 7 and didn't have to think about making miles anymore, I would face the hardest obstacle of all.

Reintegrating into civilization.

EUROPE
BACK TO THE FUTURE

It always seems impossible, until it's done.

—NELSON MANDELA

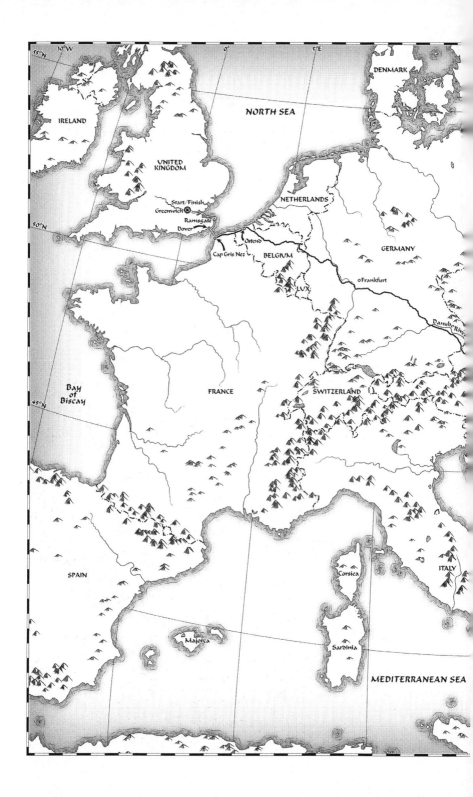

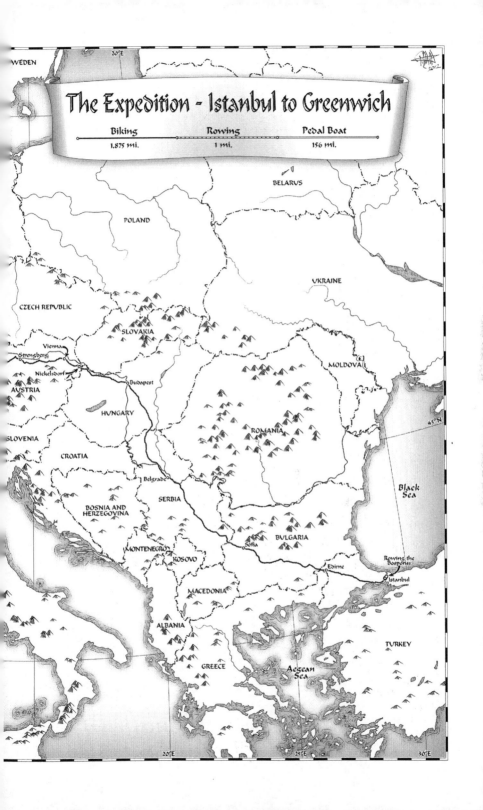

A LINE OF CARS and lorries a mile long choked the border between Turkey and Bulgaria, so we went straight to the front, of course. It was the only way to deal with queues in the Asia-Pacific region. But this wasn't Asia. Nor was it Africa. Having crossed the Bosphorus, I was now officially in Europe, poised to re-enter the European Union. The driver of a BMW I'd horned in on took exception to this, swung his wheel and missed my foot by a whisker.

"Crazy bastard nearly ran over my foot!" I hollered over my shoulder to Merlin.

Polite and well mannered, my cousin looked the consummate Englishman in his white Tilley hat, bookish glasses, and sun-famished complexion. He was taking a short holiday from his job as a country solicitor to ride with me from Edirne to Budapest.

"This isn't the Sudan, Jason." He laughed. "You'll have to start behaving yourself now we're about to enter Christendom."

It was a view apparently shared with the occupants of the BMW. A hairy, troll-like thing, presumably the daughter of the even hairier driver, put her head out of the passenger-side window, and whinnied, "I can understand English, you know."

"Good," I replied. "Then tell the driver to get his eyes checked. Is he fucking blind?"

A week earlier, I'd crossed from Syria into Turkey, encountering neat rows of viridescent crops, modern farm machinery, and prices three to four times that of other Middle Eastern countries. Social proprieties were also on the rise. I couldn't just stop and pee off the side of the bike whenever I felt like it or dive into the nearest bush for a number two. Blowing my nose al fresco, between thumb and forefinger, also drew reproachful stares from passers-by. In Ceyhan, I was grilled by the police for drinking a beer outside the store I'd purchased it from.

But any reservations I had of returning to European law and order were temporarily forgotten when I saw the brightly painted pinewood caïque waiting for me on the east shore of the Bosphorus, a traditional fishing skiff with green trim laid on by the Turkish Rowing Federation. The Turkish-born adventurer Erden Eruç had arranged this, as well as mobilizing a local support network of family and friends. As I rowed the busy waterway with Asia narrowing in the caïque's wake, Erden was preparing for his own voyage, albeit a slightly longer one, rowing across the Pacific.

The deeper Merlin and I pressed into eastern Bulgaria, the more I was convinced that my run-in with the BMW driver had been more than a mere accident. A good proportion of the men looked like they'd just dropped out of the trees—hulking brutes with close-cropped, odd-shaped heads, their hands the size of dinner plates. The women, by contrast, became less hairy the farther west we travelled, until, by the time we reached Sofia, passing billboard after billboard of naked beauties selling everything from microchips to washing machines, they looked so utterly different as to belong to a different species.

Which wasn't a million miles from the truth, as it turned out. "Slav women, they different, they proud," a young male petrol pump attendant told me when I asked why the local women dressed like supermodels, while the average Balkan male looked like he'd just been dragged out of bed. "They make competition weez each other. They want to look their best for the boys."

He then refused to sell me half a litre of fuel for my stove bottle. "Maybe you make bomb?" he suggested.

Rows of cheap liquor filled the shelves inside the forecourt shop. "Let me get this straight," I said. "You can't sell me any petrol because I'm on a bicycle. But you can sell every driver that comes through here enough booze to turn their vehicle into a cruise missile?"

He shrugged. "Iz rool."

Bloody bureaucracy, I thought, and rode away.

With the Borat jokes coming thick and fast ("Number fifty-three prostitute in all Bulgaristan!"), Merlin and I crossed into Serbia and cycled through a region that could have passed for England's West Country were it not for the Cyrillic signage. The hedgerows teemed with greenery, comprising many native trees and plants I hadn't seen in years—elderflowers and oaks among them. We then found ourselves transported to the set of the Benny Hill Show (actually, Belgrade) with short waddling men in wife-beaters chasing überbabes in miniskirts.

Pushing on, we entered Hungary, where, for the first time in as long as I could remember, I was stung by a Eurasian stinging nettle. This alerted me to the EU proper: drivers actually stopped at red lights and the roads had manhole covers in place—they hadn't all been nicked. A Tesco supermarket appeared, and in a roadside café in Kiskunfélegy-háza, I found unambiguous proof of having left Asia behind: the salt shakers contained salt and the pepper shakers contained pepper, not the other way around.

By the time we parted ways in Budapest, Merlin looked quite different to how he'd stepped off the bus ten days earlier. Gone were the hat, the glasses, and the clean-shaven image. My cousin had gone native: stubbly, phlegmatic, and donning a sweat-stained wife-beater. Although our time together had been brief, we'd forged a connection outside of family protocol, laying the foundation for a long-lasting friendship.

In Nickelsdorf, the first town inside the Austrian border, I stopped at a coffee shop to warm up. Europe was in the grips of an unseasonably cold snap.

"Coffee is finished at twelve," said the stony-faced waitress.

The clock on the wall said 11:56 am. "Wonderful," I replied. "Then I'm just in time."

"Clock is five minutes slow. "

I checked my watch. It read 12:01 pm.

"Can't you make a small exception?" I said. "I'm very cold."

She shook her head. "Weekend licensing rules."

Bloody regulations, I thought, and rode away.

Like Singapore, everything worked in Austria, everything was spotless, and everyone toed the line. The roadside lavatories were more luxurious than any third-world jiggy motel I'd stayed in. But where was the edge? It seemed to me the homogenizing effect of Europeanization dulled cultures into achromatic shadows of their former selves, seducing people into that cosy grey indifference that comes with social affluence. I missed the colour and chaos of the Middle East and having to think on my feet. I longed to run a red light just to see what might happen. And on the outskirts of Vienna, when I saw a hugely obese man leave a McDonald's hugging a sack of fast food, I had the overwhelming urge to go up and push him over.

West of Vienna, the undulating landscape gathered into neat, rectangular fields framed by immaculate hedges. Corn and pumpkins were in abundance, pawed at by the giant paddles of electricity-generating windmills. The temperature dropped to single digits. Then it started to rain. Torrentially. Six days later it was still raining and snowing above a thousand metres. I celebrated my fortieth birthday the way I had my previous three in Tibet, Indonesia, and Australia: in my tent, hunched over a pan of noodles, staring at my feet. Only this time, I'd pushed the boat out with a two-euro bottle of plonk.

Having anticipated pleasant end of summer weather for the ride through Europe to finish, I'd made no provision for winter conditions. Any waterproofing capability my Chinese-made "K2 Summit" rain jacket ever had was long gone, and the rest of my gear was falling apart. My gloves had disintegrated in Egypt. The welds on my trailer had cracked in Sudan—the frame was now held together with pieces of blue string. The tyres on my steel-framed Ridgeback, the same bike I'd ridden away from Greenwich on, were worn well past the tread mark. For now, though, the whole rig moved.

I stopped at the first bike shop in Amstetten to pick up some cold-weather gear, but six hundred euros for a pair of shoes and Gore-Tex trousers put me back on my heels. The outdoor industry in Europe had clearly gone high-end since the early nineties. I settled for some socks to wear with my sandals and a pair of gloves on sale with only three fingers on each hand, apparently designed with amphibians in mind.

In Germany, I opted to ride on the road instead of the designated bike paths, which, being thick with joggers and dog walkers, I found treacherous to negotiate with full panniers and a loaded trailer. The paths were also deliberately tangential, taking off on impromptu excursions along the scenic Danube or oblique detours into residential neighbourhoods. However, the departure from trail etiquette didn't go down well with my fellow road-users, sending many of them into fits of finger-stabbing hysterics. Drivers would pull up beside me, wind down their windows, and give me an earful of phlegmy German: "Aussteigen die Straße, trottel!" Get off the road, moron! To which I would fondly recollect the chaos of roads in places like India—the dogs, cats, cows, goats, pedestrians, and trumpeting trucks missing each other by inches and the live-and-let-live attitude of the locals in general—then tell the driver to go fuck himself.

Bike-lane bullies behind me, I entered Belgium bound for Ostend where *Moksha* would be waiting. Since returning from Djibouti, Nathalie had worked tirelessly through a mire of EU import bureaucracy to have the boat shipped in a container and stored in the driveway of her friends Robin and Kathleen in Rotterdam. Online followers of the expedition blog had generously raised the transportation cost of $5,761.

On the afternoon of September 21, I turned onto a wharf belonging to the Royal North Sea Yacht Club and found *Moksha* looking frayed and battered on the little wheeled cradle that John Andrews had built for her in Australia. Beyond, past the breakwater and a covey of mewling seagulls, the muddy brown Channel beckoned. The ride through Africa, the Middle East, and Europe was over, leaving one last "wet bit."

All I had to do was cross the Channel, pedal up the River Thames to Greenwich, and continue on foot to the Royal Observatory from where Steve and I set off. The first human-powered circumnavigation of the globe would then be complete.

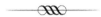

Cap Gris Nez, France. Sept 30, 2007
TODAY WAS THE day. The wind was light, the swell less than one metre. The conditions were as good as they were going to get for an autumn crossing. The morning mist clinging to the water gradually dissipated as the sun climbed. I stood on *Moksha's* trailer, monitoring the same Traffic Separation Scheme that Steve and I had negotiated thirteen years earlier. A steady stream of ships, faintly visible in the murk, slipped past in ghostly silence. Then the fog lifted completely and there, blazing in the morning sunlight, were the White Cliffs of Dover topped by the green fields of England.

I called to a figure hunched over *Moksha's* cockpit. "How's it going, Chris?"

The boat builder had returned from a job in Tunisia to assist in the closing stages and to have one last ride in his creation before she was retired. He was using a plane to bevel the edges of a replacement Perspex window to the original he'd fitted in Exeter in 1994, now scratched and clouded from wear and tear.

"The usual," he replied, frowning with concentration.

"As in?"

He looked up and smirked. "Frantic, last-minute, kick-bollock scramble!"

We had just five hours to prepare the boat for a beach launch, something we'd never had to do before. There was a perfectly good crane ten miles away in Calais, but we'd been warned against leaving from the busy ferry port. Thirteen years on, it was still illegal to operate "unorthodox craft" in French territorial waters. Being turned back was a very real possibility.

"Eez a yelloo submareen!" cried a voice, one of several local residents taking advantage of the low tide to collect cockles and mussels. A shelf of wicked black rocks known as Dragon Teeth Rocks stretched to the water's edge, bisected by a narrow channel through which Chris and I would attempt to pilot *Moksha* once the tide came in.

Chris laughed. "Yes, The Beatles. We don't all live in it, though. Just separately on occasion."

A short distance away, Kenny was filming Eilbhe. She'd arrived from Dublin to give *Moksha* a Celtic figurehead to guide her on the last leg home. A mysterious looking creature was taking shape on the bow, with the head of a Gorgon, the body of a scaled serpent, and the feet of a chicken. Eilbhe stepped back to admire her masterpiece, art brushes bristling from her fist.

"What's that?" said Kenny from behind his camera.

"Mary. She's a dragon."

Elsewhere, other members of the extended expedition family were lending a hand. Nathalie's two young sons had given *Moksha* a new lick of paint in Ostend, and an events coordinator from Southampton University was supervising the Greenwich completion. Lee and his team faced a formidable mountain of red tape. The Metropolitan Police Service required detailed risk-assessment plans, as did the Thames River Police, the Port of London Authority, the Greenwich Harbour Master's office, Greenwich Council, and Greenwich Park. Special security arrangements needed to be made with the Royalty Protection Branch for HRH the Duke of Gloucester, who would be there at the finish. The National Maritime Museum, having initially baulked at letting me complete the circumnavigation at the Royal Observatory on health and safety grounds, finally conceded after a concerted campaign of letter writing, including one from The Right Honourable Oliver Letwin, Member of Parliament.

Meanwhile, the story was gaining "legs" in the media, fuelled by a double page spread in *The Daily Mail* and regular press releases circulated by Alex Foley PR and Chris Court from the Press Association. I now had two mobile phones on the go, taking calls from journalists as far away as Beijing.

By 11:30 am, there was still no sign of the tractor we'd reserved to launch *Moksha*. The window for floating her off the trailer was fast approaching.

"Useless, bloody, Frenchies," I cursed under my breath.

A family returning from the beach stopped in front of *Moksha*, their buckets brimming with shiny black molluscs. "Quel genre de bateau est-ce?" asked the father, a wiry, middle-aged man with sandy hair. What kind of boat is this?

Nathalie, who'd just arrived with Sher, explained in French.

"Ask them if they know of someone with a tractor," said Kenny.

The father's name was Jean Calais. "Mais bien sûr!" he cried. "J'en ai un!"

Ten minutes later, he came bouncing down the road in his blue-and-white tractor, orange light flashing, and hitched up to *Moksha's* trailer. His daughter, Chantelle, grabbed my arm. "From zer last windows." She pointed to the restaurant above the cliff and then out to sea. "You go straight."

Down on the beach, sandy waves were churning over Dragon Teeth Rocks, a sign that it was nearing high tide. Seeing the turbulent water, my mind clouded with uncertainty. Attaching the rudder was hard enough to do on dry land. How on earth would we manage it with *Moksha* plunging and rolling in the swell and without her running aground on the rocks?

Jean Calais had the trailer turned around and was waiting for the signal. He shouted something from his cab. Nathalie translated: "He says you have a few minutes before the waves get big again."

The sea suddenly went flat.

"Fuck it," I said to Chris, slipping on my ocean ring. "Let's do it."

Jean began reversing *Moksha* into the surf as Chris, Chantelle, and I took up positions either side. A hundred metres out, the tractor reached as far as it could go without swamping the engine. The three of us tried pulling the boat off her trailer, but she wouldn't budge—there wasn't enough water under the hull. Moments later, the sea responded with a torrent of water crashing over the stern deck, soaking Chantelle in her skin-tight jeans and black top. On the count of three, we heaved—Chris on the stern, Chantelle and me on the bow—and with a groan of complaint *Moksha* slid into the water.

Pushing and pulling as one, we set about turning the craft 180 degrees to face her in the right direction. As she came parallel to the breakers, a wall of water slammed into her seaward side, sending her on her beam-ends and Chris and Chantelle sprawling into the water. The next wave did the same. Jean Calais leapt out of his cab to lend a hand, and together we spun the bow the remaining ninety degrees and pushed the boat out into deeper water.

Chris climbed aboard to slide the centreboard into the place while I wrestled with the rudder. Just as I'd feared, I could barely keep my footing in the chest-high water let alone marry up the four rudder pintles with the gudgeons.

A minute passed. "How are you going?" Chris shouted anxiously from the hatch.

"Not on yet," I shouted back.

I struggled some more. Another minute passed. The boat was drifting dangerously near the rocks. "On now! Let's go!"

Scrambling aboard, I clamped the pedal mechanism into place and started pedalling furiously. A foot of water was sloshing inside the main cabin. As Chris bailed with a saucepan, I picked up speed and watched the Dragon Teeth Rocks slip past the port side window. When the water turned from silty brown to the opaque green of deeper water, Chris let out a whoop.

"Unbelievable!" I cried, clawing off my shirt—I was sweating from all the exertion. "Got away with it by the skin of our teeth, didn't we?"

Chris was still bailing. "Yeah, I was worried about Jean Calais."

"Me, too," I said. "He almost got mown over on her leeward side, didn't he?"

"Yeah. Lucky."

"What a way to start the day!" I said.

"And we didn't even have a cup o' tea yet, either," said Chris.

Once safely offshore, we stood up in the hatch and waved to Jean and Chantelle. Our French heroes were back on the beach, drenched but smiling. The words "bon voyage!" came echoing across the water.

"Those guys did us proud," I said.

"Good people," agreed Chris.

"Who'd have thunk it, Frenchies saving the day?"

"Hang on." Chris was pointing at something in the water heading our way. "We forgot somebody."

The original idea was to give Our Man Brown a ride so he could film the crossing, but in the confusion of the launch, he'd got left behind. The plucky Scotsman was now swimming out to sea, towing all his camera gear in a dry bag.

I remembered the first day that Steve and I met him in the Chandos pub off Trafalgar Square:

"Soonds loch an amazin' adventure yetois haegot gonnae thur."

"Um, I'm sorry?"

"So when daeyetois think yoo'll beheadin' aff 'en?"

"Eh? What was that again?"

Fifteen years on, we still could barely understand a word Kenny said, but one thing was beyond question. The filmmaker had remained loyal throughout, sticking with the expedition through thick and thin, using his own savings to keep it documented.

Six hours later, Dover's chalk cliffs loomed ghostly pale in the half-light. I steered *Moksha* inside the harbour and the night shrank before us under the ferry terminal floodlights. Guided by the flashing green and red marker lights, we nosed our way into a space on the wharf usually reserved for lifeboats.

A phone rang. It was my dad. "We've just arrived!" I chuckled as I stepped onto the wharf.

One of the more unexpected rewards of the expedition was the close bond I now had with my father. Often I'd wondered how things would have turned out if I'd followed his advice and pursued a career in the armed services or some other starchy institution. As a young maverick still unsure of his own convictions, likely I would have ended up in a line of work that I didn't particularly enjoy and therefore wasn't very good at, and I would have become resentful, driving the wedge even deeper between father and son. As it was, despite justified reservations about the sanity of the expedition, my father had to his credit pitched in with logistics, an area familiar to him from his army days, and over time a mutual respect and camaraderie had grown between us. I came to see the paradox faced by many nonconforming sons and daughters, that to be happy within yourself but also close with your parents, you need to live your own life, not the life they may have imagined for you—even if it takes a while for them to come around.

Kenny had his camera trained on Chris. "So, did you expect to see this boat return to England?"

Chris nodded. "Yeah, I did. I always knew it would come back. Definitely." He paused, his expression deadpan. "Or bits of it, anyway."

"WHAT I FIND most appealing about this trip is that it's still not that different from when I hooked up eleven years ago."

Sher was sitting opposite me in a blue Belgium Sailing Team top, grinning and eating a cheese sandwich. Another *Moksha* veteran, he'd been invited to accompany me on a farewell voyage from Dover to Ramsgate.

"Remind me of how we met again?" I was pedalling on the spot outside the entrance to Ramsgate harbour, holding ground against the northerly tide until the evening ferry departed for Ostend.

"I read an article in the *San Francisco Chronicle* by Carl Nolte and came along to the talk you did at Stanford, remember?"

"Right. You used to come up at the weekends to help get the boat ready for the Hawaii crossing."

A voice interrupted us on the VHF: the port controller giving *Moksha* permission to enter the harbour.

Sher continued. "So yeah, that's really the essence of this trip for me. The people that it's brought together."

It was an apt observation in light of the task that awaited us. Within the hour, *Moksha* was back on her trailer and parked in a shed at the top of the boat ramp. 1,868 vinyl names of expedition supporters had just arrived from the printer. While Eilbhe put the finishing touches to her creation, the rest of us—Chris, Nathalie, Kenny, Sher, our former North American coordinator Nancy Sanford, and myself—set about adding the names to the side of the boat, using hairdryers to get the adhesive to stick. It took all night.

Words took human form as I pressed each letter to the hull, triggering my memory of how each person had helped the expedition move forward over the years. Some had contributed money, others expertise or simply a roof.

Ed Apodaca: Stopping after a hit-and-run driver ran me over in Pueblo, Colorado.

Norlia Carruthers: Volunteering her house as a base camp in Cairns, Australia.

Hobsons Family: Donating £20 at the London Boat Show in 1994.

Gretchin Lair: Providing backend support for the expedition360.com website.

Nancy Sanford rode upriver with me to Erith, reciprocating a twelve-year-old favour of equipping the expedition with Escapade pedal boats to cross Tampa Bay in 1995. The last time I saw her she was wearing a grass hula skirt and white orchid leis as Steve and I pedalled into Hilo, Hawaii.

"Happy, Nancy?" I asked.

She smiled broadly. "Very happy. Waited a long time for this, but it was worth the wait."

It was a gorgeous day on the Thames, the sun glancing off the water as we breezed past oozing mudflats, bickering gulls, and sheets of corrugated tin daubed with clumsy white letters that clamoured "Save our Shoreline!" The dereliction of the lower docklands—its hangdog cranes, idle warehouses, and rusting barges—soon slipped astern. A chemical tanker, the *Oriental Kerria*, rolled us with wash as she bullied her way downstream. Beyond Greenhithe, the cable-stayed Queen Elizabeth II Bridge soared overhead, girders fanning out like eagle wings. The buildings overlooking the river became more lavish as the afternoon rolled on, concentric waves of luxury flats rippling out from the financial heart of the metropolis, and by close of day the Legoland vista of Canary Wharf had taken centre stage against a fiery sunset.

Moksha rode out the ebb on a swinging mooring while our company, its number growing daily, slumped exhausted on the deck of an old Norwegian roll-on roll-off ferry, since reincarnated as the convivial Erith Yacht Club. Next morning, it was Casey's turn. Behind the facial hair of an academic, the Californian hadn't aged a day since our last encounter—December 1998, all of us blue with hypothermia after rescuing *Moksha* from her near fatal capsize in San Simeon cove.

"Better not bloody sink it this time, Casey," I joked as he clambered aboard.

He broke into his familiar schoolboy grin. "Wow, I can't believe the expedition is coming to a close. It's always been out there in the world, like an institution. I'm sad to see it finishing."

Conversation turned to the white-knuckle days he and John had spent tethered to the sea anchor, drifting towards the Big Sur coast. How strange it felt to be on a tiny boat again, he noted, very different to the big research vessels he now worked on as an assistant professor of ecology and evolutionary biology at Brown University.

"All the little things are the same. I can even tell which bolts were here ten years ago, staring at them for those ten days in that storm."

"Were you out there for that long?"

"Yah, ten days."

"You need to scratch those into the timbers," I said. "We've got every voyage marked apart from that one."

"I'm worried I might jinx the boat."

"Good point. Do it just before you get off."

It was another brisk, gin-clear day, perfect for messing about in a boat on the river. April joined me downstream of the Thames Flood Barrier, shuttled from shore in a rigid inflatable. She'd arrived that morning from Colorado where she was midway through the winter semester, teaching fifth grade, as she had been when I'd shuffled in on my walking frame to give a presentation to her class. *The invisible hand of serendipity,* I thought. *How it brings the unlikeliest of people together.* Of all the chance encounters, the one with April had born the most fruit in terms of educational outreach.

"Wish I'd had a pint of Guinness before coming out," she chuckled to Eilbhe, who'd ridden out with her.

We embraced between the two boats. Then she stepped gingerly aboard.

"How many years since you pedalled her?" I asked.

"Coral Sea. That was the last time, my goodness, yes. When was that … 2000? I think it was. But it's got to be like riding a horse. Once you've learned how, you just get on and go, right?"

No High Seas Hair this time. No emaciating effects of starvation. April looked fit and healthy, quite different to how she'd arrived on Lizard Island after thirty-two days of seasickness.

Escorted by Chris in his blue kayak, we passed between the Norman helmet-shaped buttresses of the flood barrier and into one last sunset together. A carpet of glazed, caramel light rolled out to meet us like gold leaf poured over liquid glass, and I had the distinct impression of time slowing down, of stopping, turning backwards, and transporting us up Marlow's river of dreams to where the whole thing started. On a dark pier up ahead, a lone figure was waiting, munching on an apple.

I steered alongside, and we made the switch.

Eight years before, he'd stood on the deck of *Goodwinde* thirty miles west of Hawaii, watching *Moksha* disappear into the Great Blue Never. Like the protagonist in Herman Hesse's *Siddhartha,* Steve had since continued his own quest, becoming an ordained Zen Buddhist monk, and in doing so come full circle: back to life on a small boat plying the sea, eking out a living as a simple ferryman taking people back and forth across the Salcombe Estuary in Devon.

He reached for the steering toggles. "She feels great. I reckon she could go around again."

I looked for any trace of regret in my old friend's face, but there was none. He was at peace with his decision. Then I remembered something I'd wanted to ask him for a long time.

"When we reached Hawaii in 1998, how did you feel stepping off *Moksha* for the last time?"

He was thoughtful for a few seconds before leaning forward and lobbing his apple core over the side. "Really quite glad to see the back of her, to be honest."

We both laughed.

"No." His expression turned serious. "I try not to be too sentimental. I'm just glad that she's brought you safely home."

6:00 am. October 6, 2007

I AWOKE IN darkness, salt smarting in my nostrils. It took me a moment to work out where I was.

Ah yes. The Rathole. The guest dock of the Greenwich Yacht Club.

Heaving myself out, I boiled some water for tea and added the Union Jack to a long line of flags attached to the wind generator pole, representing thirty-seven countries the expedition had passed through on its long parabola around the world. According to my calculations, I'd been gone for thirteen years, two months, and twenty-three days, covering 46,505 miles across five continents, two oceans, and one sea.

But the journey wasn't over yet.

At 9:30 am, I slipped the mooring lines. Apart from a lone seabird crying, it was quiet out on the river. For the first time in fifteen years, I felt relaxed and prepared, not an ounce of stress in my body. I was ready to draw closure to my little odyssey.

A crane was parked at the narrow slipway beside the Old Royal Naval College, waiting to pull *Moksha* from the water. But there was a problem. With the tide already on the ebb, the boat was out of the crane's reach.

Just as the situation looked hopeless, a tattooed pirate pushed through the crowd armed with a wooden fence post. Ponytail reaching even farther down his back since I'd last seen him and moustache still very much waxed, Hugo shoved his Roman roller under the bow and marshalled the team of helpers to heave. Up she came, inch-by-inch. Clearing the adjacent buildings by a red one, *Moksha* was lifted up and onto her wheeled trolley.

It was time to close the circle, the last mile of the last degree up the hill to the Royal Observatory, and *Moksha* was coming, too. Having delivered her crews safely across every body of water she'd been aimed at, leaving the expedition's heart and soul behind at this point was unthinkable.

Faces from the near and distant past materialized from the waiting throng and pressed their hands to the gunwales: Stuart in his gnarled leather hat, Ollie and Carole from France, Shirley from San Francisco, Jim Brady and Mike Roney from the Australian leg, Jane Koca, who'd rung me for morale-boosting chats as I pedalled on the spot in the doldrums, *Moksha's* designer Alan Boswell, my cousin Merlin and his son Huw, Edwina from the Guildford Street Gang …

And there were other, smaller hands pushing, some belonging to relatives I'd never even met.

Chaperoned by the Greenwich Police, we spirited *Moksha* along Romney Road and into Greenwich Park. Dappled sunshine splashed through the boughs of Spanish chestnuts overhead. The first bronzed leaves of autumn were falling, bouncing down the path and skittering under our feet.

"Come on, Lewis!" Hugo shouted from the back. "Pull harder."

At the summit, we stopped to rest at the junction of Blackheath Avenue where Steve and I had taken a wrong turn on July 12, 1994. The right fork would have taken us to the A21 and straight out of London. We'd taken the left fork instead and become horribly lost, equipped as we were with every map and nautical chart known to man except a London A to Z road atlas. I mused at the machinations of destiny and how our lives are steered by the briefest decisions: the right fork would have cut at least an hour off the trip; Wilbur Ladd would have missed me on Highway 50 in Colorado; I would have met up with Steve nine months earlier in San Francisco. Then, who knows?

Pressing on towards the observatory's red time ball, now visible above the trees, a quote from the legendary French circumnavigator, Bernard Moitessier, came to mind. "There are two terrible things for a man: not to have fulfilled his dream, and to have fulfilled it." *How true,* I thought. The expedition was never about crossing the line. The line was only there to make the journey possible.

A mass of people lined the final approach to the courtyard. Through the wrought-iron gates, looking a little older but neatly dressed and standing proudly next to the Duke, I recognized my mother, my father, sisters Julia and Vicky, and the rest of my family.

At exactly 12:42 pm, I recrossed the metal strip embedded in the cobblestones, *Moksha* two paces behind.

The journey was done.

A sea of camera lenses and scribbling journos closed in. A Sky News reporter thrust a microphone in my face. "What took you so long, Jason? Thirteen years!"

Cheeky bastard, I thought.

There was the accident in Colorado, the months of fundraising in umpteen cities, a year lost to El Niño in Central America, eight months resurrecting *Moksha* after the San Simeon debacle, and myriad other setbacks. But that wasn't what the reporter wanted to hear. He wanted a short, pithy sound bite. Three to four seconds. Five tops.

"It's been a long trip," I said, my eyes brimming with tears. "It's good to be back."

"COULDN'T HAVE FINISHED it without you, Hugh," I said. "I'd still be in Singapore, washing dishes or something."

Hugh Young and his wife, Lina, had been present at the completion. Grass-roots funding had got the expedition two-thirds of the way around the planet, but the support of Aberdeen Asset Management had come at a crucial point, when the prospect of going back to scrabbling around in shopping malls for funds had sapped my resolve to keep going. Hugh was also covering the cost of the completion party, now kicking off in the upstairs bar of the Globe Rowing Club.

Champagne and whisky were flowing. Jimbo Trout was treating the assembly of family, friends, and supporters to a foot-stomping dose of Appalachian bluegrass before handing off to DJ Jimmy Squall from the Guildford Street Gang. Only a handful of those present had met before, but with the expedition in common, it was like a reunion of old friends. Seeing the smiles and hearing the laughter as people recounted their experiences, I felt myself swell with pride. Of all the memories, this would be the most precious.

As the evening wore on, though, I grew pensive, thinking how we were meeting for the first and last time. This wasn't just the end of the journey. It was the end of our fellowship. In the morning, people would go back to their homes and their regular lives.

It was time to bring another alliance to a close. I stepped onto the balcony overlooking the river and pulled off my ocean ring. The water was black as the night and fathomless as the deepest ocean. Hearing the chattering current, I imagined all the ships that had passed this way down the centuries, clippers and East Indiamen striking out for foreign shores. Their holds would have been empty, but what of the hopes burning in the hearts of the crew?

"To spices!" they would toast at Deptford.

"To new lands!" at Woolwich.

"To adventure!" at Gravesend.

So much good fortune in that ring, I thought. One day, someone would find it on a beach, and it would bring them the same luck. Reaching in my pocket, I fished for the champagne cork from the bottle used to toast *Moksha* at the meridian, pressed the ring into the top, and hurled it into the night. A splash, and the cork appeared briefly, pirouetting in a whorl of turbulence. Then it was gone, riding the ancient waterway that recoiled like a giant serpent to the waiting sea.

EPILOGUE

A man travels the world in search of what he needs and returns home to find it.

—GEORGE A MOORE

If you don't tell the truth, why bother to write the book?

—SALMAN RUSHDIE

ROWING UP IN A tiny village in deepest, darkest Dorset, I re-member staring out of my bedroom window at night, imagin-ing what it would be like to travel through the interstellar void and set foot on some distant planet for the first time. What would be my first impressions of this strange new world, and what bizarre life forms might I encounter? Little did I know that years later I would indeed get to slip through the void, not in a metal canister belching carbon, but in a lovely old rocket ship made of wood. And the older questioning me, still striving to see the big picture, would gaze up at the stars with a mug of hot tea in his hands, and instead imagine a space traveller visit-ing Earth for the first time. What would be its first impressions of the blue planet? And what would it make of us, *Homo sapiens*, the so-called "wise" species? Perhaps, seeing our greed and destruction, gobbling up the planet's resources exponentially, the visitor would conclude we were actually rather stupid and short-sighted, and I wondered whether we humans could learn anything from an alien's-eye view of our world

That was a bit like how I felt returning to England after thirteen years, a traveller from another dimension observing my homeland with fresh eyes. Some things were refreshingly familiar: the wry humour, the cosy pubs, and my long-suffering family, of course. Otherwise, much had changed. It was all teen stabbings on the news, stealth taxes, po-litical finger pointing, and an almost pathological infatuation with ce-lebrity out of all proportion to anything I remembered. The country twitched and convulsed to the whims of tabloid narcissism, an obses-sive-compulsive hunger for dirty laundry fuelled by the gods of reality TV. Captured on camera an average of three hundred and ninety-two times a day by the nation's burgeoning arsenal of CCTV cameras, now everyone was a status-seeking whore in the making.

Climate change and global warming, terms that had produced sunny indifference when Steve and I aired them pre-1994, were now fashionable household terms. A taxi driver boasted to me that he was carbon-footprint free, his vehicle's emissions "offset to zero." What did that mean? That he never started the damn engine? No, it was clever marketing semantics for "carry on polluting guilt free."

And the place was awash with money. The elbowing bankers had their snouts firmly in the trough, skimming from the labour of others. The church was up to its nuts in kiddy fiddling. The spineless politicians were, as usual, spineless, selling the public with manicured spin and faux sincerity.

I thought: *Where's the integrity here?*

What few values there once were had gone, leaving people gaping into the abyss. With the old markers washed away and nothing to set its moral compass by, western civilization appeared to be dismantling itself from the inside out. *A new creed is needed here,* I wrote in my journal. *A new set of rules. A new religion to ride out the coming storm.** And a year later in 2008 when the global economy went into meltdown, I knew I wasn't completely off my rocker.

But the biggest surprise was discovering how little I had in common with regular people anymore. Amused glances would be furtively thrown when I extolled the virtues of silence to be found a thousand miles from land, and the conversation promptly turned to the latest episode of *X Factor.*

"What's *X Factor?*" I would ask.

Nor had I watched *Strictly Come Dancing, Come Dine With Me,* or *I'm A Celebrity … Get Me Out of Here!* For all the years I'd travelled through

---

* In March 2009, the UK Government Chief Scientific Advisor, Professor John Beddington, predicted the world faced a "perfect storm" of food, water, and energy shortages as the global population rises to 8.5 billion by 2030. The overpopulation of Rapa Nui island in the South Pacific offers clues as to how this scenario might play out, albeit on a larger scale and over a longer period of time: fierce competition for resources, leading to mass migrations, social upheaval, warfare, and famine. At the current rate of biodiversity loss, scientists believe the Earth's sixth mass extinction event, the man-induced Holocene extinction, is already well underway with a projected loss of over seventy-five per cent of the world's species.

distant lands, I never felt so lost as in my own. My estrangement was complete sharing a railway carriage with several hundred weary London commuters riding the 17:10 from Paddington to Reading.

"This is not a valid ticket," the inspector said, handing me back my stub.

"But I only bought it fifteen minutes ago," I protested.

He looked at me like I was an imbecile. "It's a receipt. Not a ticket."

Examining the stub closer, I realized what had happened. Since the last time I bought a train ticket, machines had largely replaced humans, and now the self-service kiosks on station platforms produced not only tickets, they apparently spat out receipts as well. I'd left the ticket in the dispensing tray by mistake.

I explained my oversight, but the inspector remained unimpressed. The passengers around me kept their noses firmly glued to their Black-Berrys and evening papers—British indifference at its best.

Tapping the receipt, I said, "But this shows I bought a ticket for £18.20 at 16:52. That's less than twenty minutes ago."

"It doesn't indicate the route," replied the inspector. "You could be going anywhere."

"Well, obviously I'm going where this train is going, from London to Reading."

"There's no way to prove that without a valid ticket, though, is there?"

The ridiculousness of the conversation triggered a corresponding rise in my blood pressure. "Let me ask you something," I said, changing tack. "How much is a single fare from Paddington to Reading at this time of day?"

The inspector consulted the ticket machine hanging around his neck. "Eighteen pounds and twenty pence."

I felt like we'd made a breakthrough. "Precisely! So, if that's the amount on the receipt, and I'm currently on a journey between two stations that costs that exact amount, then don't you think it more than likely that the route marked on the original ticket was from London to Reading?"

My reasoning, however, fell on deaf ears. "I need to see a valid ticket," the inspector parroted. "If you cannot produce a valid ticket, you will be required to pay the penalty fare of two full singles."

After nearly a decade and a half of dealing with rather more formidable opponents—a saltwater crocodile, Sumatran bandits, Egyptian military intelligence—this pasty-faced goon had got the best of me in less than a minute. Being forced to pay triple for a legitimate mistake put me over the edge.

"Really?" I said. "Well, I'm NOT BLOODY PAYING!"

I was kicked off the train at Slough, the next station, not far from where I used to work as a window cleaner. The irony of the situation wasn't lost on me; I'd come full circle, literally. Watching the train pull away, I met the gaze of a female passenger. She was smiling at me in pity, and in that moment something twigged. It wasn't adventurers who were the bravest, most patient, tenacious, or level-headed—as I had been described in media interviews since recrossing the prime meridian. It was people with conventional occupations the world over who endured the petty humiliations of modern life, indignities that frequently involved the inflexibility and discrimination of mass transit employees, many of whom appeared to have undergone personality-bypass operations. With grace and aplomb, these nine-to-fivers held down a job, raised a family, put food on the table, and rode the 17:10 from London to Reading five times a week.

My story sold for six figures. I would be collaborating with a co-writer, striking what my new literary agent assured me would be the perfect balance between an honest account of the journey and one that had the commercial weight of one of the world's biggest publishing houses behind it. The advance would be enough to get a place, somewhere to just be, without having to move on all the time.

But as chapters from my co-author began trickling in, I realized that apart from a hasty interview over a tape recorder, no one actually intended for me to be involved in the writing of my story. The book was trash, a cheap and tacky rendition churned out in a few weeks for the Christmas market. Mainstream publishers had a tried-and-tested formula for making money from adventure stories: match the media's flavour of the minute with a unique selling point, slap on an eye-catching dust jacket, and give it an edgy title. Who cared what was between the covers? Story was incidental, rattled off by a ghostwriter while the "talent" became a knobhead on TV. Turning down such a high advance would result in the story being blacklisted by other publishers, warned my agent, making self-publishing the only other option. I was left with two choices: take the money and hand over my dignity, or walk away and try to write the thing myself.

Fuck 'em, I thought, and tore up the contract.

If you go away long enough, there is no coming back. Home will always be somewhere else. Ruined financially and betrayed by those I had entrusted fifteen years of my life to, I felt too demoralized to stay. So I completed my media duties, and I went away.

Meenakshi met me in San Jose, California. We could stay in Sher's apartment while he was in India for a few months, allowing us to live cheaply. The task of collating the expedition story was immense: forty-four handwritten journals, thousands of blog entries, and hundreds of hours of audio and videotape to wade through. After Christmas, delving deeper into archival material, things started to go awry. I couldn't sleep. I lost my temper easily. Occasionally, and without warning, I was overcome by anxiety, my heart pounding uncontrollably. Like a cartoon character running off the end of a cliff, I was in a state of suspended animation—legs whirling in mid-air, gravity yet to take hold. I withdrew; even answering the phone filled me with dread. For Meenakshi, used to the warmth and vibrancy of Mumbai, adapting to dull

American suburbia was equally difficult. We clung to each other like two lost souls adrift in the wastes of Silicon Valley.

Then the flashbacks started. Walking beside a busy road one afternoon, I found myself balled up on the pavement, legs smashed by an imaginary vehicle. I started drinking. Meenakshi and I started fighting. I was "confused and unreliable," she said. And she was right. The delicate mechanism of the human brain can suppress acute stress for only so long. The journey ends, and the doors to the mind's innermost chambers swing open, releasing any raw, unprocessed artefacts.

When I became violent, she packed up her things and returned to India.

It would be several months before I was diagnosed with chronic post-traumatic stress. In the meantime, I ran full tilt down the path of self-destruction, drinking more and more as my head continued to unravel. And all the while I was plagued by a nagging sense of failure. That after thirteen years, my search for a unifying Philosophy for Life, a way of living with a big-picture perspective to guide right behaviour on an overcrowded planet, had come to nothing. How do you live your life so you're part of the solution to a sustainable future, not part of the problem? What would be the ideal lifestyle for that to become a reality? What would you eat? Where would you live? How would you get around? These were the overarching questions that had driven me forward over the years.

I was the first to circumnavigate the planet by human power. But so what? I'd returned to civilization empty-handed with nothing useful to show for my prodigal efforts. The faith that had kept me going all those years was a hollow, indulgent faith, I told myself, a shadowy reflection of my own deluded vanity. When all was said and done, the expedition had been an elaborate excuse to avoid responsibilities back home. *Much harder to stay put and face real life,* I thought. *That takes true grit.*

The breakdown, when it came, was like sitting behind the wheel of a runaway vehicle, hurtling towards a precipice. Tipping over the edge, I just remember tying one end of my laptop cable to a hook in the ceiling and the other around my neck, thinking: *Why carry on when the only thing keeping you alive is the air in your lungs?*

The stool was too low. I went to the kitchen to fetch a chair.

Then the doorbell rang.

It was a United Parcel Service driver delivering a box containing my father's expedition logbooks, totalling 4,834 entries painstakingly recorded in his jerky penmanship, listing mileages, weather conditions, and other details for every day I was out there. Those few seconds were enough, an impromptu bucket of oil flung under the juggernaut wheels of destiny. I slumped to the floor and sobbed—and slept.

In the dream, I was kneeling on a beach, water lapping the shore. Laughter roused me from my dark reverie. There was the girl with the sprig of white Frangipani blossom in her hair, sitting in the shade of a pandanus tree. She was smiling at me, a wide, beatific, South Pacific island smile, radiating like a lighthouse shining from an ocean of darkness. And beyond her, out past the swell, a little boat was bobbing alone and vulnerable in the vast Pacific, a speck of possibility in a cosmos of never-ending blue.

Then it came to me, a point I'd been moving towards all my life, taking me on a journey I was meant to take, leading me to an answer that had been under my nose all along.

The Earth is a boat crossing a turbulent sea, a life-support machine suspended in the watery darkness of space.

On *Moksha*, it didn't matter what country you were from, or whether you were white, black, or anything in between. It didn't matter if you were Christian, Muslim, animist, or atheist, liberal or conservative. These were just vestigial tribal attributes, molecules and memes, redundant traces of evolutionary geography, nothing more. What mattered was nurturing the cooperation needed to sustain the long voyage, seeing through the illusions of separateness to the underlying chemistry that connects us all, fields of molecular energy by which everything in the universe can be understood as a variation of itself—patterns and metaphors repeated over and over. The secret to living on a crowded planet was learning how to survive on a small boat. You either adapted to life in a closed system, using Critical Eye to consciously eschew unsustainable behaviour, or surrendered to the blind executioner's hand of natural selection and risked becoming extinct.

I knew then that the far country I'd been working my way back to was actually a country within, one that had been growing inside me as I inched my way around the world—a place free of conceptual borders, fibbing politicians, greedy bankers, predatory priests, and self-serving do-gooders. It was a world defined by a voluntary Vow of Simplicity, and to be part of it, and so part of the solution, I needed to stop thinking as an individual and start acting as a species.

Freeing the power cord, I reached for my laptop and started to write. The quickest way of bringing such a world into being was to start living it, breathing it, writing it from the inside out, for you never know how you will change the future by simply living out your truth. Writing, in its simplest form, is also the process of letting go, of self-healing, a device for exorcising the demons snapping at the tortured soul. I had glimpsed enlightenment on the expedition. I had fallen in love. I had made a fortune and left it all behind. I had gambled my sanity. I had gambled my life. I had plumbed the depths and taken it to the brink. Had it all been worth it? Only time would tell. For now, I could draw comfort knowing that there is always hope, and where there is hope, there is the strength to carry on.

Besides, a journey isn't over until it's told.

CALL TO ACTION

SINCE MY EPIPHANY ON global sustainability, namely scaling the fantastically complex issue of planetary self-reliance down to the more fathomable model of a boat on the ocean, I have tried my best to apply the lessons learnt aboard *Moksha* to my life back on land. Underpinning this life philosophy is the realization that many of the adaptions needed to survive on a small vessel isolated by water are the same behaviour modifications we, as a species, need to make on an overpopulated world isolated by space.

The good news is you don't have to spend 13 years in a glorified broom closet to come to a similar conclusion. If, having come this far with the expedition story, you're inspired to become part of the solution to a sustainable future not part of the problem, join me in making seven easy lifestyle changes guaranteed to reap rewards for both you and the planet.

1. Adopt a plant-based diet

TAKING ANIMAL PRODUCTS off the menu is the single, most impactful choice you can make. The livestock sector is responsible for 18% of global greenhouse gas emissions, more than all cars, trains, planes and ships combined.* Eliminating meat and dairy will not only alleviate collective harms such as climate change, habitat loss, and related species extinctions, for you personally it can mean living a longer, healthier life by reducing preventable diseases such as heart attack, cancer, stroke, diabetes, and obesity.

---

* UN Food and Agriculture Organization, 2006. More recent analysis by World Bank environmental advisors Robert Goodland and Jeff Anhang puts the figure as high as 51%.

Notable vegans include Brad Pitt, Beyoncé, Alec Baldwin, Thom York, Ellen DeGeneres, boxer David Haye, ironman triathlete John Joseph, Olympic gold medallist Carl Lewis, tennis champions Venus and Serena Williams, footballer Jason Roberts, marathon runner Fiona Oakes, and Sir Paul McCartney.

- Buy organic, locally sourced, seasonal produce if possible.
- Supplement by learning how to grow and forage your own food.
- Check out urban and vertical gardening solutions if living space is tight, or start a community garden project.
- Find recipes and support online to make your transition to a plant-based diet as smooth as possible.

2. Use human power to get around more

NEXT TIME YOU grab the car keys or plan to take public transport, ask yourself: "Could I walk or bike this journey instead?" Half of all journeys taken in the US are three miles or less. If 50% of those journeys were completed by human power, over 24 billion gallons of gasoline would be saved each year and the emissions kept out of our atmosphere.[*]

Moreover, by the time you factor in road congestion and finding a parking space or delays on mass transit, often it's quicker and easier to use human power. It's less stressful, you'll save money, and get in shape—studies show you can lose 13 pounds in the first year of riding to and from work.[†]

- Buy a (used) bicycle.
- Fit it with panniers or a trailer for shopping.
- On journeys where human power or public transport isn't practical, consider using a ridesharing scheme instead of driving.
- If you live in a rural area, start a supply relay with your neighbours.

---

[*]   Environmental Defense Fund.
[†]   UKCRC Centre for Diet and Activity Research.

3. Fix stuff when it breaks

GLOBAL SUSTAINABILITY IS about much more than global warming and climate change. One way to help reduce the extraction, production, and consumption processes that drive environmental degradation is to learn how to fix things when they break—a skill our grandparents once nurtured out of economic necessity and millions of impoverished people still do today. Every item you fix is one less item that will wind up in a landfill, or worse, shipped off to the other side of the planet where the world's poorest can often be found shredding, burning, and dismantling discarded equipment, exposing themselves and their families to toxic chemicals.

Buying new clothes instead of mending what you already have also has far reaching consequences. It can take 20,000 litres of water to produce a mere 1kg of cotton, equivalent to a single tee shirt and a pair of jeans. Unsustainable cotton farming has already caused the destruction of entire ecosystems, like the Aral Sea in Central Asia, once the world's fourth largest lake. Now the lake is almost entirely gone, leaving only desert, and the livelihoods of the local people have been destroyed— just so we can wear cheap cotton.*

On planet *Moksha,* we taught ourselves how to mend clothes, dismantle and repair mechanical equipment, re-solder electronics, and so on—Created Value tasks, as I came to know them. The act of bringing something back to life generates (in my experience) a sense of fulfilment that lasts well beyond the junkie thrill of clicking Add to Cart. It's better for the health of the planet, not to mention your bank account.

- Tried every video on YouTube and still can't get the toaster to pop up? Ask around if there's a jack-of-all-trades in your neighbourhood. If he or she fixes the toaster, offer to take their dog for a walk. Barter exchanges like this go a long way to foster a sense of community and personal pride.

---

* WWF report: *The Impact of Cotton on Freshwater Resources and Ecosystems.*

- Start a neighbourhood Freecycle—a simple little shed where people can bring items in good shape they no longer want, or pick up something they might otherwise have to buy. The cabin Tammie and I caretake in Colorado is largely furnished with items that were otherwise destined for landfill: cutlery, dishes, bedding, furniture, garden tools, camping supplies—the list goes on. If Jack can't fix the toaster, you might find one there.
- Look online for recycling co-ops. You might find that toaster yet.

4. Use water sparingly

PUMP A DESALINATOR handle for an hour to produce just one gallon of salt-free H_2O, and you really appreciate how precious clean drinking water is. Water security is already one of the biggest challenges to global sustainability as aquifers continue to be over pumped, rivers dry up, and wetlands disappear to development. On *Moksha*, we survived comfortably on two gallons per person per day, significantly less than the 30-100 gallons the average Westerner fritters away each day. Hygiene and laundry was admittedly a little basic at times, but the point remains that we can all get away with using a lot less water than we might think.

- Take shorter showers and fit a low-flow showerhead (washing your hair less also maintains natural shine and prevents split ends).
- Modify your toilet to dual flush (don't waste money and resources buying a new one).
- Turn the tap/faucet off when brushing teeth or washing dishes.
- Choose xeriscaping over traditional lawn irrigation.

5. Cut down on waste

THOSE OF US living in affluent countries generate an average of 4.3 pounds of waste per day, contributing to a staggering three *trillion* tonnes of refuse globally each year—the vast majority of which ends up in landfills.* Half of this waste is organic (mainly food), and a quarter of it paper and plastic. On planet *Moksha,* the daily 0.25 pounds of waste each crewmember produced was never far from our minds (or nostrils) as it mouldered in the stern cabin, waiting to be recycled at the next port of call. Food was rarely wasted as every calorie burned took us one step closer to making landfall.

- Buy only a few days of produce at a time.
- Compost leftover food scraps, use vermicomposting (with worms) for apartment settings, or donate to local gardening initiatives.
- Never buy bottled water unless you absolutely have to—it takes 3 litres of water and 0.25 litres of petroleum to produce only 1 litre of bottled water. Invest in a reusable bottle, a water filter if needed, and drink tap water.
- Shop with reusable bags.
- Boycott goods with excessive packaging.

6. Switch to renewable energy

To AVOID THE potentially catastrophic effects of Earth's climate heating beyond two degrees Celsius, the world needs to transition to a low-carbon economy, and fast. We can all do our bit by powering our homes with renewable energy and reducing the amount of electricity we actually use.

On planet *Moksha,* with no access to fossil fuels, our energy needs were met using solar panels and a wind turbine. The same technology is widely available for domestic uses, and with a little investment it is possible to power your home exclusively by renewable energy. Alternatively, if you don't fancy the upfront installation costs, you can purchase green power as you go from a growing range of renewable energy suppliers.

---

* The World Bank.

Of equal importance is usage. On *Moksha*, we became acutely aware of conserving and prioritizing our limited quota of stored power. The question "Do we really need to?" was always privately asked before switching on a light, electronic device, or any other appliance. At night, for example, we would only turn on the navigation lights if we saw a ship coming towards us. Otherwise, we would pedal in darkness.

- Add or remove layers of clothing instead of automatically reaching for the thermostat.
- Turn off lights and appliances when not in use.
- Air-dry laundry.
- Fill dishwater completely and skip the rinsing before you load.

7. Join the sharing economy

IMAGINE A WORLD where resources are pooled instead of being individually owned. That reality is fast becoming an option with the digital age; it is now possible to share seldom used goods and services like automobiles (which otherwise spend an average of 22.8 hours a day parked in a garage), skills, accommodation, tools, tasks, sporting goods, furniture, meals, clothing, gardening implements, even children's toys. Resource-consuming property represents a quarter of household expenditure and a third of all our waste. Research shows that participating in collaborative consumption initiatives can save up to 7% of a household budget and reduce waste by 20%.*

- Sharing is not environmentally sustainable by nature; we make it sustainable by *how* we share. So, for instance, instead of ridesharing apps being an alternative to biking or taking public transport, use them as a supplement on short essential trips, such as from the nearest railway station to your workplace.

---

* The Institute for Sustainable Development and International Relations (IDDRI).

The journey continues

MICROEARTHS.COM

ACKNOWLEDGEMENTS

FOR ME WRITING IS a hellish process. Wrestling with a particularly unruly sentence in *The Expedition* manuscript, often it occurred to me that the physical journey I was attempting to describe was merely a warm-up for the literary one, both exercises being slow and tedious with no apparent end in sight. More than once I cursed my obstinacy for turning down the money and insisting on writing the story myself.

But, as I should have known from the journey itself, gut decisions have an uncanny way of being correct. I've since learned that narrative writing is an effective treatment for PTSD, a way of defusing emotional responses to traumatic events by externalizing them and reassigning to a box labelled *The Past*. So, although financially ruinous at the time, rejecting the ghostwriter and penning the story myself turned out to be the right decision, if only to set me on the path to recovery.

I am tremendously grateful to those who offered shelter in the early days of writing, when I was flat broke and living rough in the mountains above Santa Cruz. In particular I'd like to thank Auspet Jordan and Lara Summer for letting me stay in their delightful home in return for token house decorating.

Early chapter drafts received sensitive and insightful editing from my friend Anthony DiMatteo. Others who read portions of the manuscript and offered valuable suggestions include Sandra Cain, Pete Roper, Sharon Kessler, Michelle Cisney, Margaret DiMatteo, Mark and Carol Rickman, Pat and Sally Mara, Rella Abernathy, Susan Reep, Mark Smith, Anne Goddard, Elektra Macdonald, and Ian Macalpine-Leny. Lana Woodruff and Juliann Feuerbacher deserve a special mention for all their efforts.

The manuscript would never have been finished without my dear partner Tammie, who, as well as doing a fine job as editor, magically conjured up places for me to keep writing—random houses, empty garages, even gardens where I could pitch a tent. She proposed setting up BillyFish Books to publish the title in three parts, a strategy dismissed as too risky by other publishers, and worked a job she hated for eight months to raise the starting capital. Since then, she has worked tirelessly to bring the story to life, and in doing so built the framework to publish other authors so often overlooked or ignored by the larger publishing houses.

Finally, a note of thanks to my family, who have been tremendously supportive throughout, and to you, the reader, for waiting patiently for all three books to be released. It was your early patronage buying *Dark Waters* and *The Seed Buried Deep* that allowed me to keep scribbling.

To all of you, I express my heartfelt thanks.

Glossary of Nautical Terms & British Vernacular

Admiralty chart	Nautical chart issued by the UK Hydrographic Office
Aft	Towards the rear of a boat
Amidships	The middle section of a ship
Astern	Backwards or toward the rear of a ship
Backsheesh	Small amount of money, often given as a tip or bribe
Beam-ends (on her)	Leaning over to the point of imminent capsize
Berth	Sleeping compartment
Billabong	Stagnant pool formed by a river during flood
Billycan	Tin can for boiling tea on a campfire
Biscuit	Cookie
Bitumen	Asphalt, tarmac
Bloody	Expletive used in anger, shock, or surprise
Blue Water	Open ocean
Boil a billy	Make tea in a billycan
Bommie	Outcrop of coral higher than the surrounding reef
Bore	Water well. Also tiresome person
Bow (sounding like cow)	Front end of a boat
Bugger off	Get lost
Bull dust	Powdery dust
Bunk (as in done a)	Cut and run
Bush tucker	Wild plants or animals used as food
Bushwhack	Blaze a trail
Buggered	Tired out, exhausted
Bulkhead	Partition between sections of a ship
Bursary	Grant, endowment
Bwana	Boss or master in Swahili
Catching a crab	Miss an oar or paddle stroke
Centreboard	Retractable keel giving stability to a boat

Channel 16	Marine radio frequency used for broadcasting distress calls
Damper	Traditional Australian soda bread baked in campfire coals
Dhow	Lateen-rigged trading vessel
Dory	Flat-bottomed rowing boat
Dragon Boat	Boat propelled with paddles by a large crew and used for racing
Esplanade	Promenade
Felucca	Vessel moved by oars or lateen sails, typically on the Nile
Flotsam	Wreckage
Folbot	Collapsible kayak
Foredeck	Deck at the foremost part of a ship
Fortnight	Two weeks
Freeboard	Height of a ship's side between the waterline and deck
Gaff	Pole with a hook for landing large fish
Gantry	Raised platform
Ghat	Flight of steps leading down to a river
Gudgeon	Socket at the stern of a boat into which the rudder is fitted
Hawser	Thick rope or cable
Helm	Tiller or wheel for steering a ship
Hookah	Oriental tobacco pipe with flexible tube that draws the smoke through water
Hove to	Bring a vessel to a stop
Key Stage	Fixed stages of UK national curriculum
Khat	Leaves of an Arabian shrub, which are chewed as a stimulant
Knob	Idiot
Knots	Nautical miles per hour
Lariam	Trademark for mefloquine, used for malaria prevention and treatment
Lateen sail	Triangular sail on a long beam set at 45° to the mast
Lee	Shelter
Listing	Leaning over
Lorry	Semi truck
Losmen	Budget accommodation (Indonesia)

Make fast	Secure firmly
Mullet	Hair cut short at the front and sides and left long at the back
Neap tide	Moon phase when there is least difference between high and low water
Northing	Distance travelled or measured northward
Ocean sentry	Radar target enhancer
Ocker	Australian redneck
Outriggers	Long poles on a fishing boat to keep tackle separate. Also beams projecting from the side of a vessel for stability
Pak	Mr (Indonesia)
Pintles	Pins on a rudder that fit into the gudgeons and suspend the rudder
Plonk	Poor quality wine
Port	Left side of a boat looking towards the bow
Pram	Baby stroller
Prow	Front end of a boat
Punter	Customer. Also highly paid ball player doing very little
Push the boat out	Splash out
Put the boot in	Give someone a hard time
Quango	Quasi-autonomous non-governmental organisation
Queue	Wait in line
RIB	Rigid inflatable boat
Ringer	Stockman, ranch hand
Roundabout	Traffic circle
Row (sounding like cow)	Shouting match
Rowlock	Fitting on gunwale that serves as a fulcrum for an oar
Runnel	Small stream
Scroggin	Trail mix
Selat	Strait
Shingle	Small round pebbles on a beach
Shipping water	Taking in water over the side
Shoal	Sandbank
Skiff	Flat-bottomed open boat with sharp bow and square stern
Slipway	Boat ramp

Sloop	One-masted sailboat with fore-and-aft mainsail and jib
Smoko	Rest from work for a smoke, a tea break
Sod 'em	To hell with them
Sosbud visa	Social cultural visa (Indonesia)
Spindrift	Spray blown from the crests of waves
Spinnaker	Large three-cornered sail at the front of a yacht
Spoil area	Area where dredged material is deposited
Sprats	Small fishes
Spring tide	Moon phase when there is greatest difference between high and low water
Starboard	Right side of a boat looking towards the bow
Stern	Rear end of a boat
Stooks	Sheaves of grain stood on end
Stubbie bin	Container for empty beer cans (Australia)
Tender	Small boat used to ferry people and supplies
Tidal Stream	Currents associated with tides, usually near a coastline
Tiller	Lever or wheel connected to the rudder for steering a boat
Tindal	Trained seaman
Transom	Stern section of a square-ended boat
Tsampa	Barley flour mixed with yak butter tea (Tibet)
Wallah	Person involved with a specified thing or business (India)
Whinge	Complain
Wild camping	Camping in non-authorized areas. Not an orgy in the woods
Windscreen	Windshield

CONVERSIONS
1 pound sterling = 1.61 US dollars (approximate)
1 nautical mile = 1.151 statute miles
1 statute mile = 1.609 kilometres

Made in the USA
Middletown, DE
09 May 2017